D1198133

Contents

Contributors

Coeditor and Author of Chapters 8, 14 and 15:

Christopher Nobes Professor of Accounting at the University of Strathclyde. Has also taught in England, the USA, Australia and New Zealand. Is a member of a committee of the *Groupe d'Etudes des Experts Comptables de la CEE*.

Coeditor and Author of Chapters 4, 6 and 10:

Robert Parker Professor of Accountancy at the University of Exeter. Editor of *Accounting and Business Research*. Has also practised and taught in Nigeria, Australia, France and Scotland.

Authors of Other Chapters:

Bryan Carsberg Professor of Accounting at the London School of Economics and Research Director of the Institute of Chartered Accountants in England and Wales; formerly Assistant Research Director of the Financial Accounting Standards Board of the USA. (Chapter 2)

Peter Standish Professor of Accounting at the University of Tasmania, Australia. Has also taught in the UK and the USA. (Chapter 3)

Klaus Macharzina Professor of Business Administration, University of Hohenheim at Stuttgart, Germany. Managing Editor of *Management International Review*. Previously, Professor of International Accounting at the University of Lancaster, England. (Chapter 5)

Les Campbell Accounting Research Manager with Deloitte Haskins & Sells, London. Held a Fulbright Fellowship at New York University in 1985. (Chapter 7)

Adolf Enthoven Professor of Accounting and Director of the Center for International Accounting Development, University of Texas at Dallas, USA. (Chapter 9)

Patrick Kirkman Senior Lecturer in Accountancy at the University of Exeter. Has also taught in the USA, Australia and New Zealand. (Chapter 11)

John Flower Commission of the European Communities, Brussels, Belgium. Formerly, Professor of Accounting at the University of Bristol, England. (Chapter 12)

David Walker Vice President of the Bankers Trust International. (Chapter 13)

Preface

Preface to Second Edition

Much has changed in the world of comparative accounting since 1981. The most obvious single source of change has been the implementation in several countries of the EEC's fourth Directive on company law. This second edition is intended to be up to date as at the middle of 1985.

The book is structured along similar lines to those of the first edition. Nothing has happened since 1981 to persuade us that it is sensible to study comparative accounting problems without first obtaining a detailed grasp of the reasons for, and nature of, international differences in financial reporting practices. It is not sufficient, in our opinion, to rely upon general and inevitably superficial survey data. Two new chapters have been added: a country study of Japan, and the problem area of the management of foreign exchange risk. We have also standardised on short appendices to the country studies chapters, containing specimen financial statements.

In addition to those mentioned in the preface to the first edition, we are very grateful for much help and advice from many distinguished colleagues, including Janet Debman of Arthur Young, London; Michael Glautier of ESSEC; Horst Kaminski of the Institut der Wirtschaftsprüfer; Geoff Mitchell of the Institute of Chartered Accountants in England and Wales; Hein Schreuder of the State University of Limburg; and Otto Volgenant, Jr. of NIVRA.

We are also grateful for excellent secretarial help from Susanne Robertson, Elvy Ibbotson and Hilary Ireland. Any errors or obscurities which remain, however, are entirely our responsibility.

C.W. Nobes   Universities of Strathclyde
R.H. Parker   and Exeter 1985

Preface to the First Edition

This book is intended for undergraduate and graduate courses in comparative and international accounting. Its primary markets are expected to be in English-speaking countries, not only because of the language in which it is written, but also because readers in these countries will have somewhat similar accounting backgrounds. Thus, for example, students in Britain or North America should find that Chapters 2 or 3 (on each other's countries) will enable them to establish a common Anglo-Saxon background from which to approach the remaining chapters on other countries.

The book was conceived during the teaching of a course on comparative international accounting at the University of Exeter. It was our experience that, despite much written material on aspects of this subject, there was no 'text book'. Also, some writings are heavily biased towards readers of a particular country, for example the USA, and may misinterpret or mislead because of lack of detailed local knowledge. Therefore, our intention has been to produce a book which covers (or, it is to be hoped, 'uncovers'!) many of the important areas of comparative international financial reporting. Further, we have tried to gain from the experience of those with local knowledge.

For example, the chapter on North America was co-authored by a British professor who is also the Assistant Research Director of the American Financial Accounting Standards Board. His knowledge of US accounting is thus interpreted through and for British readers. This seems the most likely way to highlight differences and to avoid missing important points through over-familiarity. Similarly, the chapter on Britain and Australia was written by an Australian professor who has held posts in London and Harvard; and the chapter on West Germany by a German professor who has taught in Britain.

The list of chapters and of contributors is an illustration of our attempt to provide a fairly comprehensive coverage and to obtain expert knowledge which is intelligible to Anglo-Saxon readers. However, we hope that our book may also be of interest and use in many countries outside the world of Anglo-Saxon accounting.

It is partly because of the distinguished nature of our contributors that we have not tried to force each chapter into a common mould. However, there is a stronger reason, which may be illustrated by referring to the 'country' Chapters 2 to 6. It would not be sensible to adopt a common format or section headings because, for example, company law is all-important in Germany, fairly important in the UK, but of little importance in France or the USA; accounting standards are very important in the UK and the USA, but of virtually no importance in France and West Germany.

These 'country' chapters provide some of the detail on the topics which are discussed more broadly and comparatively in Part II: 'problem areas'. We have tried to insert information and predictions about the changes to law in several of these countries in 1981–2 which result from the EEC's fourth Directive on company law; Chapter 12 on 'harmonisation' is thus not very detailed on this point. The 'country' chapters on France, West Germany and the Netherlands have appendices containing extracts from annual reports, which are referred to in the text. Readers or teachers should have no difficulty in obtaining other annual reports of listed companies, particularly as illustrations for Chapters 2 and 3. In these 'country' chapters and in some others, many institutions, laws, etc. are mentioned which may usefully be abbreviated; a list is provided on page 369. References at the end of chapters are listed in two parts by type of author; individuals first, and then institutions.

We are grateful to Edward Stamp for writing a Foreword. Professor Stamp is an English-born Canadian CA, who has been a practising auditor in Canada and has held chairs in New Zealand, Scotland and England. His own career demonstrates the degree to which accounting has become international.

We have received great help and much useful advice from many distinguished colleagues in addition to our contributors. We would like especially to thank Jan Klaassen of the Free University of Amsterdam; Andrew Brown and Jules Muis of the Continental office in Brussels of Ernst & Whinney; Paul Rutteman and Michael Timms of the London office of Arthur Young McClelland Moores & Co; the Paris office of Peat Marwick Mitchell & Co; M. Turq; and, for financial help for Chapter 9, the Research Sub-committee of the Institute of Chartered Accountants in England and Wales. Also, we acknowledge the kind permission of the officers of two companies to reprint parts of their companies' reports. Finally, we are very grateful for the secretarial help provided by Mrs Elvy Ibbotson, Mrs Hilary Ireland and Mrs Margaret Baldwin. Despite the efforts of all these worthies, we have no doubt that errors and obscurities remain, for which we are culpable jointly and severally.

C.W. Nobes
R.H. Parker   University of Exeter, 1981

Foreword

Financial Reporting is a subject of great importance to many groups of people. Investors and potential investors, industrialists, legislators, governmental regulatory agencies, employees, and accounting practitioners all have a vital interest in the reporting standards and practices of the countries in which they live. So of course do academic accountants and their students. The needs of all these people have been served for many years by a comprehensive literature of textbooks, professional publications, journals and so on. Yet virtually all of this literature, throughout the developed world, has concentrated on the issues and problems of the specific country in which it happens to be published. Accounting textbooks in particular have largely ignored the international ramifications of financial reporting; as a result they have failed to reflect the growing importance of comparative international studies in accounting.

The present volume thus fills an important need. Accounting is the language of commerce, and the growth of international trade and investment makes it imperative that all the interest groups specified above should be well informed about the problems of international financial reporting. It is particularly important for today's students – who are, after all, tomorrow's leaders – to have a mastery of these issues.

Language barriers are by no means the only obstacle to the goal of international harmonisation, as this book makes abundantly clear. Considerable differences in theory, legislation, policies and practice

exist among the various English-speaking countries, and language differences are only a minor factor in the gap that exists between (for
example) British, German, French and Dutch reporting practices.
There are good reasons for the differences, and unless these reasons are
properly understood by tomorrow's business and professional leaders
there is little chance of their being successful in the process of
harmonisation.

This is a field in which I have been interested for many years. The
authors of the various chapters of this book, whom I know and for all of
whom I have a high regard, share this interest. I hope that this book will
be widely read (in the English-speaking countries and in the rest of the
world) and that the result of this will be a much broader understanding
of the international differences that now exist, and of the need to do all
we can to narrow them in the future.

Edward Stamp   International Centre for Research in Accounting
                      University of Lancaster   January 1981

1

Introduction

R.H. PARKER
C.W. NOBES

This book is concerned with the international and comparative aspects of corporate financial reporting. In this introductory chapter we explain why we think the comparative approach is important; we justify the choice of the countries whose financial reporting practices are considered in detail; and we outline the main causes of the differences to be found in these practices. In the process of doing this we provide in tabular form some basic statistical information relevant to comparative accounting.

The rest of the book is divided into three parts. Part I contains country studies. There are six chapters on financial reporting in various developed countries. In Chapter 8 we discuss the classification of financial reporting systems. This chapter can, if desired, be read at an earlier stage. It is placed where it is because the analysis in it is firmly based on the factual material presented in the previous chapters. In Chapter 9 accounting in developing countries is considered.

With this background, it is possible to proceed in Part II to the comparative analysis of important problem areas. The ones we have chosen are consolidation, inflation accounting, foreign currency translation and foreign exchange risk management. These are all of great topical interest.

Part III is an examination of the purposes, difficulties and progress of the international (both world-wide and regional) harmonisation of financial reporting and corporate taxation. It is in this part of the book that we discuss international accounting organisations and institutions.

1.1   Importance of Comparative Accounting

There are at least four reasons why the study of comparative international accounting is important. They may be called the historical
reason, the multinational reason, the comparative reason and the harmonisation reason (Parker 1983). Although it is convenient for
pedagogic purposes to discuss them separately, the four reasons are
closely linked.

Historically, a number of countries have made important contributions to the development of accounting. In the fourteenth and fifteenth
centuries the Italian city states were the leaders. The 'Italian method' of
bookkeeping by double entry spread first to the rest of Europe and eventually round the whole world. One lasting result of this dominance is the
number of accounting and financial words in English which are of
Italian origin. Some examples are bank, capital, cash, debit, credit,
folio, imprest and journal.

In the nineteenth century, Britain took the lead in accounting matters, to be followed in this century by the USA. As a result English has
become established as the world's language of accounting. As shown by
Table 1.4 the modern accountancy profession developed first in
Scotland and England. Table 1.5 demonstrates the overwhelmingly
British and American origins of most of the thirteen largest international
accounting firms. The concepts and practices of management accounting throughout the non-Communist industrialised world owe much to
American initiatives.

Multinational companies (MNCs) may be broadly defined as those
which produce a good or a service in two or more countries. Much of the
dramatic increase in world trade since the Second World War (see Table
1.1) can be ascribed to the development of the MNC. MNCs have
played a major role in the transfer of accounting technology from one
country to another. Their existence has given a new dimension to problems such as transfer pricing which already exist at the domestic level.
Other problems such as the translation of foreign currencies in the
preparation of consolidated financial statements (see Chapter 12) are
peculiar to multinational companies. Since MNCs produce financial

Table 1.1   International Trade 1950 – 1980

	1950	1960	1970	1980
Annual exports (US $ billion)	61	128	314	2,002
Index	100	210	515	3,282
Periodic increase (in money terms)	—	210%	245%	637%

Source: United National Statistical Year Books, 1979/80, Table 136; and 1981, Table 178.

statements in accordance with the laws and practices of their home countries, investors in and lenders to them need to become experts in the financial reporting systems of more than one country.

The comparative reason is perhaps the most important of all. It is possible for a country to improve its own accounting by observing how other countries have reacted and are reacting to problems which, especially in industrial nations, may not differ markedly from those of the observer's home country. It is also possible to satisfy oneself that, where accounting methods do differ, the differences are justified by differences in the economic, legal and social environment and are not merely the accidents of history. Such accidents are unlikely seriously to impede harmonisation (see below). More fundamental differences are likely to be much more difficult to deal with.

Until quite recently accountants have tended to discuss accounting problems on a national basis only, paying little attention to practices in other countries. They have ignored the fact that accounting methods and institutions which are proposed but not yet practised or established in one country are often already in use in another. In the UK and USA, for instance, there have at times been calls for greater uniformity in the layout of financial statements and in valuation principles; for a closer connection between accounting profit and taxable income; and for the establishment of an accounting court. American accountants have on occasion argued for stronger company legislation; and some British accountants have recommended the establishment of a governmental regulatory body with power over accounting matters.

All these proposals have already been adopted in one country or another and descriptions and assessments of them are to be found in the chapters that follow. France and West Germany provide good examples of uniformity, in one case by means of a national accounting plan, in the other through statute law. The same two countries also provide examples of a very close connection between the rules of financial accounting and the rules for corporate taxation. Dutch financial reporting has neither of these characteristics, but the Netherlands is the only country which operates an accounting court.

American accountants who wish to study the role of company legislation in financial reporting can look not only at the British and German experiences – both of long standing – but also at the Netherlands where company legislation has grown from a minor to a major influence since 1970. British accountants in search of a regulatory body have the obvious precedent of the American Securities and Exchange Commission (SEC), but it is possible that a study of the French Commission des Opérations de Bourse (COB) might prove just as relevant.

The harmonisation reason has grown steadily in importance in recent years. Harmonisation may be defined as a process of increasing the compatibility of accounting practices by setting bounds to their degree of variation. The arguments for and against harmonisation are considered in Chapter 14. At this point it may be noted that, as is demonstrated in Chapters 10, 11 and 12, major problems such as consolidation accounting, inflation accounting and foreign currency translation have been tackled in different countries in many different ways, although a pattern may sometimes be discerned. Solutions devised by American accountants, the most numerous and the most powerful group, have been very influential but have not always been accepted. Indeed, one argument for international harmonisation has been to prevent the wholesale adoption of American accounting principles. Within the EEC, all the major countries have found their own solutions challenged and have had to accept compromises of both a technical and a political nature.

It is clear that any attempt to harmonise financial reporting touches on wider issues than accounting alone. In section 1.3 we look at some of the underlying reasons for the differences that exist. First of all, however, we shall attempt to justify the list of countries whose financial reporting systems we have chosen for detailed discussion.

1.2   Choice of Country Studies

In choosing which countries' financial reporting practices to consider in detail we make use of the concept of 'vital countries' advanced by Mason (1978). It is Mason's contention that harmonisation of financial reporting can only be achieved with the support of certain countries. A list of such countries can be established by the use of the criteria of economic significance and accounting significance. These criteria are of course to some extent interdependent. A strong accountancy profession is unlikely to grow up in a country of little economic importance.

In the present context economic significance can best be judged by

Table 1.2   Share of the World's Top
50 Companies

USA	25
Japan	11
German Federal Republic	4
UK/Netherlands	2
UK	2
France	2
Italy	2
Netherlands	1
Venezuela	1
	50

Source: Allen (1984), p.7.

listing the home countries of the world's largest companies and the world's largest stock exchanges. Table 1.2 lists those countries which are represented in the world's top fifty industrial groupings as reported in *The Times 1,000 1984–1985* (Allen 1984). Table 1.3 lists those stock exchanges with more than 200 domestic listed companies.

Table 1.3 Stock Exchanges, 1983

	Number of domestic companies with equity shares	Domestic equity shares: market valuation in £m.	Domestic equity shares: market valuation as % of UK
Amsterdam	215	23,331	15
Australia	930	41,438	27
(Association of Exchanges)			
Barcelona	386	6,278	4
Madrid	394	7,477	5
Basle	341	27,014	17
Zurich	341	30,520	20
Brussels	204	7,497	5
W. Germany	442	57,289	37
(Association of Exchanges)			
Johannesburg	501	57,200	37
New York	1,500	1,048,007	673
American	774	27,459	18
Paris	736	26,344	17
Tokyo	1,441	369,871	238
Toronto	808	96,458	62
United Kingdom	2,217	155,692	100

Source: Stock Exchange Companies (1984), The Stock Exchange, London, Table 6.

More direct measures of 'vitality' are the size of a country's accountancy profession, whether or not its accountancy firms have grown into international firms, founder membership of the International Accounting Standards Committee (IASC) and acting as host to an international congress of accountants. Table 1.4 gives details of public accountancy bodies; Table 1.5 lists in alphabetical order the 13 largest international accountancy firms and their countries of origin; Table 1.6 lists in alphabetical order the nine founder countries of the IASC; and Table 1.7 lists the international congresses of accountants.

From these six tables the following list of fifteen possible vital countries can be drawn up:

Australia	Italy	UK
Belgium	Venezuela	France
German Federal Republic	Canada	Mexico
Netherlands	Japan	Spain
Switzerland	South Africa	USA

Table 1.4 Public Accountancy Bodies, Age and Size

Country	Body	Founding date*	Approximate nos. in thousands 1983/84
United States	American Institute of Certified Public Accountants	1887	200
Canada	Canadian Institute of Chartered Accountants	1902(1880)	38
United Kingdom	Institute of Chartered Accountants in England and Wales	1880(1870)	78
	Institute of Chartered Accountants of Scotland	1951(1854)	11
	Chartered Association of Certified Accountants	1939(1891)	26
	Institute of Chartered Accountants in Ireland	1888	5
Australia	Australian Society of Accountants	1952(1887)	50
	Institute of Chartered Accountants in Australia	1928(1886)	14
France	Ordre des Experts Comptables et des Comptables Agréés	1942	10
W. Germany	Institut der Wirtschaftsprüfer	1931	5
Netherlands	Nederlands Instituut van Register-accountants	1895	5

* Dates of earliest predecessor bodies in brackets.

Table 1.5 Leading International Accountancy Firms

	Main countries of origin
Arthur Andersen & Co.	USA
Arthur Young	USA, UK
Binder Dijker Otte & Co.	UK, Netherlands
Coopers & Lybrand	UK, USA
Deloitte Haskins & Sells	UK, USA
Ernst & Whinney	USA, UK
Fox Moore International	USA, UK
Grant Thornton International	USA, UK
Horwath & Horwath International	USA
Klynveld Main Goerdeler	Netherlands, USA, W. Germany
Peat, Marwick, Mitchell & Co.	UK, USA
Price Waterhouse	UK, USA
Touche Ross & Co.	UK, USA, Canada

Source: Bavishi and Wyman (1983).

Table 1.6 Founder Countries of the International Accounting Standards Committee

Australia	German Federal Republic	Netherlands
Canada	Japan	UK and Ireland
France	Mexico	USA

Table 1.7 International Congresses of Accountants

1904	St. Louis	1957	Amsterdam
1926	Amsterdam	1962	New York
1927	New York	1967	Paris
1933	London	1972	Sydney
1937	Berlin	1977	Munich
1952	London	1982	Mexico City
		1987	Tokyo (projected)

Only the USA, the UK, the Netherlands and the German Federal Republic appear in all six tables; at the other extreme South Africa, Mexico, Venezuela, Spain, Switzerland, Italy and Belgium appear in two or fewer of the tables. If we omit these, the list of vital countries is reduced to eight. Canada and Australia are, however, unlikely to take any action to forestall an international accounting endeavour supported by both the USA and the UK, and we support Mason's contention (1978, p.77) that the six vital countries are therefore the USA, the UK, West Germany, France, the Netherlands and Japan. These are the countries on which most information is provided in this book, although some material is also included on Canada and Australia.

1.3 Differences in Financial Reporting

The factors that may be seen as having been important in shaping the principles and practice of accounting in various countries include the nature of the legal system, the prevalent types of business organisation and the ways in which they obtain their finance, the influence of taxation and the strength of the accountancy profession. The accidents of history may also have played a part.

Some countries have a legal system which relies upon a limited amount of statute law which is then interpreted by courts which build up large amounts of case law to supplement the statutes. Such a system allows for flexibility and the exercise of judgment. However, in some ways it is inefficient. The UK and the USA operate in this way. This of course influences British company law, which does not prescribe a very large number of all-embracing rules to cover what companies should do or how they should calculate and publish accounting information. Other countries have a legal background of *dirigisme* where the rules attempt to cover all eventualities. Such countries are France and West Germany, where company law and other government controls precisely prescribe rules of asset valuation, income measurement and the format of reports. As a result of the fourth EEC Directive on Company Law (see Chapter

14 and Gray and Coenenberg 1984), the UK has recently moved closer to continental European countries in the matter of rules and formats, whilst at the same time the latter have adopted the British concept of a 'true and fair view'. Major differences of outlook still remain, however.

The prevalent types of business organisation also differ. It is clear that, if most companies in a country are small family businesses, as in France, the need for a strong accountancy profession and detailed comparable published accounts is less. If most of the shares in public companies are owned or controlled by banks, as in West Germany, it is again the case that the need for 'true and fair' comparative information for private shareholders is reduced. If, on the other hand, there are many public listed companies whose ownership is widely spread, as in the UK and the USA (see Table 1.3), published accounting information which has been prepared and audited for shareholders in, what we will call, an Anglo-Saxon way becomes useful and necessary.

The influence of taxation on accounting practice can also be considerable. In many EEC countries, including France, West Germany and Italy, if expenses are claimed for tax purposes they must usually be charged in the financial statements as well. The most obvious example of this is the necessity to show accelerated depreciation as allowed for tax purposes in the financial statements. This affects the profit figure because the company must charge not the depreciation it considers appropriate, but the larger amount claimed for tax purposes.

The strength, size and competence of the accountancy profession in a country may follow to a large extent from the various factors outlined above. The lack of a substantial body of private shareholders of public companies in some EEC countries means that the need for auditors is much smaller than it is in the UK or the USA. Consequently, the profession is much smaller in continental European countries, as shown in Table 1.4. Even so, the figures in this table may seem surprising at first sight. It should be realised, however, that in West Germany, for example, there is a separate profession of tax experts; accountants may only be members of the *Institut* if they are in practice; and the training period is longer than in the UK or the USA, meaning that some German 'students' should be included in the numbers for comparability. Despite this, the above point – on the different type of work for accountants – is of great importance in explaining the figures.

In turn, the lack of a large and influential profession means that it is more difficult to introduce elaborate auditing or accounting methods in some countries. This factor and the others discussed above, coupled with the accidents of history which push law and practice in various directions, have combined to create a considerable diversity of accounting systems, as we will see.

By considering these underlying factors it may become easier to explain differences in accounting practices, for example different degrees of conservatism or propensity to disclose information. Again, the fact that different practices spring from different underlying backgrounds may cast light on the desirability – and difficulty – of any attempt to harmonise practices.

1.4 Summary

The study of comparative accounting is important for four reasons: the historical fact that several countries have contributed to the development of accounting; the growth of world trade and multinational enterprises; the adoption in some countries of solutions not yet tried in others; and the insight it gives into how successful and useful attempts at harmonisation are likely to be.

Six countries can be identified as vital in any attempt at worldwide harmonisation, that is, the USA, the UK, the German Federal Republic, France, the Netherlands and Japan. At present even these six have quite widely different financial reporting systems. These existing differences can be largely explained in terms of legal systems, types of business organisation and sources of finance, the influence of taxation and the strength of the accountancy profession.

References

Allen, M. (ed.) (1984) *The Times 1,000 1984–1985. The World's Top Companies,* Times Books, London.

Bavishi, V.B. and Wyman, H.E. (1983) *Who Audits the World,* University of Connecticut.

Gray, S.J. and Coenenberg, A.G. (eds.) (1984) *EEC Accounting Harmonisation: Implementation and Impact of the Fourth Directive,* North-Holland, Amsterdam.

Mason, A.K. (1978) *The Development of International Financial Reporting Standards,* ICRA Paper No.17, Lancaster.

Parker, R.H. (1983) 'Some international aspects of accounting', in S.J. Gray, *International Accounting and Transnational Decisions,* Butterworths.

Part I

Country Studies

2

Financial Reporting in North America

BRYAN CARSBERG*

2.1 Introduction

A volume of great length would be required to present a comprehensive description and analysis of financial accounting and reporting practices in North America. In discussing those practices in a single chapter, I have had to be highly selective. I have focused on topics in which the choice of acceptable practice may be expected to affect significantly the amounts of income and net worth reported by an enterprise; I have commented on areas that seem to be controversial; and I have attempted to identify practices that differ significantly from those used in the United Kingdom. In order to keep the length of the chapter within reasonable bounds, I have given main emphasis to practices in the United States of America and I have commented on practices in Canada only when they differ significantly from those applied in the United States.

The reader who expects to find dramatic differences between British and US accounting is likely to be disappointed. If an accountant crosses the Atlantic, he may experience an initial sense of shock at the discovery that the balance sheet appears to be presented upside down and that the financial statements are written in what seems to be a partially foreign

* This chapter is a revised version of a chapter in the first edition, written by Bryan Carsberg and Alf Eastergard, both of whom worked for the Financial Accounting Standards Board at the time.

language. However, after he has learned the language, he is likely to conclude that the similarities between British and American accounting greatly outweigh the differences. He will not find that he has to master an alien accounting philosophy. Another factor is likely to make the traveller feel at home: a large proportion of the audits of public companies in the US is undertaken by eight firms of accountants – 'the big eight'. The names of those firms are equally prominent in British practice even though most of the British firms are formally separate from their American counterparts.

The transatlantic commuter should notice that there is no legal distinction between public and private companies in the US. However, corporations that wish there to be a public market in their securities (i.e. those analogous to public companies in other countries) must be registered with a government agency: the Securities and Exchange Commission (see later). He may notice that American accountants tend to give a greater relative emphasis than their British counterparts to the needs of investors and creditors as users of financial reports; however, he will probably fail to trace important differences of practice to that different emphasis. If the British traveller has imagined the United States to be a country in which private enterprise is less constrained by public control than at home, he may need to revise his opinion considerably; he will be surprised by the amount of detailed regulation of financial accounting and reporting. The United States has many accounting regulations which typically contain quite detailed provisions. By contrast, the United Kingdom has fewer regulations and its regulations are more general in nature. This difference may be attributed partly to differences between the legal and economic environments in the two countries. However, it must also be admitted that the British accounting profession became involved in regulation more recently than the American and that the volume of regulation in Britain may be catching up. We shall discuss the American system of accounting regulation in some detail.

It is difficult to detect systematic differences between the United Kingdom and the United States in the methods accepted for accounting measurements. If there is one pervasive difference affecting the primary financial statements, it is perhaps a greater reluctance in the United States to depart from measurements based on historical prices. For example, companies are not permitted to revalue fixed assets to an amount higher than cost. Other measurement differences discussed in this chapter have the appearance of being attributable to chance factors rather than being part of some consistent pattern. However, the United States has regulations that call for very detailed disclosures of financial information by public companies – probably more than any other country in the world.

2.2   The Setting and Enforcement of Standards

The United States is a federation of 50 individual states, each of which has its own legislative body with extensive powers to control business activity and levy taxes within its own boundaries. The right to practise as a public accountant is also conferred by the individual states and the requirements for conferring that right differ slightly from state to state; membership of the national body, the American Institute of Certified Public Accountants (AICPA), is not required as a condition for exercising the right to practise and many practitioners elect not to become members.

Laws governing transactions in securities were first introduced by individual states, beginning with Kansas in 1911. Such state laws became widespread; they are generally knows as 'blue sky laws', after a quip to the effect that unscrupulous Kansas dealers were trying to sell the blue sky. They normally require registration of a proposal to offer securities for sale, and disclosure of information; in some cases they confer on a state official the right to refuse permission for the proposal to go ahead.

The most important regulations for the control of dealings in securities are now enforced at the federal level of government under the Securities Act of 1933 and the Securities Exchange Act of 1934, which were passed after the financial crises of 1929 onwards. However, neither these statutes nor any others contain detailed provisions relating to financial accounting and reporting. The United States has no statutory requirements for accounting in a form that is comparable to the accounting sections of the UK Companies Act. The United States has dealt with the need for accounting regulations in a different way. The federal securities legislation established a Securities and Exchange Commission (SEC) to administer the securities regulations. The primary function of the SEC is to ensure that investors are furnished with information necessary for informed investment decisions. It requires publication and receives registration of prospectuses and periodic financial reports. It also has the power to prescribe the methods to be followed in the preparation of financial reports and to prescribe the form and content of those reports. One vital point is that it is only the minority of US companies which are SEC-registered and have to obey its accounting and auditing rules. Other companies have no compulsory audit or published financial reporting requirements.

The Securities and Exchange Commission

The Commission comprises five members appointed by the President of the United States and acts as an independent regulatory body with quasi-judicial powers. It has issued a large number of statements containing regulations and opinions on accounting matters, notably in its 'Accounting Series Releases' and in its more recent 'Staff Accounting Bulletins'. However, these statements have related mainly to the details of registration requirements rather than to general accounting standards. *Regulation S-X* contains rules for the preparation of financial reports by registered companies. Form *10-K*, containing the reports and extra information, must be filed annually.

The Commission since its inception has tended to limit the exercise of its accounting standard-setting authority to a supervisory role, permitting and encouraging the private sector, currently through the FASB, to maintain leadership in the standard-setting process.

In 1973 the SEC issued Accounting Series Release No. 150, *Statement of Policy on the Establishment and Improvement of Accounting Principles and Standards*, in which it reaffirmed its intention to maintain a supervisory role:

> In meeting this statutory responsibility effectively, in recognition of the expertise, energy and resources of the accounting profession, and without abdicating its responsibilities, the Commission has historically looked to the standard-setting bodies designated by the profession to provide leadership in establishing and improving accounting principles. The determinations by these bodies have been regarded by the Commission, with minor exceptions, as being responsive to the needs of investors.
>
> The body presently designated by the Council of the American Institute of Certified Public Accountants (AICPA) to establish accounting principles is the Financial Accounting Standards Board (FASB). . . . The Commission intends to continue its policy of looking to the private sector for leadership in establishing and improving accounting principles. . . .
>
> . . . For purposes of this policy, principles, standards and practices promulgated by the FASB in its Statements and Interpretations will be considered by the Commission as having substantial authoritative support, and those contrary to such FASB promulgations will be considered to have no such support.

In the course of monitoring the performance of the FASB in the standard-setting process, the staff of the SEC maintain regular communications with the staff of the FASB. The Commission might have reached different conclusions from those reached by the FASB on some of the topics on which the Board has issued pronouncements. However, the Commission has interfered in matters that fall within the terms of reference of the Board only in a few special cases, notably:

(a) In March 1976, the Commission issued Accounting Series Release No. 190, requiring large public companies to disclose information about inventories, cost of goods sold, productive capacity, and depreciation expense on a replacement cost basis. That action, discussed further below, effectively (i) delayed the progress of the FASB towards establishing a requirement for the introduction of 'constant dollar accounting' (accounting for changes in purchasing power of the dollar), but (ii) accelerated the progress towards an FASB requirement for the introduction of 'current cost accounting' (accounting for changes in prices of specific assets owned).

(b) In 1978, the Commission effectively overruled part of an FASB standard for oil and gas accounting. That standard (Statement No. 19) required the use of the 'successful efforts method' for measurement of the historical cost of oil and gas reserves and outlawed use of the 'full cost method'. Under Statement 19, all companies would have been required to treat the costs of abortive exploration as expenses when they were determined to have no future economic benefit. However, the SEC concluded that neither cost-based method provided information that was satisfactory for the needs of investors. It decided to study the feasibility of a method of measuring the value of oil and gas reserves and gave companies permission to use either the full cost method or the successful efforts method until a more permanent solution could be found. In 1979, the Commission adopted rules requiring oil and gas companies to present supplementary information according to 'Reserve Recognition Accounting', a method under which proved oil and gas reserves are measured at the net present value of their estimated future cash flows. Cash flows are to be estimated without regard to future price or cost changes and discounted at a fixed rate of 10% per annum. These restrictions avoid some of the more subjective elements of the valuation but at a cost of producing a number that may differ significantly from the market value of the reserves.

However, the FASB regained the initiative to some extent in 1981. By this time, it was generally agreed that the disclosure requirements for oil and gas companies – which included reports of the effects of changing prices as well as extensive information about mineral reserves – had become too onerous. FASB took on the job of reviewing the requirements with the intention of reducing them after being informed that the SEC would probably support their findings. Late in 1982, the FASB adopted Statement 69 which contained requirements for information about the net present value of reserves as well as about the effects of changing prices, while simplifying both; and the SEC did indeed support them. However, the full cost method and the successful efforts method remain acceptable alternative costing methods for the main financial statements – the FASB have not shown any inclination to revisit that thorny issue.

The SEC's ventures into the two areas described above have been interesting for their strategic implications as well as for their direct contribution to accounting practice. Both initiatives concerned topics that were controversial. It would have been difficult for a private sector organisation to introduce the new requirements because a private sector organisation must have the broad support of the people who will implement the requirements and that support is not readily given for innovative types of reporting that put a burden on the preparers of financial reports. The SEC used its legislative authority to hasten the adoption of new practices. However, it made clear its wish that the FASB should take over the job of further standard setting in the areas concerned; and that wish has been implemented with the adoption by the FASB of Statement No. 33, *Financial Reporting and Changing Prices* and Statement No. 69, *Disclosures about Oil and Gas Producing Activities*.

One other controversial issue that has been addressed by the SEC is worthy of discussion here because it shows a significant difference between US and UK reporting practices. In the UK, forecasts of future results have been a standard part of a prospectus for several years. Until recently, the SEC refused to accept forecasts in financial reports that it received for filing. In effect, its refusal meant that forecasts could not be included in a prospectus. Forecasts were often made by company officials in statements that were not filed, and fairly recently the SEC reviewed its practice in order to find a way of bringing forecasts within its control. It decided to reverse its previous position and adopt a position that was distinctly encouraging to the publication of forecasts although it stopped short of demanding it.

The United States Congress

The US legislative authority – the Congress – has rarely taken a direct interest in accounting matters. It has usually relied on the SEC to look after the public interest. However, two exceptions to that practice are noteworthy.

The first concerned the investment credit, a provision of tax law designed to give an incentive for the purchase of productive assets. The credit is a deduction of a percentage of the cost of new assets from the tax liability for the year in which the assets were first used. The introduction of the credit led to a controversy about the timing of its recognition in earnings. Some believed that the credit should be added to earnings in the year for which it was given; others believed that it should be spread over the life of the asset concerned. Eventually, the private sector standard-setting authority proposed to require the use of one method – the spreading of the credit over the asset's life. However, before that proposal was finalised, the Congress passed legislation (the Revenue Act of 1971) to prevent any standard-setting body from limiting the acceptable methods of accounting for the investment credit in reports filed with any government agency, including the SEC.

This action of Congress was apparently motivated by a concern not to reduce the incentive effect of the tax credit. Congress recognised that it would be unfortunate if accounting standards were to produce an unfavourable pattern of earnings when optimal decisions were taken and hence to give an incentive to the taking of 'uneconomic decisions'. Today, it is widely accepted that accounting standards should, as far as possible, have a neutral effect on economic decisions. The FASB has sponsored research to estimate the economic consequences of its standards. The action of Congress may be seen as the forerunner of the concern about the neutrality of standards.

The second occasion on which Congress concerned itself with the affairs of the accounting profession has broader implications. It came at a time of public questioning of the role of the accounting profession, following some dramatic failures of large corporations. The debate raised the issue of whether the profession could do more to protect the public from losses involved in such failures. In early 1977, responding to the general concern, the staff of a US Senate Subcommittee (chaired by Senator Metcalf) published a report which cricitised, among other things, the role of the FASB in setting accounting standards. The report argued that the FASB tended to serve the interests of the managers of large corporations rather than the interests of the users of financial reports because it obtained its financial support from the corporations and their auditors.

The Senate Subcommittee held hearings during which it received evidence to contradict its staff report; the evidence suggested that FASB standards tended to reflect the positions taken by the users of financial reports rather than the positions of corporations, in cases of conflict. The final report (the Metcalf Report) was much concerned with the independence of auditors but gave little emphasis to the need for change at the FASB, except in supporting some proposals that had already been developed by the Foundation responsible for supervision of the FASB's activities.

Private Sector Standard-Setting Bodies

The first private sector body to become involved with the systematic development of US accounting standards was the Committee on Accounting Procedure established by the AICPA at about the same time as the SEC was established (1934). The Committee produced 51 publications known as 'Accounting Research Bulletins' during the period 1939–1959. The Committee was replaced by the Accounting Principles Board (APB) in 1959 and the Board published 31 Opinions and 4 Statements up to 1973. Pronouncements of the Committee and of the APB remain in force if they have not been amended or superseded by action of the FASB.

In 1971 growing dissatisfaction with the procedures for setting accounting standards led the AICPA to establish two committees to review those procedures. One source of dissatisfaction was that the APB was dominated by the accounting profession; there were insufficient provisions to ensure that the opinions of other interested parties were taken into account. The Wheat Committee was given the task of studying that problem. Its 1972 report, *Establishing Financial Accounting Standards*, led to the formation of three new bodies: the Financial Accounting Standards Board, responsible for setting standards; the Financial Accounting Foundation responsible for appointing members of the Board and for raising finance; and an advisory body, the Financial Accounting Standards Advisory Council. A second source of dissatisfaction was the limited progress of the APB in identifying fundamental concepts that would put the development of accounting standards on a surer foundation. The Trueblood Committee was formed to prepare a report on the objectives of financial reporting – a first step in the development of concepts. The report that resulted was to lead to one of the most important projects ever undertaken by an authoritative accounting body – the FASB's conceptual framework project.

Financial Accounting Standards Board

Since 1973, the Financial Accounting Standards Board has been the designated organisation in the private sector for establishing standards of financial accounting and reporting in the US. It is financed by voluntary contributions from public accounting firms, industry, investor and creditor organisations and various related organisations and individuals. Each annual contribution is limited to ensure the Board's independence from undue influence.

The seven members of the Financial Accounting Standards Board serve full time and are required to sever all previous business or professional connections before joining the Board. They have diverse backgrounds; only three of the present members were recruited directly from public accounting practices.

The FASB issues 'Statements of Financial Accounting Standards', 'Statements of Concepts' and 'Interpretations'. Statements of Standards establish new standards or amend those previously issued. Concepts Statements establish general concepts that will be used to guide the development of standards, but do not contain standards for direct application in themselves. Interpretations clarify, explain or elaborate on existing standards.

Before it issues a Statement, the FASB is required by its rules to follow extensive 'due process' procedures. In connection with each of its major projects, the Board:

(a) appoints a task force of technical experts representing a broad spectrum of preparers, auditors, and users of financial information to advise on the project;
(b) studies existing literature on the subject and conducts such additional research as may be necessary;
(c) publishes a comprehensive discussion of issues and possible solutions as a basis for public comment;
(d) conducts a public hearing;
(e) gives a broad distribution to an exposure draft of the proposed Statement for public comment.

The Board currently has an annual budget of about $10 million. Its technical staff works directly with the Board. It conducts research, participates in public hearings, analyses oral and written comments received from the public, and prepares recommendations and drafts of documents for consideration by the Board. At the time of writing, the Board has published 81 Statements.

Canadian Institute of Chartered Accountants

In Canada, the accounting profession has direct responsibility for authoritative statements of acceptable accounting practice. In 1945, the profession formed an 'Accounting and Auditing Research Committee' to formulate such statements; that Committee was divided into an 'Auditing Standards Committee' and an 'Accounting Research Committee' in 1973. The Accounting Research Committee issues 'Accounting Recommendations', for incorporation into the Canadian Institute's *Handbook*. Recommendations can be issued only if they have the support of a two-thirds majority of the Committee's members and only after the Committee has published an exposure draft for public comment. For many years, the main sanction against failure to follow accounting Recommendations was qualification of the audit report. However, additional legal backing for those Recommendations was introduced with the passing of the Canada Business Corporations Act of 1975. The Act does not contain direct provisions for financial reporting, instead it gives the government power to introduce such provisions by 'regulation'; and the regulations presently consist almost entirely of adoption of the Recommendations of the Canadian Institute.

Enforcement

As already noted, FASB standards are officially recognised in the US as authoritative by the Securities and Exchange Commission. Further assurance of the enforcement of FASB standards is provided by the AICPA rules. We noted above that membership of the AICPA is not a prerequisite of the right to practise. However, state authorities that control the right to practise have generally adopted the AICPA rules. Rule 203 of the AICPA's Code of Professional Ethics states:

> A member shall not express an opinion that financial statements are presented in conformity with generally accepted accounting principles if such statements contain any departure from an accounting principle promulgated by the [FASB] ... which has a material effect on the statements taken as a whole, unless the member can demonstrate that due to unusual circumstances the financial statements would otherwise have been misleading. In such cases his report must describe the departure, the approximate effects thereof, if practicable, and the reasons why compliance with the principles would result in a misleading statement.

The AICPA's Rules of Conduct also provide that 'the Trial Board may, after a hearing, admonish, suspend, or expel a member [of the AICPA] who is found guilty of infringing ... any provisions of the Rules of Conduct'. Accordingly, a Certified Public Accountant who condones a departure from an FASB pronouncement is subject to loss of his standing in the profession and, assuming that the licensing authorities concur with the conclusions of the AICPA Trial Board, loss of his legal authority to attest to the fairness of an enterprise's financial statement presentation.

Reports of Independent Auditors

The report of independent auditors can be an important source of information for the reader of financial reports. It explains what the independent auditor has done to satisfy himself as to the fairness of the financial statements and states his opinion regarding their fairness in the context of generally accepted accounting principles. The standard form of the audit report in the United States is expressed differently from audit reports in the United Kingdom. The AICPA's Statement on Auditing Standards No. 15, *Reports on Comparative Financial Statements*, suggests the following wording for the standard report:

> We have examined the balance sheet of *X* Company as of December 31, 1985 and 1984, and the related statements of income, retained earnings and changes in financial position for the years then ended. Our examinations were made in accordance with generally accepted auditing standards and,

accordingly, included such tests of the accounting records and such other auditing procedures as we considered necessary in the circumstances.

In our opinion, the financial statements referred to above present fairly the financial position of X Company as of December 31, 1985 and 1984, and the results of its operations and the changes in its financial position for the years then ended, in conformity with generally accepted accounting principles applied on a consistent basis.

The key words in the above opinion are 'fairly . . . in conformity with generally accepted accounting principles'. Those words contrast with the words used in audit reports that comply with British company law: 'The accounts show a true and fair view . . .' It is impossible to reach a full understanding of the significance of the forms of words without undertaking a detailed analysis of law cases in which they have been interpreted. To some extent, the words may simply represent different 'codes' for expressing a given idea. To establish what represents a 'true and fair view' would certainly involve reference to evidence about accounting standards and practice followed by other accountants. However, the reference to generally accepted accounting principles (GAAP) in the US report may reflect a greater reliance than in the UK on authoritative literature including standards.

2.3 Accounting Standards – Conceptual Framework

Since its inception, the FASB has devoted a significant portion of its resources towards the development of what has been referred to as a 'Conceptual Framework for Financial Accounting and Reporting'. As noted above, the need for a conceptual framework was one of the primary considerations in the studies that led to the establishment of the FASB, and the work undertaken by the Trueblood Committee made an important contribution to the development of a key statement on the objectives of financial reporting. One of the documents issued by the FASB on this subject explains the significance of that framework:

> Perhaps because accounting in general and financial statements in particular exude an aura of precision and exactitude, many persons are astonished to learn that a conceptual framework for financial accounting and reporting has not been articulated authoritatively. Though many organizations, committees, and individuals have published their own constructs of conceptual framework or aspects of a framework, none by itself has come to be universally accepted and relied on in practice. Notable among those efforts is Accounting Principles Board Statement No. 4 'Basic Concepts and Accounting Principles Underlying Financial Statements of Business Enterprises' (1970), but it purports primarily to describe the way things are and not to prescribe how they ought to be.

A conceptual framework is a constitution, a coherent system of inter-related objectives and fundamentals that can lead to consistent standards and that prescribes the nature, function, and limits of financial accounting and financial statements. The objectives are to identify the goals and pur-poses of accounting. The fundamentals are the underlying concepts of accounting, concepts that guide the selection of events to be accounted for, the measurement of those events, and the means of summarizing and com-municating them to interested parties.

Pressure for development of a conceptual framework came from many quarters, including accountants in public practice who saw it as a means of reducing the difficulty of judgments that have to be made about the relative desirability of accounting alternatives in areas that were not already covered by well-defined standards. However, it should not be supposed that the development of a conceptual framework will mean that all subsequent accounting standards can be determined easily by much the same process as that involved when using an algebraic formula. Discussions about standards involve the assessment of the benefits and costs of accounting alternatives and that assessment will continue to be partly subjective because of conflicts of interest and the lack of firm evidence about the level of both costs and benefits.

The development of a conceptual framework for accounting has been a challenging task. The FASB has been working on the project con-tinuously since its formation. At the present time, the Board's conclu-sions about the framework are expected to be contained in concepts statements as follows:

1. Concepts Statement No. 1 describes the fundamental objectives of financial reporting for business enterprises; a separate statement (No. 4) gives the objectives for non-business organisations.

2. Concepts Statement No. 2 describes the qualities that make accounting information useful.

3. Concepts Statement No. 3 gives definitions for the main elements of financial statements – components such as assets, liabilities, revenues and expenses. This statement, like No. 2, focuses on the business enterprise. The Board is expected to finalise an extension of these two statements to non-business enterprises in the near future.

4. A concepts statement to be published will deal with criteria for recognising and measuring the elements of financial statements, and with some of the issues that arise in relation to the presentation of information in financial reports. An exposure draft of this state-ment was issued in December 1983 and a final statement is expected to be issued in 1985. At one time, it seemed likely that a separate statement would be issued to deal with the presentation of information but the Board now intends to deal with presentational

issues briefly in a statement focusing mainly on recognition and measurement; and to deal with other presentational issues by issuing standards, if necessary.

The prospects created by a conceptual framework project are exciting. The Statement on the Objectives of Financial Reporting contains the conclusion that financial reports should provide a basis for assessing future cash flows. It opens the way for accounting to make more effective use of scientific method. Consider the following questions: do the users of financial reports wish to assess future cash flows? (to confirm the conclusions of the objectives Statement) and: which of specified accounting alternatives is more useful for the assessment of future cash flows? (to implement the conclusions). Answers to those questions can be formed – at least partially – by referring to objective evidence; the questions embody testable hypotheses. They represent great advances over the abstract type of question that used to be considered in the formulation of accounting standards, for example: which method represents an appropriate matching of costs and revenues?

However, the FASB has been criticised for its slow rate of progress. It had particular difficulty with the project on recognition and measurement because Board members were unable to agree on any conclusions. For a time, the Board was thought likely to abandon the project and thus admit that it would not complete its conceptual framework. Such a failure would have been widely regarded as serious – by the SEC among others; it would have lowered the Board's standing and perhaps threatened its medium-term survival. Recognising this danger, the Board renewed its efforts and succeeded in issuing the exposure draft, mentioned above. The draft has been strongly criticised. To obtain agreement, the Board had to blur its conclusions with compromises, with the result that some difficult issues were largely avoided and the quality of the conceptual analysis was severely impaired. Nevertheless, finalisation of the draft, expected with little change, will enable FASB to claim that it has completed its plan of work; and perhaps to work quietly – with less public pressure – to produce an improvement at some time in the future.

Objectives of Financial Reporting

The FASB issued the first in its series of Statements of Financial Accounting Concepts in November 1978. That Statement, entitled *Objectives of Financial Reporting by Business Enterprises*, contains the following major conclusions:

(a) Financial reporting is intended to provide information that is useful in making business and economic decisions.

(b) The objectives state that:
   (i) Financial reporting should provide information that is useful to present and potential investors and creditors and other users in making rational investment, credit, and similar decisions. The information should be comprehensible to those who have a reasonable understanding of business and economic activities and are willing to study the information with reasonable diligence.
   (ii) Financial reporting should provide information to help present and potential investors and creditors and other users in assessing the amounts, timing, and uncertainty of prospective cash receipts from dividends or interest and the proceeds from the sale, redemption, or maturity of securities or loans.
   (iii) Financial reporting should provide information about the economic resources of an enterprise, the claims to those resources (obligations of the enterprise to transfer resources to other entities and owners' equity), and the effects of transactions, events, and circumstances that change its resources and claims to those resources.
(c) Information about enterprise earnings based on accrual accounting generally provides a better indication of an enterprise's present and continuing ability to generate favourable cash flows than information limited to the financial effects of cash receipts and payments.
(d) Financial reporting is expected to provide information about an enterprise's financial performance during a period and about how management of an enterprise has discharged its stewardship responsibility to owners.

The Qualitative Characteristics of Accounting Information

The Statement on qualitative characteristics aims to identify the specific qualities that make accounting information useful. It adopts the framework of a cost – benefit test: accounting information is costly to provide and should be provided only if the benefits from use can be judged to outweigh the costs; the optimal amount of information is that which brings about the greatest possible surplus of benefits over costs. However, the Statement also acknowledges that the test can be applied only roughly at the present time, using subjective judgment.

The Statement emphasises the importance of making accounting information understandable; but pride of place, among the qualities that make the information useful, is reserved for relevance and reliability. Information is not worth presenting unless it has some minimum level of both relevance and reliability. Once those minima have been reached, a trade-off may be necessary: to gain relevance, some sacrifice of reliability may be required, or vice versa.

Relevance comprises three subsidiary qualities: predictive value, feedback value and timeliness. The quality of predictive value is defined in a way that echoes the main point of the objectives statement: information is useful if it helps the assessment of future cash flows. Feedback value is related to predictive value. Users will require information about actual results in areas where they have previously made predictions so that they can consider the efficiency of their predictive processes and improve them if they are found to be deficient. The quality of timeliness emphasises that information must be available in good time to be useful.

Reliability also consists of three subsidiary qualities: verifiability, representational faithfulness and neutrality. Verifiability indicates that the numbers should be capable of independent checking by people using an agreed method. Representational faithfulness means that accounting information should represent what it purports to represent: in other words, it should be true. Neutrality implies the desirability of avoiding bias. Although bias may be difficult to detect in practice, at least information should not be chosen with a view to supporting the interests of some parties to the accounting process at the expense of others.

2.4 Accounting for Assets

The international differences in accounting practices related to fixed assets stem from different perceptions about how fixed assets should be measured and how, if at all, the carrying value of fixed assets should be allocated to accounting periods.

Measuring Fixed Assets

North American accounting practices reflect a long-standing adherence to the historical cost basis of accounting and to the notion that revenues and gains are recognised only when an objective 'arm's length' transaction with another party has occurred. Accordingly, in both the US and Canada, the financial statement carrying value of fixed assets is almost never increased on the basis of appraisals or changes in prices because those events are not 'transactions'.

Moreover, it is unusual for any changes to be made to the measurement of fixed assets before their disposal, except for changes associated with the normal application of methods of depreciation. For example, if an enterprise builds a plant whose cost after completion exceeds its fair market value and if management plans to operate the plant, the cost of that plant generally is allocated to the periods during which it is operated; the asset is not normally written down to fair market value. The issue is addressed in paragraph 183 of APB Statement No. 4:

> Reductions in the utility of productive facilities caused by obsolescence due to technological, economic, or other change are usually recognized over the remaining productive lives of the assets. If the productive facilities have become worthless the entire loss is then recognized ... In unusual circumstances, pervasive evidence may exist of impairment of the utility of productive facilities indicative of an inability to recover cost ... The amount at which those facilities are carried is sometimes reduced to recoverable cost and a loss recorded prior to disposition or expiration of the useful life of the facilities.

As suggested by this reference to authoritative literature, accounting practices are not entirely uniform. While *increases* in the carrying value of fixed assets are prohibited in the US and discouraged in Canada, *decreases* in the carrying value of fixed assets do occur occasionally. This asymmetry in accounting practice is attributable to the concept of conservatism.

Allocating Costs of Fixed Assets

It is universal practice in North America to allocate the cost of fixed assets over their useful lives. Paragraph 5 of Accounting Research Bulletin (ARB) No. 43, Chapter 9C, states the position in the US:

> The cost of a productive facility is one of the costs of the services it renders during its useful economic life. Generally accepted accounting principles require that this cost be spread over the expected useful life of the facility in such a way as to allocate it as equitably as possible to the periods during which services are obtained from the use of the facility. This procedure is known as depreciation accounting, a system of accounting which aims to distribute the cost or other basic value of tangible capital assets, less salvage (if any), over the estimated useful life of the unit (which may be a group of assets) in a systematic and rational manner. It is a process of allocation, not of valuation.

It is important to emphasise that there are no exceptions to this rule, as there are in the UK, for example for investment properties.

As in most countries, several methods are accepted for the computation of depreciation. The straight-line method is most common but various methods of providing accelerated charges are also accepted including the reducing balance method and the sum-of-the-years'-digits method. Authoritative literature in the United States recognises the existence of inflation as a good reason for choosing an accelerated depreciation method. The rationale of that decision is that accelerated depreciation will lead to an increase in the depreciation expense in most practical situations so that the income statement will include some adjustment for inflation even though the balance sheet value will become smaller and less reflective of current prices.

Leases

For thirty years, the US has had accounting and reporting requirements dealing with leasing arrangements. Comparable requirements exist in Canada and, since 1984, in the UK. What began in 1949 as a relatively simple requirement that lessees (a) disclose the amounts and timing of annual rental payments and (b) assess whether certain leases might be considered a capitalisable asset has evolved into a comprehensive, sometimes complex, network of accounting and reporting criteria related to leasing activities from the perspectives of both the lessee and the lessor.

Current accounting and reporting practices relating to leases are governed by FASB Statement No. 13, *Accounting for Leases*. Although it was issued in 1976, it did not become fully operative until January 1, 1982. The FASB selected that lengthy period of transition because of the practical problems associated with the accumulation of the data necessary for implementation of the Statement; additionally many enterprises needed time during which they could resolve any problems that might arise in connection with restrictions included in their loan indentures or other agreements.

In spite of the complexity of the pronouncement, the concept under-lying the FASB's conclusions reflected in Statement No. 13 is simple: if the risks and rewards associated with ownership of the leased asset accrue to the lessee, the lessor reports the lease as a sale of that asset (sales-type or direct financing lease), while the lessee reports the lease as a purchase (capital lease). Otherwise, both the lessee and the lessor report the lease as an 'operating lease'.

The idea that a lease should be a basis for reporting both an asset and a liability of equal amounts has acquired considerable importance in recent years. It is designed to reflect 'substance over form', i.e. economic reality rather than legal formality. In the US, the use of leasing agreements as a financing mechanism has grown very rapidly over the last decades. In certain industries (such as the manufacture of photostatic or electronic computing equipment) 'leasing' has overtaken the traditional 'sale' as a means of marketing finished products.

The fundamental accounting requirements may be summarised as follows: a capital lease, at a minimum, represents an intangible right to the exclusive use of a specific item for a specific period of time and, possibly, may represent a sales contract calling for 'rental' payments in lieu of 'loan' payments. The right to use the item is regarded as an asset having a value equal to the *present value* of the cash payments (or other consideration) exchanged for that right.

Inventories

Inventories are generally measured at the lower of cost and market value in Canada and the United States. In both countries, overhead costs must be included in the measurement of cost of manufactured inventory. In the United States, a write-down of inventory to market value might not be reversed, subsequently, if market value increases.

The most notable feature of accounting for inventory in North America is the acceptance of LIFO (last-in, first-out) as a 'flow assumption' for identifying the cost of inventory. The FIFO assumption (first-in, first-out) is used about as frequently. The popularity of LIFO in the United States stems from the fact that it normally produces lower income numbers when prices are increasing. US tax laws allow the use of LIFO for the computation of taxable income, but only provided that it is also used in the primary financial statements of the enterprise. When prices are rising, use of LIFO can lead to very unrealistically low figures for inventories in balance sheets. This will normally be identifiable in the notes to financial reports.

2.5   Accounting for Corporate Taxes

It is well known that the income of a company, measured according to generally accepted accounting principles, normally differs from the income on which taxes are payable. The most common reason for the difference is that accelerated depreciation allowances are deductible in the computation of taxable income regardless of the methods used to compute depreciation expense in the income statements. Consequently, when the assets of a company are relatively new, or when a company is expanding or when prices are rising, its reported pre-tax profit is likely to exceed its taxable income. The accounting issue that arises in such a case is the need to choose between the following main alternatives: (a) calculate income tax expense on the full amount of income on which tax will be payable now or at some time in the future and regard the difference between that amount and the amount payable currently as a 'quasi-long-term-liability'; or (b) limit corporate tax expense to the amount payable currently. In the United States and Canada, alternative (a), 'comprehensive tax allocation', is required. This contrasts with the 'partial tax allocation' required in the United Kingdom, which is a middle ground between alternatives (a) and (b): the 'quasi-long-term-liability' will reflect only taxes likely to become payable within three to five years. This difference seriously affects comparisons of post-tax income between US and UK companies.

Deferral and Liability Methods

Two main methods are available for the comprehensive allocation of taxes: the deferral method and the liability method. APB Opinion No. 11, *Accounting for Income Taxes*, requires the use of the deferral method in the United States. (The deferral method is also used in Canada.) It describes the two methods of accounting for corporate taxes, as follows:

> Interperiod tax allocation under the *deferred method* is a procedure whereby the tax effects of current timing differences are deferred currently and allocated to income tax expense of future periods when the timing differences reverse. The deferred method emphasizes the tax effects of timing differences on income of the period in which the differences originate. The deferred taxes are determined on the basis of the tax rates in effect at the time the timing differences originate and are not adjusted for subsequent changes in tax rates or to reflect the imposition of new taxes. The tax effects of transactions which reduce taxes currently payable are treated as deferred credits; the tax effects of transactions which increase taxes currently payable are treated as deferred charges. Amortization of these deferred taxes to income tax expense in future periods is based upon the nature of the transactions producing the tax effects and upon the manner in which these transactions enter into the determination of pretax accounting income in relation to taxable income.
>
> Interperiod tax allocation under the *liability method* is a procedure whereby the income taxes expected to be paid on pretax accounting income are accrued currently. The taxes on components of pretax accounting income may be computed at different rates, depending upon the period in which the components were, or are expected to be, included in taxable income. The difference between income tax expense and income taxes payable in the periods in which the timing differences originate are either liabilities for taxes payable in the future or assets for prepaid taxes. The estimated amounts of future tax liabilities and prepaid taxes are computed at the tax rates expected to be in effect in the periods in which the timing differences reverse. Under the liability method the initial computations are considered to be tentative and are subject to future adjustment if tax rates change or new taxes are imposed.

The treatment of income taxes is currently being reviewed by FASB. Current indications are that the liability method may be adopted in place of the deferred method, but that comprehensive allocation will be continued.

Comparative Example

Suppose that (a) Companies *A* and *B* both have, at the end of 1983, deferred taxes payable in the amount of $10,000, reflecting a past tax rate of 40% on $25,000 of deferred items, (b) in 1984, tax rates changed from 40% to 45%, and (c) in 1985 the difference between financial and taxable earnings reverses. Under the deferral method, corporate tax expense in 1983 would be increased by adding $10,000 to the amount of tax payable on income for the year. In 1985, corporate tax expense would be reduced as a result of the elimination of the $10,000 'liability' but it would include $1,250 as a result of the change in tax rate. Under the liability method, the adjustments would be similar except that the expense component of $1,250 would be recognised in 1984, rather than in 1985.

2.6   Accounting for Pension Costs

FASB has been working on a project to improve accounting for pension costs for more than five years. The issues have proved to be highly controversial – perhaps the most controversial of any currently on the agenda – and the outcome of the Board's deliberations cannot yet be predicted with confidence. The controversy is attributable to the fact that alternative methods of accounting can make large differences to earnings and to numbers shown on the balance sheets, given the large scale of modern pension plans. Companies are reluctant to accept changes that will make their financial position and performance seem less strong on the face of the financial statements, and some have even threatened that they would have to review the benefits provided under their schemes if certain accounting proposals were adopted.

Two issues have dominated the debate. The first is the suggestion that full provision should be made in the accounts for any pension obligation that is not fully funded. For example, if the benefits under a pension plan are improved so that employees become entitled to higher benefits on the basis of past service, a liability would have to be shown representing the value of the obligation to the extent that it was unfunded. At the same time, an 'intangible asset' might be created, representing the 'goodwill' generated by the change in plan, and this asset might be amortised over the remaining expected service life of employees. At present, such items do not have to be shown on the balance sheet, provided a plan for funding the obligation exists and meets certain conditions; unfunded liabilities are, however, shown as a note to the accounts. The second issue is the suggestion that a standard method should be used for calculating unfunded liabilities.

The Board has conducted a field test of proposals for accounting for pensions to assess the impact on reported results and it is expected to publish an exposure draft in the near future.

2.7 Accounting for Business Combinations

A detailed discussion of practice on the preparation of consolidated accounts and alternative methods of accounting for mergers and acquisitions is given in Chapter 10.

For the past decade, US accounting practices related to business combinations have been determined on the basis of APB Opinion No. 16, entitled *Business Combinations*. That Opinion provides for the use of two previously established methods of acounting: the 'purchase method' and the 'pooling of interests method'.

Purchase Method

Under the purchase method, which is broadly similar to the standard UK acquisition method, the accounting basis for the acquired enterprise's assets is changed from (a) historical cost (adjusted for depreciation) to (b) fair value at the time of the business combination. Paragraph 11 of APB Opinion No. 16 describes the essence of the purchase method, as follows:

The purchase method accounts for a business combination as the acquisition of one company by another. The acquiring corporation records at its cost the acquired assets less liabilities assumed. A difference between the cost of an acquired company and the sum of the fair values of tangible and identifiable intangible assets less liabilities is recorded as goodwill. The reported income of an acquiring corporation includes the operations of the acquired company after acquisition, based on the cost to the acquiring corporation.

The Opinion requires that any amount recorded as goodwill in relation to business combinations initiated after October 1, 1970 must be amortised over a period not exceeding 40 years.

Pooling of Interests Method

Under the pooling of interests method, the accounting basis of the acquired enterprise remains unchanged, and the historical cost (adjusted for depreciation) of its assets is combined with that of the acquiring enterprise's assets. Opinion No. 16 describes in paragraph 12 the pooling of interests method, as follows:

The pooling of interests method accounts for a business combination as the uniting of the ownership interests of two or more companies by exchange of equity securities. No acquisition is recognized because the combination is accomplished without disbursing resources of the constituents. Ownership interests continue and the former bases of accounting are retained. The recorded assets and liabilities of the constituents are carried forward to the combined corporation at their recorded amounts. Income of the combined corporation includes income of the constituents for the entire fiscal period in which the combination occurs. The reported income of the constituents for prior periods is combined and restated as income of the combined corporation.

In periods of rising prices, the purchase method can be expected to produce the following two main differences from the pooling of interest method: (1) the fixed assets will tend to be reported at greater amounts, and an intangible asset, goodwill, may be created; (2) net income reported after the business combination will tend to be less under the purchase method because the depreciation of the higher carrying amounts of the fixed assets and the amortisation of goodwill (both of which are reported as expenses) are deducted in the determination of net income.

The reader of the financial reports of a North American enterprise involved in a business combination generally can expect it to be accounted for on the basis of the purchase method. Canadian business combinations are almost always accounted for on that basis. However a significant minority (about one-fifth) of US business combinations meet certain conditions set out in the authoritative literature that enable them to be accounted for under the pooling of interests method. A similar standard (SSAP 23) was adopted in the UK in 1985.

The choice of method for translation of the financial Statements of foreign subsidiaries has been very controversial in North America. This is discussed in detail in Chapter 12.

2.8   Financial Reporting and Changing Prices

As noted in Chapter 11, methods of reporting the effects of changing prices on business enterprises have been debated in North America for many years. On several occasions, authoritative US publications by the Committee on Accounting Procedure and the APB encouraged companies to provide supplementary information on the effects of inflation. The first authoritative attempt to encourage the presentation of comprehensive information on the effect of inflation was made in 1969 with the publication of APB Statement No. 3. That Statement called for the presentation of supplementary information in which financial statements would be expressed in stabilised measuring units as a result of adjustments for changes in the general price level. Implementation of the Statement was voluntary and few companies followed its recommendations.

Subsequent attempts in the United States to establish a system for reporting the effects of changing prices have involved the problems, familiar in several industrialised countries, of achieving significant changes in a complex subject during a short period of time. It is interesting to compare the progress that has been made in the United States and in the United Kingdom. In both countries, the private sector standard-setting bodies began by developing systems based on adjustments for changes in the general price level; in both countries, public sector bodies intervened to advance systems based on the measurement of specific price changes and the private sector took over the further development of those systems.

In the United States, the FASB published in 1974 an exposure draft of a Statement that would require the presentation of supplementary financial statements based on adjustments for general inflation – the method that has become known as 'constant dollar accounting'. However, the exposure draft never became a final Statement. In 1976, the SEC introduced a requirement for large companies to file information on the replacement cost of inventories, cost of goods sold, productive capacity, and depreciation expense. The FASB concluded that agreement on a single system would not be possible at least until new evidence was available. Consequently, it decided to require companies to provide information experimentally on both a current cost basis and a constant dollar basis. That requirement was contained in Statement No. 33, *Financial Reporting and Changing Prices*, published in September 1979. It applied initially to about 1,200 of the largest US companies and calls for supplementary financial statements in which revised measurements are presented of net assets and income from continuing operations incorporating adjustments to inventories, property, plant and equipment, and related expenses.

Between 1979 and 1984, the Board sponsored a good deal of research on the usefulness of Statement 33. It found limited use of both current cost information and constant dollar information. However, use of the constant dollar information seemed the less, and that approach to accounting also involved some difficulties of reconciliation with methods of foreign currency translation. Rather than abandon all forms of information about the effects of changing prices, the Board decided, late in 1984, to remove the requirement for constant dollar information for companies that provide current cost information.

Developments in Canada have followed a similar course to those in the US and the UK. First efforts focused on methods of accounting for changes in general prices but opinion began to move towards a preference for current cost accounting in the late 1970s, spurred on by a provincial government report, *Report of the Ontario Committee on Inflation Accounting*, in 1977. In 1979, the Canadian Institute produced an Exposure Draft calling for the publication of current cost information by most large public companies; it was on similar lines to the British proposals but differed considerably from the requirements adopted in the US Statement 33. The differences from the US standard were a cause for concern, given the close economic links between Canada and the United States and, in due course, a revised exposure draft was published, adopting a compromise between the US requirements and the British requirements. This compromise survived into the Standard finalised in 1982.

2.9   Presentation of Financial Statements

We noted, in the introduction to this chapter, that the layout of North American financial statements differs considerably from the layout usually found in the United Kingdom. Two other matters of presentation are the subjects of rather more substantial differences:

(a) In North America, the financial report of a parent company is likely to include only consolidated financial statements without separate statements for the parent company.
(b) Restatement of prior period income items is usually undertaken in Canada but rarely in the United States, where a prior period adjustment is included in the computations for the current year.

Financial statements differ substantially from company to company, but a reasonably representative set is included as Appendix 2.

2.10   Summary

There are substantial similarities between North American and British financial reporting. Although some terminology is different, the underlying philosophy is the same. Despite the lack of Companies Acts, financial reporting for SEC-registered companies is subject to more detailed regulation in the USA. As for measurement rules, these are professionally set and broadly similar in the USA and the UK, although the profession has been setting standards for a longer period in the USA.

In the USA, government regulation is based on the Securities Acts of the 1930s which set up the SEC. This body at present delegates standard setting to the FASB. However, the SEC has its own registration requirements. It also occasionally intervenes in the process of setting standards, for example on oil and gas. In addition, there are rare occurences of direct action by Congress.

Private standard setting has fulfilled an even larger role in the USA than in the UK, first through the AICPA's Committee on Accounting Procedure, then its Accounting Principles Board, and since 1973 through the independent FASB. This latter body has very substantial resources compared to the UK's Accounting Standards Committee, and has the authoritative backing of the SEC. It has progressed further than the ASC into 'conceptual framework' analysis.

In Canada, the government delegates standard setting to the Accounting Research Committee of the Canadian ICA.

Auditors perform a similar role in North America to that in the UK. Auditors in the USA report whether a company's financial statements are drawn up 'fairly . . . in conformity with generally accepted accounting principles (GAAP)'.

Turning to more detailed accounting matters, it should be noted that GAAP requires a stricter adherence to historical cost accounting than is customary in the UK. The list of other differences is shrinking, but important among them is the continuing insistence in North America on full accounting for deferred taxation. Developments in accounting for changing prices have been similar on both sides of the Atlantic. Current cost accounting is the preferred method, but its usefulness is disputed and its long-term future uncertain.

Further Reading

Publications intended to compare North American and United Kingdom accounting practices:

Benston, G.J. (1975) 'Accounting standards in the United States and the United Kingdom: their nature, causes and consequences', *Vanderbilt Law Review*, (Symposium on Accounting and Federal Securities Laws), vol. 28, January, pp. 235 – 268.

Benston, G.J. (1976, reprinted 1978), *Corporate Financial Disclosure in the UK and the USA*, Saxon House for the Institute of Chartered Accountants in England and Wales.

Benston, G.J. (1976) 'Public (US) compared to private (UK) regulation of corporate financial disclosure', *Accounting Review*, vol. 51, July, pp. 483 – 498.

Nobes, C.W. (1984) 'An insight into US accounting', *Accountancy*, February, pp. 129 – 131.

Zeff, S.A. (1972) *Forging Accounting Principles in Five Countries: A History and an Analysis of Trends* (Arthur Andersen & Co. Lecture Series, University of Edinburgh 1971), Stipes Publishing Co., Champaign, Illinois.

Accountants' International Study Group, *Comparative Glossary of Accounting Terms*; and many other comparative publications, but none since 1975.

Publications intended to compare various countries' accounting practices, including North America and United Kingdom:

Fitzgerald, R.D., Stickler, A.D. and Watts, T.R. (eds) (1979) *International Survey of Accounting Principles and Reporting Practices* (compiled for Price Waterhouse International by Price Waterhouse & Co., Canada), Butterworth, Ontario.

American Institute of Certified Public Accountants (1975) *Professional Accounting in 30 Countries*, AICPA, New York.

Publications intended primarily to catalogue individual countries' current accounting practices:

American Institute of Certified Public Accountants, *Accounting Trends and Techniques*, issued annually, AICPA, New York.

Canadian Institute of Chartered Accountants, *Financial Reporting in Canada* (latest edition), CICA, Toronto.

Appendix 2
Specimen Financial Statements of an SEC-registered Company

Accountants' Report

Price, Sells and Ross
CERTIFIED PUBLIC ACCOUNTANTS

We have examined the Consolidated Balance Sheet of General Corporation and consolidated subsidiaries as of December 31, 1985 and 1984 and the related Statements of Consolidated Income and Changes in Consolidated Financial Position for each of the three years in the period ended December 31, 1985. Our examinations were made in accordance with generally accepted auditing standards and, accordingly, included such tests of the accounting records and such other auditing procedures as we considered necessary in the circumstances.

In our opinion, these financial statements present fairly the financial position of the companies at December 31, 1985 and 1984 and the results of their operations and the changes in their financial position for each of the three years in the period ended December 31, 1985, in conformity with generally accepted accounting principles consistently applied during the period except for the change in 1985, with which we concur, in the method of accounting for foreign currency translation as described in Note 1 to the Financial Statements.

Consolidated Balance Sheet (in $m.)
December 31.

ASSETS	1985	1984
Current assets		
Cash	369.5	279.6
United States Government and other marketable securities and time deposits – at cost	5,847.4	2,846.6
Total cash and marketable securities	6,216.9	3,126.2
Accounts and notes receivable less allowances	6,964.2	2,864.5
Inventories (less allowances)	6,621.5	6,184.2
Prepaid expenses and deferred income taxes	997.2	1,868.2
Total current assets	20,799.8	14,043.1
Equity in net assets of nonconsolidated subsidiaries and associates	4,450.8	4,231.1
Other investments and miscellaneous assets – at cost (less allowances)	1,222.5	1,550.0
Common stock held for the incentive program	56.3	35.2
Property		
Real estate, plants and equipment – at cost	37,777.8	37,687.2
Less accumulated depreciation	20,116.8	18,148.9
Net real estate, plants and equipment	17,661.0	19,538.3
Special tools – at cost (less amortization)	1,504.1	2,000.1
Total property	19,165.1	21,538.4
Total assets	45,694.5	41,397.8

LIABILITIES AND STOCKHOLDERS' EQUITY

Current liabilities		
Accounts payable (principally trade)	4,642.3	3,600.7
Loans payable (principally overseas)	1,255.2	1,182.5
Accrued liabilities	9,011.5	7,601.8
Total current liabilities	14,909.0	12,385.0
Long-term debt	3,137.2	4,452.0
Capitalized leases	384.6	293.1
Other liabilities	4,698.2	4,259.8
Deferred credits	1,798.9	1,720.8
Stockholders' equity		
Preferred stocks ($5.00 series, $183.6; $3.75 series, $100.0)	283.6	283.6
Common stock (issued, 315,711,299 and 312,363,657 shares)	526.2	520.6
Capital surplus (principally additional paid-in capital)	2,136.8	1,930.4
Net income retained for use in the business	18,390.5	15,552.5
Subtotal	21,337.1	18,287.1
Accumulated foreign currency translation and other adjustments	(570.5)	—
Total stockholders' equity	20,766.6	18,287.1
Total liabilities and stockholders' equity	45,694.5	41,397.8

Statement of Consolidated Income (in $m.)
For the years ended December 31.

	1985	1984	1983
Net sales	74,581.6	60,025.6	62,698.5
Costs and expenses			
Cost of sales and other operating charges, exclusive of items listed below	60,718.8	51,548.3	55,185.2
Selling, general and administrative expenses	3,234.8	2,964.9	2,715.0
Depreciation of real estate, plants and equipment	2,569.7	2,403.0	1,837.3
Amortization of special tools	2,549.9	2,147.5	2,568.9
Total costs and expenses	69,073.2	59,063.7	62,306.4
Operating income	5,508.4	961.9	392.1
Other income less income deductions – net	815.8	476.3	367.7
Interest expense	(1,352.7)	(1,415.4)	(897.9)
Income (loss) before income taxes	4,971.5	22.8	(138.1)
United States, foreign and other income taxes (credit)	2,223.8	(252.2)	(123.1)
Income (loss) after income taxes	2,747.7	275.0	(15.0)
Equity in earnings of nonconsolidated subsidiaries and associates	982.5	687.7	348.4
Net income	3,730.2	962.7	333.4
Dividends on preferred stocks	12.9	12.9	12.9
Earnings on common stock	3,717.3	949.8	320.5
Average number of shares of common stock outstanding (in millions)	313.9	307.4	299.1
Earnings per share of common stock	11.84	3.09	1.07

Statement of Changes in Consolidated Financial Position (in $m.)

For the years ended December 31.

	1985	1984	1983
Source of funds			
Net income	3,730.2	962.7	333.4
Depreciation of real estate, plant and equipment	2,569.7	2,403.0	1,837.3
Amortization of special tools	2,549.9	2,147.5	2,568.9
Deferred income taxes, undistributed earnings of nonconsolidated subsidiaries and associates, etc. – net	645.5	75.8	68.0
Total funds provided by current operations	9,495.3	5,589.0	4,807.6
Increase in long-term debt	3,177.1	2,497.4	2,172.7
Proceeds from sale of newly issued common stock	212.0	353.5	303.6
Other – net	772.8	1,459.2	1,703.3
Total	13,657.2	9,899.1	8,987.2
Use of funds			
Dividends paid to stockholders	892.2	750.2	730.5
Decrease in long-term debt	4,491.9	1,846.5	257.6
Expenditures for real estate, plants and equipment	1,923.0	3,611.1	6,563.3
Expenditures for special tools	2,083.7	2,601.0	3,178.1
Increase (decrease) in other working capital items	1,142.0	(1,306.2)	341.2
Investments in nonconsolidated subsidiaries and associates	33.7	591.0	311.0
Total	10,566.5	8,093.6	11,381.7
Increase (decrease) in cash and marketable securities	3,090.7	1,805.5	(2,394.5)
Cash and marketable securities at beginning of the year	3,126.2	1,320.7	3,715.2
Cash and marketable securities at end of the year	6,216.9	3,126.2	1,320.7
Increase (decrease) in other working capital items by element			
Accounts and notes receivable	4,099.7	(788.8)	(125.1)
Inventories	437.3	(1,038.5)	(72.3)
Prepaid expenses and deferred income taxes	(871.0)	341.1	820.6
Accounts payable	(1,041.6)	99.0	268.0
Loans payable	(72.7)	545.3	(51.3)
Accrued liabilities	(1,409.7)	(474.3)	(498.7)
Increase (decrease) in other working capital items	1,142.0	(1,306.2)	341.2

3

Financial Reporting in Britain and Australia

PETER STANDISH

3.1 Introduction

This chapter considers financial reporting practices and standards in Britain and Australia, taking account of past experiences, current issues and controversies, and possible future directions of development. When classifying financial reporting by country, it is natural to associate with Britain those other countries having economic systems, financial institutions and commercial law derived in various ways from British practice (see Chapter 8). As well as Australia, that association includes New Zealand, Canada and other countries or colonies formerly subject to British rule. But these countries also have unique aspects of their system for financial reporting which make perilous any attempt at broad generalisations about the whole set of British-influenced countries.

For this reason, this chapter is confined explicitly to Britain and Australia. In some important aspects, developments in the two countries are currently on diverging pathways. British business enterprise and the accounting profession are having to adjust to the realities of other national influences within the European Economic Community where very different legal and accounting traditions are found. At the same time Australia seeks to find better ways of establishing and supervising financial reporting standards in a geographically large and politically federated nation, for which purpose some aspects of American experience appear relevant.

Attention here is limited to financial reporting required by the relevant company laws. In both countries, much economic activity is conducted by entities outside the scope of the company law, principally:

(i)   unincorporated business (e.g. sole traders and partnerships) for which the only requirements relating to financial reporting are those found in the income tax law;

(ii) not-for-profit organisations which are subject to a wide variety of laws, in many instances specific to a given organisation;

(iii) public sector agencies and enterprises, many of which also report under specific laws.

Although company law requirements have provided useful models for financial reporting by these other categories of entities, different information needs and concepts of accountability mean that financial reporting practices and standards applicable to companies may have only limited application to them.

Finally, in the list of exclusions, this chapter does not address financial reporting other than through the annual report to shareholders. There have been calls for companies to cater more explicitly for various special interest groups, most notably for employee reporting; or for annual accounts to be rearranged in ways that would convey different messages, e.g. as is claimed for value added statements. Whilst in recent years there has been a degree of voluntary experimentation by the companies in presenting special purpose accounts, whether as part of the annual report or in separate documents, the issue of special purpose reporting remains unsettled, and contingent on the resolution of political debates about the responsibility and accountability of the business corporation.

3.2   The Road to the Present

The British Model of Financial Regulation

The economic systems of Britain and Australia continue to be dominated by the private enterprise sector. As such, these systems retain a number of key elements pioneered in Britain in the nineteenth century and further developed in this century, notably:

(i)   the right of incorporation of limited liability companies being available generally to citizens;

(ii) statutory requirements for incorporated companies to present annual accounts to their shareholders;

(iii) the requirement for annual accounts to be independently audited;

(iv) establishment of the accounting profession, characterised by non-governmental institutions having control over admission and disciplining of members;

(v) emergence of large-scale public accounting firms, organised as partnerships without limited liability, offering services to clients through national and international networks of offices;

(vi) development of the stock exchanges as a mechanism for facilitating purchase and sale of securities in quoted companies.

British developments in these respects were exported around the world, particularly to those countries largely peopled from Britain itself or governed under British laws. Thus, well before recent interest in international harmonisation of financial reporting, there was effectively an accounting *lingua franca* within the then British Empire. Throughout that domain the general appearance and content of annual accounts would have been widely familiar, while auditing services were available from well-known accounting firms operating directly or through agents in most of the countries concerned. At the same time the laws relating to companies and trading in securities created shared expectations about codes of conduct and fair dealing between parties at arm's length.

None of this is to imply a world of ordered tranquillity or perfection. The economic expansion of Britain in the nineteenth and early twentieth centuries was certainly not inward-looking, and its overseas trade and investment reached around the globe. Most of the influence on development of financial reporting practices in other countries was one way, partly the result of British self-confidence in ideas and practices of corporate accountability, and partly reflecting the fact that many other countries did not at that stage possess their own well developed ideas and practices in financial reporting.

Thus, although there was little direct foreign influence on British financial reporting, at least before Britain joined the EEC, the system for determining standards of accountability was in a phase of dynamic evolution, with repeated changes to relevant sections of the company law and to the role that the accountancy profession sought to exercise in developing standards. Frauds and scandals, of which the Royal Mail Case (1931) was particularly notable, have been one stimulus to change, but others are rooted in the development of additional forms of corporate activity and operation, and changing economic conditions. Some of the major internal influences on the British model have been:

(i) the growth of corporate groups, leading to consolidated accounts;

(ii) the rise of British-based multinationals, with implications for

translation of foreign currency investment and transactions;
(iii) high rates of price inflation within Britain, leading to questioning
of the historic cost basis of accounting and experimentation with
various forms of price variation accounting.

The Role of the Auditor

What sharply distinguished British financial reporting from concurrent
practices and developments in many other countries was the pivotal role
of the auditor. In effect, the state has struck a bargain with the citizenry
over the principle of limited liability. Persons wishing to take advantage
of risk investment with limited personal liability have to accept that the
annual accounts of companies must be audited and published. In the
nineteenth century, however, auditing was voluntary for most companies. Those that volunteered were able to use the newly emerging
institutions of the accountancy profession, commencing with the Edinburgh Society of Accountants (Royal Charter, 1854). By 1880, The
Institute of Chartered Accountants in England and Wales had been
founded, whereas by contrast the counterpart French body, L'Ordre
des Experts Comptables et des Comptables Agréés, was not founded till
1942.

Although membership of the present British professional institutions
was never restricted solely to auditors, the latter exercised a dominant
role in the various Chartered Institutes of accountants. British audit
expertise proved to be much in demand in other countries and highly
exportable, whether through expansion of public accounting firms
(noted earlier) or by example and influence, as in the United States.
Even at the present time, nearly all the recognised major international
accounting firms are Anglo-American in origin (see Chapter 1).

The significance of the role of the auditor has been profound.
Whatever shortcomings have occurred from time to time in actual financial reporting practices, the ideals and objectives underlying the audit
function have been to:

(i) place constraints on the freedom available to directors in drawing
up the accounts;
(ii) promote ideas of truth and fairness in accounts, expressed
through efforts to achieve greater comprehensibility and comparability.

Without the development of the external audit function as it now
operates, it is difficult to imagine that there would have been the same
growth of investment in risk securities, especially across national
boundaries.

The Role of the Stock Exchanges

Within the major industrial nations there are significant differences in the importance of stock exchanges in risk capital formation, *vis-à-vis* the role played by the banking system. In both Britain and Australia, the stock exchange occupies the central place in arrangements for pricing and trading in securities, and for this reason there is a long history of stock exchange involvement in the development of financial reporting standards for listed companies. The role of the stock exchanges has also meant, as in the United States, that many of the debates about financial reporting are couched in terms of claims about the information needs of investors, whether considered as individuals or as portfolio fund managers acting on behalf of individuals. Finally, the system of active trading in securities has been associated with the emergence of a vigorous financial press, quick to pounce on what it sees as examples of obscure or misleading financial reporting.

This section has outlined some of the key elements in the development of financial reporting in Britain. Those same elements were transplanted to Australia. It is now desirable to give some more specific facts and sources of information, and to record the emerging differences between the two countries in their systems of corporate financial reporting.

3.3   Structure of the Accountancy Profession

Britain was the first country in the world to develop an accountancy profession as that would now be interpreted. Although the function of audit in relation to systems for controlling and verifying public expenditure is quite ancient, there had been no comparable development of auditing skills for private enterprise prior to the Industrial Revolution. But this changed rapidly within a century from about 1780 onwards, with the establishment of the present-day professional institutions or their direct antecedents.

For purposes of educating and training accountants, literature on accounting was still in a fairly embryonic state until the 1880s. Texts on bookkeeping and some of the basic accounting issues had existed in one form or another at least since the fifteenth century in Italy and since the mid-sixteenth century in England, but by and large these were full of prescriptive detail and were intellectually unambitious. Accounting as an academic discipline did not exist in universities in Britain, where it has become established only within the past twenty-five years. Inevitably, if the profession was to secure control over the admission and qualification of members, it had to develop its own educational programmes and conduct examination of candidates for membership. With

World War Two and its aftermath, accountants and auditors faced increasingly complex issues of financial measurement in conditions of inflation and accelerating technological change. To assist them, the professional institutions became increasingly drawn into the process of offering guidance to members on the best accounting practice, and of more recent years to lay down accounting and auditing standards which members are obliged to follow in carrying out their professional duties. In other words, the profession has sought to perform the role of arbiter on the substantive practice issues in financial accounting and auditing.

The role of the accounting profession in specifying standards has been exacting and at times distinctly uncomfortable, as will be seen later in the chapter. In contrast, it is noteworthy that the approach of the profession towards practice standards differs fundamentally from that of other professions. For example, medical schools came to be established before the present-day institutions of the medical profession. Technical progress and advancement of standards in that field have flowed from the insights of gifted individuals and, increasingly, organised research in medical schools and specialist institutes. The professional institutions (e.g. the British Medical Association) do not make recommendations on how members should carry out their professional responsibilities, let alone seek to impose compulsory standards.

Four of the present institutions of the profession in the UK are shown in Table 1.4 in Chapter 1. The three Institutes of Chartered Accountants and the Chartered Association have members engaged in all principal areas of accounting in the private sector. A significant proportion of members is in public practice, either as principals or staff of accounting firms, but many members are employed in commerce and industry. The governing councils and the Presidents of the Chartered Institutes have mostly been drawn from firms of chartered accountants and in particular from the audit area. The Chartered Association has developed a particular role in offering a route for obtaining professional qualifications in third-world countries, and has a large register of overseas candidates.

There are also two further major bodies whose members cannot act as auditors. The Institute of Cost and Management Accountants (ICMA), which had about 24,000 members in 1984, particularly caters for accountants engaged in management accounting in commerce and industry. The Chartered Institute of Public Finance and Accountancy (CIPFA) had about 9,000 members in 1984, predominantly employed in local and central government.

The structure of the profession in Britain reflects historical events rather than any overall planned coverage of membership and distribution of functions. For a country having in all significant respects common company and tax laws, the existence of the six professional bodies creates what could be termed system redundancy, with major effort being required to coordinate their views and resolve conflict, which in a unified structure would perforce occur as part of the internal policy process of the profession. An attempt to integrate the profession in 1971 failed, and since then a rather uneasy coordination has been attempted through the Consultative Committee of Accountancy Bodies (CCAB).

The two major Australian accountancy bodies (see Table 1.4) also have substantially overlapping roles, though with these differences in emphasis:

(i) The ICAA has always been closely identified with audit and public practice generally, and a much higher proportion of its membership is in these fields than is the case with ASA membership.

(ii) A significant proportion of ASA members is employed in the public sector.

Within the last twenty years there have been two major attempts to achieve integration of the two bodies, but each failed for want of sufficient support from the ICAA membership. According to whether the two bodies have been in a phase of wooing each other, or getting over broken engagements, they have tended to collaborate closely or to compete with each other in seeking to attract members and advance their public image.

3.4 Company Law

The basic principle of company law in Britain and in Australia is that it shall apply to all companies incorporated within the relevant jurisdiction. For most purposes, the law does not differentiate between companies according to size or nature of their activity, with a major exception relating to the distinction between public companies, which are permitted to issue shares and other securities to the public, and private (proprietary) companies, which may not do so. In general, the company law in each country relates to:

(i) a procedure for the incorporation of companies with limited personal liability for shareholders;

(ii) the powers and duties of directors in regard to management of the affairs of the company;

(iii) the accountability of directors to the shareholders, particularly through the presentation of annual accounts and the directors' report thereon;

(iv) audit of the annual accounts by recognised, independent accountants;

(v) procedures for the conduct of affairs of companies which become insolvent, leading either to their continuance under the direction of a receiver, or to liquidation.

As regards financial reporting and audit, the law in both countries requires annual presentation by companies to shareholders of the following:

(i) a balance sheet and profit and loss account, together with notes as required, and a directors' report;

(ii) in the case of a holding company, a consolidated balance sheet and profit and loss account, as well as its own balance sheet and, in Australia, its own profit and loss account;

(iii) the auditor's report on the accounts, except under certain conditions for proprietary companies in Australia.

The overriding requirement for the annual accounts in both countries is that they show a true and fair view, and the auditors must indicate whether in their opinion that is the case. Some of the implications of this requirement are considered later. Some more detailed aspects of the respective company laws, particularly relating to accounts and audit, are noted below.

Britain

Company law was consolidated in the 1985 Companies Act. This was made necessary partly because of many changes to law that affected accounting as a result of the implementation of EEC company law Directives. The changes included:

(1) Companies Act 1980

In accordance with the intentions of the second Directive, a company may only distribute dividends from profits lawfully available for that purpose, which are its accumulated net realised profits. It may not distribute dividends from unrealised capital profits, e.g. resulting from a revaluation of fixed assets. However, additional depreciation charges resulting from revaluation of fixed assets must be added back to the realised profits available for distribution. Also, the 1980 Act introduced the designation 'public limited company' or 'plc'.

(2) Companies Act 1981

This Act introduced important changes as a result of the fourth Directive:

(a)   Layout of the Annual Accounts

Whereas, previously, there was no statutory requirement for companies to lay out the annual accounts in any particular way, the 1981 Act introduced standardised formats, long a feature in other major EEC countries. For this purpose, a company may choose between two alternative balance sheet layouts and four alternative profit and loss account formats (now to be found in Schedule 4 of the 1985 Act; examples of these formats are shown in Appendix 3). There is some flexibility of presentation.

(b)   Accounting Principles

The Act sets out five principles as a basis for drawing up the accounts:

(i)   the presumption that a business is being conducted as a going concern;
(ii)   the requirement that accounting policies be conducted consistently from year to year;
(iii) the need for amounts of items to be determined prudently, and in particular by bringing to account only realised profits but all known liabilities and losses;
(iv)   the matching of income and expenditure on an accrual basis;
(v)   separate valuation of individual assets and liabilities within each asset or liability class.

(c)   Basic Accounting Convention

The Act allows accounts to be drawn up either on the historical cost convention, or on a current cost basis, or on a historical cost basis except for ad hoc revaluations. Prior to adoption by the EEC of the Fourth Directive, there were wide differences between the various member states on the question of whether and under what conditions departures should be allowed from the historical cost convention. In West Germany, no departure was allowed; in France and Italy, departure was constrained by tax laws; in Britain and the Netherlands it has been accepted practice that companies may legally replace historical cost accounting by current cost or replacement value accounting (CCA or RVA). As this proved to be an issue on which opposed views were deeply held, the fourth Directive represented a compromise, allowing member states to permit CCA or RVA, provided that where a company adopts any such basis in relation to fixed assets, it must show the comparable historical cost and the consequent amount transferred to the asset revaluation reserve.

The law also contains a very large number of detailed disclosure requirements. However, companies that fall within specified limits of turnover, gross assets or numbers of employees, so that they are deemed to be either small or medium-sized, may file modified (abbreviated) accounts and present fewer categories of information. They must, however, continue to present full audited accounts to their shareholders.

Australia

Prior to Federation in 1901, separate company laws were enacted in each of the six Australian colonies. For the most part they were closely modelled on successive British Companies Acts. After Federation, the States (as now termed) continued to legislate in this field, while separate laws were enacted for the Commonwealth Territories. With changes over time, the laws were far from uniform and the history of evolution of company law in Australia within the past generation is one of effort to achieve a uniform or common law relating to companies.

Given its federated political structure, one may wonder why there has been impetus in Australia towards uniform company law. By contrast, there has been no comparable movement in the USA where the fifty States have basic jurisdiction in relation to companies, but where federal regulations apply to companies having securities quoted on the stock exchanges. Possibly an answer lies in differences in economic structure, with business activity and corporate control widely dispersed in the USA but more concentrated in Australia, especially in the major States of New South Wales and Victoria. Differences in relative size of the two economies may be another factor, with the additional costs associated with non-uniform company laws being regarded as burdensome and undesirable.

To achieve uniformity, the Commonwealth and the States agreed upon a cooperative scheme, whereby each State would adopt for its jurisdiction the company law applicable to the Australian Capital Territory, in which is located Canberra, the national capital. The resulting law, known as the Companies Act and Code, came into effect in 1982, with further important amendments in 1984. In design and character, the Code is similar to preceding Australian company law and continues to bear basic similarities to British law.

Financial reporting requirements are contained in Schedule 7 of the Regulations attached to the Code. Although a number of changes were made at the time of introducing the Schedule and the Code, there has been no major revision of the reporting requirements since the early 1960s. At present, and by contrast with British law, there are no specified formats for the annual accounts, and companies are *not* required to disclose:

(1) turnover, or a broad classification of costs;
(2) disaggregated information on segments of overall operations;
(3) movements in fixed assets and investments.

The Code does not contain similar provisions to the British ones relating to accounting principles underlying the accounts, the basic accounting convention, or a prohibition on payment of dividends from unrealised profits. A major 'green' paper on possible reforms to the financial reporting requirements of the Code and the Seventh Schedule, issued in 1983, has not yet been acted upon.

The 1984 amendments to the Code do, however, contain a significant change with the introduction of the concept of legal recognition for specific accounting standards. The Code refers to approved accounting standards and, while retaining the overriding requirement that the accounts must show a true and fair view, further requires that:

(1)   The report by the directors on the accounts must state:

(a) whether the accounts comply with approved accounting standards;
(b) if the accounts do not so comply:
   (i) why the accounts, had they complied, would not have given a true and fair view;
   (ii) the quantified financial effect on the accounts of non-compliance.

(2)   The auditor is required to report:

(a) whether the accounts are in accordance with approved accounting standards;
(b) if the accounts do not comply with approved accounting standards:
   (i)   whether the accounts would have given a true and fair view had they complied;
   (ii) his opinion on why the accounts would not have given a true and fair view, had they complied;
   (iii) his opinion on the quantified effect of non-compliance, or his estimate of that effect in the event of a failure to comply.

In addition, and no doubt with the intention of reinforcing the objectives of the Code, the auditor is required to report to the regulatory authority any failure to comply with the Code where he is satisfied that the matter is not adequately dealt with in his report on the accounts or by bringing it to the notice of the directors, or any instance of accounts not in compliance with approved accounting standards.

The Historical Cost Convention and Current Valuation of Assets

The British Companies Act 1985 gives specific legal authorisation for the practice of basing annual accounts on the historical cost convention. It also authorises the alternative adoption by companies of what may be termed current cost accounting. Recognition of historical cost accounting represents a continuation of a well-established basis on which companies and unincorporated businesses measure profit and establish the balance sheet. Although the Australian Companies Code is silent on the matter, the historical cost convention is generally followed in Australia as well.

Yet the historical cost convention as a concept or set of agreed accounting rules is anything but precise. It might once have been thought to preclude the practice of revaluing fixed assets and long-term investments and of bringing unrealised capital gains to account. Indeed, such is the practice today in the USA and West Germany, for example. Despite this, the circumstances of inflation and takeover offers directed at companies with apparently undervalued net assets have long since created a kind of Trojan horse, by which some of the practices of current cost accounting, if not its explicitly recognised concepts, have been introduced into the citadel of historical cost accounting.

For directors of companies this has perhaps become a mixed blessing. On the one hand, discretionary asset revaluation is handy in the armoury of defensive strategy against corporate raiders, and is also a well-understood means of signalling the likelihood of bonus issues of shares, achieved by capitalisation of asset revaluation reserves, and of possible future increased dividend payments (Standish and Ung 1982). On the other hand, the legislators have decided that, if directors can have regard to undervalued assets, they should also have regard to the possibility of overvalued or underdepreciated assets. This appears in a number of ways:

(1) Britain, Companies Act 1985

(a) Restrictions on payment of dividend in the event of a serious loss of capital mean that the directors need to be satisfied that net assets are not in that case overvalued. Moreover, for public companies, a dividend distribution is permissible only if net assets of the company exceed paid-up capital plus undistributable reserves. Effectively, before paying a dividend, the company must bring to account any existing unrealised losses.

(b) Fixed assets with a limited useful economic life are to be depreciated systematically over that life. In addition, any reduction in fixed asset values expected to be permanent must be accounted for by a charge against profits. Current assets are to be shown at their net realisable value if lower than purchase price or production cost.

(2) Australia, Companies Code 1984

Directors are required, before the accounts are made out, to ascertain that:

(a) adequate provision is made for bad and doubtful debts;
(b) current assets are not included in the accounts at amounts greater than their realisable value in the ordinary course of business;
(c) non-current assets are not included at a greater amount than their replacement cost.

Regulation of Financial Disclosure

Statutory requirements for presentation of annual accounts impose considerable costs on companies. Against this are to be set the benefits from constraining abuse of the concession of limited liability and providing an information flow of acceptable quality to external parties not able to obtain that information by other means. For all the importance attached to the system, its operation has until recently been largely unsupervised, with redress for claims of financial loss as a result of relying on misleading accounts being left to action by shareholders in the civil courts.

In Britain, copies of the annual accounts are required to be filed with the Registrar of Companies and in Australia with the various State Corporate Affairs Commissions, as delegates for the overall national authority, the National Companies and Securities Commission (NCSC). For British companies, the Department of Trade and Industry caused some surprise at its action in the Argyll Foods Case (1981) by prosecuting a company for presenting consolidated accounts not in accordance with the Act (see articles in *Accountancy* in August 1981, February and June 1982). As far as is known, the DTI does not check accounts filed with it for compliance with the Act, and this was a rare instance of court action by the statutory authority. In Australia, some of the Commissions in the larger States, notably New South Wales, have at times carried out checks for compliance with the law and issued requisitions to companies for further information, but there have been no reported prosecutions on the issue of compliance. The number of incorporated companies in each country, shown in Table 3.1, would make compliance checks a daunting task. In any event, the regulatory

Table 3.1 Number of Companies Incorporated in Britain and Australia

Britain	Public limited companies	6,508	
(1.1.84)	Private limited companies	949,903	
Australia	Limited liability companies:		
(30.6.84)	Public	6,900	
	Proprietary	587,300	594,200
	Other categories		7,500
	Total		601,700

authority is not effectively in a position to determine whether or not accounts are true and fair.

When Things Go Wrong

Both in Britain and Australia, the Companies Acts confer powers on the government to appoint inspectors into the affairs of companies. These powers are not used frequently because of the cost involved, but usually their impact on companies or officers of companies under investigation is momentous. They are ordinarily employed to investigate what are believed to be scandalous states of affairs, where there has been mis-appropriation of funds on a massive scale, or gross financial mal-administration, or a gross discrepancy between reported states of affairs and the actual position of companies. For example, on 16 September 1974, a major Australian finance and property development company, Cambridge Credit Corporation Limited, incorporated in New South Wales, released its Annual Report and Accounts for the year ended 30 June 1974, showing a 33% increase in after-tax profit over the previous year, and recommending a final dividend of 7½%, making 15% for the year. On 30 September 1974, the company was placed in receivership by the trustees for its debenture holders, having defaulted on payment of interest then due. In other words, the company was insolvent.

This triggered the appointment by the New South Wales Corporate Affairs Commission of a team of inspectors, who to date have produced a series of reports on that company and various related companies. These reports, as in other such cases, do not amount to an indictment of the company or its officers, but obviously are intended to yield information which would assist the government of the day in deciding whether or not to launch prosecutions, under the Companies Acts or various criminal laws, against directors or other officers. The process of

Table 3.2   Major Reports of Investigations into Company Affairs

Country	Name of company	Date (Final report)
Britain:	Vehicle and General Insurance	1976
	London and County Securities	1976
	Court Line	1978
	Darjeeling Holdings	1980
	Data Investments	1980
Australia:	Sydney Guarantee Corporation (NSW)	1964
	Reid Murray Holdings (Vic)	1966
	Stanhill Development (Vic)	1967
	Cambridge Credit (NSW)	1977
	Gollin Holdings (NSW)	1979

investigation, reporting, prosecution, trial and conviction of wrongdoers has proved to be highly expensive of scarce resources, time consuming and frustrating to those who feel that the sanctions against manipulating accounts and misappropriating funds are on the whole less effective than those against shoplifters. Still, there have in some cases been convictions and the processes of investigation under the Companies Acts most probably do act as a deterrent. For students of company affairs and accounting peccadilloes, the various inspectors' reports are a fascinating mine of information and insights. Table 3.2 lists some important British and Australian inspectors' reports from the viewpoint of financial practice, accounting and disclosure.

3.5   Accounting Standards: Objectives, Establishment and Application

The issue that transcends all others in the affairs of the accounting profession in Britain and Australia in the past fifteen to twenty years is that of accounting standards: why they are needed, how they are to be established, and whether and in what way they are to be binding on professional accountants. Though the profession may have come to regard standard setting as a natural or, at least, inevitable task, one will search in vain for examples of other professions acting in the same way. Indeed the idea of imposing practice standards on members of a profession runs counter to ideas about professional practice as an exercise in the use of individual skill and judgement. In this section, the objective is to look briefly at how the profession has come to assume this task, what has been achieved and what problems lie unresolved.

The Road to Standard Setting

The move to standard setting in both Britain and Australia occurred in response to what were widely regarded as damaging examples of misleading annual accounts and sustained, hostile criticism of the profession, particularly by sections of the media. The reaction was therefore natural enough: to defuse criticism by being seen to address the problems and to retain or capture moral authority. The formative events took place in the 1960s. In Britain, the AEI – GEC takeover battle and the Pergamon – Leasco affair contributed to a declining confidence in the utility of financial reports to external parties, while in Australia the collapse of several major finance and property development companies, notably Reid Murray, had similar effects. As a result, organisations with responsibility for developing statements of accounting standards were developed:

(1) *Britain* The Accounting Standards Steering Committee was established in 1970 by the ICAEW, with the other five professional institutions in Britain later joining in its constitution and operation. Subsequently renamed, the Accounting Standards Committee (ASC) comprises 20 members nominated by the six bodies, with provision for up to five members being representatives of users of accounts but who need not necessarily be accountants. The role of the ASC is confined to developing statements of standard accounting practice with adoption and enforcement remaining the responsibility of the six professional bodies, any one of which has an effective power of veto.

(2) *Australia* The two professional institutions, the ASA and ICAA, agreed in 1965 to establish the Accountancy Research Foundation to develop statements of accounting principles. For various reasons, the Foundation did not begin operations till 1969. Subsequently renamed, the Australian Accounting Research Foundation (AARF) is jointly funded by the two bodies which have equal representation on its various boards and committees. Within the AARF, the specific task of developing statements of accounting standards is assigned to its Accounting Standards Board, but the ASA and ICAA retain separate responsibility for their adoption and enforcement.

The system for producing and adopting standards is therefore similar in both countries, if allowance is made for differences in the institutional structure of the profession. In both countries, all accounting standards issued to date have endorsement by their respective professional bodies. Having regard to the troubled history of standard setting, it is worth seeking a deeper understanding of why the profession assumed this role. The following are some likely factors:

(a) *Accounting standards as the business of accountants* In both countries there is a long history of caution or even outright mistrust regarding the role of government in business affairs. The accounting profession was established before there was a body of income tax law and before it was thought desirable for government to play the part in economic affairs now more generally expected. Even now government in Britain and Australia is not highly directive towards business in the same way that it is often said to be, for example, in Japan or France. Thus there never seemed to be a case for the kind of structure that has produced the French national accounting plan (*le Plan comptable général*) under the overall direction of government. Indeed, the profession in both countries is largely unaware of the French system as an alternative model for arriving at prescribed accounting standards.

These same conditions and attitudes also explain why concepts and bases for determining taxable income have never come to be regarded as *ipso facto* accounting standards for commercial purposes, as in West Germany. The earlier establishment of the accounting profession, its perceived standing in the community, and the confidence of accountants in the suitability of their notions of profit measurement and asset valuation (however much those ideas might be argued about within the club) all led to the conviction that the accountants themselves should determine what constitute acceptable accounting principles and standards. If government needs to involve itself in the area of accounting concepts for fiscal purposes or overall development of economic policy, it should confine itself strictly to these questions, preferably with some good advice from the accountants.

(b) *Sources of ideas and authority* As noted earlier in the chapter, the profession was organised, and undertook examination of potential members, before accounting emerged as an academic discipline. Even at the time of establishment of the two standard setting bodies there were few professors of accounting in either country, and graduates in accounting were much in the minority among professionally qualified accountants. The prevalent view was that accounting is the business of practical men of affairs. There was no tradition of research as understood in some other social sciences (even the idea that accounting could be characterised as a social science would seem strange), nor was the profession itself a scholarly one in the way that the legal profession would regard itself in searching for precedents and valuing book learning. This has helped to bring about a rather *ad hoc* and unconceptual approach to the setting of standards in the UK and Australia.

(c) *Accounting standards and risk avoidance* The stakes in the game of financial reporting are high. Those with statutory responsibilities, the directors and auditors, can win or lose reputations and fortunes. Auditors in both countries bear unlimited personal liability for losses suffered by those to whom they owe a duty of care, if accounts are judged not to be true or fair. Professional indemnity insurance offers a way of controlling risk and passing the cost on to the consumer, but there is always the possibility that insurance cover may turn out to be insufficient in specific cases.

Small wonder then, in times of greater willingness by the law to prosecute directors and auditors and by shareholders to sue auditors, that the profession should seek to create a shield. If the advent of standards implies a reduction in professional independence, it also provides the possibility of defence, using the likely view of the courts that accounts based on accepted accounting standards will be true and fair. One should not be too critical of the appeal of standards in this context. The accountant and the auditor have all too often been caught in the middle: under pressure by corporate management to paint or accept a favourable picture of its financial performance, but knowing well that they may be subsequent targets for disgruntled investors.

Travelling Along the Standard Setting Road

With hindsight it is clear that the accounting profession established a structure for standard setting without understanding what was involved or the troubles that lay ahead. There were some early standards achieved without much fuss and the whole activity probably seemed worthwhile.

Table 3.3 Statements of Accounting Standards in Britain and Australia at 31.8.1985

Britain (SSAP)

1	Accounting for associated companies
2	Disclosure of accounting policies
3	Earnings per share
4	The accounting treatment of government grants
5	Accounting for value added tax
6	Extraordinary items and prior year adjustments
8	The treatment of taxation under the imputation system in the accounts of companies
9	Stocks and work in progress
10	Statements of source and application of funds
12	Accounting for depreciation
13	Accounting for research and development
14	Group accounts
15	Accounting for deferred taxation
16	Current cost accounting
17	Accounting for post balance sheet events
18	Accounting for contingencies
19	Accounting for investment properties
20	Foreign currency translation
21	Accounting for leases and hire purchase contracts
22	Accounting for goodwill
23	Accounting for acquisitions and mergers

Australia (AAS)

1	Profit and loss statements
2	Valuation and presentation of inventories in the context of the historical cost system
3	Accounting for company income tax (tax-effect accounting)
4	Depreciation of non-current assets
5	Materiality in financial statements
6	Accounting policies: determination, application and disclosure
7	Accounting for the extractive industries
8	Events occurring after balance date
9	Expenditure carried forward to subsequent accounting periods
10	Accounting for the revaluation of non-current assets
11	Accounting for construction contracts
12	Statement of sources and applications of funds
13	Accounting for research and development costs
14	Equity method of accounting
15	Disclosure of revenue
16	Financial reporting by segments
17	Accounting for leases
18	Accounting for goodwill

Table 3.3 records the standards issued in each country up to the time of writing. The missing numbers in the British list are those superseded by later standards on the same subject, namely deferred tax and current cost accounting. SSAP16 lapsed during 1985.

The problems encountered in standard setting have been of several kinds:

(1) *Standard setting as a process of political bargaining* The profession seems to have believed that standards could be set in a reasonable way, through exchange of reasonable views, given that the training of accountants instils in them the same ideas, practices and experiences. But the reality of the context causes standard setting to operate differently. Financial information is the lubricant of economic decisions. The stories conveyed by annual reports confirm or disappoint investor expectations and have the power to move millions (whether of money or persons). For all the bloodless image that accounting may have, people really care about the way the financial score is kept.

Establishment of standard setting agencies therefore quickly created a means for exposure, possibly even for exacerbation, of sectional interests. The niceties of argument may have mattered but political clout counted for even more. Companies that one day favoured deferred tax accounting because it shielded operating cash inflows from pressures for dividend distribution could and did change their minds once it seemed that mounting deferred tax provisions would adversely affect the debt/equity ratio. Multinational companies, unhappy at the instability of currency translation gains and losses arising from a standard (in this case, American) consistent with historical cost accounting, could bring influence to have it jettisoned.

None of this is reprehensible and none of it would surprise professional politicians. But the profession repeatedly seemed surprised and aggrieved at outbreaks of sectional lobbying and the delight with which stories were served up by emerging newspapers in the accounting field (notably *Accountancy Age* in Britain and *Business Review Weekly* in Australia). The result has been repeated redesign of the organisational structure and elaboration of the process for developing standards, with more stages to the process, more committees and working parties, more position papers, exposure drafts, defences and counter proposals. The struggle to establish a standard on current cost accounting has been both a cause and an expression of these developments.

In the sphere of politics and law making, clashing sectional interests are dealt with in the end by political force using weight of numbers or by negotiated compromise. The former route is not sustainable for the accounting profession which is not in a position to make or enforce laws of its own devising. The most telling example of this is in the Keymer-Haslam 1977 victory of ICAEW members over the ASC on the proposed

British standard on current cost accounting, and its near repeat in 1982. The alternative route for resolution of conflict, namely by compromise, inevitably implies recognition of the reasonableness of diversity in practice (e.g. as has occurred in arriving at the more contentious EEC Directives). But this is anathema to those who want standards in the first place.

(2) *The battle of the accounting theories* The 1960s and 1970s saw a remarkable upsurge in the enunciation of deductive or *a priori* theories of accounting, especially relating to income measurement and asset valuation. Though much of this occurred in the United States, there were also major contributions in Australia, notably through the work of Professors Chambers and Mathews, and in Britain by Professor Baxter. Many of these theories have been offered as the 'best' or, even more assertively, the sole intellectually tenable theory on the particular subject. Since academic reputations and intellectual power have been on the line, it is not surprising that there have been passionate debates in search of what in Britain has been termed the Holy Grail of accounting, or in Australia would be better understood as the Golden Boomerang. While the theorists battled on, the various sectional interests found that the theories could be used to provide better arguments with which to advance their causes (Watts and Zimmerman 1979). Again, in the context of current cost accounting, practical men of affairs, who would once have been innocent of accounting theory, have taken to theoretical argumentation on issues of replacement value theory, capital maintenance concepts, net present value, etc.

However, most of today's theorists believe there is no Holy Grail of accounting theory. There is no one best answer. Profit, wealth, distributable income and so forth are abstract concepts of the mind, not real world artefacts. We cannot say what is the best way to measure profit. If the profession truly wishes to be helpful it needs to discover from users, or to suggest to them, what ideas would support their decision making, and then to develop the measures which best reflect those ideas. But this is for the long haul, and not nearly so dramatic as winning the next round in the accounting theory heavyweight match.

(3) *The search for a conceptual framework* Time and again, critics of financial reporting practices and the activities of the standard setting bodies have been able to make capital out of the charge that those bodies merely deal with brush fires (i.e. urgent problems) and have no overall set of interlocking ideas on accountability and measurement.

The American response, noted elsewhere, has been to devote major effort to developing statements of a conceptual framework for financial measurement and reporting. By contrast, neither standard setting agency in Britain or Australia has followed suit with the same zeal. The search for an agreed conceptual framework could be regarded as essential to orderly standard setting and a responsible way for the relevant agency to act. More cynically, it could be regarded as a stratagem for distracting critics while getting on with the real issues (i.e. urgent problems). Although the British and Australian agencies have each sponsored conceptual framework investigations (Macve 1981, Barton 1982), they perhaps wisely felt that major commitment of resources might result in substantial duplication of American effort or might fail to have a noticeable impact on standard setting. A significant aspect is that neither agency is funded on anything like the same scale as the US Financial Accounting Standards Board, and therefore each has less latitude to deal with other than pressing issues.

(4) *What are standards supposed to achieve?* Standards and proposals for standards issued to date vary greatly in character. Some are broad in coverage as, for example, the British ED18, *Current Cost Accounting*, which almost amounted to a complete rewriting of accepted practices of income measurement and asset valuation. Others deal with a limited, specific issue; for example, the Australian AAS15 is confined to stating that the profit and loss account should disclose sales revenue and other operating revenue. Some allow more than one method of accounting for a particular type of transaction or disclosure, whereas others do not. For example, SSAP12 on depreciation specifically allows choice of basis of depreciation; AAS17 on lease accounting is highly prescriptive, and replete with decision trees comparable to the consolidated American standard on the same subject. This diversity can partly be explained by intrinsic differences in the topics dealt with by particular standards. But it also points to the uncertainty about their place in the spectrum of issues facing accountants.

Consider the structure of professional response to the objective of producing audited annual accounts, as shown in Figure 3.1. Levels 1 and 4

Information needs		*Decision*
1.	Accounting literature and data Examples: Concepts, theories, surveys of practice	Choose method most applicable to particular circumstances
2.	Professional recommendations	Apply if appropriate
3.	Accounting standards	Apply as intended, exercising choice where available
4.	Company law	Compliance

Figure 3.1 *Decision Stages in Financial Reporting*

may be regarded as constant factors: there is always a body of common knowledge (level 1) and company law is part of the general social contract for private enterprise. Level 2 is an option: for example, between 1942 and 1969 the ICAEW issued to members a series of recommendations on accounting practices. The ASC has now recommenced a similar practice by issuing Statements of Recommended Accounting Practice (SORPs). Standards (level 3) can only hover uncertainly between having the character of recommendations, in those cases where choices are permissible within the application of a standard, or presenting law-like statements but without the force of law.

Just as there is no clear dividing line between professional recommendations and standards, neither is there a clear line between the latter and what might reasonably be contained within the law. For example, the Australian AAS1 in effect calls for an all-inclusive income statement, but this might just as easily be written into the Companies Code. The British SSAP2 on disclosure of accounting policies or SSAP17 on accounting for post balance date events both deal with matters now embodied in the Companies Act 1985.

The Struggle for Authority

The history of standard setting in the two countries is in essence a struggle about who shall have authority over financial reporting. The profession has repeatedly been a bit like Germany in two world wars, fighting its wars on two fronts. At one extreme, its role is opposed by those who want a *laissez-faire* approach, allowing accountants and auditors as much room as possible for the exercise of individual professional judgement. This should not be dismissed as a reckless road to fraud and misleading information, given that the sanctions of the law are still there in relation to accounts judged not to be true or fair. At the other extreme are some politicians and bureaucrats who, for whatever reasons, want to expand the ambit of company law and regulation, and for whom accounting standards issued by the profession are superfluous.

In their respective responses to this situation, the two countries are proceeding in opposite directions. In Britain, the position may be stated as follows:

(1) *Legal recognition* SSAPs do not have legal force, in that they are not referred to in the Companies Act. It is generally held that accounts prepared in accordance with SSAPs are presumptively true and fair and that statements not so prepared are less likely to be regarded by the courts as true or fair (Arden and Hoffman 1983). The Gower Report (1984), drawing attention to the indeterminate status of accounting

standards in Britain, felt that the time would come for them to be given legal recognition, but accepted that the time had not yet arrived.

(2) *The profession's bitter fruit* A 1983 report by the ASC recommended, as noted above, that in future it issue SORPs. It further recommended that standards (SSAPs):

> ... deal only with matters of major and fundamental importance affecting the generality of companies, and will therefore be few in number.

Since that report, the British profession (and ASC in particular) has undergone a further grinding ordeal in the long and, as may be predicted, fruitless quest for an inflation or a current cost accounting standard, the struggle for which has revealed major disagreements among the professional bodies and threatens the structure for setting standards.

In Australia the profession has also wished to hold the high ground in standard setting, but it has been pushed aside by the lawmakers and regulators through the 1984 amendment to the Code dealing with approved standards. The task of approval has been handed to a statutory agency created for this purpose, namely the Accounting Standards Review Board (ASRB) which is answerable to the Ministerial Council (Commonwealth and State) responsible for company law. The regulatory authority on companies and securities, the National Companies and Securities Commission, has an obvious interest in financial reporting and has already issued two key green papers in this area. Accordingly, one would expect that it will wish to have an input to the work of ASRB, though it has no authority over the latter.

The ASRB is empowered to seek or consider proposals for accounting standards emanating from any source (e.g. shareholder associations, industry groups). There is an expectation that it will in practice rely heavily on the accounting profession through the AARF to provide technical expertise and develop proposed statements. In other words, a relationship could develop analogous to that between the American SEC and FASB. If so, the AARF will carry out the detailed work of developing and issuing standards, but presumably will have some influence with the ASRB in determining priorities for standards – what issues to proceed with and which to avoid. It may also suffer the fate of being unsupported in efforts to develop standards, as has sometimes happened to the FASB.

The structure for standard setting in Australia has as a result become more complex, following the creation of additional layers of decision making and possibilities for exerting influence. It is summarised in Figure 3.2. The likely outcome from these developments in Australia is that accounting standards will become an adjunct of the law (i.e. effectively part of level 4, in Figure 3.1), and that the profession will not issue

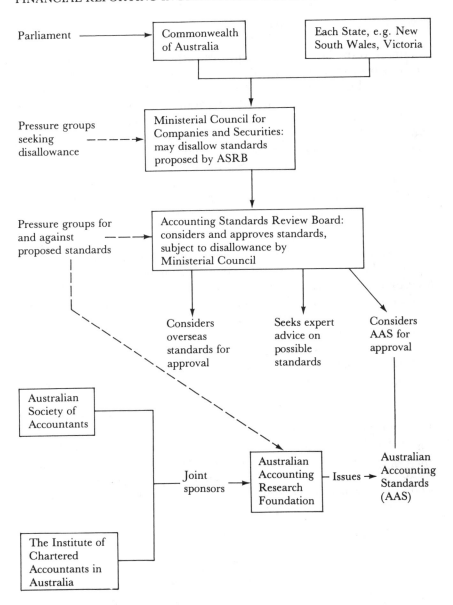

Figure 3.2 *System for Legislative Recognition of Australian Accounting Standards*

standards other than those to be approved by ASRB. In both countries, standards at level 3 may become less important, in Britain because of recommendations and because of more detailed law, and in Australia because of regulatory approval of standards.

Implications of a 'True and Fair View'

Common to the law of both countries is the requirement that annual
accounts present 'a true and fair view'. The phrase was written into the
EEC fourth Directive largely at British insistence and since that time has
become a matter of concern to the accounting profession in various of
the other EEC member states which did not previously have a comparable statutory requirement. Since the British insisted on retaining it,
other European accountants have naturally wanted to know how best to
interpret it. Unfortunately, neither the British nor the Australians can
give any definitive answers. Several broad possibilities can be discerned,
in relation to other disclosure requirements in the company law and to
professional recommendations or statements of standards.

(1)   *Statutory disclosure requirements but no extant recommendations or standards*
This position existed in both countries, prior to 1942 in Britain and 1946
in Australia when the first professional recommendations were issued.
Statutory disclosure requirements at the time were considerably simpler
or abbreviated compared with those now in force. In those conditions,
assessing whether accounts present a true and fair view is inevitably an
exercise in which accountants, directors and auditors are thrown back
on their respective sense of professional responsibility to convey adequately the financial position of the company. Given the theoretical
developments that have since occurred in accounting and related areas
(e.g. the efficient capital market hypothesis, studies in human information processing), the professional response to a situation of company law
unsupported by recommendations and standards would be at level 1 in
Figure 3.1. In other words, accountants and others affected would need
to be abreast of ideas and research findings, much in the same way as
occurs in other professions. Any challenge to whether particular
accounts were true or fair would have to be assessed solely on the facts of
that case.

(2)   *Statutory disclosure requirements and professional recommendations, but no*
standards   This state of affairs existed in both countries prior to the
operation of ASC and AARF. The existence of recommendations
becomes a significant source of information for all concerned including
the courts. Given the status of recommendations there is still a place for
an overriding criterion of true and fair, since the decision of those concerned is whether a true and fair view would be obtained if particular
recommendations were implemented or disregarded.

(3)   *Statutory disclosure requirements and standards*   The advent of standards that do not have the force of law somewhat weakens the meaning
to be attached to a true and fair view. Although particular standards can
be disregarded if it can be argued that this is required in order to arrive

at a true and fair view, the risks for accountants and auditors of non-compliance are much greater. Moreover, the whole intent of issuing standards is to reduce diversity in financial reporting practices by securing compliance. In relation to those aspects of financial reporting for which there are relevant statements of standards, it would seem sufficient to require that accounts be presented fairly, in accordance with standards, as occurs in the USA. In the UK, the recent detailed incursions of law into the territory previously held by standards has led to conflict (Tweedie 1983).

(4)   *Statutory disclosure requirements and legally approved accounting standards* Although this structure now exists in Australia, it may be a considerable time before the combination of statutory requirements and approved accounting standards covers all important aspects of financial reporting. If and when that occurs, it is difficult to see how there will be a place or meaning for the concept of a true and fair view, since the emphasis in the system would then have tilted overwhelmingly toward compliance, rather than legitimising the exercise of individual professional judgement. Prior to arriving at that state of affairs, there may be reasons for continuing with a true and fair criterion in relation to aspects of reporting not covered in either the law or the approved standards. Put another way, the approval of standards will effectively override application of the criterion in relation to the matters dealt with by that standard.

In summary, it is significant to note that the British accounting profession seems insistent on retaining an overall true and fair criterion for accounts, consistent with a possible move away from issuing standards in favour of recommendations on practice. Conversely, the Australian profession, faced with statutory approval of standards and possible reforms to the disclosure requirements of the Code, has argued strongly for abandonment of the true and fair criterion, in recognition of the greater emphasis on compliance.

3.6   Summary and Conclusion

Financial reporting by companies in Britain and Australia is an important social function aimed at assisting the movement of risk capital toward profitable use and at encouraging a high sense of responsibility in accountants, directors and auditors, in relation to the accountability of incorporated business enterprise. Although company laws dealing with presentation of annual accounts have existed in both countries since the nineteenth century, the accounting profession has emerged as the principal interpreter of the needs of the community for reported financial information and as its supplier. The reassessment and development of standards of financial reporting has been stimulated in recent years by circumstances of inflation and changing social expectations about business performance.

The role of the profession has been under challenge. Fairly or not, the accounting profession has been seen as too closely identified with management to be fully effective in raising reporting standards if the result of doing so is to make life more difficult for directors and managers. The concepts of income measurement and asset valuation traditionally used by accountants have been criticised as inappropriate for inflationary conditions. The work of the profession in seeking to develop and impose accounting standards has been impeded by internal disagreements and a lack of legitimate authority, at least in the eyes of some lawmakers.

Seeking to cope with these criticisms and changed conditions, the profession has developed more elaborate systems for producing standards, requiring more consultation and more research into ideas and alternatives. The response in both countries has in these regards been similar in kind to that of the American profession, if different in degree. As yet the profession in Britain and Australia shows less confidence in the outcome from accounting research and experimentation, as a basis for addressing disputes, than does the American profession. Whether for this reason or not, the profession in the two countries has not been able to achieve or sustain the same authority in standard setting as accomplished by the FASB. In Britain, following the Gower Report, it is not clear whether the profession will recapture its position or whether specification of accounting standards will eventually move under the control of government. In Australia, the latter has now happened and the profession will be seeking to reassess its role in determining accounting standards and to influence the lawmakers.

Variants on these themes are being played out in many countries. The British voice in financial reporting practices and standards has been of great importance in the past and no doubt will continue to be in the future. For the profession in both countries, and indeed elsewhere, the key issue is to clarify the role of professional integrity and judgement within the context of a more regulated environment for business enterprise.

References and Further Reading

General

Standish, P. E. M. (1984) 'The rationale for accounting standards setting', in M. J. R. Gaffikin, *Contemporary Accounting Thought*, Prentice-Hall, Melbourne.

Britain

Accounting Standards Committee (1983) *Review of the Standard Setting Process*, Accounting Standards Committee, London.

Arden, M. and Hoffman, L. (1983) 'Counsels' opinion on true and fair', *Accountancy*, November.

Gower, L. C. B. (1984) *Review of Investor Protection, Report: Part 1*, Cmnd. 9125, HMSO.

Leach, Sir R. and Stamp, E. (eds) (1981) *British Accounting Standards: The First 10 Years*, Woodhead-Faulkner, Cambridge.

Lee, T. A. and Parker, R. H. (1979) *The Evolution of Corporate Reporting*, Nelson.

McKinnon, S. M. (1983) *Consolidated Accounts: The Seventh EEC Directive*, Amsa and Arthur Young International.

Macve, R. (1981) *A Conceptual Framework for Financial Accounting and Reporting*, ICAEW, London.

Nobes, C. W. (1983) 'The evolution of the harmonising provisions of the 1980 and 1981 Companies Acts', *Accounting and Business Research*, Winter.

Standish, P. E. M. and Ung, S.-I. (1982) 'Corporate signaling, asset revaluations and the stock prices of British companies', *Accounting Review*, October.

Sutcliffe, C. E. T. and Patient, M. L. (1984) *Accounting Problems of the Companies Acts*, Deloitte Haskins & Sells and Tolley Publishing, London.

Tweedie, D. (1983) 'True and fair rules', *Accountant's Magazine*, November.

Tweedie, D. and Whittington, G. (1984) *The Debate on Inflation Accounting*, Chapters 4–6, Cambridge University Press.

Watts, R.L. and Zimmerman, J.L. (1979) 'The demand for and the supply of accounting theories: the market for excuses', *Accounting Review*, April.

Zeff, S. A. (1972) *Forging Accounting Principles in Five Countries*, Chapter 1, Stipes Publishing, Champaign, Illinois.

Proposed statements of standard accounting practice are issued as exposure drafts by the Accounting Standards Committee. Statements once adopted are issued in the SSAP series by the respective professional bodies.

Surveys of financial reporting by British companies have been published by ICAEW for a number of years in the series *Financial Reporting* (previously, *Survey of Published Accounts*).

Australia

Australian Accounting Research Foundation (1984) 'The auditor's report on financial statements' in *Statement of Auditing Practice AUP3*, AARF, Melbourne.

Australian National Companies and Securities Legislation, Vol. 1 (1984), CCH, Sydney.

Barton, A.D. (1982) *Objectives and Basic Concepts of Accounting*, Accounting Theory Monograph No. 2, Australian Accounting Research Foundation, Melbourne.

National Companies and Securities Commission (1983) *Financial Reporting Requirements of the Companies Acts and Codes*, NCSC, Melbourne.

National Companies and Securities Commission (1984) *'A True and Fair View' and the Reporting Obligations of Directors and Auditors*, NCSC, Melbourne.

Ryan, F. J. O. (1976) *Towards Better Company Reporting*, ASA, Melbourne.

Standish, P. E. M. (1975) 'Proposals for reform of Australian company financial disclosure requirements' in *Australian Company Financial Reporting*, Bulletin No. 18, ASA, Melbourne.

Tweedie, D. and Whittington, G. (1984) *The Debate on Inflation Accounting*, Chapter 8, Cambridge University Press.

Zeff, S. A. (1973) *Forging Accounting Principles in Australia*, Bulletin No. 14, ASA, Melbourne.

Proposed statements of accounting standards are issued as exposure drafts by the Australian Accounting Research Foundation. Statements once adopted are issued in the AUS series by the respective professional bodies.

Several surveys of financial reporting by Australian companies have been published by AARF, the most recent being in 1980.

The National Companies and Securities Commission publishes from time to time statements of its policies and requirements relating to the Companies Code, issued as Releases for the NCSC Manual.

The Accounting Standards Review Board issues publications (commencing December 1984) of the following series:

(1)   Statements and Commentaries (Release Series 100)
        Policy statements including statements on criteria for the evaluation of accounting standards and discussion papers on technical matters.
(2)   General Releases (Release Series 200)
        Statements on procedural matters, including procedures for the approval of accounting standards.
(3)   Progress Reports (Release Series 300)
        Reports on activities and plans of the Board.

Appendix 3
1985 Companies Act, Balance Sheet Format 1*

A.   *Called up share capital not paid*

B.   *Fixed assets*

I   Intangible assets
   1. Development costs
   2. Concessions, patents, licences, trade marks and similar rights and assets
   3. Goodwill
   4. Payments on account

II   Tangible assets
   1. Land and buildings
   2. Plant and machinery
   3. Fixtures, fittings, tools and equipment
   4. Payments on account and assets in course of construction

III   Investments
   1. Shares in group companies
   2. Loans to group companies
   3. Shares in related companies
   4. Loans to related companies
   5. Other investments other than loans
   6. Other loans
   7. Own shares

C.   *Current assets*

I   Stocks
   1. Raw materials and consumables
   2. Work in progress
   3. Finished goods and goods for resale
   4. Payments on account

II   Debtors
   1. Trade debtors
   2. Amounts owed by group companies
   3. Amounts owed by related companies
   4. Other debtors
   5. Called up share capital not paid
   6. Prepayments and accrued income

III   Investments
   1. Shares in group companies
   2. Own shares
   3. Other investments

IV   Cash at bank and in hand

D.   *Prepayments and accrued income*

E.   *Creditors: amounts falling due within one year*
   1. Debendure loans
   2. Bank loans and overdrafts
   3. Payments received on account
   4. Trade creditors
   5. Bills of exchange payable
   6. Amounts owed to group companies
   7. Amounts owed to related companies
   8. Other creditors including taxation and social security
   9. Accruals and deferred income

F.   *Net current assets (liabilities)*

G.   *Total assets less current liabilities*

H.   *Creditors: amounts falling due after more than one year*
   1. Debenture loans
   2. Bank loans and overdrafts
   3. Payments received on account
   4. Trade creditors
   5. Bills of exchange payable
   6. Amounts owed to group companies
   7. Amounts owed to related companies
   8. Other creditors including taxation and social security
   9. Accruals and deferred income

I.   *Provisions for liabilities and charges*
   1. Pensions and similar obligations
   2. Taxation, including deferred taxation
   3. Other provisions

J.   *Accruals and deferred income*

K.   *Capital and reserves*

I   Called up share capital

II   Share premium account

III   Revaluation reserve

IV   Other reserves
   1. Capital redemption reserve
   2. Reserve for own shares
   3. Reserves provided for by the articles of association
   4. Other reserves

V   Profit and loss account

---

* Arabic number heading may be shown in notes. Letters and numbers are for reference only.

Profit and loss account formats

Format 1

1. Turnover
2. Cost of sales
3. Gross profit or loss
4. Distribution costs
5. Administrative expenses
6. Other operating income
7. Income from shares in group companies
8. Income from shares in related companies
9. Income from other fixed asset investments
10. Other interest receivable and similar income
11. Amounts written off investments
12. Interest payable and similar charges
13. Tax on profit or loss on ordinary activities
14. Profit or loss on ordinary activities after taxation
15. Extraordinary income
16. Extraordinary charges
17. Extraordinary profit or loss
18. Tax on extraordinary profit or loss
19. Other taxes not shown under the above items
20. Profit or loss for the financial year

Format 2

1. Turnover
2. Change in stocks of finished goods and in work in progress
3. Own work capitalised
4. Other operating income
5. (a) Raw materials and consumables
   (b) Other external charges
6. Staff costs:
   (a) wages and salaries
   (b) social security costs
   (c) other pension costs
7. (a) Depreciation and other amounts written off tangible and intangible fixed assets
   (b) Exceptional amounts written off current assets
8. Other operating charges
9. Income from shares in group companies
10. Incomes from shares in related companies
11. Income from other fixed asset investments
12. Other interest receivable and similar income
13. Amounts written off investments
14. Interest payable and similar charges
15. Tax on profit or loss on ordinary activities
16. Profit or loss on ordinary activities after taxation
17. Extraordinary income
18. Extraordinary charges
19. Extraordinary profit or loss
20. Tax on extraordinary profit or loss
21. Other taxes not shown under the above items
22. Profit or loss for the financial year

4

Financial Reporting in France

R. H. PARKER

In this chapter we begin to look at financial reporting in a number of Continental European countries. Despite the company law directives of the EEC and the issue of numerous international accounting standards (see Chapter 14) there are still important differences between, say, British accounting and French accounting. In recent years, however, these differences have narrowed and there is a better understanding of what differences exist and why. There are several reasons why they continue to exist: the seventh EEC Directive on consolidated accounts has yet to be implemented; the fourth EEC Directive on (unconsolidated) accounts contains numerous options among which member states have been able to choose; member states have been allowed to adopt varying degrees of flexibility even where there are no options as such; and, finally, company law is not the only influence on financial reporting.

It is generally believed that French financial statements are prepared in a much more standardised manner than British. This is indeed true of unconsolidated financial statements, even though British statements are more standardised than they used to be. It is by no means yet true of French consolidated statements. Some of these are still very French in concept; but others have been much influenced by Anglo-Saxon ideas and practices, a trend which will be strengthened when the seventh EEC Directive is implemented.

We shall concentrate in this chapter mainly on indigenous influences. We shall refer on a number of occasions to the annual report of Compagnie Française des Pétroles (CFP) for 1983. CFP's financial statements are, in the English translation that the company provides as well as in the French original, a better guide to normal French practice than those of many other leading French companies.

4.1 Forms of Business Organisation

The most important forms of business organisation in France are the *société anonyme* (SA), the *société à responsabilité limitée* (Sàrl) and the *société en nom collectif* (partnership). Relevant legislation includes the Commercial Code*; the Law of 24 July 1966 and related decrees and amendments, including, in an accounting context, the Decree of 23 March 1967; the Law of 30 April 1983 and the related Decree of 29 November 1983; and the Law of 3 January 1985. The 1983 Law and Decree, in conjunction with the revised national accounting plan (see section 4.2 below), implement the EEC fourth Directive. SAs are roughly equivalent to the British public company, and Sàrls to the British private company. The Sàrl was originally based on the German GmbH (see Chapter 5) and, like it, has some of the aspects of a partnership. On January 1, 1983, there were 128,396 SAs in France and 320,690 Sàrls (INSEE, 1983). Most French companies have a single Board of Directors *(Conseil d'Administration)* but it is also possible for French companies to adopt a variation of the German two-tier system referred to in Chapter 5, although few have done so. Those which have, Peugeot-Citroën for example, have both a Supervisory Board *(Conseil de Surveillance)* and a Management Board *(Directoire)*.

4.2 Influences on Accounting

French financial reporting is much influenced by the government, especially through the tax system, company legislation and the national accounting plan (which is administered by a National Accounting Council). The rules relating to mergers *(fusions)* have important accounting consequences. Other influences, which have grown in importance in recent years, are a stock exchange regulatory body (the

---

* In continental European countries it is normal for distinct branches of the law to be set out in Codes, whose function it is to replace and supersede all previously existing legal rules (whether of customary law, case law or statute). Most such Codes are based on those promulgated by Napoleon.

COB) and the accountancy profession. The Stock Exchange itself is not an important direct influence.

Capital Market

The Paris Bourse is relatively small, as is demonstrated in Table 1.3 in Chapter 1. Loan capital is more important than in the UK; most shares are bearer shares; many large groups are still dominated by family holdings; and contested takeover bids are rare. The nationalisation of large companies since 1981 has severely reduced the number of listed companies. There has therefore been relatively little emphasis in France on disclosure of information to equity shareholders. Vigorous attempts to change this in recent years have been made by the *Commission des Opérations de Bourse* (COB), an organisation modelled on the American SEC, but lacking some of the latter's powers. The COB has a great influence on prospectuses and has been the driving force behind the publication of more consolidated financial statements. These have only been compulsory for listed companies for financial years ending after 31 December 1984 (see section 4.4).

Taxation

In the absence of a strong capital market, taxation has long been one of the major reasons in France for the preparation and publication of accounts. The French corporation tax system is based on an imputation system which is not too different from (and, indeed, served in part as a model for) that which is now in force in the UK, but taxable income is calculated differently. Details are given in Chapter 15. The importance of tax for an understanding of French financial statements is twofold:
  (a) The rules for measuring reported accounting profit do not differ significantly from those for measuring taxable income.
  (b) Expenses are only allowable as deductions for tax purposes if they are included in the books of account.
The following two notes from the Prospectus of Compagnie Française des Pétroles when it gained a quotation on the London Stock Exchange in 1973 illustrate how important an influence French tax regulations are:
  (i) If a French company incorporates in its accounts any revaluation of fixed assets, the amounts added to the asset values must be dealt with as exceptional profits and are then subjected to corporation tax; it is not, therefore, the practice of CFP to revalue its assets. (But see section 4.5 below.)

FINANCIAL ACCOUNTING								COST ACCOUNTING
Balance sheet accounts					Management accounts		Special accounts	
Class 1	Class 2	Class 3	Class 4	Class 5	Class 6	Class 7	Class 8	Class 9
Capital accounts (capital, loans and similar creditors)	Fixed asset accounts	Stock and Work-in-progress accounts	Personal accounts	Financial accounts	Expense accounts	Income accounts	Special accounts	Cost accounts
10 Capital and reserves	20 Intangible assets	30	40 Suppliers and related accounts	50 Trade investments	60 Purchases and stock movements (supplies and goods for resale)	70 Sales of goods and services	80 Contingent assets and liabilities	90 Reciprocal accounts
11 Profit or loss brought forward	21 Tangible assets	31 Raw materials	41 Trade debtors and related accounts	51 Banks, financial and similar institutions	61 Purchases from sub-contractors and external charges (related to investment)	71 Movements in finished goods during the accounting period	81[a]	91 Cost re-classifications
12 Profit or loss for the financial year	22 Fixed assets under concession	32 Other consumables	42 Employees and related accounts	52	62 Other external charges (related to operations)	72 Work performed by the undertaking for its own purposes and capitalised	82[a]	92 Cost analysis centres
13 Investment grants	23 Fixed assets in course of construction	33 work-in-progress (goods)	43 Social security and other public agencies	53 Cash in hand	63 Taxes, direct and indirect	73 Net income recognised on long-term contracts	83[a]	93 Manufacturing costs

14 Provisions created for tax purposes	24	34 Work-in-progress (services)	44 The Government and other public bodies	54 Imprest accounts and credits	64 Staff costs	74 Operating subsidies	84(a)	94 Stocks
15 Provisions for liabilities and charges	25	35 Finished goods	45 Accounts current — group companies and proprietors	55	65 Other operating charges	75 Other operating income	85(a)	95 Cost of goods sold
16 Loans and similar creditors	26 Participating interests and debts relating thereto	36	46 Sundry debtors and creditors	56	66 Financial costs	76 Financial income	86 Intra-company exchanges of goods and services (charges)	96 Standard cost variances
17 Debts related to participating interests	27 Other financial assets	37 Goods for resale	47 Suspense accounts	57 Internal transfers	67 Extra-ordinary	77 Extra-ordinary	87 Intra-company exchanges of goods and services (income)	97 Difference in accounting treatments
18 Branch and inter company accounts	28 Provisions for depreciation of fixed assets	38	48 Prepayments and accruals	58	68 Depreciation, amortisation, transfers to provisions	78 Depreciation and provisions written back	88	98 Manufacturing profit and loss account
19	29 Provisions for loss in value of fixed assets	39 Provisions for loss of value of stocks and work-in-progress	49 Provisions for loss in value on personal accounts	59 Provisions for loss in value on financial accounts	69 Profit sharing by employees, taxes on profits and and similar items	79 Charges transferred	89	99 Internal transfers

Figure 4.1 French *Plan Comptable Général*: Chart of Accounts
Note: (a) Accounts for possible use in connection with consolidated balance sheet and profit and loss account

(ii)   ...Depreciation is an allowable deduction for tax purposes only to the extent that it is recorded in the accounts; conversely, any depreciation charged in the accounts in excess of the fiscal rates is disallowed for tax purposes. It is the policy of the company to apply the maximum fiscal rates. No adjustments have been made to the balance sheet figures already published.

Also, as will be seen in section 4.5, accounting for inflation in France is mainly a matter of following taxation regulations.

The Accounting Plan

The national accounting plan has a very important influence on French accounting. Far from being merely a chart or classified list of ledger accounts, it is a very detailed accounting guide. Included within it are definitions of accounting terms, valuation and measurement rules and model financial statements. There is also a substantial section on cost accounting. There is an abridged system designed for small enterprises, a basic system for medium and large enterprises and an advanced system to facilitate management accounting. Accounting text books are based on the plan; so are the requirements for the annual tax return. It is also used for national and local government accounting and for the production of detailed national statistics. Accounting plans (*plans professionnels*) are prepared for each industry. The first plan was produced in 1947; an improved version in 1957; and a revised plan (*plan comptable révisé*), taking into account the provisions of the EEC fourth Directive, in 1982 (Pérochon, 1982). The revised plan came into force for accounting periods commencing on or after 1 January, 1984. It is administered by the *Conseil national de la comptabilité* (National Accounting Council). Both the Council and the professional accounting bodies produce accounting standards (*normes comptables*). The Council's members include accountants, industrialists and civil servants. It is organised and controlled by the government and advises on any question regarding accounting, its teaching and its practice, both commercial and public.

The basis of the plan is a decimalised chart of accounts, the official diagram of which is reproduced in English translation (which follows as far as possible the terms used in the English text of the EEC fourth Directive) as Figure 4.1. The nine major account categories are:

1. Capital accounts.
2. Fixed asset accounts.
3. Stock and work-in-progress accounts.
4. Personal accounts.
5. Financial accounts.
6. Expense accounts.
7. Income accounts.
8. Special accounts
9. Cost accounts.

The plan owes much to the influence of ideas which were put into practice in Germany in the interwar years. The consequent uniformity for which French accounting is famous is very useful in an economy which is centralised and closely regulated by the government.

Prudence, Regularity, Sincerity and a True and Fair View

Before the implementation of the fourth EEC Directive, the emphasis in French accounting was on *prudence, régularité* and *sincérité*.

Prudence (conservatism) has been and remains a greater influence on French financial statements than it is on British or American (Gray 1980). This has consequences for both the valuation of assets and the measurement of profit. What are regarded as reserves (appropriations profit) in France. *Régularité* means conforming with the rules and procedures in force and *sincérité*, although a less precise concept, may be thought of as the application of the spirit of the rules and procedures.

To these French concepts the fourth Directive has added the British idea of a true and fair view (*une image fidèle*). French financial statements must now be not only regular and sincere, but must also give a true and fair view of a company's assets, financial situation and profit or loss. Since a true and fair view is an imported concept with no precisely defined meaning in its country of origin, there has been much discussion in France of its significance (Pham 1984). The introduction of a requirement to show a true and fair view has been regarded by some French accountants as merely a change in terminology; others have regarded it as a means of escaping from restrictive rules. It is likely that practice will settle down somewhere between these two extremes, with the balance sheet and profit and loss account following the detail of the regulations, and the Notes (*Annexe*) being used to give any further information necessary for a true and fair view.

Fusions

A further very important, but rather hidden, influence on published reports is the *fusion*. *Fusions* are not takeovers in the British sense but agreed amalgamations, worked out in all their details beforehand, which have subsequently to be submitted for approval to extraordinary general meetings of both companies. One of the two companies is liquidated and absorbed; it does not continue as a wholly-owned subsidiary. Assets of the absorbed company are nearly always revalued when the merger takes place although this is not required by legislation. The revaluation is taxable, being considered for fiscal purposes as the disposal of assets by one company to another at a capital gain. The tax on the gain can, however, be spread over several years and depreciation can be charged on the revalued amounts. There is no tax assessed on non-depreciable assets unless they are resold. Information not available in the annual accounts is often disclosed after a *fusion*. *Fusions* have the following accounting consequences in subsequent years:

(a) There are no strict regulations regarding the uses to which the share premiums arising may be put.
(b) A company may hive off some of its assets to a subsidiary at a revalued figure and credit the capital gain to its profit and loss account.
(c) The fixed assets acquired by the absorbing company are taken in 'net' but shown in the 'gross' assets column in the balance sheet.
(d) Most important of all, most French balance sheets contain assets which have been revalued on mergers. However, unless the merger has taken place in the current year, there will be no indication at all of the revaluations.

Professional Bodies

There are two professional accounting bodies, the *Ordre des Experts Comptables at des Comptables Agréés* and the *Compagnie Nationale des Commissaires aux Comptes*. The former is roughly equivalent to a professional accounting body in the UK, but is less powerful and less independent of government control. There are about 11,000 *experts comptables*.

Members of the other body referred to above are known as *commissaires aux comptes* or state registered auditors. Many, but not all, of these are *experts comptables*. SAs and larger Sàrls must be audited by one of more *commissaires aux comptes* (see the end of section 4.3).

Outside Influences

Large French companies quoted on overseas stock exchanges have to take notice of the requirements of other countries. Compagnie Française des Pétroles, for example, has chosen to retain a very French approach to accounting but includes in the annexes to its annual report a 'Chartered Accountants' Opinion' pointing out the major differences between French and UK financial reporting (see below). At the other extreme, French companies may, whilst remaining within the minimum requirements of French law, adopt foreign and especially American accounting principles, particularly for consolidation.

4.3   Annual Reports

Formats

Unlike the UK, prescribed formats for balance sheets and profit and loss accounts in France are not an innovation introduced by the EEC fourth Directive, but a practice of long standing. Implementation of the directive did bring about some changes, however and, in particular, the disappearance of the, to British eyes, old-fashioned horizontal trading account (*compte d'exploitation générale*) and horizontal profit and loss account (*compte des pertes et profits*) and their replacement by a single income statement (*compte de résultat*).   France has not, however, adopted the profit and loss accounts in which expenses are classified by type of operation (distribution costs etc., as in Format 1 of the UK's 1985 Act). Nor has the Directive's possibility of a distinction between medium and large enterprises, for the purposes of reduced publication requirements for the former, been implemented.

French companies must prepare a balance sheet in horizontal format, but are given a choice of two profit and loss accounts, one vertical and one horizontal. Translations of the horizontal versions of the balance sheet and profit and loss account formats are given in Appendix 4. There is a clear similarity, resulting, of course, from the EEC fourth Directive, to the formats of British and Dutch statements shown in Chapters 3 and 6. It should be emphasised, however, that whilst in the UK and the Netherlands much of the detail is shown in the Notes, this is not so in France, although the Notes (called the *Annexe*) have greatly increased in importance since 1984 because of the Directive.

Balance Sheets

French companies normally publish balance sheets with two columns on the capital and liabilities (*passif*) side: one before and one after the distribution (*répartition*) of profits. This can be regarded as a typical French compromise between the law-abiding German practice of not recognising proposed dividends at all and the 'substance over form' approach in the UK of giving them full recognition. The French practice can be illustrated by CFP's balance sheet at 31 December 1983. The items varying between 'before and after' distribution are (using the English translations provided by CFP):

	Before	*After*	*Difference*
	(FF 000)	*(FF 000)*	*(FF 000)*
Legal reserve	136,440	136,441	+ 1
Carry forward	279,483	367,315	+ 87,832
Sundry creditors	1,373,195	1,809,806	+ 436,611
Net income for the year	524,444	—	– 524,444
	2,313,562	2,313,562	NIL

It is clear that it is proposed that the net income for the year should be partly distributed in dividends (FF 436,611,000), partly carried forward (FF 87,832,000) and partly (FF 1,000) transferred to a 'legal reserve' (see below).

Details of the composition of any item in the formats can be obtained from the plan. For example, the first of the intangible fixed assets listed, *frais d'établissement*, includes not only formation costs (the approximate English translation) but also the cost of issuing shares or debentures. All must be amortised over a period not exceeding five years. The cost of pure research may not be capitalised, but other R & D costs may be amortised over a period not longer than their economic life, in exceptional circumstances. Goodwill on consolidation is discussed in section 4.4 below.

It will be noted under tangible fixed assets that land and buildings are shown separately. There is a good tax reason for this: buildings can be depreciated, land cannot. The French word for depreciation is not, as the English-speaking reader might expect, *dépréciation* (which means loss in value) but *amortissement* (applied to both tangible and intangible fixed assets). The amount of depreciation charged is strongly influenced by tax regulations. Details of methods and rates, not usually disclosed in the past, will now be given in the Notes. The valuation of stocks and work in progress is similarly influenced by tax considerations. As in other countries, the lower of cost or market rule is followed. Cost is measured by the FIFO or weighted average methods; LIFO is not permitted. The amount of detail provided on the face of the balance sheet about the other current assets is large compared with British or American practice.

The other side of the balance sheet contains numerous items under the heading of capital and reserves (*capitaux propres*). A consolidated balance sheet would also include items relating to consolidation differences (see section 4.4 below).

The item briefly translated as share premiums is made up of *primes d'émission* arising from an issue of shares for cash; *primes d'apport* arising from an issue of shares for a consideration other than cash; and *primes de fusion* arising on the issue of shares when absorbing another company.

The legal reserve arises from the obligation of French companies to retain 5% of each year's profit, less losses brought forward, until an amount of 10% of share capital is reached. Such legal reserves, which are common in Continental Europe, are intended to protect creditors from excessive distribution of profits to shareholders. Reserves may also need to be established pursuant to a company's articles of association (*statuts*), or to take advantage of tax benefits.

An innovation introduced by the recent changes in French accounting regulations is the showing of the profit or loss for the accounting period as part of the capital and reserves instead of at the foot of the capital and liabilities side (if a profit) or the assets side (if a loss). As a result, it is now possible to show in the balance sheet after distribution a sub-total for net worth (*situation nette*). Not regarded as part of the net worth are investment subsidies (*subventions d'investissement*). They are recorded net of transfers to date to the profit and loss account. Operating subsidies (*subventions d'exploitation*) are taken straight to the profit and loss account. 'Revaluation differences' and 'provisions required by regulations' are explained in section 4.5 below on inflation accounting.

The next important section on the capital and liabilities side of a French balance sheet is provision for liabilities and charges (*provisions pour risques et charges*), a heading which has become familiar to British accountants, although not to those of other English-speaking countries, since 1981. These provisions provide some scope for income smoothing. They do not in France usually include any deferred taxation (as they would in the UK) because of the very close link in France between tax accounting and financial reporting.

The new prescribed balance format, unlike that in the 1957 plan, does not distinguish on its face between long-term, medium-term and current liabilites. Both are included under the general heading of creditors. In the Notes, however, they are divided into either long-term (more than five years), medium-term (more than one year to less then five years) and short-term (less than one year), or into the two categories of 'more than a year' and 'less than a year'. The classification of creditors according to their nature is given in more detail on the face of the balance sheet than is the practice in the UK or USA.   Appended to French balance sheets are details of both contingent liabilities and contingent assets.

Income Statements

Under the revised plan, income statement items are regarded as operating, financial or extraordinary (for which the French word is, to the possible confusion of British and American readers, *exceptionnel*). Although it is in conformity with the fourth Directive, the French income statement is not very similar to the typical British profit and loss account. There are three reasons for this. The first is the amount of the detail on the face of the statement rather than in the Notes. The second is the emphasis in the mandatory formats on goods produced as well as sold. Thus an item appears, for example, for work performed for own purposes and capitalised (*production immobilisée*). The third is that French companies are not permitted to use the format from the fourth Directive most frequently adopted by UK companies (who have a choice), that is, the format which discloses cost of sales, distribution costs and administrative expenses.

The expense item 'profit share of employees' (*participation des salariés aux fruits de l'expansion*) records a company's tax-deductible contribution to a compulsory employee share purchase scheme.   The credit (liability) side of the entry is included under 'Creditors: taxation and social security'.

Funds Statements

Publication of a funds statement (*tableau de financement*) is obligatory from 1986.   It had already become common practice for large companies. The statement is divided into two parts. The first part shares the long-term sources of funds (*stables*) and the long-term uses of funds (*durables*). The balance represents the change in working capital (*fonds de roulement*) which is analysed in the second part of the statement.

The analysis distinguishes between operating funds (stocks, trade debtors, trade creditors) and non-operating funds (other debtors and creditors) with a sub-total. The balance then represents changes in net liquid funds (*trésorerie*). The statement is normally constructed before profit distribution, so that uses of funds include dividends *paid* during the accounting period. The sources side is headed by *autofinancement* (essentially net profit after adding back depreciation).

Notes (Annexe)

Before the implementation of the fourth Directive, French financial statements were accompanied by very few Notes as understood in the UK and USA. As a result of the implementing legislation, they are now much more detailed and represent a substantial increase on previous amounts of disclosure in French financial statements. Part of the data provided is obligatory, irrespective of its materiality; part need only be provided if of material importance. The former includes such matters as the following: additional information necessary in order to give a true and fair view; details of any departure from the rules in order to give a true and fair view; description and justification for any changes in methods of presentation and valuation methods; explanation of the treatment of intangible assets; details of leasing transactions. The latter includes such matters as accounting policies; depreciation methods; revaluations and the accounting and fiscal consequences thereof; maturity dates of loans; the differences between the book and replacement value of stocks; analysis of the share capital; the identity of any company which has fully consolidated the financial statements of the reporting company; pension information; global data on directors' remuneration; details of convertible debentures; analysis of the tax change into that relating to ordinary and extraordinary activities; analysis of the turnover by business sector and geographical market; details of the labour force; the effect of the application of fiscal rules on the determination of the profit or loss; details of deferred tax; and data concerning subsidiaries and affiliated companies.

Other Contents

Two useful tables are included not in the Notes but elsewhere in the annual report. Attached to the report of the directors is a table giving the financial results of the parent company for the last five accounting periods. This is divided into four sections and gives not only balance sheet and income statement figures but also earnings per share, dividends per share and employee information. Earnings per share figures are *not* adjusted for extraordinary or prior year items.

An inventory of securities held in portfolio is obligatory disclosure for listed companies and certain of their subsidiaries. Many listed companies also provide stock exchange data relating to their shares.

Additional Requirements for Listed Companies

Listed companies are required to publish their annual financial statements in the *Bulletin des annonces légales obligatoires* (BALO) and also to publish half-yearly turnover and profit information and quarterly turnover figures.

Exemptions for Small Companies

Companies and other enterprises below a certain size are allowed, as in other EEC countries, to present their balance sheet, income statement and Notes in a simplified form. Unlike the UK, these exemptions apply for all purposes and the criteria differ as between balance sheet and income statement on the one hand and the Notes on the other.

A company may use the abridged system in the revised accounting plan for its balance sheet and income statement if it satisfies two of the three following criteria and does not go beyond the limits for two successive periods:

Balance sheet total	FF 900,000 or less
Turnover	FF 1,800,000 or less
Permanent employees	7 or less

For the Notes the upper limits are higher:

Balance sheet total	FF 5,000,000 or less
Turnover	FF 10,000,000 or less
Permanent employees	50 or less

Under the abridged system the balance sheet is drawn up before distribution of profit and includes only the headings marked with an asterisk in Appendix 4. Similarly, the income statement includes the headings marked with an asterisk in Appendix 4 plus one heading only for purchases and one heading only for variation in stocks.

Small companies are required to disclose in their Notes all of the data which is required irrespective of materiality, but need publish only certain items of those to be included if of material importance.

Audit Reports

In their report to the annual general meeting of shareholders, the *commissaires aux comptes* must, under the new legislation (unless qualifying their report), certify that the annual accounts of the parent company and the consolidated accounts annexed to them are 'regular' and 'sincere' and give a true and fair view of the profit or loss of the accounting period, as well as of the assets and financial situation of the company and the enterprises included in the consolidation at the end of the period. They must also state that the directors' report and other documents included in the annual report are 'sincere' and in agreement with the annual accounts.

Auditing in France is still relatively underdeveloped by British and American standards and is not dominated by the international accounting firms. Standards of practice are steadily improving. As noted in section 4.2, audit is compulsory for SAs and for the larger Sàrls. More Sàrls will be subject to obligatory audit when the fourth Directive is fully implemented.

4.4 Consolidation and Currency Translation

As recently as the late 1960s consolidated financial statements were almost unknown in France. During the 1970s the number of listed companies publishing such statements increased rapidly with the encouragement of COB and the CNC. The latter issued in 1968 an influential report on consolidation principles which was approved, but not made mandatory, by the Ministry of Economics and Finance. A revised report, taking into account International Accounting Standard No. 3 and the (then) proposed seventh EEC Directive, was issued in 1978 and carries much weight although it has never been formally approved. COB has, since 1 July 1971, required consolidated statements from any parent company newly applying for a listing on the stock exchange or making a public issue to increase its capital.

Anticipating the seventh Directive, the law of 3 January 1985 concerning the development of private investment and the protection of investors requires listed companies to publish consolidated accounts for financial years ending after 31 December 1984. Details will be set out in a decree to be issued after consultation with the CNC.

Techniques of consolidation have been increasingly influenced in recent years by those practised in the UK and USA, but are by no means identical with them (see Chapter 10). Consolidation may be global, proportional or by *mise en équivalence*. Global consolidation is, subject to the remarks below, similar to British practice for subsidiaries. Proportional consolidation (i.e. inclusion of assets, liabilities, revenues and expenses on a pro rata basis) is used for joint ventures. *Mise en équivalence* is similar to the British equity method of dealing with associated companies. Until the law of 30 April 1983 there was no legal obligation for consolidated statements to be audited.

French consolidation techniques have in the past differed from those in the UK in that a comparison has been made *each year* between the net value of a subsidiary according to its own books and the cost of the investment in the parent company's books. The difference thus arising includes, in British terminology, not only goodwill on consolidation, but also the excess of the fair values of tangible net assets over their book values, and undistributed profits of subsidiaries since acquisition. The CNC recommends that goodwill on consolidation be calculated as in the UK, but some French companies base it on the excess over book values rather than fair values, or even simply report the consolidation difference as a single figure. These treatments are not likely to be permissible in the future. Further, it will become necessary, as the CNC recommends, to write off goodwill on consolidation over a reasonable period.

Consolidated accounts are not important for French tax purposes and have only recently been prescribed by law. As a result, presentation and techniques have varied more than is the case in the UK, Germany and the USA. Some have retained a French flavour, such as those of CFP; others have been much influenced by Anglo-Saxon accounting methods, such as those of St. Gobain-Pont-à-Mousson.

CFP described its general principles of consolidation in 1983 as follows:

As in previous years, the Total Group's consolidated accounts have been prepared in accordance with recommendations set forth by the 'Conseil National de la Comptabilité'.

General Principles of Consolidation
Companies eligible for consolidation are those over which Compagnie Française des Pétrole's control is at least 20%. The parent company's share of the equity of such companies or the TOTAL Group's investment therein (investments and long-term loans) must in addition represent at least F 10 million after revaluation.

The minimum value criterion is not applied to certain companies due to the importance of their operations to the Group, nor in the case of sub-subsidiaries whose accounts are already included in the consolidated sub-group of a subsidiary.

Full consolidation is applied in the case of companies which are more than 50% controlled by the Group and whose activity falls within the main activities of the Group. Exceptions to this rule may be made in the case of subsidiaries which are less than 50% controlled but whose operations form part of the Group's integrated activities, and over the management of which the Group has a significant influence. The most important of these exceptions in 1983 is Total Petroleum (North America). Consolidation is, however, proportional, based on percentage of control by the Group, and is applied accordingly to the following companies:

'joint interest' companies (in which operations are shared on the basis of each partner's interest);

companies controlled jointly on a 50/50 basis by the TOTAL Group and a single other shareholder.

All other companies have been accounted for on an equity basis. The TOTAL Group's share of these companies' earnings is included in the consolidated statement of income.

In accordance with the above consolidation methods, the TOTAL Group is made up of 195 companies: 149 are fully consolidated, 13 are consolidated on a proportional basis and 33 are accounted for under the equity method.

Reciprocal items
All intercompany transactions have been eliminated.

The seventh Directive will have an important impact on French consolidation law and practice. Most companies, rather than just listed companies, are likely to have to provide consolidated statements; the statements will become much more uniform, and they will have to be audited. There will be more use of equity accounting and, in general, more disclosure of information on a consolidated basis.

Methods of foreign currency translation have not been standardised in France, although the closing rate method appears to be the most common, with average rates used in the income statement. Translation differences are also dealt with in various ways: CFP passes those on non-current assets through reserves and those on net monetary assets and stocks through the income statement.

4.5 Inflation Accounting

Because of the close relationship between tax accounting and financial reporting, inflation accounting practice in France has always been closely linked with tax law. Thus, whilst in principle French companies have always been allowed to revalue assets, in practice they have not done so because, as explained in the CFP's 1973 Prospectus (in section 4.2 above), an increase in the value of depreciable assets would be taxed. The special case of *fusions* has already been discussed.

However, the Finance Acts of 1978 and 1979 suspended this 'free' revaluation and made revaluation obligatory for companies officially listed on the Stock Exchange, for other companies in which such companies hold a participation large enough for consolidation, and for other commercial companies which solicit funds from the general public (van Waardenburg 1979). It is optional for most other business enterprises.

Whether or not an asset is depreciable for tax purposes, it is still eligible for revaluation. Non-depreciable assets (e.g. land and goodwill) were revalued to their use value (i.e. estimated cost of acquisition or construction) as at 31 December 1976, with a corresponding credit to a revaluation reserve. This credit is not taxable but may be distributed; it can be capitalised.

Similar rules apply to depreciable assets, except that the new book values may not exceed the old book values multiplied by a coefficient determined by the decree of 24 March 1978. The credit is to a special revaluation provision account (one of the 'provisions required by regulation' in the balance sheet format). An amount equal to the extra depreciation resulting each year from the revaluation is debited to the special revaluation provision account and credited to profit and loss account, thus removing the tax benefit.

Fixed assets acquired since 31 December 1976 are valued at their historical cost.

There are no accounting standards in France on inflation accounting, but professional accountants and others are aware of the deficiencies of historical cost accounting and have made recommendations. In 1976 a working party connected with the preparation of the national economic plan drew attention to the problem and recommended the use of general price level accounting. In March 1981 the council of OECCA stated that French financial statements ought to be supplemented by information on the effects of inflation and of variations in specific prices. A number of leading French companies have experimented with inflation accounting in collaboration with the *Association des directeurs de comptabilité* (association of directors of accounting).

OECCA and the *Association* have recently recommended what they consider to be a workable, although not conceptually perfect, solution to the problem of inflation accounting (OECCA 1984). The procedures they favour can be summarised as follows : having adjusted the balance sheet and income statement so that they are based on pure historical costs (i.e. having eliminated the effect of any fiscal 'distortions'), (1) debit or credit the income statement for adjustments for depreciation, cost of sales, and gain or loss on net monetary assets; and (2) adjust the figures for stocks, tangible fixed assets, and reserves in the balance sheet.

Tangible fixed assets and depreciation thereon are, for simplicity, revalued by the use of *general* price indices. Stocks in the balance sheet are valued at the lower of current replacement cost or net realisable value; the cost of sales adjustment is the difference between FIFO and LIFO cost of sales. The gain or loss on net monetary assets is calculated using a general price index. There is no gearing adjustment.

4.6 Social Balance Sheets

In 1975 a Report on Company Law Reform recommended the publication each year by companies of a *bilan social* (Sudreau 1975). The literal translation of *bilan social* is 'social balance sheet' but the term is perhaps best translated as 'social report' since information produced by French companies in this area is not in any way related to their financial statements.   French companies provide various translations in the English versions of their annual reports; CFP, for example, uses the phrase 'staff relations'.   CFP's translation is revealing. As will be seen below, not all aspects of social responsibility are covered and what is provided could well be described as an employment report.

The recommendation of the Sudreau Report was implemented by the Law of 12 July 1977 and the related decree of 8 December 1977 (Kapp and Petitguyot 1978).   Information has to be provided by undertakings with 300 or more employees on the following matters : employment; wages and related costs; health and safety conditions; other working conditions; training; industrial relations; and other relevant conditions of life within the undertaking. The information provided is very detailed and specific and French law and practice in the aspects of social reporting listed above are in advance of those of other countries.

4.7 Summary

The main influences on French company financial reporting are the close relationship between tax accounting and financial accounting, the national accounting plan, and the COB. The influence of the accountancy profession is growing but is less than in the UK or USA.

The financial statements of parent companies are more uniform than those in the UK and USA but this uniformity does not yet extend to consolidated statements. Auditing is becoming more important. A form of inflation accounting has been introduced through fiscal legislation. The publication of social balance sheets is more advanced in France than in the USA or the other member states of the EEC.

The seventh EEC Directive will have a great impact, with consolidation on a uniform basis eventually becoming the norm for most companies.

References

Gray, S.J. (1980) 'The impact of international accounting differences from a security-analysis perspective: Some European evidence', *Journal of Accounting Research*, Spring.

Kapp, B. and Petitguyot, B. (1978) *Le Bilan Social, son Application Légale; Loi du 12 Juillet 1977, Décret et Arrêtés d'Application du 8 Décembre 1977*, Editions Sirey, Paris.

OECCA (1984) *Corriger les Comptes des Variations de Prix: Pourquoi? Comment?* Economica, Paris.

Pérochon, C. (with the collaboration of Prost, A.) (1982) *Guide d'Application. Plan Comptable Général 1982*, Les Editions Foucher, Paris.

Pham, D. (1984) 'A true and fair view: a French perspective', in S.J. Gray and A.G. Coenenberg, *EEC Accounting Harmonisation: Implementation and Impact of the Fourth Directive*, North-Holland, Amsterdam.

Sudreau, P. (Chairman) (1975) *Rapport du Comité d'Etude pour la Réforme de l'Entreprise*, La Documentation Française, Paris.

Waardenburg, D.A. van (1979) 'France: The Finance Law 1979', *European Taxation*, No. 4.

Institut National de la Statistique et des Etudes Economiques (INSEE) (1983), *Annuaire Statistique de la France 1983*, Paris.

Further Reading

Beeny, J. (1976) *European Financial Reporting II: France*, ICAEW, London.

Boussard, D. and Rey, F. (1984) 'Accounting institutions and accounting research in France', in A.G. Hopwood and H. Schreuder (eds) *European Contributions to Accounting Research*, Free University Press, Amsterdam.

Ernst & Whinney (1984) *The Impact of the Seventh Directive*, Chapters 4 and 6, Financial Times Business Information.

Glautier, M.W.E. and Roy, J.L. (1981) 'Social responsibility reporting', in T.A. Lee (ed.) *Developments in Financial Reporting*, Philip Allan.

Le Gall, J. (1974) *French Company Law*, Oyez Publishing.

McKinnon, S.M. (1983) *Consolidated Accounts: The Seventh EEC Directive*, Arthur Young, London, ch.6.

Peat Marwick (1984) *Consolidated Accounts: Seventh Directive*, Peat Marwick, Mitchell, Brussels, ch.13.

Commission des Opérations de Bourse, *Annual Reports*, in French. Abridged reports also published in English.

Compagnie Nationale des Commissaires aux Comptes (1983) *Guide des Commissaires aux Comptes*, Paris.

Conseil National de la Comptabilité (1982) *Plan Comptable Général*, Paris.

Memento pratique Francis Lefebvre – Comptable (1985), 4th edn., Editions F. Lefebvre, Paris.

Ordre des Experts Comptables et des Comptables Agréés (1981) *Les Rapports Annuels des Sociétés Françaises*, Masson, Paris.

Société Fiduciaire du Marché Commun (1979) 'A new tool for measuring the social situation of French businesses: the social balance sheet', *Journal UEC*, No. 4, 1978-81.

Appendix 4

Uniform Formats for French Financial Statements

BALANCE SHEET

*ASSETS

Issued share capital not called

*Fixed Assets
  * Intangible fixed assets
    Formation costs
    Research and development costs
    Concessions, patents, licences,
      trademarks, and similar rights
      and assets
    * Goodwill
    * Other intangible fixed assets
    Payments on account

  * Tangible fixed assets
    Land
    Buildings
    Plant, machinery, tools
    Other tangible fixed assets
    Tangible fixed assets in course of construction
    Payments on account

  * Investments
    Shares in group and related companies
    Amounts owed by group and related companies
    Other fixed asset investments
    Other loans
    Other investments

*Current Assets
  * Stocks and work in progress
    Raw materials and consumables
    Work in progress (goods and services)
    Intermediate and finished goods
    Goods for resale

  * Payments on account and deposits

  * Debtors
    * Trade debtors
    * Other debtors
    Called up share capital not paid

  * Investments
    Own shares
    Other investments

  * Cash at bank and in hand

  Prepayments and Accrued Income
    Prepayments
    Accrued income

Debenture redemption premiums

Translation differences

*CAPITAL AND LIABILITIES

Capital and Reserves
  Share capital (of which paid up ....)
  Share premiums
  * Revaluation reserves
  * Reserves:
    * Legal reserve
    Reserves required by articles or by contract
    * Reserves required by regulations
    * Other (optional) reserves
  * Carry forward from profit and loss account
    (credit or debit balance)
  * Profit or loss for the accounting period
    Sub-total: Net worth
    Investment subsidies
  * Provisions required by regulations

*Provisions for Liabilities and Charges
  Provisions for liabilities
  Provisions for charges

* Creditors
  Convertible debenture loans
  Other debenture loans
  * Loans and sundry creditors
  * Payments received on account
  * Trade creditors
  Taxation and social security
  Debts relating to fixed assets
  * Other creditors
  Accruals and deferred income

Translation differences

INCOME STATEMENT

EXPENSES   **INCOME**

* *Operating expenses*
   Purchases of goods for resale
     Variation in stocks thereof
   Purchases of raw materials and consumables
     Variation in stocks thereof
  * Other purchases and external charges
  * Taxes and similar payments
  * Wages and salaries
  * Social security costs
   Valuation adjustments
     on fixed assets: depreciation
     on fixed assets: other amounts written off
     on current assets: amounts written off
     relating to provisions for liabilities and charges
  * Other operating expenses

       TOTAL operating expenses

Share of loss on joint ventures

Financial expenses
   Value adjustments
   Interest and similar expenses
   Losses on foreign exchange
   Net expenses on transfers of securities held as
     fixed assets

       TOTAL financial expenses

* *Extrordinary expenses*
   Operating
   Non-operating
   Depreciation and other amounts written off

       TOTAL extraordinary expenses

Profit share of employees

* *Tax on profit*

       TOTAL expenses

     Balance = profit

     SUM TOTAL

* *Operating income*
  * Sales of goods bought for resale
  * Sales of goods and services produced
     Net turnover
     (including exports)
  * Variation in stocks of
     finished goods and work in progress
   Work performed for own purposes and capitalised
  * Operating subsidies
   Provisions written back
  * Other operating income

       TOTAL operating income

Share of profit on joint ventures

* *Financial income:*
   From participating interests
   From other investments and loans
     forming part of the fixed assets
   Other interest receivable and similar income
   Provisions written back
   Gains on foreign exchange
   Net income from transfers of securities held as
     fixed assets

       TOTAL financial income

* *Extraordinary income:*
   Operating
   Non-operating
   Provisions written back

       TOTAL extraordinary income

       TOTAL income

     Balance = loss

     SUM TOTAL

5

Financial Reporting in
West Germany

KLAUS MACHARZINA*

An analysis of German financial reporting invariably involves references to a number of laws and names of different types of businesses. For a useful list of abbreviations, see the Glossary on p. 371. As with the preceding chapter, there is an Appendix containing excerpts from the annual report of a company; readers may find it useful to refer to this.

5.1 General Characteristics of the German System

To the British or American user or student of German corporate financial reporting, the accounting practices and authoritative requirements will seem to be unorthodox: the fashion of drawing up financial statements and the underlying accounting methods may seem difficult and confusing.

In detail, some of the features of German accounting and auditing which are rather different from Anglo-Saxon type accounting requirements are:

(a) strong influence of tax law and regulations;

---

* The author is indebted to Professor Chris Nobes and to WP/StB Horst Kaminski (Executive Director of the IdW) for useful comments on a draft of this chapter.

(b) lack of formally codified auditing standards, although there are professional pronouncements to which the auditor would normally adhere;

(c) a much greater degree of disclosure for public than for private companies;

(d) possibilities for smoothing profit figures especially with respect to movements on undisclosed reserves;

(e) financial reporting founded on a 'true-accurate-complete' basis;

(f) overall reference to 'proper accounting principles' which are not codified but indirectly established by court decisions;

(g) inflexibility of accounting requirements in response to environmental developments;

(h) a lower level of disclosure for certain types of companies;

(i) absence of binding requirements on additional statements like funds flow statements, employment reports, social reports, earnings per share information, information on pension funds, segment information, and information on directors' interests;

(j) different requirements concerning consolidations; for example, foreign subsidiaries are not required to be included.

Comparative Model

In order to understand the German financial reporting system better, the Anglo-Saxon reader may find it useful to consider the objectives, means, context and efficiency of accounting. The objectives of financial reporting in Germany are nowhere explicitly stated. There is, however, a rather flexible requirement contained in the public companies law which could be interpreted as the *informational purpose* of annual financial statements. Under s.149 (1) of the *Aktiengesetz (AktG)*, such statements should disclose a company's results and net assets as reliably as possible within the framework of the valuation requirements. Furthermore, there is a secondary objective of annual financial statements which relates to the *determination* of a company's annual *income*. From the standpoint of conflicting interests among shareholders, creditors and management, this could be interpreted as a conflict-regulating mechanism. On the one hand, the distribution of the annual profit is limited by allowing the management board to retain up to 50% of it (ss.58 (2), 150 (2), 1 *AktG*) and, on the other hand, a minimum distribution to minority shareholders is guaranteed (ss.58 (1), (2), (4), 254 (1) *AktG*).

There is a built-in conflict between these basic purposes of financial statements which the law does not resolve. Moreover, compared to Anglo-Saxon developments towards improving financial statements as information devices for users, German objectives appear to be rather conservative. This may be partly due to the greater influence of bankers and other lenders.

From country to country there are different environments which influence the various national financial reporting systems. Variables such as the level of industrialisation, the level of international integration, and the quality of the capital market may be taken as general influences on national accounting systems. Apart from the latter, which does differ between Britain and Germany, there are not many differences. Therefore, in order to explain variances between the two systems, it is better to use a class of variables which have a direct influence on national systems and which will be referred to as 'financial reporting authorities'.

Financial Reporting Authorities

In Germany, there are three major sources of authoritative rules:

(1) Commercial and tax law (see Table 5.1)
(2) Accounting practice
(3) The profession

Legal requirements date back to the first Commercial Code of 1897; present laws in force include the Companies Act of 1965 and the Publicity Act of 1969. The German requirement that financial accounts should agree with the constantly changing tax requirements leads to changes in financial reporting.

The impact of 'accounting practice' is also felt because of a reference in law to established 'principles of orderly bookkeeping' (see section

Table 5.1 Commercial and Tax Law Requirements

Commercial Code (1897)

Law on Public Companies (1965) (*Aktiengesetz*)

Law on Private Companies (1892, amended 1980) (*GmbH-Gesetz*)

Law on Cooperative Associations (1889)

Law on Financial Accounting by Certain Enterprises and Related Enterprises (1969)

Income Tax Law (1939*)

Income Tax Regulations (1967*)

Regulations of Tax Administration and Procedure (1937*)

Note: *Tax laws are continually amended.

5.3). Obviously, the major reason why these principles are not codified is to allow for a certain flexibility and a feedback between law and practice. A more direct interaction is achieved by practising accountants commenting on legal requirements and initiating new developments in financial reporting, such as corporate social reporting.

The German accounting profession is a rather small body of about 5,000 members. The *Institut der Wirtscaftsprüfer in Deutschland e. V.* (IdW) was formed in 1931 following the provisions of the Companies Act 1931. Whereas membership is voluntary and about 90% of German *Wirtschaftsprüfer* (WP) have joined the Institute, there is a legally required membership of the *Wirtschaftsprüferkammer* (chamber of accountants) which was introduced by the law regulating the accountancy profession (*Wirtschaftsprüferordnung*) of 1971. The chamber's legally imposed function is to observe professional standards and to educate accountants. The latter function, however, has been left in the hands of the Institute which, besides this task, aims to advance the profession and to protect the interests of its members. Educational standards are high: either a university degree in business administration, economics or law plus five years' accountancy experience; or ten years' practical experience if the candidate for the Institute's examinations has no university degree. In either case at least four years' experience (out of the five or ten years) have to be with a WP or a partnership of WPs.

The influence of the German Institute is mainly by recommendation and non-mandatory releases but also by consultation in the process of lawmaking. In their audit function, qualified accountants (WPs) mainly check and confirm the compliance of corporate financial reports with legal requirements and the company statutes. They also exercise judgment as regards economic valuations and compliance with 'proper accounting principles'. Under the Companies Act of 1965 all public companies and, under the Publicity Act of 1969, certain other types of business are required to be audited by WPs.

Authorities such as the Stock Exchange and trade unions, who exercise direct influence in other countries, are of less importance to accounting in Germany, but they take part in discussions on the setting of rules. This is also true of accounting academics – although there is a long tradition and great variety of different approaches offered by German accounting theory.

5.2 Forms of Business Organisation

Financial reporting and disclosure requirements depend on the organisational form of the business. Among the variety of forms available under commercial and company law, it is particularly those involving limited liability which lead to exacting requirements, mainly because of the protection necessary for third parties. For this reason, and because it is these types of business which readers of this book are most likely to encounter, the limited company form is given particular attention.

Public Company – Aktiengesellschaft (AG)

The limitation of liability of an AG is stated in s.1 (1) of the *AktG*. An AG's capital is divided into shares which are freely transferable. Registered shares are uncommon, although they are permitted. Normally shares are 'bearer'. The founders (at least five in number) subscribe for the whole of the capital, which amounts to at least DM 100,000 (s.7 *AktG*); there is no distinction – as for instance in Great Britain – between subscribed and issued capital. The company must have its own articles (*Gesellschaftsvertrag*) by which legal requirements may be modified or expanded. There is also a memorandum which is very similar to the one required by the British Companies Act with the exception that limited liability of shareholders need not be mentioned separately. Moreover the nominal value, the ascribed value (i.e. the issuing price) and the classes into which shares are divided must be confirmed by a notarial deed which is a constituent part of the articles.

In the legally prescribed organisational structure of an AG the decision-making power and responsibility are concentrated within the management board (*Vorstand*) (s.76 (1) *AktG*). In addition there is a supervisory board (*Aufsichtsrat*) (s.100 *AktG*), half of whose members are appointed by the shareholders' meeting (*Hauptversammlung*), and half by the workforce (*Mitbestimmungsgesetz* 1976). The function of this board, which is unknown to British law but has parallels in France and the Netherlands, is to appoint and dismiss the members of the management board, to supervise the latter body, and to approve the annual financial statements.

Kommanditgesellschaft auf Aktien (KGaA)

There is a modified form of public company which has a separate legal personality like the AG but in which at least one shareholder, the general partner (*Komplementär*), is personally liable for the company's obligations to its creditors; the remaining shareholders (*Kommanditaktionäre*) are liable only to the extent of their interest in the company (s.278 *AktG*). The KGaA is – as its name indicates – a mixture of the limited partnership and the corporation. Although its major characteristics are certainly closer to those of a corporation and the respective legal requirements are embodied in ss.278–90 of the *AktG*, there are some distinct elements of partnership organisation. The regulations of the Commercial and Civil Codes are especially relevant for the personally liable shareholders (who, by the way, are *ipso facto* managers of the company). The KGaA is always treated as a commercial public company.

The importance of the KGaA, which is unknown in Anglo-Saxon countries, has decreased since its introduction (from France) into various German states in the eighteenth century. The reasons for this are difficulties arising from the complex legislation, the reluctance of small businesses to choose this form because of the high minimum capital requirement, which is the same as that for the AG, and because of its *unlimited liability* element.

There may, however, be a revival of this form in the future on the grounds of certain advantages regarding co-determination (*Mitbestimmung*) legislation. For instance, the KGaA's management is protected from the influence of the supervisory board in hiring and firing them and thus protected also from the influence of workers' representatives, who constitute half of such boards.

Gesellschaft mit beschränkter Haftung (GmbH)

The *Gesellschaft mit beschränkter Haftung* (GmbH) under German law is fully liable to the extent of its total assets for its obligations to creditors, whereas a direct liability on the part of its shareholders does not exist at all (s.13 (2) *GmbHG*). Before the *GmbHG* of 1980 the crucial question was whether the low legal minimum capital requirement of DM 20,000 and the consequent 'under-capitalisation' of some private companies restricted their liability unreasonably. This problem was solved by the 1980 GmbH Act, which provides for a minimum share capital of DM 50,000 (s.5 *GmbHG*), in line with the second EEC Directive on company law. This requirement has operated since the start of 1985.

The GmbH is quite similar to the AG in its basic legal characteristics such as separate legal personality and the nature of the company (although it has partnership aspects). However, it has some quite distinct features, particularly the less restrictive legal regulations. Accordingly, the company's formation is much simpler and cheaper than that of the AG. There is no requirement to establish a supervisory board unless the workforce exceeds 500 in number. Shareholders are allowed to take decisions outside a formally constituted meeting and without the presence of a notary public.

Altogether, there is much more flexibility and contractual freedom as far as the articles are concerned, because there are fewer legal requirements than in public company law. However, this causes greater risks for shareholders and creditors. In practice, inappropriate company formation and management, and a great number of insolvencies and bankruptcies have shown the implicit problems of this type of company, particularly in times of economic crises. As a result it is more difficult for the GmbH to raise funds in the form of loans from banks, for example. This has led to the German coinage 'Gesellschaft mit beschränkter Hochachtung' (literally, company with limited trustworthiness).

Managers (*Geschäftsführer*) need not have any shares in the company (*Drittorganschaft*), depending on the articles or a resolution of the shareholders (ss.6, 46 *GmbHG*). Each member's share in the business must have a nominal value of DM 500 or a higher amount which is a multiple of DM 100 (s.5 (1), (3) *GmbHG*). This must be fully subscribed on the formation of the company but may be paid in fractions by calls that are made on the shareholders. The company's assets include the amounts unpaid on its shares, and the transfer of shares requires a notarial deed. There is no possibility of Stock Exchange dealings, and shares are not in bearer form, nor are they negotiable like shares in an AG.

It is often suggested that the GmbH is roughly the equivalent of the British private company. However, there are some substantial differences. The principal difference is that there is a separate body of private company law in Germany. The impossibility of admission to the Stock Exchange is a consequence of the GmbH's structure and the Stock Exchange regulations, and not the original intention of the lawmakers. The GmbH can be converted into an AG only subject to a formal procedure detailed in a special section of the company law.

Other Forms

To complete the description of the situation in Germany, some other forms will be mentioned briefly. There are business organisations in the form of the 'Registered co-operative association' (*Eingetragene Genossenschaft*). As far as its legal nature is concerned, this is similar to the GmbH. It is governed by a separate law of 1889 (*Genossenschaftsgesetz, GenG*).

Other popular forms are the GmbH & Co and the GmbH & Co KG, equivalents of which are unknown in Britain. A GmbH & Co is a partnership (OHG), whereas the GmbH & Co KG is a *limited* partnership in which the GmbH as the general partner (*Komplementär*) is liable without limit for the partnership's debts, while the shareholders of the GmbH are limited partners (*Kommanditisten*) who again are only liable to the extent of their approved contribution (s.161 *Handelsgesetzbuch*).

Although it has often been suggested that the major reasons for choosing this form are tax-orientated (e.g. Pennington 1970), originally there seemed to be a major economic motive, because there are no legal provisions which would explicitly allow for a 'private limited partnership'

(*Personen* GmbH). It was only a legal decision of the Supreme Court of 1922 which allowed a GmbH to become a partner in a KG (*RGZ* 105/101). Yet it was not until the 1950s that tax courts also recognised this form as a partnership.

Another common form is the one-man company, public as well as private, which is legally sanctioned under s.1 of the new Act. In contrast to the British Companies Acts, German law does not provide any restrictions on, or even requirements for the winding up of, a company if and when the membership decreases below the minimum number required for its formation, that is, five with the AG and one with the GmbH. The restriction under the old Act that a one-man company might not be incorporated had been circumvented in practice by means of straw formations, which were a popular device particularly for overseas investors such as multi-national oil and other companies. This device is no longer necessary, although it is still permitted.

Economic Importance

AGs have decreased from a total of about 17,000 in 1926 to a fairly constant level of about 2,000 over the last fifteen years. The GmbHs have risen from about 20,000 in 1911 to about 260,000 in 1983, with an increase of more than 100,000 within the last decade. Medium and small businesses seem to prefer the GmbH, whereas the AG is reserved for big business. In 1984, the largest 100 industrial enterprises by turnover were 71AGs, 20 GmbHs, 2 KGaAs, 4 KGs, 1 OHG and 2 private foundations.

Summary

All business entities including sole proprietorships and partnerships (general or limited) are subject to the accounting requirements of the Commercial Code (ss.38 *et seq. HGB*). In addition, private companies are subject to accounting requirements laid down in the private limited company law (ss. 41 *et seq. GmbHG*). Moreover, public companies are required to follow the financial reporting and disclosure requirements of the Companies Act (ss.148–77 *AktG*). Larger companies (see Section 5.5) also fall within the scope of the publication requirements of the 1969 Publicity Law (*PublG*).

5.3   Accounting Principles and Theories

Accounting Principles

The German understanding of 'accounting principles' is not quite comparable to what is meant in Britain. In fact it simply seems to be a wrong translation which is even used in official documents, and legal and accounting texts (e.g. Mueller and Galbraith 1966). This set of basic norms may be referred to as 'principles of orderly bookkeeping' – *Grundsätze ordnungsmässiger Buchführung (GoB)*. There are three main sources of these requirements: company, commercial and tax law and regulations. The German Commercial Code (*HGB*, ss.38 *et seq.*), Public Company Law (*AktG*, ss.149, (1), 1), Income Tax Law (*EStG*, s.5), and Income Tax Regulations (*EStR*, 29) provide that all legal entities (including branches of foreign companies) operating in Germany are to comply with these principles.

According to the commercial code (s.38 *HGB*), all *merchants* (i.e. sole proprietorships, partnerships either in general, limited or partly limited form, private or public companies) are required to keep accounts and provide annual financial statements subject to the provisions of the tax order (*Abgabenordnung, AO*). Under s.141 of the *AO*, even a sole proprietor who has

(a) an annual turnover of more than DM 360,000, or
(b) total assets of more than DM 100,000, or
(c) an annual business income of more than DM 36,000

is obliged to keep proper books of account and to file tax statements (s.5 *EStG*).

Income Tax Regulations in particular leave no doubt whatsoever that the term involves the keeping of books required by other laws, and *makes it quite clear that all tax allowances, including the carry forward of losses, will be disallowed if the tax audit reveals that principles have not been adhered to.* There is, however, the problem that these principles are neither defined nor codified. One has rather to deduce them from the various laws, especially the company law, and even from decisions in several tax cases. The consequence is that commercial accounts are very much orientated towards tax calculation. Since the Saxon Income Tax Law of 1874 there is the paramount principle (*Massgeblichkeitsprinzip*) that commercial and tax statements should agree. Valuation for tax purposes has to comply with the *GoB* which are followed in the financial statements (s.5 (1) *EStG*). A corollary to this is that, in order to obtain the maximum benefit from tax allowances, the most favourable tax-oriented valuations have to be taken up in the financial statements as well. This principle also explains the absence of deferred tax accounting in German financial reports.

Under s.38 of the *HGB* and s.149 of the *AktG*, books of account and financial statements are to be drawn up in compliance with the *GoB*. Such deductively derived principles were first mentioned in the Prussian Civil Code of 1793. Additional *inductively* determined principles are the conventions followed by 'reputable businessmen' in practice. The latter have been subject to criticism mainly because of the ambiguity of the measurement criteria of 'reputable' businessmen and the delay and difficulty involved in identifying in detail what they are. A commission of

German accountancy professors has suggested that the task of establishing an explicit set of accounting principles be given to an independent board similar to the FASB. As civil legislation has been reluctant to fulfil this legally imposed responsibility, it is largely tax courts which determine such principles – naturally in a tax-biased manner.

Fundamental accounting conventions can be identified: they comprise the accounting entity principle, the accounting period principle and the historical cost principle. Accounting should be performed from the standpoint of an economic *entity*, in between two balance sheet dates, and based on *historical cost*. There is also a German *accruals* principle which combines the British accruals and going concern concepts. The *consistency* principle implies the requirement that closing figures be the same as in the subsequent opening balance sheet; the principle covers disclosure of balance sheet items and valuation methods. Moreover, extraordinary items have to be reported separately in the income statement. The *conservatism* principle means the use of the lowest value attributable to any asset item. It includes two other principles which are referred to as the *realisation* and *inequality* principles. According to the former, income must be realised before profit can be taken up. This principle, which obviously limits the accruals concept, is the main authority for the historical cost convention. The inequality principle requires that, while profits must not be anticipated, any potential future losses must be provided for in the accounts.

One might summarise the differences between German and Anglo-Saxon principles by saying that *conservatism* is stronger and *accruals* weaker in German accounting.

5.4   Structure and Contents of Corporate Accounts

German financial statements present a rather confusing picture to the British reader, particularly because of the lack of cross-referencing which would link balance sheet items with notes or comments in the directors' report. There are strict legal requirements as to the form and contents of company financial statements and reports. There are some merits in such inflexible schemes: intercompany comparison is made easier, and the regrouping of items in order to present a year's figures in a more favourable way is prevented. (See section 5.6 and Chapter 10 for details of consolidation practices.)

For GmbHs an accompanying report is required only from entities which are within the scope of the Publicity Law. This report must contain details about the firm's development, business situation in the accounting period, and events which occurred after the closing date, as well as disclosure of valuation methods and capital relationships with other firms.

The form, contents and organisation of the various items in the income statement and the balance sheet are shown by the typical set of German financial statements in Appendix 5. It is an English translation of part of the 1983 Annual Report of Daimler–Benz AG. The structure and contents of the income statement are governed by ss.157 and 158 of the *AktG*, and those of the balance sheet by ss.151 and 152. These formats were the basis of the formats in the EEC's fourth Directive, and are similar to the No. 2 formats in British company law. The valuation rules are in ss.153–6 of the *AktG*. S.160 of the *AktG* includes the requirements concerning the management report. By s.161 of the *AktG* the Department of Law and the Department of Economy issue *special formats* for financial institutions, building societies, transport businesses, and so on.

Balance Sheet

Striking differences from British practice are:

(a) more *detailed breakdown* of captions on the face of the balance sheet, and often inclusion of *negligible items* simply because of mandatory regulations;

(b) the recording of *capital subscriptions outstanding* which show the amount due for payment *on the assets side*;

(c) *shareholders' equity* does not appear as a sub-total; rather it is divided under various headings;

(d) the *balance on the income statement* is always shown as the *last item* on the balance sheet, if it is a loss it will appear on the assets side;

(e) *reserve accounting* is not permitted. All movements must be passed through the income statement, as must tax-allowed reserves;

(f) provision for future *pension* payments is optional, although most companies take this option;

(g) apart from a few exceptions, such as prepayments for a period close to the balance sheet date, there is not much *deferred accounting*. Many charges relating to the future must be treated as expenses in the year in which they are incurred;

(h) there is no clear identification of '*current items*'. Prepayments and current liabilities such as provisions, accruals, loans, deferred income are shown separately. In addition there is also a one-year cut-off for *trade debt receivable* and a four-year cut-off on *loans*.

There are three criteria according to which a balance sheet is structured: liquidity, legal nature and production process. Under the liquidity principle, assets are ranked in decreasing order according to their maturity dates. The underlying rationale is to indicate in the balance sheet the time horizon within which assets will earn cash returns for a business and liabilities will lead to cash expenditure. Structuring the balance sheet items according to their *legal nature* will result in grouping them into rights, real estate, etc. or according to their nature as equity or loans. Finally, ordering the various items with respect to the *production process* will lead to the classification of fixed and current items, raw materials and supplies, unfinished and finished products. The above criteria are included in the structure of the example of German financial statements (see Appendix 5); it is in agreement with the minimum requirements which are mandatory under s.151 (1) of the *AktG*. Regrouping of items is not allowed; further grouping of individual items into subsections is possible, however. The prescribed format must be followed literally, with no flexibility allowed even for non-material items.

Under s.152 (1) *AktG*, items can be taken as assets only if they are determined to be permanently in use by the business at the balance sheet date. There are also some special features as regards the various balance sheet items which may be interesting to the British or American reader:

(A)   Fixed Assets and Intangibles

Under the *AktG* the movement on fixed assets during the period has to be shown. Fixed assets are shown net as at the beginning of the period, followed by the changes during the period, and the balance at the balance sheet date. There *is no disclosure of the original cost amounts*. A special feature are additions (*Zuschreibungen*) to fixed assets. These normally result from a realignment of the commercial accounts to the values attributed to fixed assets for tax purposes. The adjustment is made to avoid the need for keeping two sets of fixed asset records. An example would be if depreciation of repairs and renewals as revenue expenditure were disallowed by the tax authorities; this would lead to an adjustment of assets.

Construction in progress and payments on account of fixed assets will often be found to be an important item. The reason for this is that normally projects are recorded 'in progress' and not transferred to a specific fixed asset account until they are completed. Intangibles, if purchased, will be recorded at cost along with amortisation charges over a period of five years (s.153 (3) *AktG*). Preliminary expenses may also be taken up and amortised in the same way (s.153 (4), 2, 3 *AktG*). The same is true of goodwill purchased (*derivativer Firmenwert*) on acquisition of a business but not of a goodwill created by a business over time (s.153 (5) *AktG*).

Equity accounting is not permitted at present under German law (see section 5.7). Investments are shown as 'Interests/Investments' (*Beteiligungen*) and 'Securities' (*Wertpapiere*). If an investment is long-term it will be taken as a fixed asset. The underlying purpose rather than the size of the participation is important. It is, however, presumed that an investment of 25% may qualify for definition as a long-term interest; but this presumption is rebuttable (s.152 (2) *AktG*). The 'interests' section in German accounts covers both the British associated company and the unconsolidated subsidiary. Loans with less than an original term of four years are taken as current assets. Movements of investments held as fixed assets are reported exactly as for other fixed assets.

(B) Accounts Receivable

This heading includes all accounts receivable originally due within a period of more than one year from companies other than related businesses. The non-current portion must be disclosed. Adequate provisions for bad debts must be made, but these will be shown on the liabilities side.

(C) Share Capital and Reserves

The capital of a business includes any financial resources which are invested in the business by the owners without any time limit, including retained earnings. Several capital definitions are suggested in German literature: 'nominal capital' which is equivalent to the share capital, 'calculated capital' which includes share capital, reserves (*Rücklagen*) and unappropriated surplus, and 'effective capital' which comprises the calculated capital plus undisclosed reserves.

A peculiarity of limited companies in Germany is that in constrast to other organisational forms they must have a so-called 'constant equity'. Under ss.6 *et seq.*, 152 (3), 156 (1) of the *AktG* for the public company and under s.5 (1) of the *GmbHG* for the private company, there is a requirement to record the full amount of the nominal capital with a counter-entry on the assets side showing the amount of capital subscriptions due for payment. The nominal capital account will not be changed unless the shareholders' meeting approves this by a three-quarters majority. Changes in a company's equity, caused for example by losses or non-distribution of profits, have to be disclosed as separate items.

Several kinds of reserves may be distinguished: *open reserves* such as legal reserve, statutory reserve with or without a certain purpose, reserve for equalisation of burdens levy, reserve for purchase of own shares, free reserves with or without a certain purpose; *special accounts with a reserve element* (i.e. tax-free reserves), and finally *secret reserves* which are not disclosed but included in various assets or liabilities. Under the *Aktiengesetz* there are three kinds of reserves: legal reserve, reserve for own shares, and other (free) reserves. Public companies (including KGaA and Co-operatives) are required to maintain a legal reserve. Transfers to this reserve of 5% of net profits per year are mandatory until the reserve equals 10% of the share capital. It may be used only to absorb losses incurred by the company (s.150 (3), (4) of the *AktG*). Only an amount of the legal reserve in excess of 10% of share capital may be used in order to increase capital (ss.207 – 20 *AktG*). Out of the remaining profit for the period, the board of management may, with the approval of the supervisory board, appropriate a share up to 50% of the period's net profit to the so-called 'free' reserves. These are available for distribution to the shareholders at the discretion of the board of management and are similar to retained earnings. Any share premium is also part of the legal reserve.

Since 1 July 1979, as a result of the inclusion of the second EEC Directive into German company legislation, there is a requirement to maintain a reserve for a company's own shares equivalent to the value of such shares in the assets section. This provision is for creditors' protection.

One might well criticise the Continental European accounting practice for creating secret reserves by undervaluing assets or overvaluing liabilities. There are three fundamental ways of creating them:

1. by neglecting mandatory requirements;
2. by taking advantage of certain options in valuation regulations and accounting requirements, e.g. simply by following a conservative valuation principle;
3. by legal requirements with respect to accounting and valuation, e.g. the historical cost rule or the exclusion of intangibles other than those purchased.

The first option is clearly in conflict with law and might lead to a special tax audit or nullity of the financial statements (ss.256, 158 *et seq.* *AktG*). The possibility of creating secret reserves by ultra-conservative valuation is compensated for to a certain extent by the requirement to disclose valuation and depreciation methods in the management report. Moreover, the so-called 'fixed value' principle in company law, which involves a constant valuation policy for certain items over time, is a useful barrier against creating secret reserves. On the other hand, conservatism is legally enforced in some cases. This is a particular handicap when trying to present a true and fair view of the company's financial position, for example in the cases of land and buildings and long-term investments.

Thus, a complication in arriving at shareholders' equity is the tax-allowed reserves which are partly deferred taxation and partly shareholders' funds. The difficulty is that the rate of tax which will have to be paid when the reserves are released is not known. This is because the reserves can in certain circumstances be deducted from non-depreciable assets such as land or investments, leading to an almost permanent postponement of taxation. Even where this is not the case, the amount of taxation payable depends on the company's future dividend policy. Clearly, therefore, an investment analyst's assumption that tax-allowed reserves should be split equally between shareholders' funds and taxation liabilities, for example, will rarely be correct.

(D) Provisions for Accruals

There is a clear distinction between value adjustments (*Wert-berichtigungen*) and provisions for accruals (*Rückstellungen*). Value adjustments can be made only against specific fixed assets and trade debtors. The major example is the *general* bad debt provision which is shown as a liability, whereas specific bad debt provisions and most stock provisions are deducted from the assets in question. Accruals in Germany have the same meaning as 'provisions' under the British Companies Act definition, that is, they do not relate specifically to assets included in the balance sheet such as pension, tax and guarantee provisions.

In s.152 (7) of the *AktG* there are requirements with respect to provisions for accruals; in connection with s.151 of the *AktG* provisions for pensions, for repairs and renewals expenditure, and for guarantees are to be shown separately. Other accruals may be grouped as one item. The last two items above are exceptions from the general rule that neither accruals for contingent creditors without legal basis nor accruals for (internal) business expenditures are allowed. Since equalisation accounting for such expenditures as repairs and renewals is not permitted, the law provides an exemption for expenditure anticipated within the subsequent accounting period. Also, as for accounting for purchased goodwill and for preliminary expenses, accounting for pensions is optional (Supreme Federal Court, 27 February 1961, *BGHZ*, Vol. 34, p. 324, and Supreme Tax Court, 24 May 1963, *BFH*, *BStBl* III, p. 489). It is normal practice for German companies which have established their own funds to provide for pension liabilities in the accounts.

Other provisions contain in particular the tax charge based on the annual profit. Agreed tax liabilities appear in sundry creditors.

(E) Creditors

The division of creditors is between those with an *original* period of over four years and the others. Of the former, a total of the amount due within four years is to be reported.

The different kinds of liabilities as taken up in the model set of financial statements (see Appendix 5) are stated in s.151 (1) of the *AktG*. It should be mentioned that the off-setting of liabilities against receivables is not permitted (s.152 (8) *AktG*). The only exception is the case of debtors and creditors relating to a customer/supplier when debtors and creditors are due at the same point in time.

'Balance Sheet Profit' (*Bilanzgewinn*) is the final figure on the income statement, after appropriation to reserves and before any dividends payable for the accounting period. A loss would be recorded at the foot of the assets side.

Income Statement

The income statement should provide information on the characteristics, the amount and the sources of the components of a business's results in terms of its (positive or negative) income and expense. The accruals concept is generally used. Another feature is the requirement included in the Companies Act of 1965 (s.157 *AktG*) to use the vertical report form (*Staffelform*). To the British reader the detailed disclosure on the face of a German profit and loss account may come as a surprise (see Appendix 5). There are two major differences which should be taken into account when analysing a German income statement. First, whereas the British income statement can be called *sales-oriented*, the German equivalent is *production-oriented*. Secondly, German practice is to show revenues and expenses by *primary categories* (e.g. salaries, wages, depreciation, interest) and not by categories such as cost of sales, selling and administrative expenses. Clearly, the German 'gross output' is not the same as 'gross profit', i.e. the difference between sales and cost of sales, and it may be regarded as a rather meaningless figure by the British reader. Nevertheless, the British Companies Act's Format 2 is based on this German format, and some British companies use it, partly in order to avoid disclosing cost of sales. Extraordinary or prior-year items which are recorded under other income must be disclosed on the face of the income statement. The so-called 'EEV' taxes (taxes on income and capital) are grouped together. Therefore, provision for corporate income tax for the period is sometimes obscured. It should be noted that *all* movements on reserves in the balance sheet must be passed through the income statement.

Valuation

Although it is not stated explicitly, valuation requirements under company law are based on a principle equivalent to the British 'going concern' concept. Items are to be valued individually (s.39 (1), (2) *HGB*) in order explicitly to exclude the possibility of compensating value adjustments and thereby omitting necessary depreciation of individual (wasting) assets which would be possible under an aggregate (collective) valuation approach. Company and tax law require certain items to be stated at a fixed value over time (*Fixwertprinzip*).

Also, under company law and tax law there is the fundamental rule that an overstatement of net assets and income should be prevented. This policy is very much in line with the British stewardship concept. It is followed by applying the conservatism principle (ss.153, 155 *AktG*) in that generally valuation is at the 'lowest value' (*Niederstwertprinzip*) of either cost or market or any other value which can be attributed to an item. In practice, the choice is between production cost and original purchase price, net realisable value, and replacement cost. Under company law the 'lowest value principle' is applied to both fixed and current assets, but for the former this is mandatory only if an item's value has fallen permanently below cost. If this is not the case there is an option for extra depreciation in order to carry an item at the lowest value attributable to it (*gemildertes Niederstwertprinzip*) (s.154 (2) *AktG*). For current assets, however, there is a more restrictive requirement to the effect that special depreciation must be provided whether or not the impairment in value of an item is expected to be permanent. A reasonable businessman's judgment with respect to future developments may be sufficient for such exceptional depreciation (*strenges Niederstwertprinzip*) (s.155 (2) *AktG*). The extra depreciation may remain even if the underlying cause has ceased. Moreover, there is the *Realisationsprinzip* (ss.154 *et seq. AktG*) under which profits and losses may only be taken into account when realised, although downward corrections are required or permitted under the two versions of the *Niederstwertprinzip*. Income from market transactions at market prices must be realised before profit can be taken.

Tax authorities provide precise tables for 'planned' depreciation (AfA tables) which because of the 'correspondence' rule are also used for commercial purposes. Both straight line and reducing balance methods are permitted. On average, straight line rates are 10% for machinery and furniture, 20% for equipment and 25% for cars. There are also cases of accelerated depreciation because of special tax allowances based on socio-economic policy and usually for a limited time span.

Finally, under tax law (s.6 (1), (4) *EStG*) it is necessary to record additions to or withdrawals from net assets at the so-called partial value (*Teilwert*), that is, the value a businessman would allocate to the item taking into account the total value of the business as a going concern. In other words, the partial value is seen in the context of the (future) income of the business. It is very much a fictitious construct which has turned out to be rather impractical when used for tax purposes.

More precisely, there are the following valuation requirements for particular balance sheet items:

(1) Fixed assets are to be stated at cost less appropriate depreciation (s.153 (1) *AktG*). The latter must be provided in accordance with a consistent plan designed to write off the asset over its useful life. Financial accounting depreciation rates tend to follow tax rules. These allow in general a faster write-off than is usual in Britain for financial accounting.

(2) Intangible assets may be recorded only if they were acquired for a consideration from third parties (s.153 (3) *AktG*). An exception applies to preliminary expenses of newly formed companies. However, it is only an option rather than a requirement to capitalise intangible assets even when purchased.

(3) Current assets are to be stated at the lowest of cost, net realisable value or replacement cost (s.155 (2) *AktG*). The determination of cost in respect of stocks is arrived at by the usual methods such as FIFO, LIFO, average cost, etc. Average cost is, however, the most usual method as it is allowed for tax purposes. Where stocks include work-in-progress and finished goods, the manufacturing costs must include variable manufacturing costs. Lower values than those calculated by the above methods may still be attributed to stocks where diminutions in value may reasonably be anticipated within the next two years after balance sheet date or where lower values are permitted under tax rules.

(4) All liabilities including unrealised losses must be fully provided for (s.156 *AktG*); unrealised profits may not be included. This principle, which requires liabilities to be stated at the amounts which will become due on maturity, does not apply to long-term liabilities such as pension provisions which may be stated at their discounted actuarial value (s.156 (3) *AktG*). Share capital has to be recorded at the nominal value (s.156 (1) *AktG*). Provisions and accruals are to be valued according to the 'reasonable businessman's judgment' (s.156 (4) *AktG*).

5.5 Disclosure

Disclosure requirements may be found in the *Aktiengesetz* and in the Publicity Law of 1969 (*Publizitätsgesetz, PublG*). Regardless of legal form, businesses fall within the scope of the *PublG* if:

(1) balance sheet total, calculated under the regulations of company law, is equal to or exceeding DM 125 million;
(2) annual sales revenue is equal to or exceeding DM 250 million;
(3) average workforce during the accounting period is equal to or exceeding 5,000 employees.

Provided they meet two of these three criteria for three consecutive accounting periods (s.1 *PublG*), businesses are required to publish their financial statements and reports. Banks (including certain mutual insurance companies) are required to publish their financial statements only if their total business volume amounts to DM 300 million and more. Insurance companies must publish their financial statements if annual premium revenues amount to DM 100 million and more. Groups of legally autonomous entities which, regardless of their legal structure, represent economic units and can act as such, are subject to similar requirements (s.11 *PublG*); total assets are the consolidated ones, sales are from extra-group activities, and the number of 5,000 employees applies to affiliates located in Germany.

At present, there is no obligation to disclose for those private companies which are outside the scope of this law. According to ss.8, 10 *GmbHG*, with the exception of banking companies, GmbHs are only required to file annual financial statements with the Registrar (*Registerpublizität*); there are presently no statutory audit requirements for them. Those GmbHs which are within the scope of the Publicity Law (about 200 GmbHs out of a total of about 260,000 at present) and other general partnerships (11) and limited partnerships (48) must publish their annual financial statements and group accounts and have them examined by independent auditors. It should be borne in mind that these companies are still in a different position to AGs because, although they have to follow the layout of public company accounts, they do not have to apply their valuation rules. Companies outside the scope of the Publicity Law do not even have to publish profit and loss statements if they include instead a specified appendix to the balance sheet. The information given in this appendix includes sales revenues, income transferred from affiliates, wages and salaries, social expenditures, pension and relief payments, disclosure of valuation and depreciation methods applied including major changes, and the number of employees. In order to reduce inequities for partnerships and sole proprietorships, and at the same time to protect the interests of individual owners, such organisations are treated similarly to the smaller GmbH.

Management Report (Geschäftsbericht)

In order that financial statements can be interpreted and supplemented by additional information, a management report has to be provided (s.160 *AktG*) unless there are specified reasons in the interest of the general public or of the company, especially where disclosure of information would be highly disadvantageous for the company or a related enterprise (s.160 (3), (4) *AktG*). The management report is subject to audit (s.162, *AktG*) and is normally divided into two sections (s.160 (1) *AktG*):

(1) Situation of the company (*Lagebericht*), which comments on business trends, the development of the order book, sales, expenses and capital expenditure. In addition to this there is usually detailed cost information, information on the state and development of the company's products, research and development, investments, and personnel and social matters.

(2) Notes on the financial position (*Erläuterungsbericht*), which comment on the annual financial statements including details on accounting policies, valuation and depreciation methods for all major balance sheet items, changes in accounting principles where material, disclosure of depreciation relating to the fixed asset additions, details of executive and advisory board directors' remuneration, and information about contingent liabilities not included in the notes to the financial statements (ss.160 (2), 2–5, 160 (3) *AktG*).

Whereas the British reader may rightly be critical of the disclosure level of the average German management report, he has to take into account that much detailed information is included in the balance sheet or the income statement. There are, however, several items found in British balance sheets which he would search for in vain, such as gross fixed assets, market value and directors' valuation of investments, and future capital expenditure contracted for or authorised. Also, audit fees, plant hire charges and directors' and executives' emoluments do not have to be disclosed in the income statement. At least until the enactment of the EEC fourth Directive, the report will not necessarily contain any information with regard to segment reporting, nor are there some other items which British directors' reports normally include such as an opinion about the market value of properties held by the company, or charitable and political donations.

Social Reporting

There is increasing inclusion of social reporting, either in the management report or separately. In 1972, STEAG company for the first time issued a social report which was integrated into the annual financial statements. Since then a number of companies have been disclosing separate social reports.

An industrially sponsored committee (*Arbeitskreis Sozialbilanzpraxis* 1977) made some progress in the endeavour to institutionalise corporate social reporting by issuing guidelines in 1977. According to them a *report on social matters* should disclose information about goals, activities initiated to achieve them, and the degree of social efficiency. Secondly, there sould be a *value added statement* giving information on a company's contribution to national income and the allocation of the company's net value added into societal sectors. Finally, a *social statement* is recommended which would disclose socially oriented income and expenditures. Trade unions have criticised current corporate social reporting as largely corporate public relations.

There is still a great variety of concepts, contents and quantity of information in German social reports. Among the areas of social concern, employee relations are considered as being of primary relevance followed by the impact of company activities on the environment and on society and finally the relations of the company with its owners. It is interesting that company relations with customers and suppliers do not appear to be regarded as a worthwhile topic.

Inflation Accounting

Discussing the German approach to inflation accounting within the section on disclosure points to the fact that inflation adjustments are not used in the main financial statements. There is an inflation accounting recommendation by the German Institute but it is not mandatory and calls only for a supplementary disclosure to the income statement (IdW, HFA 1975). On the other hand the German government has made it quite clear that inflation adjustment will not be permitted in Germany because of its allegedly detrimental effects as a stimulant to inflation.

The HFA recommends the provision of 'capital maintenance statements'. These represent supplementary information which public companies and other companies covered by the Publicity Act should include in the management report and which other companies should add to their set of annual statements. The calculation should be taken into account when determining a company's profit distribution and reserve policy. In the case of companies which are subject to compulsory audit, the supplementary statements are to be included in the scope of the audit.

Capital maintenance statements, according to the recommendation, should relate only to an adjustment of the income statement. It is, however, appreciated that this means that the financial position of a company in a situation of changing prices is not correctly reported. The HFA has only gone so far as to recommend that 'the effects of increased replacement values on the financial position in the internal reports must be watched'. However, one must bear in mind the rigid legal situation which establishes historical cost and disallows revaluations. Its application by companies to date has been negligible. Only some large groups such as Siemens and Mannesmann have disclosed inflationary profit corrections in their directors' reports. While, for example, Siemens were able to state in 1978 – 81 and 1983 that reported profits did not include any inflationary profits because of the fullest use of tax-allowed accelerated depreciation, beginning with their 1976 report they published that 'there was no longer an adequate compensation for the price increase of our equity-financed assets'. Accordingly, DM 73 Million (DM 67 Million in 1982) out of an annual income of DM 606 Million (DM 738 Million in 1982) would have been required to offset inflationary profits in order to maintain the company's capital. These inflationary profits are calculated taking into account the proportion of fixed assets and stocks financed by equity funds.

There is, however, disagreement in German practice as to how to account for the gain or loss on monetary items. The most convincing solution advanced so far is that the gain or loss on net monetary liabilities or assets, calculated in the same way as under the current purchasing power (CPP) method, should be deducted from or added to 'gross' inflationary profits.

The Accounting Committee of the German Association of University Teachers in Business Administration issued a proposal regarding the reform of company accounting, which is mainly concerned with the integration of the fourth Directive into German company law. In this they advocate comment on the impact of inflation on the assets, financial position and results of a company in the management report. They propose a statement of the profit corrections necessary to maintain a company's equity capital.

Since the great inflation after the First World War a number of suggestions to account for the effects of inflation have been advocated by accounting theorists. These go back to the early CPP–CCA controversy of German accounting academics in the 1920s: Mahlberg (1923) and Schmalenbach (1926) on one side, and Schmidt (1921) on the other. Although the case for adjusting annual accounts by reference to current purchasing power employing general price indices was convincingly argued by the former, the problems troubling the business world at that time were related to the short and medium term control over liquidity and the ability to replace assets sold or scrapped at greatly increased prices. Accordingly, Schmidt's current cost accounting (CCA) proposal could be seen to be more relevant than a CPP type of solution, and it was again taken up in more recent writings particularly by Sommerfeld (1955), Hasenack (1966), Hax (1957), Feuerbaum (1966), and Sieben (1974). Yet the early controversy gave rise to an extreme heterogeneity of approach. Consequently it was made doubtful whether German accountants would ever arrive at a unified and practical solution to the inflation accounting problem.

Funds Flow Reporting

German financial statements are of limited use for financial analysis because they provide an imperfect insight into the net assets position and results of a company. Obviously, this deficiency has been felt, because an increasing number of major corporations voluntarily disclose information about their sources and applications of funds as supplementary information in the management report.

Coenenberg and Schmidt (1978) found that, although about 50% of a sample of about 100 German public companies with share capital in excess of DM 10 million disclosed flow of funds figures, the kind of information given was not very useful. Because of the variety of concepts used and changes in approaches, comparison is difficult to make; moreover, the majority do not provide funds statements but only comparative figures which show changes of financial resources and investments. In order to improve uniformity and usefulness of funds reporting, the technical committee of the German Institute released a proposal (IdW, HFA 1978) which includes recommendations with respect to design and disclosure of funds statements.

Two basic approaches can be distinguished:

(a) a flow of funds statement (*eigentliche Kapitalflussrechnung*), in which causes of changes in the financial position are disclosed with respect to sources and applications of funds; and

(b) a change of funds statement (*Fondsveränderungsrechnung*), in which changes of financial resources and their underlying elements in the accounting period are shown.

Transactions should be shown gross with respect to sources and applications. The proposed funds to be selected are net liquid funds, net cash (assets) and net working capital. The German Institute's proposal is very similar to IAS 7 released by the IASC. However, it may be criticised on several grounds: particularly the supplementary nature and the voluntary basis. The same is true of the options allowed for calculating the cash flow, selecting the appropriate funds, and structuring the funds statements (Coenenberg and Schmidt 1978). Moreover, it has also been doubted whether the efforts involved to provide the kind of information recommended by the Institute would be justified in terms of information value. A simple cash flow statement would possibly be more useful (Weber 1979).

In summary, the level of disclosure does not in practice go much beyond the disclosure by notes in Anglo-Saxon accounts. Disclosure of accounting policies, and particularly of changes in their application, has been required since 1967 when the *Aktiengesetz* became effective. The disclosure requirements also have a controlling effect on the managers of large public companies in that they will often have a high regard for consistency in presentation and valuation in order to avoid detailed disclosure of changes in the management report. A decrease in profit smoothing and an improvement in disclosure have been found in empirical research (Coenenberg *et al.* 1978).

5.6   Consolidation

As consolidation is dealt with in detail in Chapter 10 of this book, only the major features of the German approach will be discussed. The legal requirements are laid down in ss.329 – 35 of the *AktG*. Under these provisions public companies are required to produce group accounts by consolidating *domestic* subsidiaries in which the parent has a major interest of more than 50% (*Konsolidierungskreis* s.329 (2), 1 *AktG*), unless these would distort the information value of the group's financial statements (*Konsolidierungsverbot* s.329 (2), 3 *AktG*). There is an option to exclude companies of minor importance from the group accounts (*Konsolidierungswahlrecht* s.329 (2), 2 *AktG*). Consolidated financial statements together with a consolidated report of the board of management must be produced within five months after the year end and must be reported on by German auditors. The inclusion of overseas subsidiaries is optional. This applies to some GmbHs and to AGs, unless they are controlled in turn by a foreign company which publishes its own group accounts in the German Federal Gazette.

The major difference from British practice is the method of consolidation: in Germany the cost or acquisition method is used. This is different from methods used in the UK. *Goodwill* arising on consolidation in Britain is fixed as the difference between the purchase cost and the capital and reserves of the acquired company at the date of *acquisition*. In Germany it may fluctuate from year to year depending on movements in the subsidiaries' reserves. Also, the use of the equity method for associated companies is not allowed.

Clearly, current basic consolidation requirements in Germany are too weak to provide a fair presentation of the group's position and results. One can expect drastic changes when the seventh Directive on group accounting becomes national law. It should be noted that the Directive is very similar to British group accounting.

5.7   The Impact of EEC Directives

Directives on corporate financial reporting and disclosure form part of the programme for the coordination of the company laws of member States of the European Community. The requirements of the first Directive of 1968 on disclosure were included in the German Publicity Law. The second Directive has had little effect in Germany.

The fourth Directive of 1978 concerns the form and content of annual financial statements (see Chapter 14). The changes relevant to German financial reporting were included in proposals of a Committee of the Accounting Commission within the German Association of University Teachers of Business Administration (Accountancy Commission 1979,

1983). This statement reflects the overall impact of the fourth Directive on German accounting and also suggests further developments which seem to be necessary from an academic standpoint. By mid-1985, the German government had not implemented the fourth Directive, and according to official sources the enactment cannot be expected soon. This is mainly because of the inclusion of changes which are required by the seventh and eighth Directives, and which the German government intends to integrate in a comprehensive transformation law (*Bilanzrichtliniegesetz*). The recommendations of the Association of University Teachers with respect to changes cover the following major points, among others:

(i) The overall objective of financial reporting and disclosure should be to inform external users. Therefore, accounting information should be appropriate in terms of scope, reliable in terms of content and allow for intercompany comparison. A consolidating act is necessary to integrate the diverse accounting regulations included in several laws. Ideally, this should lean on the present company law and do away with different legal requirements for different organisational forms of business. In order to take into account special needs, variations may be allowed as regards size or industry. As an interim step, the present reporting and valuation requirements should become mandatory for unincorporated businesses within the scope of the Publicity Law.

(ii) Voluntary supplements to annual financial statements should be called for.

(iii) The principle that financial statements should accord with tax statements should be changed in order to be able to present a true and fair view of the financial position and results of a company. Tax statements should, however, continue to be drawn up according to commercial accounts.

(iv) The equity method of consolidation should be introduced.

(v) Downward correction of fixed assets should be permitted only if the impairment of the value of an asset is expected to be permanent, in which case correction should be mandatory.

(vi) Large companies should disclose information on the past development of the company by presenting at least a three years' summary of selected figures which must be comparable.

(vii) The impact of price changes on a company's net assets, financial position and results, i.e. on maintenance of capital, should be explained by notes in the management report.

(viii) For large companies it should be mandatory to disclose segment information as regards sales and investments in tangible assets in the notes, broken down by divisions and regions.

Although some of these recommendations were taken up while drafting the law, the Association was not influential in the design of the major requirements. The draft of the *Bilanzrichtliniegesetz* is based on the concept that there will be no general accounting law but rather a major integration of the new requirements into the Commercial Code. The changes will be particularly important for the small GmbH which represents the German equivalent of the private limited company. Changes in other related laws, such as the Laws on Public and Private Companies, and on Cooperative Associations, will be kept to a minimum.

The implementation of the fourth Directive will have no direct tax effects. In particular, the basic principle that financial and tax accounts should agree will be maintained. National options will principally be exercised in such a way that companies should benefit from the respective rules. Although the present draft will still be subject to change, it can be expected that at least the requirements set out below will be implemented.

From the fourth Directive (see von Wysocki 1984):

(1) The annual accounts shall give a true and fair view of the company's assets, liabilities, financial position and profit or loss (Busse von Colbe 1984).
(2) The notes are an integral part of the annual accounts including far-reaching disclosure requirements.
(3) Provisions for pensions have to be shown either in the balance sheet or in the notes.
(4) Intangible assets must be taken up if they were acquired for valuable consideration.
(5) General valuation principles will be codified, and in particular:
    (a) valuation is to be based on the principle of purchase price or production cost;
    (b) valuation at lower values may not be continued if the reasons for which the value adjustments were made have ceased to apply (only for public and private companies).
(6) The requirement that more than 20,000 private limited companies will, for the first time, be obliged to publish audited accounts can be regarded as a major challenge for Germany.

From the seventh Directive:

(1) New conditions for the preparation of consolidated accounts for undertakings which have:
    (a) the majority of the voting rights or
    (b) the right to appoint or remove a majority of the members of

the administrative, management or supervisory body or
  (c) the right to exercise a dominant influence over another undertaking.
(2) Consolidated accounts include foreign as well as domestic subsidiaries.
(3) Equity accounting for holdings in associated companies.

5.8 Summary

There are many differences in practice between German and Anglo-Saxon accounting. To a large extent, these may be traced from differences in the objectives and environments of accounting. Some aspects of the economic environment in Germany are similar to the UK or USA, although capital markets are certainly more developed in the latter countries. More obvious variation may be seen in the relative importance of company law and professional rule making. For example, in Germany, law is important and there is a requirement that financial statements should follow tax requirements. On the other hand, the profession is smaller and less influential than in Anglo-Saxon countries.

Financial reporting and disclosure requirements vary by type and size of business. A public company (AG) has a minimum capital requirement and, usually, bearer shares. It has a supervisory board as well as a management board. The private company (GmbH) is subject to different, less restrictive laws.

German accounting runs on 'principles of orderly bookkeeping' which derive from three sources: company, commercial and tax laws. Also, historical cost and conservatism are clearly strong conventions. Financial statements are more uniform than in the UK or the USA and there is a lack of application of materiality. Some items will appear as assets in German balance sheets which would be negative liabilities or capital in an Anglo-Saxon balance sheet, e.g. unpaid capital or a balancing loss on revenue account. Also, current liabilities are shown differently. Further, although disclosure is very detailed, there is no requirement to show the original cost of assets.

An important area of difference is the large number of 'reserves' in German accounting; some of these are treated as provisions. It is also normal to find some 'secret reserves' due to undervaluation of assets and the use of a strict historical cost system. Depreciation may be more lavish than in Anglo-Saxon countries in order to gain tax reductions.

Small companies (regardless of legal form) are substantially exempted from disclosure, and social reporting is becoming increasingly common. However, despite academic suggestions, there are very few examples in practice of notes about inflation accounting. Funds flow reporting is more common, but by no means universal.

Important differences in practice are found in the area of consolidation. German companies are not yet allowed to use the equity method, and tend not to consolidate foreign subsidiaries. Further, the definition of a group is based on control, not ownership, and the method of consolidation involves yearly recalculation of goodwill.

The introduction of the requirements of the EEC's fourth and seventh Directives into German law should give rise to a number of important changes. These may be supplemented by some of the recommendations from German accountancy professors. The results should narrow the areas of difference between German and Anglo-Saxon accounting.

References

Busse von Colbe, W. (1984) 'A true and fair view: A German perspective', in S.J. Gray and A. G. Coenenberg (eds) (1984), *EEC Accounting Harmonisation: Implementation and Impact of the Fourth Directive*, North-Holland, Amsterdam.

Coenenberg, A. G., Berndsen, H. P., Möller, P., Schmidt, F. and Schönbrodt, N. (1978) 'Empirische Bilanzforschung in Deutschland', *Die Betriebswirtschaft*, vol. 38, no. 4, pp. 495–507.

Coenenberg, A. G. and Schmidt, F. (1978) 'Die Kapitalflussrechnung als Ergänzungsrechnung des veröffentlichten Jahresabschlusses', *Zeitschrift für Betriebswirtschaft*, vol. 38, no. 6, pp. 507–516.

Feuerbaum, E. (1966) *Die polare Bilanz*, Duncker & Humblot, Berlin.

Gray, S. J. and Coenenberg, A. G. (eds) (1984) *EEC Accounting Harmonisation: Implementation and Impact of the Fourth Directive*, North-Holland, Amsterdam.

Hasenack, E. (1966) 'Der bilanztheoretische Streit Riegers gegen Schmalenbach im Licht von zwei Briefwechseln', *Betriebswirtschaftliche Forschung und Praxis*, vol. 18, no. 9, pp. 484–498.

Hax, K. (1957) *Die Substanzerhaltung der Betriebe*, Westdeutscher Verlag, Köln-Opladen.

Mahlberg, W. (1923) *Bilanztechnik und Bewertung bei schwankenden Währungen*, 3rd edn, Gloeckner, Leipzig.

Mueller, R. and Galbraith, E. G. (1976) *The German Stock Corporation Law*, 2nd edn, Knapp, Frankfurt.

Pennington, R. R. (1970) *Companies in the Common Market*, 2nd edn, Oyez, London.

Schmalenbach, E. (1926) *Dynamische Bilanz*, 4th edn, Gloeckner, Leipzig, pp. 217–273.

Schmidt, F. (1921) *Die organische Bilanz im Rahmen der Wirtschaft*, Gloeckner, Leipzig. (See also *Die organische Tageswertbilanz*, reprint of 3rd edn (1951) Gabler, Wiesbaden.)

Sieben, G. (1974) 'Kritische Würdigung der externen Rechnungslegung unter besonderer Berücksichtigung von Scheingewinnen', *Zeitschrift für betriebswirtschaftliche Forschung*, vol. 26, pp. 153–168.

Sommerfeld, H. (1955) *Eudynamische Bilanz*, in K. Bott (ed.), *Lexikon des kaufmännischen Rechnungswesens*, 2nd edn, Muth, Stuttgart, col. 980 *et seq.*

Weber, H. K. (1979) 'Die Kapitalflussrechnung als Ergänzung des Jahresabschlusses? Kritik der Stellungnahme 1/1978 des Hauptfachausschusses (HFA) des Instituts der Wirtschaftsprüfer', *Der Betrieb*, vol. 32, no. 13, pp. 609–614.

Wysocki, K. von (1984) 'The fourth Directive and Germany', in S.J. Gray and A.G. Coenenberg (eds) (1984), *EEC Accounting Harmonisation. Implementation and Impact of the Fourth Directive*, North-Holland, Amsterdam.

Accountancy Commission (1979) (in the Association of Professors in Business Administration) 'Proposals for the reform of commercial accounting law in Germany', *Journal of Business Finance & Accounting*, vol. 6, no. 3, pp. 331–337.

Accountancy Commission (*Kommission Rechnungswesen im Verband der Hochschullehrer für Betriebswirtschaft e. V.*) (1983) 'Stellungnahme zum Regierungsentwurf eines Bilanzrichtlinie-Gesetz', *Die Betriebswirtschaft*, vol. 43, no. 1, pp. 5–45.

Arbeitskreis Sozialbilanz-Praxis (1977) *Sozialbilanz heute, Empfehlungen des Arbeitskreises Sozialbilanz-Praxis zur aktuellen Gestaltung gesellschaftsbezogener Unternehmensrechnung.*

Institut der Wirtschaftsprüfer, HFA (1975) 'Zur Berücksichtigung der Substanzerhaltung bei der Ermittlung des Jahresergebnisses, Stellungnahme HFA 2/1975', *IdW Fachnachrichten*, no. 12, pp. 193–194.

Institut der Wirtschaftsprüfer (1981) *Wirtschaftsprüfer-Handbuch*, Düsseldorf.

Institut der Wirtschaftsprüfer, HFA (1978) 'Die Kapitalflussrechnung als Ergänzung des Jahresabschlusses, Stellungnahme HFA 1/1978', *IdW Fachnachrichten*, no. 4, pp. 99–101.

Further Reading

Beeny, J. H. (1975) *European Financial Reporting: West Germany*, ICAEW, London.

Busse von Colbe, W. and Ordelheide, D. (1984) *Konzernabschlüsse*, 5th edn, Gabler, Wiesbaden.

Coenenberg, A. G. (1984) *Jahresabschluss und Jahresabschlussanalyse*, 7th edn, Moderne Industrie, München.

Leffson, U. (1982) *Die Grundsätze ordnungsmässiger Buchführung*, 6th edn, Institut der Wirtschaftsprüfer, Düsseldorf.

McKinnon, S. M. (1983) *Consolidated Accounts*, Chapter 7, Arthur Young, London.

Mueller, R. and Galbraith, E. G. (1976) *The German Stock Corporation Law*, 2nd edn, Knapp, Frankfurt.

Appendix 5
Excerpts from the 1983 Annual Report and Accounts of Daimler-Benz AG.

ASSETS

	Balance Dec. 31, 1983 DM
I. Fixed and financial assets	
Property, plant and equipment	
Land and equivalent titles	
with office, factory and other buildings	2,202,599,408
with residential buildings	10,061,991
without buildings	1,630,433
Buildings on land owned by others	91,858,274
Machinery and plant	1,363,112,223
Factory and office equipment	501,190,814
Construction in progress and advance payments relating to buildings and plants	700,847,603
	4,871,300,746
Financial assets	
Investments in subsidiary and affiliated companies	978,031,949
Investments in long-term securities	106,630,197
Loans made for a term of at least four years	1,025,340
of which secured by mortgage DM 814,323 (last year DM 935,497)	
	1,085,687,486
	5,956,988,232

II. **Current assets**

Inventories

Raw materials and supplies	707,763,691
Work in process	695,844,425
Finished goods and goods purchased for resale	1,065,591,755
Spare parts	428,685,315
	2,897,885,186

Other current assets

Advance payments to suppliers other than for fixed assets		36,430,177
Receivables for goods sold and services rendered		1,628,487,350
Including receivables maturing in more than one year	DM 22,897,179 (last year DM 18,305,464)	
Notes receivable		449,518,995
of which: discountable at German Federal Reserve Bank	DM 24,933,744 (last year DM 36,005,291)	
notes receivable maturing in more than one year	DM 12,838,314 (last year DM 26,274,763)	
from affiliated companies	DM 309,954,515 (last year DM 156,737,946)	
Checks		1,454,797
Cash on hand, in German Federal Reserve Bank and in post office checking accounts		3,584,782
Cash in banks		1,381,940,972
Temporary investments in securities		1,676,756,455
Treasury stock	Par value DM 2,897,750 (last year DM 4,097,100)	17,943,605
Receivables from affiliated companies		1,347,213,686
Receivables from members of the Board of Management etc. (Section 89 of the Company Act)		11,859,958
Other current assets		2,672,224,540
		9,227,415,317

III. **Prepaid and deferred charges** | 7,734,394

Total assets | 18,090,023,129

STOCKHOLDERS' EQUITY AND LIABILITIES

		DM	Balance Dec. 31, 1983 DM
I.	**Capital stock**		
	Common stock	33,935,460 votes	1,696,773,000
	Preferred stock	38,430 votes	1,921,500
	in special cases of Section 17 of the bylaws	1,152,900 votes	
			1,698,694,500
II.	**Retained earnings, as allocated**		
	Allocated under statute		
	·Balance at beginning of period	156,338,214	
	Capital contributed for shares in excess of par value	3,734,921	
	Transfer from net income	9,796,315	
	Allocated for treasury stock		169,869,450
	Balance at beginning of period	12,782,952	
	Transfer from net income	5,160,653	
	Unallocated		17,943,605
	Balance at beginning of period	2,908,815,745	
	Transfer from net income	340,295,880	
			3,249,111,625
III.	**Special equity reserves**		**3,436,924,680**
	Reserves in accordance with Section 3 of the Foreign Investment Law, Section 1 of the Tax Law with respect to Developing Countries, Section 74 of the Income Tax Regulation, Section 6b of the Income Tax Act, Subsection 35 of the Income Tax Guidelines		295,626,050
IV.	**Lump-sum allowance for doubtful accounts**		**157,100,000**
V.	**Provisions**		
	Old-age pensions		4,365,873,839
	Deferred maintenance		124,500,000
	Other		3,891,122,000
			8,381,495,839

VI.	**Liabilities with a term of at least four years**			
	Liabilities to banks	DM 131,879,368 (last year DM 123,700,533)		131,879,368
	of which secured by mortgage	DM 1,021,966 (last year DM 1,445,379)		
	Other liabilities			8,281,559
	of which secured by mortgage	DM 73,481,981 (last year DM 72,663,995)		
	Due within four year			
				140,160,927
VII.	**Liabilities to the Daimler-Benz Unterstützungskasse GmbH, Stuttgart**			52,268,621
VIII.	**Other liabilities**			
	Accounts payable – trade			1,819,640,072
	Notes payable			4,322,000
	Advance payments received			137,135,136
	Accounts payable to affiliated companies			57,057,619
	Other liabilities			1,551,265,463
				3,569,420,290
IX.	**Deferred credits**			3,079,370
X.	**Unappropriated surplus**			355,252,852

	1983	1982
	DM	DM
Contingent liabilities from:		
Trade acceptances	13,855,015	27,629,664
of which to affiliated companies	(8,119)	(2,668,815)
Guaranty of payment	135,901,486	241,049,333
Payment guarantees for bonds of		
Daimler-Benz Finanz-Holding S.A., Luxemburg		
DM-bond	30,000,000	45,000,000
lfr-bond – lfr 250,000,000 –	12,272,500	12,710,000

Total stockholders' equity and liabilities   18,090,023,129

STATEMENT OF INCOME

	1983	
	DM	DM
Sales		31,991,793,909
Decrease of work in process and finished goods inventories including spare parts	32,178,639,442	
Other capitalized in-house output	186,845,533	147,529,697
Total revenue		32,139,323,606
Cost of raw materials and supplies and of goods purchased for resale		15,999,663,759
Excess of total revenue over cost of raw materials etc.		16,139,659,847
Income transferred from affiliated companies under profit and loss pooling agreements	9,348,142	
Income from investments in affiliated companies	51,589,603	
Income from other financial investments	10,070,350	
Other interest and similar income	586,363,560	
Gain from disposal of fixed assets	31,239,719	
Gain from reduction of lump-sum allowance for doubtful accounts	7,900,000	
Gain from dissolution of provisions	187,394,057	
Gain from dissolution of special equity reserves	30,155,224	
Other income	191,211,090	
		1,105,271,745
		17,244,931,592
of which extraordinary	DM 48,749,504 (last year DM 35,102,452)	

Wages and salaries		7,334,250,133
Social levies		1,134,014,168
Expenditures for old-age pension and support payments to dependants		770,190,714
Depreciation of fixed assets		2,093,287,678
Write-down of financial assets		108,955,456
Losses from reduction in value of or from sale of current assets, excluding inventories		68,800,788
Losses from disposal of fixed assets		6,920,383
Interest and similar charges		51,270,472
Taxes		
a) on income, trade and property	DM 2,538,868,845	
of which payments for prior years which were covered by other provisions	DM 18,296,790	
	DM 2,520,572,055	
of which charged to parent companies	DM 19,495,043	
b) other		2,501,077,012
Losses transferred from affiliated companies under profit and loss pooling agreements		8,347,036
Additions to special equity reserves		569,972
Other expenses		38,415,496
		16,534,425,892
Net Income		2,418,326,584
Withdrawal from retained earnings allocated for treasury stock		710,505,700
		—
		710,505,700
Transfer from net income to:		
Retained earnings allocated under statute	9,796,315	
Retained earnings allocated for treasury stock	5,160,653	
Unallocated retained earnings	340,295,880	355,252,848
Unappropriated surplus		355,252,852

6

Financial Reporting in
the Netherlands

R. H. PARKER

6.1 Influences on Accounting

As in the United Kingdom, the main direct influences on Dutch financial reporting are company law and the accountancy profession.
Taxation is relatively unimportant as an influence, there is no national
accounting plan and there is no equivalent of the American SEC or the
French COB. The similarities with the UK must not be pressed too
hard: there are important differences, as the rest of this chapter will
make clear. On the other hand, the EEC's Directives on company law
are bringing financial reporting practices closer together in all member
states. This harmonisation hardly extends to inflation accounting,
however, and Dutch theory and practice in this area are likely to remain
rather distinct, although as a result of the fourth Directive the minority
of Dutch companies which previously reported only current cost data
must now report some historical cost information as well.

Company Law

The influence of company law has steadily increased since the early
1970s. Before the Act of 10 September 1970 on the Annual Accounts of

Enterprises there was practically no legislation at all on the form and contents of published financial statements. The Act was incorporated in the Civil Code[1] in 1975 and substantially amended by the Act of 7 December 1983 which introduced into Dutch law the provisions of the EEC fourth Directive. The relevant legislation is now contained in Title 8, Book 2 of the Dutch Civil Code and two decrees on asset valuation and annual accounts formats (for an English translation see Moret and Limperg 1984).

As a result of other company legislation, passed in anticipation of the EEC second Directive, the most important forms of business organisation in the Netherlands since 1971 from the point of view of financial reporting have been the *Naamloze Vennootschap* (NV) or 'public' company, which has existed for many years, and the relatively new *Besloten Vennootschap met Beperkte Aansprakelijheid* (BV) or 'private' company. In 1984 there were less than 4,000 NVs and approximately 150,000 BVs. Other forms of business organisation include sole proprietorships, civil partnerships, general partnerships, limited partnerships, cooperatives and mutual guarantee associations. These forms are not dealt with in this chapter but it should be noted that much of the legislation relating to company financial statements applies to cooperatives and mutual guarantee associations as well as to NVs and BVs. The legislation refers to these four types of organisation as 'corporate bodies'.

Large companies, whether NVs or BVs, must normally have not only a board of managerial directors (*Raad van Bestuur*) but also a supervisory board (*Raad van Commissarissen*) of at least three persons (no maximum number is set). For other companies, a supervisory board is optional. Three interested parties, the general meeting of shareholders, the works council (*Ondernemingsraad*) and the board of managerial directors may recommend appointees to the supervisory board; the first two must be informed who is chosen, and have rights of objection and appeal. It is the supervisory board which appoints the board of management, adopts the accounts and submits them to the shareholders' meeting, the works council and the local trade registry. This Dutch system of two-tier boards can be compared to the systems operating in Germany and France (see Chapters 5 and 4).

A large company in this context is one which satisfies all the following criteria:

(i) it has issued share capital and reserves totalling at least fl 20 million;

(ii) it, or any other company in which it holds at least half of the issued share capital directly or indirectly for its own benefit, has, pursuant to a legal obligation, formed a works council; and

---

1. Unlike France, the Netherlands does not have a separate Commercial Code.

(iii) it, or any such other company together employ, as a rule, at least 100 persons in the Netherlands.

Both NVs and BVs must deposit for public inspection, within eight days of their being approved by the annual general meeting, a copy of their annual accounts, directors' report and supplementary information at the trade registry at which they are registered. Before 1984, BVs were, with some exceptions, exempt from these requirements. The content of the documents filed may, as explained in section 6.5, differ according to whether the company is large, medium or small as measured by balance sheet total, turnover and number of employees.

As in Germany and France, most listed shares in the Netherlands are in bearer rather than registered form. The shares of BVs cannot be listed and cannot be in bearer form. As well as ordinary shares, Dutch companies may have fixed dividend preference shares and priority shares (*Prioriteitsaandelen*). These last are peculiar to Dutch law and have the effect of strengthening the power of directors against takeover bids. For example, the priority shares of Akzo NV, one of the largest Dutch companies, are held by the Akzo Foundation which is controlled by members of the supervisory board and the board of managerial directors.

The general purpose of a set of accounts is defined in the Code as the provision, in accordance with generally acceptable accounting principles, of such information that a responsible opinion can be formed regarding the financial position and profit or loss; and, to the extent to which annual accounts permit, regarding solvency and liquidity (article 362 (1)). It should be noted that reference is made not to generally *accepted* accounting principles but to generally *acceptable* accounting principles. The criterion (still used in income tax law) of 'sound business practice' (*goed koopmansgebruik*) was deliberately avoided in 1971 as having acquired too wide a meaning. The balance sheet and the profit and loss account, together with the notes thereto, must reflect 'fairly, consistently and clearly' the financial position and its breakdown into assets and liabilities as at the end of the financial year, and the amount of the profit or loss for the financial year and its derivation from the items of income and expense (article 362(2)(3)).

The above provisions require what in British company legislation is referred to as a true and fair view. Later articles of the Code and the Decrees contain regulations as to disclosure, valuation and format. Where these are insufficient to provide the information required in article 362(1), a company must disclose additional information in its annual accounts and, if necessary, depart from the regulations. The reasons for such a departure must be stated in the notes, where necessary with an indication of its impact on the financial position and profit or loss (article 362(4)).

Accounting Standards and the Accountancy Profession

Guidance as to what are generally acceptable accounting principles is provided by the guidelines (*richtlijnen*; formerly *beschouwingen*, considerations) published by the Council for Annual Reporting (*Raad voor de Jaarverslaggeving*). As its former name (*Tripartiete Overleg*, Tripartite Accounting Standards Committee) indicates, the Council is composed of representatives of employers (Council of the Dutch Employers Federations), employees (Dutch Trade Union Federation and Protestant National Trade Union Federation) and accountants (Dutch Institute of Registered Accountants, *Nederlands Instituut van Registeraccountants* or NIVRA). The Council was formed at the request of the Dutch government after the enactment of the 1970 Act on Annual Accounts. The authority of the Council has been strengthened by placing it under the Social and Economic Council (*Sociaal-Economische Raad*), the main governmental advisory body in the Netherlands on social and economic matters, but it is still less than that of the FASB in the USA or the ASC in the UK. The Council has, however, ceased to be a totally private organisation and is now aiming to formulate 'positive pronouncements' (*stellige uitspraken*). Companies are not obliged to follow the guidelines (although most of them do so), nor need they or their auditors state that they have been followed; audit reports are not qualified for this reason.

In many respects the guidelines are akin to the Recommendations issued by the Institute of Chartered Accountants in England and Wales from 1942 to 1969, i.e. they are the authoritative opinions of an influential private group. The group is not, as it was in England and Wales, confined to accountants. The inclusion of employees in its membership is indicative (as are the works councils) of the importance of organised labour in Dutch economic life. It is the Dutch system of informing and consulting employees which has served as a model to the EEC for the Vredeling proposals (see Chapter 14). It is noteworthy, however, that by no means all users are represented on the Council; for example, there are no direct representatives of shareholders or of the Amsterdam Stock Exchange, although efforts are being made to include them.

As in the USA and the UK, pronouncements are issued in exposure draft form first. Since NIVRA mostly prepares the proposals for the new pronouncements, it is quite influential within the Council. The Dutch accountancy profession is thus an important influence on financial statements.

NIVRA is the result of the merger in 1967 of the Nederlands Instituut van Accountants (NIVA), formed in 1927, and the more academically oriented *Vereniging van Academisch Gevormde Accountants* (VAGA), set up by a breakaway group in 1927. The standards of entrance to and training for the profession are very high and NIVRA, although relatively small (about 5,000 members, of whom approximately half are in public practice), has an international reputation. NIVRA enforces a rigorous code of ethics. High standards are also ensured by the provisions of the Registered Accountants Act of 1962.

The Enterprise Chamber

The Code provides that interested parties may complain to the Enterprise Chamber (*Ondernemingskamer*) of the Court of Justice in Amsterdam if they feel that the financial statements submitted do not comply with the law (Klaassen 1980). The Chamber is composed of three judges and two experts; there is no jury. The term 'interested parties' is defined broadly and includes shareholders, employees, works councils and trade unions, but not auditors. The public prosecutor may also bring proceedings. The Chamber may order rectification of the financial statements. Although the rulings of the Chamber are applicable only to the defendant company, the Chamber may indicate grounds for its decisions which may influence the reporting practices of other companies. Failure to comply with the Court's rulings may be punished by fines or imprisonment. No rulings were given by the Chamber until 1977. Since then it has given over twenty rulings dealing with accounting policies and disclosure.

Despite the fourth Directive, Dutch law and accounting standards remain more permissive and general than those in most other industrial countries. The scope for cases before the Chamber is thus large. The conclusions of the Chamber have not always supported the guidelines and indeed these have rarely been cited by companies in their defence. Proceedings have been brought against both NVs and BVs and by both shareholders and trade unions. A pressure group of shareholders called SOBI (see below) has acted as plaintiff in many of the cases.

Taxation

Taxation provisions, so important an influence in France and Germany, have always had only an indirect influence on Dutch financial reporting. The resulting divergence between financial accounting and tax accounting led to an earlier use in the Netherlands than in most other countries of the techniques of deferred tax accounting.

The Stock Exchange

Dutch companies raise capital both by share and loan issues on the

Amsterdam Stock Exchange and from the commercial banks in the form of short- and medium-term loans. The Stock Exchange is not an important direct influence on the contents of company financial statements. Although over 200 companies are listed, dealings are dominated by the five major multinational companies (Akzo, Hoogovens, Philips, Royal Dutch Shell and Unilever) which account for about 50% of the market capitalisation and turnover. Table 1.3 in Chapter 1 gives comparative statistics for the world's leading stock exchanges. The Amsterdam Exchange is relatively insignificant as a provider of new capital, but it is the most active secondary market in Continental Europe.

Pressure Groups

Corporate financial reporting in the Netherlands is monitored by a number of active pressure groups (Volten 1979), notably SOBI (*Stichting Onderzoek Bedrijfs – Informatie*, the Foundation for the Investigation of Corporate Information), SGO (*Stichting Goed Ondernemerschap*, the Foundation for Good Enterprise Behaviour) and SSA (*Stichting Sociaal Aandeelhouderschap*, the Foundation for Social Accountability). SOBI was established in 1976 with the objectives of verifying compliance with legal requirements in financial statements (annual reports, interim statements, prospectuses) and of taking action should they be deemed to be inaccurate or inadequate. It is a private-sector body whose leading light has been Pieter Lakeman. As already noted, SOBI has acted as plaintiff in many cases before the Enterprise Chamber.

SGO is chaired by Professor Slot who in 1975 led an investigation at Utrecht University into the financial statements of fifty major enterprises. SGO is a strong supporter of current value as against historical cost accounting. SSA buys shares in enterprises and uses shareholders' meetings as a platform to raise questions and promote discussion of social accountability.

International Influences

Leading Dutch companies, especially the five major multinationals, are strongly affected by accounting developments outside the Netherlands, particularly in the USA and the UK. This may help to explain why the Netherlands has been slow to establish its own definitive standards: 'A small country in which many corporations are already affected by so many, and often so diverse, foreign standards simply cannot afford the luxury of another set of rules' (Klaassen and Schreuder 1984, p. 127). On the other hand, it may regard itself as too advanced simply to adopt on a selective basis, as many less developed countries are doing, the standards promulgated by the International Accounting Standards Committee (see Chapter 14).

6.2   Current Cost vs. Historical Cost

Dutch accountants are well known for their business economics approach to accounting and their recognition of the importance of replacement values and costs. This recognition is associated at the theoretical level with the names of Theodore Limperg, Jr. (1879–1961) and his successors, and in practical application with NV Philips Gloeilampenfabrieken. The Dutch approach in this area is similar to UK current cost accounting (CCA), but a gearing adjustment is less common.

As already noted, Dutch companies practise deferred tax accounting. The permanent differences which result from the non-recognition for tax purposes of adjustments for depreciation and cost of sales are usually deducted in current cost accounts from the revaluation surpluses rather than from profit before tax. This materially reduces the effect of inflation accounting on reported net profits (van Hoepen 1981).

Before the 1983 company law amendments consequent upon the EEC fourth Directive, there were no legislative requirements or guidance as regards current values or historical costs. The guidelines, however, recommended that net operating income be shown on both a historical and a current cost basis, the company choosing which basis to use in the main statements and which in the supplementary statements.

The Civil Code, as amended in 1983, permits but does not require the use of current cost accounting, companies being required to choose between CCA and historical cost accounting (HCA). Contrary to widespread belief, HCA is in fact more common than CCA in Dutch external financial reporting. It is not permissible to use CCA accounting in the balance sheet and HCA in the profit and loss account, but HCA in the balance sheet is not regarded as incompatible with current cost depreciation in the profit and loss account. The substance, scope and method of application of CCA are regulated by the asset valuation decree of 22 December 1983 which applies only if a company chooses to use CCA. The decree provides, in effect, for the use of deprival values (termed 'value to the business' by the UK Sandilands Committee). Tangible fixed assets, fixed asset investments and stocks (inventories) may be valued at replacement value, recoverable amount or realisable value and estimates may be used if necessary. (By recoverable amount is meant not the higher of net realisable value and net present value, as in the UK, but 'the value, at the time of the valuation, of net turnover imputable to goods or system of goods, which may be generated by operating the business in which they are employed or for which they are intended'.) Tangible fixed assets are to be valued at replacement value if their replacement may reasonably be assumed, or at their recoverable amount if still in use but not intended to be replaced, and otherwise at realisable value. Stocks whose replacement may be assumed are to be valued at the lower of replacement value and realisable value; if replacement cannot reasonably be assumed they are to be valued at realisable value. Increases in current cost have to be credited to a revaluation reserve and decreases debited thereto (article 390(1)). Irrespective of whether HCA or CCA is chosen, intangible assets and current assets other than inventories are not permitted to be valued at current cost.

A number of surveys have shown that current cost accounting has been applied neither universally nor in a uniform manner. For example, NIVRA's periodic surveys of the annual reports of listed companies demonstrate that replacement value has not been the normal valuation method used in external reporting. Corporate taxation is based on historical costs, not replacement costs, although the Hofstra Report (see Muis 1978) suggested that this should be changed. The best-known practical exponent of replacement value is, of course, Philips which, in its 1984 Annual Report, describes its valuation and income calculation policies as follows:

Current value
The valuation of tangible fixed assets and inventories, as well as the depreciation and/or usage of such, is based on current value which, in general, in order to maintain continuity, represents replacement value unless the lower business value or net realisable value of an asset is required.

The replacement value is determined by taking into consideration such factors as the usage and the location of the assets, as well as the influence of technological developments. The replacement value is calculated using current prices for specific assets or, if this is not possible, using price indices for categories of assets which have been subjected to the same price influences.

The net realisable value of an asset is the amount for which that asset can be sold. The current value of a tangible fixed asset is equal to the net realisable value in the event that the net realisable value is lower than the replacement value, and the asset will no longer be of productive use in the near future. Inventories are valued based on net realisable value when the net realisable value is lower than the replacement value.

The business value of a tangible fixed asset is determined based on the expected net income to be derived from the productive employment of that asset during its remaining useful lifetime, plus the net realisable value upon discontinuation of productive employment of that asset. The current value of a tangible fixed asset is equal to the business value in the event that the business value is lower than the replacement value, and the asset will no longer be productively employed in the foreseeable future.

Changes in the replacement value, which have resulted from fluctuations in the local price level of inventories and tangible fixed assets (i.e. revaluation) are credited or debited to the revaluation surplus account. In the event that the stockholders' equity is greater than the total capital invested in inventories and tangible fixed assets, an amount is added to revaluation surplus and charged to the income account in order to preserve a properly leveraged financial structure. To the extent that the revaluation surplus is not necessary for preserving a properly leveraged financial structure, a gearing adjustment is credited to the income account. In compliance with legal regulations, this gearing adjustment is transferred to the income account in proportion to the usage and/or depreciation of the relevant assets. The deferred gearing adjustment is temporarily accounted for within revaluation surplus in the stockholders' equity section.

A provision for deferred income tax arising from a revaluation of assets is temporarily deducted from revaluation surplus. Upon usage and/or depreciation of the revalued assets, the related income tax is charged to the income account and the provision for deferred income tax is then reversed in the revaluation surplus account.

Further details of Philips' methods can be found in Enthoven (1982) and Spinosa Cattela (1983).

More typical of most Dutch listed companies is Akzo's 1984 Annual Report which follows the historical cost convention but also provides supplementary current value information. The current value of land is approximated on the basis of appraisals; that of buildings, machinery and equipment by external indices (with, additionally, a decrease in value to take account of technological advances). Inventories are shown at historical cost, unless there is a material difference with the current value at the balance sheet date.

6.3 Accounting Principles and Policies

A number of accounting principles and valuation rules apply in Dutch financial reporting irrespective of whether historical or current costs are used. The accounting principles expressly stipulated by the Civil Code (as amended in 1983) are: going concern, consistency, accruals, prudence, realisation and individual valuation.

Amortisation, depreciation and diminution in value of fixed assets must be taken into account regardless of whether a profit or loss is reported. Straight-line depreciation is the most common in practice. Buildings but not land are usually depreciated. As in the UK, depreciation for tax purposes often varies from that charged in the profit and loss account.

Intangible assets other than research and development and share issue expenses may only be capitalised if purchased. Capitalisation, which is not mandatory, must be followed by amortisation, with a maximum period of five years, although where purchased goodwill can reasonably be allocated to a substantially longer period, it may be written off over that period, provided that the latter does not exceed ten years. In practice many Dutch companies do not capitalise intangibles at all, writing off goodwill on consolidation against reserves.

If historical cost accounting is used, tangible fixed assets must be valued at acquisition or production cost, reduced by amortisation, depreciation and any other diminution in value. Acquisition cost is defined as the purchase price plus costs incidental to acquisition; production cost as the purchase price of raw material and consumables used, plus directly attributable expenses.

For current assets the lower of cost and market rule applies. Inventories must be classified according to category, either in the Notes or on the face of the balance sheet. FIFO and weighted average cost are the most popular, but LIFO is also expressly permitted (article 385(2)).

6.4 Consolidation and Currency Translation

Of the 120 listed companies included in the 1981 NIVRA Survey, 106 (88%) published a consolidated balance sheet, 12 had no subsidiaries, and in two cases there were subsidiaries but no consolidated balance sheet. 106 companies also provided notes to the consolidated balance sheet and published a consolidated profit and loss account (in 2 cases without notes). The main legal requirements relating to consolidation are set out in article 379(6) of the Civil Code which provides that financial data concerning the subsidiaries must, with or without data relating to the parent company and other group companies, be included in group annual accounts drawn up in accordance with the consolidation method.

Subsidiaries, group companies and participating interests are defined in articles 54a, 76 and 187 of Book 2 of the Civil Code. Subsidiaries include (a) corporate bodies (i.e. NVs, BVs, cooperative societies and mutual guarantee associations) more than half of whose share capital is provided or caused to be provided by another corporate body either alone or together with another subsidiary or group company; and (b) limited partnerships or general partnerships in which the parent company is a fully liable partner. A subsidiary of a subsidiary is itself a subsidiary for this purpose. A group company is a corporate body or a partnership associated in a group with a parent company. A corporate body is deemed to have a participating interest in another corporate body if the latter or its subsidiary provides or causes to be provided capital for it with the object of creating a durable link for the benefit of the first corporate body's own activities. A participating interest is presumed to exist where at least 20% of the issued capital is so provided.

Akzo sets out its principles of consolidation in its 1984 Annual Report as follows:

> The consolidated financial statements include the accounts of Akzo NV and all companies in which the interest of Akzo NV or any of its majority-owned subsidiaries separately or jointly exceeds 50% of the subscribed stock ... All of the assets, liabilities and results of the consolidated companies are included. Minority interest in Group equity and Group income is shown separately.

As can be seen from this quotation, Akzo does not use the proportional method of consolidation. This method of consolidation was, however, used by sixteen (15%) of the companies in the 1981 Survey (including Heineken, for example). Participating interests are usually valued by the 'net asset method' of equity accounting which is used in both the group accounts and the accounts of the parent company. The use of this method means that any goodwill arising is separately identified and either written off immediately to reserves or amortised through the profit and loss account. Negative goodwill must be transferred to a revaluation reserve. The first time that the associated company's net assets are valued, the valuation must be at current cost (i.e. at the equivalent of the Anglo-Saxon fair value at date of acquisition). Thereafter the associate's net assets must be valued on the same basis as those of the parent company.

The Civil Code (article 384(5)) requires companies to explain the bases for the translation of amounts expressed in foreign currencies, with disclosure of how translation and exchange differences have been dealt with. Practice in this area is not uniform. Except in relation to hyperinflationary countries, Akzo uses current rates in its consolidated balance sheet (e.g. fl 3.55 to the US dollar at 31.12.84), except for its US dollar-convertible debentures which are translated at fl 3.60 (the agreed rate for conversion purposes). Quarterly average rates of exchange (e.g. fl 3.22 to the US dollar for 1984) are used in the income statement. Translation differences are included in income except for those which result from translation of shareholders' funds of foreign companies into guilders. These are transferred to reserves. Philips, which uses current cost accounting, not historical cost accounting, in its main accounts, also uses mainly current rates but writes off translation differences as far as possible against revaluation reserves.

The EEC seventh Directive on consolidated accounts, adopted in 1983, is unlikely to be implemented in practice in the Netherlands before the early 1990s. Since consolidation is already a well-established practice, its effects will not be great, but Dutch law will have to define in more detail the requirements relating to consolidated accounts, especially with respect to the definition of a subsidiary and consolidation techniques. Fewer subgroup consolidations are likely to be required. There will also be some minor changes in disclosure requirements (Ernst & Whinney 1984; McKinnon 1984).

6.5   Formats and Exemptions

As in all member states of the EEC, mandatory balance sheet and profit and loss account formats are now laid down for Dutch companies. In accordance with the traditional flexible Dutch approach to financial reporting, however, as wide a choice of formats as is permissible under the fourth Directive has been made available (Moret and Limperg 1984).

The amount of disclosure under the formats depends upon size. Companies are classified as medium or small if they satisfy for two consecutive years two of the following criteria:

	Small	Medium (unless small)
Balance sheet total	⩽ fl 4 million	⩽ fl 17 million
Net turnover	⩽ fl 8 million	⩽ fl 35 million
Average number of employees	< 50	< 250

All other companies are classified as large in this context. In the case of a group of companies, the limits refer to the consolidated figures for the parent company and its subsidiaries.

A large company is not entitled to any exemptions from disclosure and must choose one of the two balance sheet formats (A and B) and one of the four profit and loss account formats (E, F, G and H) annexed to the Annual Accounts Formats Decree of 23 December, 1983. Format A is reproduced in Appendix 6. It is very similar, though not identical, to Format 1 in the British Companies Act 1985. Format B is Format A in horizontal instead of vertical form (and thus equivalent to the British Format 2). Formats E and F (reproduced in Appendix 6) are similar to the British profit and loss account Formats 2 and 1 respectively and are in vertical form. Formats G and H are horizontal versions of these formats.

Small corporate bodies may select instead one of the balance sheet Formats C and D (which are equivalent to Formats A and B excluding the items preceded by arabic numbers) and one of the profit and loss account Formats I and J. Format I is Format E, starting with 'gross margin' and excluding all items above 'salaries and wages'; Format J is Format F, excluding 'net turnover' and 'cost of sales'. Medium corporate bodies are treated in the same manner as large corporate bodies so far as the balance sheet is concerned, but are allowed to use the same profit and loss account formats as small corporate bodies.

The shareholders have the power, within six months from the beginning of the financial year, to decide in general meeting not to apply the above exemptions.

6.6   Notes to the Accounts

As in the UK and the USA, a great deal of information is provided by Dutch companies in the Notes. Disclosure of the following items, amongst others, as Notes is specially required by the Code:

  (i) movements in capital and reserves (article 378);
 (ii) interests in other corporate bodies (article 379);
(iii) analysis of net turnover by class of business and geographical area (article 380);
 (iv) important long-term financial commitments (article 381);
  (v) employee information (article 382);
 (vi) remuneration of, and loans and advances to, supervisory and managerial directors (article 381, 383).

6.7   Other Contents of Annual Reports

The annual reports of every corporate body must include a managerial directors' report and also supplementary information. Neither of these may be at variance with the annual accounts or with each other. The managerial directors' report (article 391) must give a true and fair view of the state of affairs on the balance sheet date and of the development of the business (including subsidiaries) during the financial year. It must also contain information in respect of significant post-balance-sheet events and expected developments and activities in the field of research and development. In reporting expected developments, special attention must be paid, to the extent that it will not be at variance with vital interests, to capital expenditure, financing and employment, and to the circumstances on which the development of turnover and profitability depend.

The supplementary information required by law to be given in the annual report includes statements regarding the following (article 392): the rules as laid down in the Articles of Association concerning the appropriation of profit; the appropriation of the year's profit or the treatment of the loss or proposals relating thereto; the number of profit-sharing certificates and similar instruments, with an indication of the rights they confer; and post-balance-sheet events having material financial consequences, with a mention of the impact of those consequences.

The auditors' report (see section 6.9) is also regarded as being part of the supplementary information. If there is no auditors' report its omission and the reason therefore must be stated, unless the corporate body is exempt from audit by reason of its size.

Article 379 of the Code requires disclosure of information relating to subsidiaries and other group companies.

The more important Dutch companies typically include in their annual reports a number of statements and items not required by law. Akzo, in its 1984 report, for example, provides the following:

(a) A consolidated statement of changes in financial position (source and application of funds statement). Funds statements are quite common in Dutch practice; 108 (= 90% of 120) are recorded in the 1981 Survey.

(b) Information relating to value added, although not a value added statement as such.

(c) A detailed ten-year financial summary.

(d) Financial highlights with earnings per share figures.

(e) The report of the supervisory board.

6.8 Social Reporting

Corporate social reporting has been established in the Netherlands since the 1970s (Schreuder 1981). In the Dutch context, social reporting refers mainly to reports about employment and personnel policies (e.g. total number of employees and subclassifications thereof; total wages paid; costs of training programmes; recreational facilities; medical services; safety and accidents) and is aimed mainly at employees but also at other users of published corporate information. Although such reporting has been encouraged by the Act on Works Councils (originally passed in 1950, revised in 1971 and 1979), it is mainly voluntary in nature. It is supported by the employers' federations and appears to have been accepted by employees as a corporate means of communication.

6.9 Audit

All NVs and BVs except those classified as small by the three size criteria are subject to audit. Transitionally, however, BVs are only subject to audit if they have an issued share capital of at least fl 500,000; are insurance companies or credit institutions; or have a balance sheet total of at least fl 8 million and employ at least 100 people (including those employed by subsidiaries, if any).

Only members of NIVRA or foreign accountants approved by the Minister of Economic Affairs are allowed to act as auditors. Auditors are in principle appointed by the annual general meeting of shareholders. Should the shareholders fail to act, the power to appoint falls first upon the supervisory directors and then upon the managerial directors. In practice the appointment is usually made by the supervisory board.

The auditors report both to the supervisory directors and to the managerial directors. There is no legally required wording of the report but the following wording (in English translation) is typical:

> We have examined the foregoing financial statements of . . . . In our opinion, these financial statements present fairly the financial position of . . . at . . . , and the results of its operations for the year then ended.

'Present fairly' is a free translation of *getrouw beeld* (faithful picture). It will be noted that there is no reference to legislation in the report, but if the annual accounts, the managerial directors' report or the supplementary information do not comply with the law, the auditor must so state.

6.10   Summary

Dutch company financial reporting differs in important respects from that in other countries, although implementation of the EEC fourth Directive has moved it significantly closer to reporting in other member states of the EEC. Outsiders have usually concentrated on Dutch theory and practice in the field of current cost accounting. Whilst this is undoubtedly important, it can be overstressed and the belief in its widespread use in *external* reporting is certainly incorrect.

Until recently, a more important feature has been the combination of almost extreme permissiveness with high professional standards. The permissiveness is being moderated by EEC directives; the high standards remain.

The nearest equivalent to an accounting standard setting institution in the Netherlands is the Council for Annual Reporting. Unlike the British ASC and the American FASB, it is not composed mainly of accountants. Its powers are also considerably less. Its Guidelines do not lead to qualified audit reports and, far from having the backing of a regulatory body, have not always been supported by that unique Dutch institution, the Enterprise Chamber ('accounting court').

On the other hand, the Netherlands does not share with France and

West Germany either their coincidence of financial accounting and tax accounting or their love of uniformity. There is no national accounting plan.

International and EEC harmonisation notwithstanding, Dutch accounting is still *sui generis*.

References and Further Reading

Ashton, R.K. (1981) *Use and Extent of Replacement Value Accounting in the Netherlands*, Institute of Chartered Accountants in England and Wales.

Beeny, J. and Chastney, J. (1978) *European Financial Reporting. The Netherlands*, Institute of Chartered Accountants in England and Wales.

Chester, M.G. and Vogelaar, F.O.W. (1974) *English/Dutch Company Law*, Kluwer-Harrap Handbooks.

Council for Annual Reporting (1985) *Netherlands Accounting Guidelines*, Amsterdam.

Enthoven, A.J.H. (1982) *Current Value Accounting. Its Concepts and Practice at N V Philips Industries, The Netherlands*, International Accounting Research Study 3, Center for International Accounting Development, The University of Texas at Dallas.

Ernst & Whinney (1984) *The Impact of the Seventh Directive*, Financial Times Business Information, Chapter 4.

Hoepen, M.A. van (1981) *Anticipated and Deferred Corporate Income Tax in Companies' Financial Statements*, Kluwer.

Klaassen, J. (1980) 'An accounting court: the impact of the Enterprise Chamber on financial reporting in the Netherlands', *Accounting Review*, April, pp. 327–341.

Klaassen, J. and Schreuder, H. (1984) 'Accounting research in the Netherlands', in A.G. Hopwood and H. Schreuder, *European Contributions to Accounting Research: The Achievements of the Last Decade*, Free University Press, Amsterdam.

McKinnon, S.M. (1984) *The Seventh Directive. Consolidated Accounts in the EEC*, Kluwer Publishing and Arthur Young International, Chapter 12.

Moret & Limperg (1984) *New Dutch Legislation on Annual Reports*, Rotterdam.

Muis, J. (1975) 'Current value accounting in the Netherlands: fact or fiction?', *Accountant's Magazine*, November, pp. 377–379.

Muis, J. (1977) 'Accounting standard setting: the pith and the pendulum', *Accounting and Business Research*, Autumn, pp. 291–294.

Muis, J.W. (1978) 'The Hofstra report – inflation accounting for tax purposes', *The Accountant's Magazine*, March.

Nederlands Instituut van Registeraccountants (1983) *Onderzoek Jaarverslagen 1981* (in Dutch only), Amsterdam.

Sanders, P. (1977) *Dutch Company Law*, Oyez Publishing.

Schreuder, H. (1981) 'Employees and the corporate report: the Dutch case', *Accounting Review*, April, pp. 294–308, reprinted in S.J. Gray (ed.) (1983) *International Accounting and Transnational Decisions*, Butterworths.

Spinosa Cattela, R.C. (1983) 'An introduction into current value accounting and its application within Philips N V', in A.J.H. Enthoven, *Current Cost Accounting – Its Aspects and Impacts*, International Accounting Research Study 4, Center for International Accounting Development, The University of Texas at Dallas.

Volten, H. (1979) 'Challenges to financial reporting in the Netherlands. How corporate reporting is monitored by social pressure groups', PILOT (Netherlands), 9, (published by NIVRA).

Appendix 6
Uniform Formats for Dutch Financial Statements

BALANCE SHEET FORMAT A

Balance sheet as at

A. Fixed assets

I. *Intangible fixed assets*
1. share issue expenses
2. research and development
3. concessions and licences
4. intellectual property rights
5. goodwill
6. payments on account

II. *Tangible fixed assets*
1. land and buildings
2. plant and machinery
3. fixtures, fittings, tools and equipment
4. in the course of construction and payments on account
5. not employed in the production process

III. *Fixed asset investments*
1. group companies
2. amounts owed by group companies
3. other participating interests

C. Current liabilities

Creditors due within one year
1. convertible debentures and other loans
2. other debentures and private loans
3. amounts owed to credit institutions
4. advance payments received on orders
5. trade creditors and trade credits
6. bills of exchange and cheques payable
7. amounts owed to group companies
8. amounts owed to related companies
9. taxation and social security
10. pensions
11. other creditors
12. accruals and deferred income

D. Net current assets

E. Total assets less current liabilities

F. Long-term liabilities

Creditors due after more than one year
1. convertible debentures and other loans
2. other debentures and private loans
3. amounts owed to credit institutions

4. amounts owed by related companies
5. other investments
6. other loans

IV. *Total fixed assets*

B. Current assets

I. *Stocks*
1. raw materials and consumables
2. work in progress
3. finished goods and goods for sale
4. payments on account

II. *Debtors*
1. trade debtors
2. amounts owed by group companies
3. amounts owed by related companies
4. other debtors
5. called up share capital not paid
6. prepayments and accrued income

III. *Investments*
1. shares, or depositary receipts thereof, in group companies
2. other investments

IV. *Cash at bank, giro and in hand*

V. *Total current assets*

4. advance payments received on orders
5. trade creditors and trade credits
6. bills of exchange and cheques payable
7. amounts owed to group companies
8. amounts owed to related companies
9. taxation and social security
10. pensions
11. other creditors
12. accruals and deferred income

G. Provisions for liabilities and charges
1. pensions
2. taxation
3. other

H. Capital and reserves

I. *Paid up and called up share capital*

II. *Share premium account*

III. *Revaluation reserve*

IV. *Statutory reserves and articles of association reserves*
1. statutory reserves
2. articles of association reserves

V. *Other reserves*

VI. *Undistributed profit*

PROFIT AND LOSS ACCOUNT FORMAT E

Profit and loss account for the year . . ./months ended . . .

Net turnover
change in stocks of finished goods and work in progress
own work capitalised
other operating income

Total operating income

raw materials and consumables
work contracted out and other external expenses
salaries and wages
social security
amortisation, depreciation and diminution in value of intangible and tangible fixed
   assets
reversals of diminution in value of intangible and tangible fixed assets
exceptional diminution in value of current assets
other operating expenses

Total operating expenses

Operating profit or loss

profit or loss on fixed asset investments
other interest receivable and similar income
profit or loss on participating interests
increase in value of remaining fixed asset investments and current investments
decrease in value of remaining fixed asset investments and current investments
interest payable and similar expenses

Balance of financial income and expense

Profit or loss on ordinary activities before taxation

tax on profit or loss on ordinary activities

Profit or loss on ordinary activities after taxation

extraordinary income
extraordinary expense

Extraordinary profit or loss before taxation

tax on extraordinary profit or loss

Extraordinary profit or loss after taxation

Profit or loss after taxation

PROFIT AND LOSS ACCOUNT FORMAT F

Profit and loss account for the year . . ./months ended . . .

Net turnover
cost of sales

Gross margin on turnover

distribution expenses
general administrative expenses

Total expenses

Net margin on turnover

other operating income

Operating profit or loss

profit or loss on fixed asset investments
other interest receivable and similar income
profit or loss on participating interests
increase in value of remaining fixed asset investments and current investments
decrease in value of remaining fixed asset investments and current investments
interest payable and similar expenses

Balance of financial income and expense

Profit or loss on ordinary activities before taxation

tax on profit or loss on ordinary activities

Profit or loss on ordinary activities after taxation

extraordinary income
extraordinary expense

Extraordinary profit or loss before taxation

tax on extraordinary profit or loss

Extraordinary profit or loss after taxation

Profit or loss after taxation

7

Financial Reporting in Japan

LES CAMPBELL

7.1 Introduction

The industrialisation of Japan began in earnest in 1868 after the Meiji Restoration. The government was responsible for encouraging and enabling the growth of industry. In 1899 the first Commercial Code was established, based on a Franco-German model and oriented towards creditors and tax collection. At least until the Second World War, the Japanese economy was controlled by a small number of *Zaibatsu*, industrial – political consortia usually involving a bank and originally based on noble families. The importance of banks and the existence of several somewhat feudal aspects of business control still continue.

Since the Second World War, Japan has developed into one of the world's economic superpowers. Japanese multinational companies are now ranked among the largest in the world. Eleven of the world's top fifty industrial groupings are based in Japan (*Times 1000* 1984). However, despite Japan's economic importance, relatively little is known of Japanese accounting requirements and practices. This chapter analyses the influences on Japanese financial reporting and comments on the main accounting requirements and practices.

An Anglo-Saxon[1] user of Japanese financial statements generally faces one immediate and important difficulty: the language barrier. He

---

1. As usual in this book, the term 'Anglo-Saxon' refers to the UK, the USA, and other developed English-speaking countries.

might face similar difficulties when reading a set of French financial statements. However, it is more likely that he will have a basic knowledge of French, and so be able to interpret the key elements of a set of French financial statements. Even if the Anglo-Saxon has no basic knowledge of French accounting terms, he may be able to make an informed guess in some cases. For example, he may correctly guess that *immobilisations* means fixed assets and that *amortissements* means depreciation.

It is obvious that, with Japanese financial statements, there are not only different *words* from English, but also a different *script*. Consequently, few Western users can even guess at the key elements of a set of Japanese financial statements. The language barrier may be overcome in several different ways. A Western firm of stockbrokers may employ Japanese nationals to translate and comment on the Japanese financial statements, and individual shareholders may benefit from this. A user interested in the financial statements of a particular Japanese company may himself employ a firm or individual who specialises in translating Japanese material.

Some large Japanese multinational companies prepare English-language versions of their annual reports. For example, a Japanese company that is listed on the New York Stock Exchange must comply with the relevant requirements of the Securities and Exchange Commission (SEC). In general, these require a set of English-language financial statements in accordance with US generally accepted accounting principles (GAAP), with the omission of segment information. However, although such financial statements may be helpful to a user, the conversion to US GAAP means that the financial statements are not a good source of information about financial reporting in Japan.

A Japanese company that is not listed on a foreign stock exchange may still prepare English-language financial statements. These are sometimes described as 'convenience translations'. A company may prepare a convenience translation as part of a public relations and marketing exercise. It usually includes the relevant amounts in yen, and translates the yen amounts into US dollars using the appropriate year-end exchange rate. The report normally emphasises that the company has translated the yen amounts into dollars solely for the convenience of the reader, which does not imply that they actually have been, or could be, translated into dollars. A convenience translation normally uses income measurement principles and asset valuation principles that are in accordance with Japanese GAAP. However, a convenience translation may include additional disclosure items that are not required by Japanese GAAP, and may reclassify some financial statement items into a form that is more familiar to non-Japanese readers. Such reclassifications normally do not affect the values of total assets, of shareholders' funds or of the profit for the year. Convenience translations provide a useful insight into some aspects of financial reporting in Japan. However, the additional disclosures and the reclassifications referred to above mean that they do not provide a completely accurate picture of financial reporting in Japan.

7.2   Forms of Business Organisation

The most common form of business organisation in Japan is the *kabushiki kaisha*. This is similar in many respects to the public limited company in the UK, particularly in that the liability of the shareholders is limited to the extent of the subscribed nominal capital. In both countries, the rights of limited liability lead to corresponding duties of reporting financial information that is available to third parties.

There are approximately 767,000 *kabushiki kaisha* in Japan. Only 2,800 of these have their stock traded publicly, and only 1,760 or so are listed on stock exchanges. Consequently, although all companies whose shares are publicly traded are *kabushiki kaisha*, by far the majority have relatively few shareholders and are relatively small.

The next most common form of business organisation in Japan is the *yugen kaisha*. The nearest equivalent in the UK would be the private limited company. The shareholders of a *yugen kaisha* have limited liability in the same way as the shareholders of a *kabushiki kaisha*. The main differences between a *yugen kaisha* and a *kabushiki kaisha* are restrictions on shareholders. A *yugen kaisha* cannot have more than fifty shareholders, whereas there is no upper limit on the number of shareholders of a *kabushiki kaisha*. A shareholder in a *yugen kaisha* may dispose of his shares only if the other shareholders give their consent. There is no such restriction for a shareholder in a *kabushiki kaisha*, although the articles of incorporation may require that shares be disposed of only with the approval of the directors.

There are two main types of partnership in Japan: a *gomei kaisha* is a general or unlimited partnership; a *goshi kaisha* is a combined limited and unlimited partnership, consisting of one or more limited partners and one or more unlimited partners.

7.3   Influences on Accounting

The government has the most significant influence on accounting in Japan. However, this comes from three separate sources, and there is little overall coordination of them. In fact, the three sources sometimes have conflicting approaches to financial reporting issues.

The first source of government influence is the Commercial Code.

This is administered by the Ministry of Justice and applies to all *kabushiki kaisha*. It has its roots in the German Commercial Code of the nineteenth century which was copied by the Japanese. However, the German influence has diminished over time as amendments have been made to the code. Shareholders and creditors may inspect, at the company's head office, the financial statements that the company has prepared under the Commercial Code (see section 7.4).

In general, the staff in the Ministry of Justice have a legal background rather than an accounting background. Consequently, the administration of the Commercial Code is influenced, as in Germany, by the apparent belief of the legal profession that the protection of creditors is at least as important as the protection of shareholders. This belief may explain why the specific accounting rules of the Commercial Code place greater emphasis on asset valuation than on income measurement.

The second source of government influence is the Securities and Exchange Law. This is administered by the Ministry of Finance, and applies only to those *kabushiki kaisha* that are publicly traded. The Securities and Exchange Law was enacted shortly after World War Two, when General MacArthur was responsible for the Allied administration of Japan. The MacArthur régime naturally took the US system of accounting regulation as the model for the revised Japanese system (Baxter 1976). The main US influences on the Japanese Securities and Exchange Law were the Securities Act of 1933 and the Securities and Exchange Act of 1934. Consequently, the functions and powers of the Ministry of Finance in relation to financial reporting are similar in many respects to those of the US Securities and Exchange Commission, though there is not a directly equivalent body in Japan.

The accounting measurement, disclosure and filing requirements of the Securities and Exchange Law are more extensive and specific than those of the Commercial Code. A company must file its financial statements with the Ministry of Finance and with any stock exchange on which it is listed. The financial statements (see section 7.4) are available for public inspection at the Ministry and at the relevant exchanges.

The Ministry of Finance has an advisory body, called the Business Accounting Deliberation Council (BADC), whose members come from a variety of backgrounds, such as industry, the accountancy profession, government and the universities. The BADC prepares accounting standards, known as Business Accounting Principles, in response to specific requests from the Ministry of Finance. The Business Accounting Principles are published by the Ministry of Finance. All companies that report to the Ministry under the Securities and Exchange Law must comply with these Principles. The members of the BADC normally have an accounting background rather than a legal background. Consequently, the financial reporting requirements of the Ministry of Finance tend to place greater emphasis on income measurement and shareholder protection than on asset valuation and creditor protection, in contrast to the Code of the Ministry of Justice referred to above.

A *kabushiki kaisha* that is publicly traded is subject to both the sources of government influence described above. Consequently, it must prepare two sets of financial statements: one in accordance with the requirements of the Commercial Code and one in accordance with the requirements of the Securities and Exchange Law. Net income will be the same in the two sets of financial statements. The principal difference is the greater amount of disclosure required under the Securities and Exchange Law. Another significant difference is that there is no requirement in the Commercial Code to prepare group accounts.

The third source of government influence arises from the tax laws and regulations. These have a significant impact on financial reporting because, as in many European countries, certain deductions for expenses and deferrals of income are only permitted for tax purposes if they are reflected in the company's statutory accounts as prepared under the Commercial Code. Examples of these deductions and deferrals are depreciation, allowances for bad debts, accrued employee severance indemnities, and profit from instalment sales.

Companies often choose an accounting practice that maximises the tax benefit, rather than one that more accurately reflects the underlying economic reality. Another influence that the tax laws have is that some non-deductible items, such as directors' bonuses, are charged by companies against retained earnings rather than against income.

So there are three distinct government influences on financial reporting. The influence of the Ministry of Finance seems to be increasing relative to that of the Ministry of Justice. Because of the fundamental difference in the attitude of the two ministries, this change in relative influence may result in a move away from a 'legal' approach to a more 'economic' approach to financial reporting requirements. Another likely change is that the three distinct government influences will become more unified. The BADC has begun this process of harmonisation.

The Japanese accounting profession has had relatively little influence on financial reporting compared to the government, and has far less influence than Anglo-Saxon professions have. The Japanese Institute of Certified Public Accountants (JICPA) was established by the Certified Public Accountants Law of 1948. It has approximately 8,400 members. The JICPA is thus of quite recent origin and is relatively small compared to the Anglo-Saxon professional bodies.

An entrant into the Japanese accounting profession must pass three levels of examinations in order to become a certified public accountant (JICPA 1982). University and college graduates are exempt from the preliminary CPA examination. The intermediate examination includes economics, bookkeeping, financial accounting, cost accounting, the Commercial Code, business administration and auditing theory. The pass rate for the intermediate examination is normally only about seven to ten per cent (Watson 1982). Those who pass the intermediate examination are referred to as 'junior CPAs' (or 'assistant CPAs'). A junior CPA then undergoes a three-year apprenticeship, consisting of one year of training and two years of practical experience, before sitting the final examination. The final examination is a test of technical competence. It includes auditing practice, financial analysis and accounting practice (including taxation), and it is a mixture of written and oral examinations. Candidates must also submit a thesis. The pass rate for the final examination is around 18 per cent (Watson 1982).

The JICPA issues recommendations on accounting matters. Although it describes the pronouncements as recommendations rather than as requirements, a company that reports to the Ministry of Finance under the Securities and Exchange Law *must* comply with the pronouncements, because non-compliance would be considered a departure from acceptable accounting practices. If the departure were material, the Ministry of Finance would require the company to amend the financial statements. However, although the JICPA pronouncements are supported by this strong sanction from the Ministry, they tend to deal with relatively minor matters. The main financial reporting issues are covered in the Business Accounting Principles of the BADC.

The relative weakness of the Japanese accounting profession is emphasised again by the fact that it is the BADC, not the JICPA, that issues auditing standards (Campbell 1985, Chapter 7). The JICPA has issued a number of auditing statements on an *ad hoc* basis. These deal with specific auditing issues such as allowances for bad debts. The Ministry of Finance has issued a regulation that states that the audit of financial statements for Securities and Exchange Law purposes must be conducted in accordance with generally recognised auditing practices, which shall be taken as meaning the auditing standards and working rules issued by the BADC (AICPA 1975). Consequently, the Ministry of Finance has delegated the responsibility for setting auditing standards to the BADC, whose standards then have legal authority. However, as mentioned earlier, the BADC includes representatives of the accounting profession. So these individual members of the JICPA may influence financial reporting by influencing the form and content of the Business Accounting Principles.

Very few members of the JICPA hold senior financial positions in industry or commerce. Consequently, the Japanese accounting profession has little influence on the preparers of financial information. This is in contrast to the UK, for example, where many of the financial directors of large companies are members of the accounting profession.

The stock exchanges in Japan are all government-regulated, rather than self-regulating as in the UK. There is no equivalent of the UK Stock Exchange Listing Agreement. Listed companies in Japan are subject to the requirements of the Securities and Exchange Law, as mentioned earlier. The stock exchanges do not impose any additional reporting requirements (Campbell 1983).

Japanese companies normally rely heavily on debt rather than equity as their principal source of finance, and banks are the main providers of this (see Table 7.1). Short-term debt finance in Japan commonly consists of fixed interest 90-day promissory notes. Longer-term financing may consist of an informal agreement to roll over these short-term notes for a number of years. Short-term debt often finances a substantial proportion of a Japanese company's fixed assets. In many cases, banks own a significant proportion of a client's shares, and may even be the largest shareholder. In general, shares in Japanese companies are held on a long-term basis. The heavy involvement of the banks and the long-term nature of share ownership means that there is less focus on short-term earnings information in Japan than in the UK or the US. The banks have direct access to their clients' accounting information, and so have relatively little influence on external financial reporting.

International influences on Japanese financial reporting include the US influence on the Securities and Exchange Law and the German influence on the original Commercial Code. Although Japan is represented on the International Accounting Standards Committee (IASC), the latter is considered to have had little influence on Japanese financial reporting. The primary reason for this is that the IASC seeks to implement its standards through the efforts of the national professional accounting bodies and, as mentioned earlier, the JICPA has a relatively weak influence on the standard-setting process in Japan.

7.4   Annual Reports

Commercial Code

The specific regulations that govern the form and content of the financial statements required under the Commercial Code are contained in the 'Regulations Concerning the Balance Sheet, Income Statement, Business Report and Supporting Schedules of Joint Stock Corporations'. The Ministry of Justice first issued these in 1963 and has subsequently amended them from time to time, including a major revision in 1982.

The financial statements prepared under the Commercial Code must include a balance sheet, a profit and loss account and a statement of proposed appropriation of earnings. A company must also present various supplementary schedules to the shareholders' meeting, including details of changes to share capital and reserves, acquisitions and disposals of fixed assets, and transactions with directors and shareholders. The

JICPA has published a specimen set of financial statements that conform to the disclosure requirements of the regulations under the Commercial Code (JICPA 1982). The specimen set is reproduced in the Appendix to this chapter.

The regulations require a balance sheet to have three sections: assets, liabilities and shareholders' equity. The balance sheet must disclose a total for each section. The key elements of the disclosure requirements for each section are as follows:

Assets
    Current Assets
    Fixed Assets:
        Tangible Fixed Assets
        Intangible Fixed Assets
        Investments and Others
    Deferred Charges
Liabilities
    Current Liabilities
    Long-term Liabilities
Shareholders' Equity
    Capital Stock
    Statutory Reserves
    Retained Earnings

Normally, a one-year period is used to distinguish between current items and non-current items; and current items are disclosed in decreasing order of liquidity.

The profit and loss account must include two main sections before arriving at the figure for income before income taxes: ordinary profit and loss, and special gain and loss. The former should include operating profit and loss and non-operating income and expense.

The JICPA publication referred to above (JICPA 1982) mentions some key differences between the form and content of financial statements prepared under the Commercial Code and the form of content of US (and UK) financial statements. These are:

1. The amount of trade notes receivable is nearly always greater than the amount of trade accounts receivable in a Japanese balance sheet. Similarly, the amount of trade notes payable is nearly always greater than trade accounts payable. Japanese companies normally issue non-interest-bearing notes for accounts receivable and payable. The notes normally have terms of 90 days or 120 days.
2. Trade accounts payable in Japan include only amounts owed to suppliers of goods and materials. Amounts owed for services are included under other accounts payable or under accrued expenses.

3. The directors may make a proposal to increase or decrease the amount of the general purpose appropriation account in the retained earnings subsection. This increase or decrease would be either from or to the unappropriated retained earnings account. The proposal of the directors is subject to approval at the shareholders' annual meeting. The amount that the directors propose to leave in the unappropriated retained earnings account often represents the extent of the dividend that the directors intend to distribute in the near future.

4. The special gain or loss section of the profit and loss account includes any credits to income that result from the reversal of a provision for a liability that the company originally set up for some specific purpose, but that the company no longer considers is necessary.

5. The special gain or loss section includes any prior-year adjustments before arriving at the profit or loss for the year. In the UK, however, companies adjust prior-year adjustments against the opening balance of reserves.

6. The special gain or loss section includes unusual gains or losses that arise when the company writes off deferred assets when there is no longer an expected future benefit, and other losses that arise from events or transactions that are not normal. Consequently, unusual gains or losses in Japan are not governed by the two criteria of expected non-recurrence and of unusual nature. These two criteria are contained in the UK and US definitions of extraordinary items.

7. Companies in Japan are subject to three different taxes, generally all based on income. One of these, a business enterprise tax, comprises approximately 20 per cent of total income taxes. Companies do not report the business enterprise tax as part of income taxes, but include it in the amount of selling, general and administrative expenses.

Securities and Exchange Law

The specific regulations that govern the form and content of the financial statements required under the Securities and Exchange Law are contained in the 'Regulations Concerning the Terminology, Forms and Preparation Methods of Financial Statements', issued by the Ministry of Finance in 1963. The financial statements prepared under the Securities and Exchange Law must include a balance sheet, a profit and loss account, a statement of proposed appropriation of earnings, certain supplementary schedules and certain additional unaudited information. The supplementary schedules include details of share capital and reserves, long-term debt, fixed assets and intra-group transactions. The additional unaudited information includes details of the company's organisational structure, employees, production and cash flows.

Items such as profit and loss for the year and shareholders' equity will be the same in the financial statements that a company prepares under the Securities and Exchange Law as in those prepared under the Commercial Code. However, the regulations of the former are the more detailed on terminology, form and content of the financial statements, and will normally require a company to disclose additional details of certain items, or to reclassify certain items disclosed in the Commercial Code financial statements.

The JICPA publication referred to above (JICPA 1982) mentions some of these additional requirements of the Securities and Exchange Law, including:

1. Listing of assets and liabilities in decreasing order of liquidity.
2. Disclosure of transactions and balances with related parties separately from other transactions and balances.
3. Use of a materiality standard of one per cent for balance sheet accounts: for example, separate disclosure of a particular class of inventory, such as raw materials, if it exceeds one per cent of total assets. The materiality standards for the profit and loss account are 10 per cent and 20 per cent. For example, a company must disclose separately sales to related parties if they exceed 20 per cent of total sales. Another example is that a company must disclose separately losses from the sale of marketable securities if they exceed 10 per cent of total non-operating expenses.
4. Disclosure of additional notes to the financial statements: for example, a detailed description of any material change in an accounting policy, including reasons for the change.
5. Disclosure of the separate components of selling, general and administrative expenses.

Fixed Assets and Depreciation

The balance sheet of a Japanese company must show fixed assets at cost (less aggregate depreciation). The regulations do not allow revaluation. This conservative approach is in line with German and US practice, but in contrast to current practice in the UK, where many companies revalue their fixed assets, particularly property, every few years. Because a Japanese company records its fixed assets at cost, it may have significant 'hidden reserves', consisting of the amounts by which the fixed assets have increased in value since acquisition. These 'reserves' may be substantial, particularly in the case of land values, because Japan is a mountainous country where suitable land for industrial development is relatively scarce and has increased substantially in value in the period of economic growth since the war.

The most common depreciation method in Japan is the reducing balance method. A recent survey of Japanese financial reporting (Gray *et al.* 1984) found that 47 of the 50 companies in the survey used the reducing balance method of depreciation. Companies generally use the depreciation rates that are prescribed in the tax laws.

Research and Development Expenditure

The Commercial Code and the Business Accounting Principles generally permit a company to defer development expenditure. However, a company may only defer development expenditure if it expects that future revenues from the project will exceed the deferred expenditure. In the UK, companies may defer development expenditure if certain conditions are met. In the US, companies are not permitted to defer development expenditure.

Ballon *et al.* (1976) suggested that some Japanese companies have adopted a flexible deferral policy and have smoothed their profits by deferring development expenditure in a bad year and writing it off in a good year. However, the survey of Japanese financial reporting (Gray *et al.* 1984) found that 80 per cent of the companies wrote off development expenditure immediately, as incurred.

Inventories

Companies measure inventories either at cost or at the lower of cost and market value. However, the Commercial Code and the Business Accounting Principles do not allow a company to measure inventories at cost where there has been a significant and irrecoverable decline in their market value. In practice, companies generally measure their inventories at cost rather than at the lower of cost and market value, as in the UK and the US. So from a UK or US perspective, inventories may appear to be overstated in Japanese balance sheets.

Where a company cannot specifically identify the actual cost of an item of inventory, the company may choose from a variety of flow assumptions: weighted average cost, first-in first-out (FIFO) or last-in first-out (LIFO). In practice, weighted average cost is more common than either FIFO or LIFO. Naturally, as in the US in this case, the method chosen for accounting must be the same as the method chosen for taxation. In the UK, LIFO is not normally acceptable for either accounting or taxation.

The Commercial Code and the Business Accounting Principles do not allow a company to use replacement cost as a means of inventory measurement. In the US, companies are allowed to use replacement cost where it is lower than cost and net realisable value. In the UK, replacement cost is permitted under the alternative accounting rules of Schedule 4 to the Companies Act, but is not permitted by SSAP 9 for historical cost accounting.

Provision for Doubtful Debts

Companies generally calculate the provision for doubtful debts in accordance with what the tax laws permit. Consequently, it may be more than the amount that a comparable UK or US company would include. A Japanese company is allowed to record a provision in excess of that allowed for tax purposes but the excess would not be tax-deductible, so few Japanese companies do this. This illustrates how the tax laws influence financial reporting in Japan.

Legal Reserve

The Commercial Code requires a company to transfer an amount equal to at least 10 per cent of its declared dividends to a legal reserve, until the reserve equals 25 per cent of the capital stock account. This is similar to, but larger than, German or French legal reserves. The specimen balance sheet in the Appendix to this chapter shows where a company should disclose the reserve. The legal reserve is undistributable, but may be capitalised, following the appropriate legal procedures, in much the same way as a UK company might use a revaluation reserve to issue bonus shares. The requirement for a legal reserve illustrates the creditor-protection orientation of the Commercial Code. The reserve ensures that the company does not adopt a profligate dividend policy at the expense of its creditors.

Deferred Taxation

As already mentioned, tax laws have a significant influence on financial reporting in Japan. Material timing differences rarely arise, because the amounts in the financial accounts normally correspond closely to the amounts in the tax accounts. For example, companies normally charge in their financial accounts the same amount of depreciation as for tax purposes, i.e. the maximum amount permitted for tax purposes. Because material timing differences are rare, the practice of deferred tax accounting has not developed in Japan. The Commercial Code does not refer specifically to deferred taxation, but its accounting rules limit the deferral of expenses to certain specified categories, not including income taxes. Consequently, the Code effectively prohibits a company from recording a deferred tax asset, though not a deferred tax liability. However, it seems inconsistent for some companies to record a deferred tax liability when other companies are prohibited from recording a deferred tax asset. So deferred tax accounting is rarely found in financial statements prepared under the Commercial Code.

A BADC statement ('Principles for Preparation of Consolidated Financial Statements') declares that companies that prepare consolidated financial statements under the Securities and Exchange Law may use deferred tax accounting. The Commercial Code does not require companies to prepare consolidated financial statements, and so they are not subject to the Code's prohibition of deferred tax assets. In practice, only a few companies use deferred tax accounting in their consolidated financial statements. The main timing differences that arise relate to consolidation adjustments.

7.5　Consolidation and Currency Translation

Group financial reporting is relatively undeveloped in Japan, compared to its use in the UK and the US. Financial reporting in Japan has traditionally emphasised parent company financial statements rather than consolidated financial statements. As has been mentioned, the Commercial Code does not require consolidated financial statements. The Securities and Exchange Law requires them only as supplementary information.

There are two sources of regulations dealing with consolidated financial statements. The first is the 'Regulations concerning Consolidated Financial Statements', issued in 1977 by the Ministry of Finance, which has also issued related interpretative rules and ordinances. The Ministry may exempt a company from these requirements (and those of the BADC, discussed below) if, prior to 1977, it was issuing consolidated financial statements prepared in accordance with standards accepted in foreign countries. Such a company is permitted to continue with this. For example, some Japanese companies still prepare their consolidated financial statements in accordance with US accounting principles.

The second source of rules is the BADC Principles which prescribe some very specific procedures for preparing consolidated financial statements. For example, companies must eliminate intra-group balances and transactions, and must recognise minority interests in consolidated subsidiaries that are not wholly owned by the group. In theory, the

Japanese principles of consolidation are similar to those in the UK or in the US. However, this may not be reflected in practice. For example, two recent surveys of international financial statements have criticised the consolidation policies of particular Japanese groups (Financial Times 1984; International Accounting Bulletin 1984). The criticisms refer particularly to the practice of omitting apparently significant subsidiaries from consolidation.

The BADC Principles permit two methods for calculating goodwill arising on consolidation: as the excess of the cost of acquiring a subsidiary over the value of the net assets acquired *at the date of acquisition* (the Anglo-Saxon method), or at the *balance sheet date* (the German method). Also, in Japan, goodwill is based on the *book value* of the net assets acquired, not on the *fair value* as in the UK or the US.

There are also considerable international differences in how groups subsequently eliminate goodwill from their balance sheets. In Japan, a group must amortise goodwill over its useful economic life. However, the amortisation period must not exceed five years. In the UK, the preferred method in SSAP 22 is for a group to write off goodwill immediately against reserves. However, a group may capitalise goodwill and amortise it over its useful economic life. SSAP 22 does not specify a maximum number of years. In the US, a group must amortise goodwill over its useful economic life, not exceeding forty years.

Until 1983, either the equity method or the cost method could be used to account for investments in associated companies, and in practice most groups used the cost method. However, since 1983, Japanese groups must use the equity method, as in the UK or the US.

The Japanese accounting treatment of foreign subsidiaries on consolidation is considerably different from that in the UK and the US. The requirements are contained in a BADC statement known as the 'Accounting Standard for Foreign Currency Transactions', which was issued in 1979 and subsequently amended, to some extent, in 1984. This requires a group to use a modified temporal method to translate the financial statements of foreign subsidiaries for consolidation purposes. Under this method, historical rates are used for assets held at historical costs, and the closing exchange rate is used for most assets and liabilities measured at current values, such as debtors, creditors and inventories carried at market value. However, rather curiously, either the closing exchange rate or historical exchange rates may be used to translate *current* monetary items in the foreign subsidiary's balance sheet. The group should use historical exchange rates to translate *non-current* monetary items. This contrasts with the UK and the US, where groups normally use the closing rate to translate all items in a foreign subsidiary's balance sheet (see Chapter 12).

As mentioned earlier, the Ministry of Finance may allow some groups to prepare their consolidated financial statements in accordance with foreign accounting standards. These groups may also use the appropriate foreign accounting practice for translating the financial statements of foreign subsidiaries. Consequently, some Japanese groups use the currency translation methods prescribed in SSAP 20 (UK) or in FAS 52 (US).

The BADC statements declare that exchange gains or losses arising on the translation of a foreign subsidiary's financial statements should be described as 'foreign currency translation adjustments' and disclosed as an asset or a liability in the balance sheet. This is unusual, internationally. In the UK and the US, a group would take such an adjustment direct to reserves. The survey of Japanese financial reporting (Gray *et al.* 1984) found that only half the groups complied with the BADC requirement. The other half took the exchange gains or losses to the profit and loss account. So it seems that the BADC's novel approach to the treatment of exchange gains and losses has yet to meet with widespread acceptance in Japan.

7.6 Other Financial Reporting Issues

This section deals with four financial reporting issues that are of interest in the Japanese context. For the first two issues, inflation accounting and segmental reporting, the level of disclosure in Japan falls some way short of that in the UK and the US. In the second two issues, cash flow statements and forecasts, Japan is perhaps ahead of the UK and the US.

Inflation Accounting

There is no legal or professional requirement in Japan to publish any form of inflation accounting information. Japanese companies rarely provide any voluntary disclosures of how price level changes have affected their business performance or financial position. Inflation accounting has not been the major issue in Japan that it has been in the English-speaking world.

Recent inflation rates of three to four per cent a year may have influenced the Japanese attitude to inflation accounting. However, in the mid-1970s, inflation reached over twenty per cent, and this caused the Ministry of Finance to ask the BADC to consider the topic. The BADC issued its opinion on accounting for price changes in 1980, by which time the inflation rate had fallen to a more acceptable level. The BADC opinion recognised that the historical cost approach had its limitations, but concluded that it was to be preferred to any form of inflation accounting. The main reason for the BADC's conclusion was that no other country had satisfactorily resolved the practical problems of inflation accounting. The BADC recommended that the issue should continue to receive attention from all interested parties. However, it seems unlikely that Japan will adopt any form of inflation accounting in the near future.

Segmental Reporting

There is no requirement in Japan for a company to disclose any segmental data in its financial statements or notes. However, a company that reports under the Securities and Exchange Law should include certain unaudited segmental data in the non-financial supplemental schedules that the company files with the Ministry of Finance. The segmental data required is a breakdown of sales by product categories and a breakdown of exports by geographical area. So from a UK or a US perspective, the amount of segmental data required is relatively low, and is given relatively little prominence in the annual report. In practice, many companies apparently ignore even the minimal segmental reporting requirements that exist, and very few companies disclose segmental data beyond that specified in the requirements. Cairns (1984) considers that segmental reporting is the second major problem area in Japanese reports (the first being consolidation). He comments that almost all Japanese companies fall short of international standards, and sees little hope that the recent international accounting standard will have much effect in Japan.

The International Accounting Bulletin (1984) survey of international financial statements considered that Japan was one of the countries that had shown the most significant improvement in the past three to five years. However, the survey commented that inflation accounting and segmental reporting were very poor.

Cash Flow Statements

There is no requirement in Japan to publish a funds statement (referred to in the US as a statement of changes in financial position). However, there is a requirement to disclose extensive cash flow information in the non-financial supplementary schedules filed with the Ministry of Finance. The level of compliance with this requirement is generally high. The format of the cash flow statement normally bears little relation to a typical UK funds statement. For example, a Japanese cash flow statement normally does not attempt to provide a link between the profit for the year and the changes in net liquid funds. It usually includes several categories of cash payments, such as for raw materials, for labour, for other expenses, for plant and equipment and for loan repayments. Typical categories of cash receipts include receipts from sales, from short-term borrowings and from long-term borrowings. A company must disclose the relevant information on a quarterly basis, as well as in total for the year. It must also disclose the cash balance at the beginning and end of each quarter. Few UK companies disclose the level of cash flow information included by a typical Japanese company in its report to the Ministry of Finance. The requirement to disclose quarterly cash flow data is relatively unusual in international terms.

Forecasts

A Japanese company that reports under the Securities and Exchange Law must provide quantified forecasts of *new capital investment, production* and *cash flows* in the supplementary non-financial schedules filed with the Ministry of Finance. The forecasts need not be audited, but the level of compliance with the requirements is generally high. The forecast of new capital investment includes details of the company's capital expenditure plans as at the balance sheet date, the amounts budgeted on each major project, and the amounts spent to date on each major project. The forecast of production covers the six months after the balance sheet date, and some companies provide a forecast for each of the first two three-month periods. Companies normally disaggregate the forecast by line of business, and will prepare it either in units (such as number of auto-mobiles or tons of steel) or in monetary amounts. The forecast of cash flows covers the six months after the balance sheet date and, as before, some companies provide it for the relevant two quarters. Many prepare it using the same headings as in the cash flow statement referred to earlier. The Japanese requirements for forecast reporting are relatively extensive in international terms. A Japanese company that reports under the Securities and Exchange Law must disclose details of what projects it intends to invest in, what the investment projects will produce, and how it intends to finance them.

Average Ratios

As a commentary on all the information that has been considered already, it is instructive to look at some average ratios for Japanese industrial companies. In Table 7.1 there is a comparison for five ratios between Japan and the US. The startling difference in size of ratios is partly a reflection of real economic differences and partly caused by accounting differences. For example, the higher debt ratio and lower liquidity of Japanese companies can be justified in a country where banks are major providers of finance and are closely related to their customers. However,

Table 7.1   Japanese and US Industrial Ratios

	Current ratio	Quick ratio	Debt ratio	Times int earned	Return on net worth
USA	1.9	1.1	0.5	6.5	0.14
Japan	1.2	0.8	0.8	1.6	0.07

Source: Choi (1983).

the lower return on net worth in Japan is probably substantially due to accounting differences.

7.7   Summary

The government is the main influence in the financial reporting environment in Japan. There are three distinct sources of government influence, namely, the Commercial Code, the Securities and Exchange Law and the tax regulations. These three sources represent different attitudes to the purposes of financial statements. The accounting profession in Japan is relatively small and has little influence on financial reporting in comparison to the long-established and powerful accounting professions in the UK and the US.

Japan has some accounting requirements and practices that may appear conservative to a UK user of financial statements. For example, Japanese companies always measure fixed assets at historical cost, never at valuation. The most common depreciation method is the reducing balance method, which is more conservative than the straight-line method (because the reducing balance method results in relatively high depreciation charges in the early years of an asset's life). Japanese companies must establish a legal reserve, which is not distributable. Many companies charge expenses in their financial accounts to the full extent permitted by the tax laws, even where this exceeds what is required by prudent accounting principles. These examples of a conservative approach to financial reporting are countered to some extent by accounting practices that may appear relatively unconservative, such as the valuation of inventories at cost rather than at the lower of cost and market value. However, on balance it seems that Japanese accounting principles are conservative, so that asset and profit figures may be understated, particularly compared to those of similar UK companies.

Japanese reporting requirements place a greater emphasis on parent company financial statements than on consolidated financial statements. Only those companies that are publicly traded are required to prepare supplementary consolidated financial statements, and the Japanese approach to foreign currency translation may appear unusual to Anglo-Saxon accountants.

In international terms, disclosure of inflation accounting information and of segmental data is relatively poor in Japan. However, the quality of cash flow reporting and of forecast reporting is relatively high.

The overall quality of financial reporting in Japan seems to have improved over the last decade or so. In particular, some of the large Japanese multinationals now provide a substantial amount of useful information. The desire to raise finance in the international capital markets may be the main influence in the quality of the financial reporting of many of these companies. Although domestic reporting requirements and practices may have improved recently, they are generally considered to be of a lower overall quality for the purposes of investors than are those of countries such as the UK, the US and the Netherlands.

References

American Institute of Certified Public Accountants (1975) *Professional Accounting in 30 Countries*, AICPA, New York.
Ballon, R.J., Tomita, I. and Usami, H. (1976) *Financial Reporting in Japan*, Kodansha International, Tokyo.
Baxter, W.T. (1976) 'Accounting in Japan', *Accountant's Magazine*, November, pp. 433–434.
Cairns, D. (1984) 'What's wrong with Japanese reporting?', *International Accounting Bulletin*, March, pp. 18–19.
Campbell, L.G. (1983) 'Current accounting practices in Japan', *Accountant's Magazine*, August, pp. 303–306.
Campbell, L.G. (1985) *International Auditing*, Macmillan.
Choi, F.D.S. *et al.* (1983) 'Analysing foreign financial statements: the use and misuse of international ratio analysis', *Journal of International Business Studies*, Spring.
Financial Times (1984) *World Accounting Survey 1984*, by Stilling, P., Norton, R. and Hopkins, L., FT Business Information, London.
Gray, S.J., Campbell, L.G. and Shaw, J.C. (eds) (1984) *International Financial Reporting*, Macmillan.
International Accounting Bulletin (1984) *Survey of Accounts and Accountants 1983–84*, by Cairns, D., Lafferty, M. and Mantle, P., Lafferty Publications, London.
Times 1000 1984–85 (1984), Times Books, London.
Watson, T.S. (1982) 'Accounting in Japan: regulation and practice', *Journal of Accountancy*, August, pp. 83–85.

Japanese Institute of Certified Public Accountants (1982) *Corporate Disclosure in Japan*, JICPA, Tokyo.

Further Reading

Dale, B. (1979) 'Accounting in Japan', *Australian Accountant*, April.

Katsuyama, S. (1976) 'Recent problems of the financial accounting system in Japan', *International Journal of Accounting*, Fall.

McKinnon, J.L. (1984) 'Application of Anglo-American principles of consolidation to corporate financial disclosure in Japan', *Abacus*, June.

Appendix 7
Uniform Formats for Japanese Financial Statements According to the JICPA

Balance Sheet

as of March 31, 198X

ASSETS

Current assets
    Cash on hand and in banks
    Notes receivable, trade
    Accounts receivable, trade
    Marketable securities
    Short-term loans
    Finished goods
    Work in progress
    Raw materials and supplies
    Prepaid expenses
    Other current assets

Fixed assets
    Tangible fixed assets
        Buildings and structures
        Machinery and equipment
        Vehicles
        Furniture and fixtures
        Land
        Construction in progress

    Intangible fixed assets
        Land rights
        Goodwill

    Investments and other
        Stock of subsidiaries
        Other investments in securities
        Long-term loans

Deferred charges
    Start-up costs
    Research and development costs
    Expenses of debt issues

Total assets

LIABILITIES

Current liabilities
    Notes payable, trade
    Accounts payable, trade
    Short-term loans
    Current portion of long-term loans
    Accounts payable other than trade
    Accrued expenses
    Accrued income taxes
    Withheld payroll taxes
    Unearned income
    Reserve for product guarantee
    Reserve for sales returns
    Other current liabilities

Long-term liabilities
    Bonds payable
    Employees' retirement and
        termination allowances

SHAREHOLDERS' EQUITY

Capital stock
Statutory reserves
    Capital reserve
    Legal reserve
Retained earnings
    General purpose appropriation
    Unappropriated
    (Net income of current period)

Total liabilities and shareholders' equity

Income Statement

for the year ended 31 March, 198X

Ordinary Profit and Loss Section
  Operating Profit and Loss Section
    Sales
    Cost of sales
    Selling, general and administrative expenses
      Operating profit (loss)
  Non-operating Income and Expense Section
    Non-operating income
    Interest income
    Dividend income
    Miscellaneous income
  Non-operating Expenses
    Interest expense and bank discount
    Miscellaneous expenses
      Ordinary profit (loss)
Special Gain and Loss Section
  Special Gains
    Prior period adjustment
    Gain from sale of fixed assets
  Special Losses
    Prior period adjustments
    Loss from disposition of fixed assets
      Income before income taxes
  Income Taxes
      Net income (loss)
  Unappropriated retained earnings (deficit), beginning
  Mid-year dividend
  Transfer to earnings reserve with respect to mid-year dividend
      Unappropriated retained earnings (deficit), ending

Proposal for Appropriations of Retained Earnings

for the year ended March 31, 198X

Unappropriated retained earnings (deficit), ending
  (This will be appropriated as indicated below)

  Earnings reserve
  Dividend (XX   per share)
  Directors' bonus
  General purpose appropriation

  Unappropriated retained earnings (deficit) to be carried forward to next year

8

International Classification of Financial Reporting

CHRISTOPHER NOBES

The previous chapters have discussed financial accounting practices in a number of important countries. This chapter is devoted to an examination of whether it is possible to classify these and other accounting systems. First, it is useful to discuss the nature of classification in natural sciences and social sciences. Secondly, the purpose of classification in accounting and the suggestions of various researchers are looked at. Finally, we draw our own conclusions about a possible classification system.

8.1 The Nature of Classification

Classification is one of the basic tools of a scientist. The Mendeleev table of elements and the Linnaean system of classification are fundamental to chemistry and biology. Classification should sharpen description and analysis. It should reveal underlying structures and enable prediction of the properties of an element based on its place in a classification. Classification may also provide an insight into what elements once existed, might exist in the future, or do exist and wait to be discovered.

It has been said that there are four properties necessary in a classification (AAA 1977, pp. 77 – 78). First, the characteristics of a classification should be adhered to consistently. That is, throughout any classification the characteristics used as the means of differentiating one element from another should be the same. Different purposes for a classification will

174

lead to the use of different characteristics. Secondly, a good classification will contain sufficient subsets to exhaust a given universe. Thirdly, all subsets will be mutually exclusive in such a way that no element may fall into more than one of them. Lastly, hierarchical integrity should be observed. For example, in the Linnaean biological classification, any specific *species* of plant or animal is always in the bottom tier of the classification, always belongs to a *genus*, which always belongs to a *family*, and so on.

Different types of classification are possible, from the simplest form of dichotomous grouping (e.g. things black versus things white) or rank ordering (e.g. by height of students in a class) to more complex dimensioning (like the periodic table) or systematising (like the Linnaean system). Two ways of grouping elements used in social science are 'multi-dimensional scaling' and 'morphological structuring'. The first uses two or more characteristics on different axes to try to find clusters of elements displaying similar characteristics. The second seeks to compose a 'morphology' which lists elements by important differentiating factors. It should then be clearer which elements are similar to each other (see, for example, Figure 8.1).

8.2   Classifications by Social Scientists

Having looked at the nature of classification and the techniques used to achieve it, it may be useful to examine traditional methods of classification in areas close to accounting. There have been classifications of political, economic and legal systems. For example, political systems have been grouped into political democracies, tutelary democracies, modernising oligarchies, totalitarian oligarchies and traditional oligarchies (Shils 1966). Economic systems have been divided into capitalism, socialism, communism and fascism. A more recent classification is: traditional economies, market economies and planned economies (Neuberger and Duffy 1976). Legal systems have also been classified (Kagan 1955; Derrett 1968; David and Brierley 1978).

One set of authors, while classifying legal systems, has supplied practical criteria for determining whether two systems are in the same group. Systems are said to be in the same group if 'someone educated in . . . one law will then be capable, without much difficulty, of handling [the other]' (David and Brierley 1978, p. 20). Such a suggestion is made about the UK and the USA at the beginning of Chapter 2. Also, the two systems must not be 'founded on opposed philosophical, political or economic principles'. The second criterion ensures that systems in the same group not only have similar superficial characteristics, but also have similar fundamental structures and are likely to react to new circumstances in similar ways. Using these criteria a four-group classification was obtained: Romano – Germanic, Common Law, Socialist and Philosophical – Religious.

In all the above examples, the type of classification used was rudimentary, involving no more than splitting systems into a few groups. The groups within the classifications were sometimes not precisely defined nor exhaustive. Also, the method used to determine and fill the groups was little more than subjective classification based on personal knowledge or descriptive literature. These shortcomings are very difficult to avoid because of the complexity and 'greyness' in the social sciences.

8.3　Financial Reporting 'Systems'

The reasons for wanting to classify financial reporting 'systems' into groups include the general reasons for classification in any science, as outlined above. In this case, classification should be an efficient way of describing and comparing different systems. It should help to chart the progress of one system as it moves from one group to another, and the progress of ideas of a dominant country's system by noting the other national systems grouped around it. The activity involved in preparing a classification (for example, multi-dimensional scaling or morphological structuring, as referred to above) should encourage precision. Moreover, in the social sciences, classification may be used to help shape development rather than merely to describe how and why things are. For example, classification should facilitate a study of the logic of and the difficulties facing harmonisation. This should be valuable both for academics and for those organising harmonisation. Classification should also assist in the training of accountants and auditors who operate internationally. Further, a developing country might be better able to understand the available types of financial reporting, and which one would be most appropriate for it, by studying a morphology and seeing which other countries use particular systems. Also, it should be possible for a country to predict the problems that it is about to face and the solutions that might work by looking at other countries in its group.

It has also been suggested that a way of changing from one accounting system to another may be to adjust the economic and political parameters to those more conducive to the desired system (AAA 1977, p. 100). However, this might seem like trying to wag a tail by moving the dog.

Early Classification and Recent Description

Early attempts at classification and more recent descriptions of different national systems form the background to modern classifications. Of the former, there is evidence for a three-group classification (UK, US and Continental) being used from the beginning of the twentieth century (Hatfield, reprinted 1966). More recent descriptions and analyses like those by Zeff (1972), Price Waterhouse (1973, 1975 and 1979) and the AICPA (1964 and 1975) provide the raw material for classification.

Mueller's Classifications

In the late 1960s, Professor Gerhard Mueller broke new ground by preparing suggested international classifications of financial reporting (Mueller 1967) and of business environments (Mueller 1968). His classification of accounting systems into four patterns of development is a simple grouping which is not accompanied by an explanation of the method used to obtain it. However, the 'range of four is considered sufficient to embrace accounting as it is presently known and practised in various parts of the globe' (Mueller 1967, p. 2). Each group is illustrated by one or two examples. It may well be that it is not reasonable to expect a more sophisticated classification, particularly in a pioneering work, and that Mueller's informed judgment was one of the best methods of classification available.

Mueller stresses that the types of accounting rules which exist in a country are a product of economic, political and other environments, which have determined the nature of the system. This also suggests that other countries' rules would not be appropriate to that country and that rules must be chosen to fit a country's needs. Consequently, doubt is cast on the possibility and usefulness of harmonisation.

Mueller's four groups, which are usefully summarised in a later work (Choi and Mueller 1984), are:

1. *Accounting within a Macroeconomic Framework.* In this case, accounting has developed as an adjunct of national economic policies. We might expect such financial accounting to stress value-added statements, to encourage income smoothing, to be equivalent to tax accounting and to include social responsibility accounting. Sweden is said to be an example.
2. *The Microeconomic Approach.* This approach can prosper in a market-oriented economy which has individual private businesses at the core of its economic affairs. The influence of microeconomics has led accounting to try to reflect economic reality in its measurements and valuations. This means that accounting rules must be sophisticated but flexible. Developments like replacement cost accounting will be accepted most readily in such systems. The Netherlands is suggested as an example.
3. *Accounting as an Independent Discipline.* Systems of this sort have

developed independently of governments or economic theories. Accounting has developed in business, has faced problems when they arrived and has adopted solutions which worked. Theory is held in little regard and turned to only in emergencies or used *ex post* in an attempt to justify practical conclusions. Expressions such as 'generally accepted accounting principles' are typical. Mueller recognises the accounting systems of the United Kingdom and the United States as examples.

4. *Uniform Accounting*. Such systems have developed where governments have used accounting as a part of the administrative control of business. Accounting can be used to measure performance, allocate funds, assess the size of industries and resources, control prices, collect taxation, manipulate sectors of business, and so on. It involves standardisation of definitions, measurements and presentation. France is cited as an example.

Mueller was not classifying financial reporting systems directly, on the basis of differences in *practices*, but indirectly, on the basis of differences in the importance of economic, governmental and business factors in the development of particular systems. However, one might expect that systems which have developed in a similar way would have similar accounting practices. To an extent, this is true. The early chapters of this book have suggested that the UK and US have similar accounting practices. Mueller's developmental classification also puts them together.

Nevertheless, there are a few problems with Mueller's classification. The fact that there are only four exclusive groups and no hierarchy reduces the usefulness of the classification. In effect, the Netherlands is the only country in one of the groups and the classification does not show whether Dutch accounting is closer to Anglo-Saxon accounting than it is to Swedish accounting. Similarly, the classification cannot include such facts as that West German accounting exhibits features which remind one of macroeconomic accounting as well as uniform accounting. Russian or Communist accounting is left out entirely. This may, of course, be sensible if the classification is dealing with published financial reporting.

Mueller's second classification (1968) is of business environments. He makes the point that different business environments need different accounting systems and that this should be considered when trying to change or standardise accounting. Using estimates of economic development, business complexity, political and social climate, and legal system, Mueller identifies ten groupings. This is not a classification of financial reporting and is perhaps too general to be of help in such a classification. For example, one group – 'the developing nations of the Near and Far East' – might be argued by some to *need* similar accounting systems, but it certainly does not have them. Also, the grouping consisting of only Israel and Mexico is surely an example of David and Brierley's second criterion being broken: that is, although these two countries may appear similar at one moment, they have such different underlying political, social, geographical and other factors that to expect them to continue similarly for economic or accounting purposes is wildly optimistic.

Morphologies

It has been mentioned that one way to obtain a classification is to draw up a morphology and to use empirical data with this to obtain clustering. Morphologies of accounting practice have been drawn up by Buckley (1974) and by the AAA (1977, p. 99). The latter's is reproduced as Figure 8.1. Although such parameters as the first two (political and economic systems) may seem less relevant than actual characteristics of accounting practice, it may well be important to include them in order to avoid misclassification based on temporary superficial similarities. As the AAA's Committee on International Accounting notes, 'Parameters P_1 and P_2 ... are viewed as being pivotal to the type of accounting system which does (or can) emerge' (p. 97). Unfortunately, these morphologies have not yet been taken further by combining them with empirical data.

Spheres of Influence

There have been some 'subjective' classifications based on 'spheres of influence'. Seidler (1967) suggested three groups: British, American and continental European. Also, the AAA's committee produced a subjective classification of 'zones of influence' on accounting systems (AAA 1977, pp. 105 and 129–130). These are:

1. British
2. Franco – Spanish – Portuguese
3. German – Dutch
4. US
5. Communist

This classification is referred to in the next chapter which discusses accounting in developing countries. It is perhaps most useful in such a context. It seems less appropriate as a third general method of classifying financial reporting, after the direct (practices) and indirect (environment) approaches mentioned above. This is because it has no hierarchy and thus does not take account, for example, of the links between British

Parameters		States of Nature			
	1	2	3	4	5
P_1 Political system	Traditional oligarchy	Totalitarian oligarchy	Modernizing oligarchy	Tutelary democracy	Political democracy
P_2 Economic system	Traditional	Market	Planned market	Plan	
P_3 Stages of economic development	Traditional society	Pre-take-off	Take-off	Drive to maturity	Mass consumption
P_4 Objectives of financial reporting	◄————— Micro —————	Management performance	Social measurement	►◄ ——— Macro ———► Sector planning & control	National policy objectives
	Investment decisions				
P_5 Source of, or authority for, standards	Executive decree	Legislative action	Government administrative unit	Public – private consortium	Private
P_6 Education, training & licensing	◄——— Public ———►◄ ——— Private ———►				
	Informal	Formal	Informal	Formal	
P_7 Enforcement of ethics & standards	Executive	Government administrative	Judicial	Private	
P_8 Client	Government	Public	◄——— Enterprises ———► Public	Private	

Source: Accounting Review Supplement to vol. 52, 1977, American Accounting Association, p. 99.

Figure 8.1   The AAA's Morphology for Comparative Accounting Systems

and US accounting. Further, to call a group 'German – Dutch' seems very inappropriate as a way of classifying developed financial reporting systems, when examined in the light of the material in Chapters 5 and 6.

Classifications using Clustering

Da Costa, Bourgeois and Lawson (1978) produced a classification directly based on accounting practices, using the Price Waterhouse (1973) *Survey in 38 Countries*. Clustering produced two groups: one contained the UK and nine former members of the British Empire. The other group contained the US, France, Germany, South American countries and all others, except for the Netherlands and Canada which were said to be unclassifiable.

Table 8.1   Classification Based on 1973 Measurement Practices

British Commonwealth model	Latin American model	Continental European model	United States model
Australia	Argentina	Belgium	Canada
Bahamas	Bolivia	France	Japan
Eire	Brazil	Germany	Mexico
Fiji	Chile	Italy	Panama
Jamaica	Columbia	Spain	Philippines
Kenya	Ethiopia	Sweden	United States
Netherlands	India	Switzerland	
New Zealand	Paraguay	Venezuela	
Pakistan	Peru		
Rhodesia	Uruguay		
Singapore			
South Africa			
Trinidad & Tobago			
United Kingdom			

Source: Nair and Frank (1980) p. 429.

Another researcher (Frank 1979) used the same data and similar (though more elaborate) analysis, but produced what seems to be a much more reasonable classification. This work has been extended by Nair and Frank (1980). Here the 1973 and the 1975 Price Waterhouse Surveys are used, and the financial reporting characteristics are divided into those relating to measurment and those relating to disclosure. This is a very useful differentiation, particularly because of the effect it has on the classification of countries like Germany which have advanced disclosure requirements. Frank (1979) classified Germany in a 'US group' but, by using 'measurement' characteristics only, Nair and Frank (1980) classify Germany in the continental European group. Table 8.1 represents the classification using 1973 measurement characteristics. As yet there is no hierarchy, but the overall results do seem very plausible and fit well with the analysis in previous chapters of this book. However, there are two major types of problem with these classifications that must now be dealt with.

The Data

Doubts have been expressed on the use of the Price Waterhouse data for the purpose of classification (Nobes 1981). Four types of problem with the 1973 data were noted: (i) straightforward mistakes; (ii) misleading answers; (iii) swamping of important questions by trivial ones; and (iv) exaggeration of the differences between the USA and the UK because of the familiarity of these countries (and thus their differences) to the compilers of the survey questions. The examples from the 1973 survey will not be repeated here, but a few errors in the 1979 survey will be mentioned.

Taking consolidation practices as an example, the survey reports that for practice 209 ('consolidated statements . . . are prepared for the shareholders') the answer is 'required' in France. The reason given for this is that the *Commission des Opérations de Bourse* (COB) 'requires' consolidation. However, as the Annual Report of COB shows, only 305 listed companies published consolidated balance sheets and profit and loss accounts in 1979 (289 in 1978). This is less than half of the listed companies, and a very much smaller proportion of 'enterprises which issue their statements to the general public', about which the survey is said to be (Price Waterhouse 1979, p. 5). Further, one wonders whether consolidation practices in Fiji, Malaysia or Trinidad are really correctly understood by suggestions in various survey practices that Standard No. 3 of the IASC (1976) is being followed.

These examples could be replicated many times over. They suggest that, at some points, the surveys report not on actual practices but on what practices might be if non-mandatory rules were obeyed or on what Price Waterhouse partners might like practices to be. This and the other types of error might suggest that the data are unsatisfactory for the purposes of classification. At the very least, substantial caution is called for when interpreting the results.

The Methodology

All the researchers cited above use cluster analysis based on the Price Waterhouse data, and appear to consider that this may be superior to previous subjective classifications. Nair and Frank state that their research is '. . . aimed at empirically assessing the validity of international classifications proposed repeatedly in the accounting literature' (p. 449).

This version of 'empiricism' must be challenged. It does not directly test a particular hypothetical classification. It classifies a mass of data which was not collected with this purpose in mind. The use of this approach leads one of the sets of researchers referred to above (da Costa *et al.* 1978, p. 79) to conclude that the country least like the UK group is the USA. In other words, accounting in Uruguay or Ethiopia is more like accounting in the UK than accounting in the USA is. While this may be a statistically sound result from the Price Waterhouse data, is is clearly a very inaccurate representation of the real world (see Chapters 2 and 3; also Mueller 1967). By itself such a result is of interest, but the researchers, who were generating a hypothesis from doubtful data rather than testing one, fell into the trap of taking their results seriously. This led them to the conclusion that a group of countries containing France, West Germany, Belgium and Italy, among others, 'follows the lead of the United States in dissociating itself from practice common to the British model'. However, it seems highly unlikely that the makers of the detailed and rigid company and tax laws that govern accounting in such countries bear in mind either that they should follow the USA or that they should dissociate themselves from the UK when legislating. The differences between the USA and continental European countries are great, and also suggest that there is no accidental or subconscious 'following' of the former by the latter (Chapters 4 and 5; and Mueller 1967).

The problem that these examples illustrate stems from the use of data which contain errors and which were not designed for the purpose in hand. Turning to the Linnaean biological system for an analogy to the extent that subjectivity and empiricism can be counterposed, the life scientists use a large measure of the former. Exactly which criteria to use for a classification of living things, and what weight to give them, is a matter of judgement. Judgement is needed to avoid such classifications as Plato's of man as a featherless biped. In fact, man is now seen to be much more closely related to most quadrupeds, and to dolphins which appear to have no feet at all. Aristotle saw this latter distinction. He referred to homologues, where organs similar in structure play different roles (e.g. human feet and dolphins' flippers), and to analogues where similar functions are performed by quite different organs (e.g. birds' wings and bees' wings, which have entirely different structures, the former being 'arms'). It is the homologues which indicate nearness.

Looking in more detail at the Linnaean biological classification one notes that, when classifying plants or animals, biologists largely ignore the most obvious characteristics. That is, they do not carry out factor analysis on animals by weight, colour, number of legs, nature of body covering, length of life, etc. This would merely lead to a classification of those data. It would put men with ostriches, dolphins with sharks, bats with owls, and so on. In fact, by concentrating on a subjective model which involves underlying (but less obvious) characteristics, biologists classify men, dolphins and bats more closely with each other than with any of the other three types of animal. It is then found that behaviour, intelligence, reproduction and ancestry begin to fit within the classification. The biological scientists, then, use a classification which is evolutionary and concentrates on underlying fundamental variables.

The analogy with classification in accounting seems clear. The danger with 'empirical' classifications is that one merely classifies data which concentrate on differences which may be ephemeral and superficial (and which may not be correctly recorded). The need is apparent for a model based on the evolution of accounting practices and upon variables which have caused differences in them. This needs to be checked against carefully measured 'structural' practices.

8.4   A Hypothetical Classification

Thus, it would be possible to criticise previous classifications for (i) lack of precision in the definition of what is to be classified; (ii) lack of a model with which to compare the statistical results; (iii) lack of hierarchy which would add more subtlety to the portrayal of the size of differences between countries; and (iv) lack of judgement in the choice of 'important' discriminating features. Can these problems be remedied? The author has attempted to solve them in his own researches (Nobes 1983).

Definition

The purpose of the research was defined as the classification of countries by the financial reporting practices of their *public companies*. The countries chosen were those of the *developed Western world*; the reporting practices were those concerned with *measurement and valuation*. The date of the classification was 1980, before the enactments in EEC countries of the fourth Directive on Company Law (see section 14.4).

It is public companies whose financial statements are generally available and whose practices can be most easily discovered. It is the international differences in reporting between such companies which are of interest to shareholders, creditors, auditing firms, taxation authorities, managements and harmonising agencies (like the International Accounting Standards Committee or the EEC Commission) (Mason 1978, Chapter 5). It is really only in developed Western countries that public companies exist in large numbers. It has been mentioned above that the Price Waterhouse data seem to suffer from the difficulties of holding this factor constant across their very broad coverage.

Measurement and valuation practices were chosen because these determine the size of the figures for profit, capital, total assets, liquidity and so on. Nair and Frank (1980, pp. 426 and 428) point out that it is useful to separate measurement from disclosure practices.

This definition of the geographical scope of the classification is obviously limited, though for good reasons. However, it would be possible to try to include more countries by widening the definition of accounting. To some extent this has been tried (Nobes 1984).

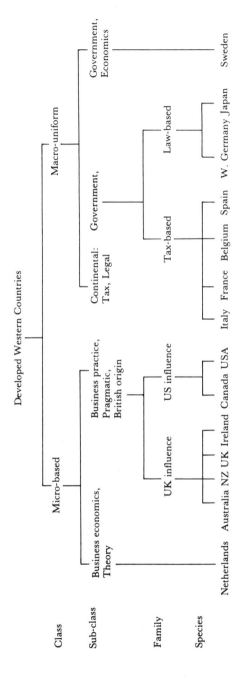

Figure 8.2   A Hypothetical Classification of Financial Reporting Measurement Practices in Developed Western Countries in 1980

A Model with a Hierarchy

The hypothetical classification shown as Figure 8.2 was based on the evolution of accounting, and the suggestions of many academics interested in comparative accounting. Some explanatory variables for differences in measurement practices were also borne in mind when drawing up this proposed classification; for example, the importance of the influence of law or of economics. Some descriptions are included at the branching points in Figure 8.2.

The number of countries is kept to fourteen, but all these are developed nations; they are all included in the Price Waterhouse Surveys and thus in the results of the above researchers; and they include all the countries identified as 'vital' by Mason (1978, Chapter 6) for the purposes of international harmonisation (i.e. France, Japan, Netherlands, UK, USA and West Germany).

Previously classifications have contained separate groups (e.g. Table 8.1) but no hierarchy which would indicate the comparative distances between the groups. It may well be reasonable to classify the UK and the USA in different groups, but it might be useful to demonstrate that these two groups are closely linked compared to, say, continental European countries. The classification in Figure 8.2 contains a hierarchy which borrows its labels from biology.

Discriminating Features

An attempt has been made to isolate those features of a country's financial reporting practices which may constitute long-run fundamental differences between countries. The result has been a selection of nine factors which, unlike the factors of most of the researchers above, are overt and thus available for inspection, criticism and amendment (see Table 8.2).

These factors are designed to operate for developed Western countries which share certain economic features. If one wished to include developing countries or Eastern bloc countries, it would be necessary to include other discriminating factors, like degree of development of economy or nature of economic systems. But such a process might not be sensible because there are few or no public companies in these other countries, so that one would have to classify something other than published financial reporting.

It was not a straightforward matter to separate measurement practices from explanatory variables. However, it was clear that at least the first two factors in Table 8.2 were examples of explanatory variables. Other factors were less clear. For example, the 'taxation' factor could have been taken as a factor explaining differences or, by asking whether particular valuations were affected by tax rules, it could have been seen as a

Table 8.2   Factors for Differentiation

---

1. Type of users of the published accounts of the listed companies
2. Degree to which law or standards prescribe in detail and exclude judgement
3. Importance of tax rules in measurement
4. Conservatism/prudence (e.g. valuation of buildings, stocks, debtors)
5. Strictness of application of historic cost (in the historic cost accounts)
6. Susceptibility to replacement cost adjustments in main or supplementary accounts
7. Consolidation practices
8. Ability to be generous with provisions (as opposed to reserves) and to smooth income
9. Uniformity between companies in application of rules

---

measurement practice. All the factors except the first two were taken in this latter sense.

The fourteen countries were scored on these nine factors, and then a large number of alternative arithmetical and computer-based tests were used to produce clusters. Very strong support was found for the 'micro/macro' split in Figure 8.2, and considerable support for the more detailed groupings (Nobes 1983).

8.5   Summary

Classification is of fundamental importance to natural scientists, and has also been used in many social sciences. It seems reasonable that we might gain from a classification exercise in comparative international accounting, and that similar rules of classification to those used by scientists might be appropriate. In accounting, such classification may aid understanding and training, and may help to chart the need for, and progress of, harmonisation.

There have been many attempts at classification in international accounting, and there has been much description and data gathering. Mueller's four-group classification of practices and later classification of environments were useful preliminary works. However, the classification of practices needs a hierarchy.

Other attempts have been made to construct morphologies and to identify zones of influence.

Most recently, attempts have been made to classify using the Price Waterhouse Survey data of 1973–79. The results seem to vary in their plausibility, and there are doubts about the suitability of the data. A new classification has been proposed by the author. This has a detailed hierarchy and has been tested in a number of ways.

References

Buckley, J.W. and Buckley, M.H. (1974) *The Accounting Profession*, Melville, Los Angeles, pp. 139 – 140.

Choi, F.D.S. and Mueller, G.G. (1984) *International Accounting*, Prentice-Hall, Chapter 2.

Da Costa, R.C., Bourgeois, J.C. and Lawson, W.M. (1978) 'A classification of international financial accounting practices', *International Journal of Accounting*, Spring.

David, R. and Brierley, J.E.C. (1978) *Major Legal Systems in the World Today*, Stevens, London.

Derrett, J.D.M. (1968) *An Introduction to Legal Systems*, Sweet and Maxwell.

Frank, W.G. (1979) 'An empirical analysis of international accounting principles', *Journal of Accounting Research*, Autumn.

Hatfield, H.R. (1966) 'Some variations in accounting practices in England, France, Germany and the US', *Journal of Accounting Research*, Autumn.

Kagan, K.K. (1955) *Three Great Systems of Jurisprudence*, Stevens, London.

Mason, A.K. (1978) *The Development of International Reporting Standards*, ICRA, Lancaster University.

Mueller, G.G. (1967) *International Accounting*, Part I, Macmillan.

Mueller, G.G. (1968) 'Accounting principles generally accepted in the US versus those generally accepted elsewhere', *International Journal of Accounting*, Spring.

Nair, R.D. and Frank, W.G. (1980) 'The impact of disclosure and measurement practices on international accounting classifications', *Accounting Review*, July.

Neuberger, E. and Duffy, W. (1976) *Comparative Economic Systems*, Allyn and Bacon, Boston, pp. 96 – 97.

Nobes, C.W. (1981) 'An empirical analysis of international accounting principles: A comment', *Journal of Accounting Research*, Spring.

Nobes, C.W. (1983) 'A judgmental international classification of financial reporting practices', *Journal of Business Finance and Accounting*, Spring.

Nobes, C.W. (1984) *International Classification of Financial Reporting*, Croom Helm, Appendices V and VI.

Price Waterhouse (1973) *Accounting Principles and Reporting Practices: A Survey in 38 Countries*, ICAEW, London.

Price Waterhouse (1975) *Accounting Principles and Reporting Practices: A Survey in 46 Countries*, ICAEW, London.

Price Waterhouse (1979) *International Survey of Accounting Principles and Reporting Practices*, Butterworth.

Shils, E. (1966) *Political Development in the New States*, Mouton, The Hague.

Seidler, L.J. (1966) 'International accounting – the ultimate theory course', *Accounting Review*, October.

Zeff, S.A. (1972) *Forging Accounting Principles in Five Countries*, Stipes Publishing, Champaign, Illinois.

AAA (1977) *Accounting Review, Supplement to Vol. 52*, American Accounting Association.

AICPA (1964) *Professional Accounting in 25 Countries*, AICPA, New York.

AICPA (1975) *Professional Accounting in 30 Countries*, AICPA, New York.

IASC (1976) *Consolidated Financial Statements*, IASC, London.

9

Accounting in Developing Countries

ADOLF ENTHOVEN

This chapter deals with accounting in Third World or developing economies. To evaluate effectively the structure and process of accounting in so-called 'developing economies', it will be useful to consider first of all two fundamental questions: (1) what is the nature of development? and (2) what is the significance and role of accounting in development? Subsequently, it will be beneficial to look at some prevailing accounting systems in developing countries, to analyse their causes and to see to what extent these 'systems' are performing a relevant socioeconomic task.

9.1 The Nature of Development

The prevalent concept of development is that it constitutes economic growth plus structural, social and economic change; structural change being composed of a whole series of social, political, legal, administrative, organisational, educational, institutional, psychological, cultural and ethical factors. According to some, structural social and economic change may be closely identified with social justice or even liberation, that is, liberation from all sorts of restrictive and suppressive socioeconomic conditions in a society. These conditions are considered to hamper the full development of man and groups of men, and are therefore regarded as detrimental to socioeconomic development.

Due emphasis should be given to a whole series of social factors and changes which might be prerequisites for rapid economic advancement to attain increased living conditions. The two aspects of development – economic and social – complement each other, and need to be integrated further into a more unified approach to guarantee sustained socio-economic development. Consequently, economic development cannot be expressed in purely quantitative economic terms alone, or be solely the working area of economists. It is a transformation process of the economy and society composed of a whole series of interlocking influences.

Economic growth by itself may be considered as principally an economic matter, referring to the annual real increase in average per capita income or output; it does not automatically lead to structural, social and economic improvements. However, many regard economic growth as synonymous with economic development on the premise that growth is fundamental to progress. But many developing countries have 'grown' economically in a satisfactory way, without having been adequately 'developed'. Therefore, *growth* may well be characterised as being more of an endogenous evolutionary process, a quantitative increase in per capita income; whilst *development* also involves exogenous factors to stimulate growth, being a process of induced change leading towards a new or better socioeconomic system.

Accordingly, economic development can be considered to be (1) a country's ability to increase its per capita income or production – i.e. a transitional process between economic stagnation and economic progress; and (2) the ability to execute a series of structural, social and economic changes and improvements – a transformation process, e.g. more equitable income distribution, improved medical services and housing, enhanced education and training, and greater employment.

Economic development can be analysed and planned by various forms of 'models'. Quantitative economic (econometric) model building helps us to know more about the working of an economy and to project systematically its structure. Accounting information systems play an important part in these economic models.

9.2   The Scope and Function of Accounting in Development

When studying development, accounting is generally identified with enterprise accounting, and therein mainly with financial accounting and auditing. Other significant versions or systems of accounting, such as management accounting, government accounting (covering public sector administration) and national income accounting (covering the national accounts) receive less attention. Auditing weaves through these accounting systems. The branches or systems of accounting (enterprise, government and national) not only play a significant role separately, but

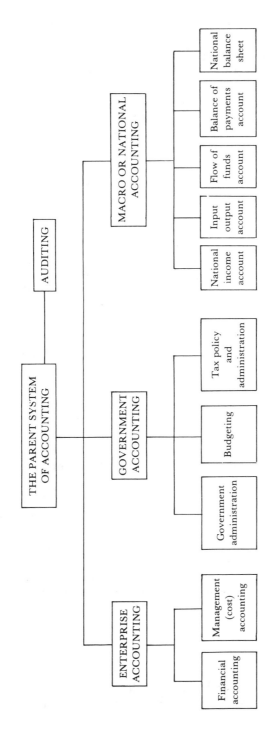

Figure 9.1 The Accounting Information Measurement System

in essence are interrelated (see Figure 9.1). Although these branches serve distinct economic functions, they work with the same raw materials, i.e. the phenomena taking place in our socioeconomic environment. They are based upon certain common accounting fundamentals and techniques, e.g. the cash and accrual system, the double entry approach, measurement criteria. Our concept of accounting also covers the vital aspect of control (auditing), and although the latter forms a separate body of knowledge, we shall treat it as part of accounting. Thus 'accounting' is an information measurement, reporting and control system covering both micro and macro economic activities.

'Accounting' has to be in tune with the economic framework in which it operates and with the socioeconomic requirements of society. Accordingly, we will have to look at accounting in a broader framework, as the identification, selection, analysis, measurement, prediction, processing, evaluation, communication and control of information about costs and benefits (both of a direct and indirect nature) to facilitate decisions about activities and resources. This concept covers private and public sector activities, and serves the micro and macro accounts. Furthermore, this broader framework is not geared only to enterprise income measurement, as the costs and benefits cover a wide range of socioeconomic activities (of a past, current and prospective nature), including measurements of externalities. Such an approach requires a sounder and more integrated theoretical foundation, for it is fair to say that we do not have as yet in accounting a coherent and economically relevant theory. (We have a series of so-called 'theories', most of them based upon practice-oriented rules or standards, but void of both inductive and deductive reasoning.)

9.3   Accounting Techniques in the Development Process

Accounting plays a significant role in measuring economic activities, and in the design of development plans and policies. We shall look at some methods and techniques applied, such as macroeconomic planning; microeconomic feasibility studies; capital formation; tax policy and administration; and accounting standardisation. We shall briefly look at these elements and the significance of accounting methods therein.

Macroeconomic Planning

Most countries require some form of economic planning or programming to allocate effectively and efficiently human, financial and material resources. For macro planning, specific measurement tools and procedures are required. These are:

(i) *Capital coefficients.* These reflect the relationship between capital formation (investment) and the resulting annual growth of the real national product. They serve as a guide for economic policy. In computing gross net or marginal capital coefficients, the composition and value of such items as fixed asets, inventories and output are of vital concern and standardised methods are desirable.

(ii) *Input – output analysis.* This is considered here since dynamic input – output models form an important element of planning. Dynamic models reflect cost inputs and outputs on a standardised basis, preferably applying current value criteria.

(iii) *Shadow prices.* These are the values of production factors under conditions in which a market equilibrium could exist and investment plans could be executed. These shadow or accounting prices portray society's preference for, and the relative scarcity of, factors of production. They constitute an important tool in framing a development plan. Accounting can supply more standardised information on the values of these factors of production.

Deficiencies in measurement and inconsistent or non-standardised data used as input for these tools may have serious economic implications.

Microeconomic Planning

A microeconomic plan consists of a series of projects which require the compilation of information relating to the production of specific goods and services. The feasibility and justifiability of such micro plans must be appraised because they are the building blocks for the macro plans.

The most rational basis for project decision making is sought. Project appraisal requires extensive present and future data, and direct and indirect quantifications and measurements. Extensive cost – benefit calculations and evaluations are incorporated in the decision model, which requires information that is economically realistic, comprehensive and standardised. The use of standard costs and tables is both desirable and feasible when, for example, relating labour input to production process, raw material requirements to tons of production, or power to scale of output. Unified investment and operating data of this sort improve the reliability of product studies. In this regard, greater uniformity of the classification system itself is required. Erroneous information may cause wrong project investment decisions. Many enterprise accounting methods are applied in this microeconomic planning phase.

Capital Formation and Capital Markets

Corporate growth, and the corporate form of organisation which enables smaller savings to be accumulated in the capital market, make heavy demands on legal, fiscal and accounting procedures. Accounting and auditing have to meet these demands; and company statements have to be reliable, helping to instil confidence in corporate operations. The necessary funds might not be forthcoming if accounting and auditing standards and practices were inadequate. The need for sound accounting, however, is not limited to the larger corporate entities. Small-scale operations might be in even greater need. The requirements of small-scale industry are too often neglected, and this can have serious repercussions on a country's potential for economic growth.

Investment by suppliers of capital presupposes an accurate financial description of the performance and potentialities of the company concerned. The evaluation of capital formation projects requires sound cost and financial accounting. With proper procedures, accurate projections may be made of the sources and applications of funds (cash flow), and the necessary feasibility studies may be made. Accounting helps to shape the climate of capital formation; well-devised systems and controls inspire investor confidence, which in turn leads to healthy growth. Thus, the role of accounting in capital formation is two-fold: first, it generates sufficient investor confidence to stimulate the flow of capital, and secondly it helps ensure the continued efficient use of capital once this has been accumulated.

In developing countries, domestic savings for long-term investment are generally in short supply. Inadequate savings may be caused by low income and inequitable income distribution, poor investment opportunities and conditions, and other institutional factors. Changes which are institutional, legal, sociocultural or ecotechnical in nature may be necessary to improve capital market mechanisms and to mobilise domestic and foreign funds into productive activities. Intermediary financial institutions can contribute greatly to better capital flows. They act not only as sources and catalysts for investment, but also provide all kinds of technical assistance, including sorely needed help in various fields of accounting.

Capital formation and development finance would clearly benefit from the professionalisation of accounting and auditing. The patronage of government and development institutions may be necessary to persuade the accounting profession to address itself to the problem and the challenges of the process of capital formation and economic development.

Closely related to capital formation and capital market enhancement in developing countries is the influential role of development banks. The role of accounting in development finance (banking) can be separated into *direct* and *indirect* functions.

Looking at the area where *direct* accounting concentration is feasible and viable, we may distinguish two such areas: internal accounting by the financial institutions and accounting at enterprises financed by them. In addition, accounting has certain general tasks in development finance:

1. satisfactory financial reporting and meaningful full and fair disclosure, for internal and external purposes, supported by sound accounting legislation, methods and practices;
2. ensuring that funds are distributed according to priority criteria, involving effective cost – benefit measurements;
3. granting accounting assistance to firms and institutions in order to help their financial and micro- and macro-economic appraisals (see Enthoven 1982).

Tax Policy and Administration

Taxation consists of two closely linked areas: tax structure formulation (including tax policy) and tax administration. Taxation has to be appraised from the points of view of equity, consistency, sound economic impact, elasticity and feasibility. Tax structure formulation, which requires an understanding of social accounting, should be conducive to capital formation (voluntary or forced). Furthermore, the revenue aspects of taxation should not be analysed independently of expenditure and its socioeconomic effects: unfortunately, too often revenue collection is a sort of 'catch as catch can' practice.

The administrative machinery may have to be strengthened before tax structure reforms and refinements can be executed, and these changes may prove more difficult and time consuming than the structural reforms themselves. Many a good intention by government to enact an equitable tax structure with a minimum of adverse economic effects is hampered by government's inability to implement it. Accounting plays an important role in improving the organisation of both the tax administration and the taxpayer, enabling more equitable and effective tax policies and procedures. Furthermore, accounting is able to assist in appraising the best forms of taxation to achieve the necessary objectives. Accounting techniques, such as information accumulation, measurement, processing, recording and verification (auditing), are all essential to a well-designed tax structure and a smoothly operating tax administration. Closer integration between taxation and accounting undoubtedly will be beneficial to the economic community as a whole and could also predispose governmental policy making to favour the interest of the private sector.

Accounting Standardisation

An aspect which is receiving greater attention in both developing and developed countries is the need for greater standardisation in accounting measurement and reporting. Measurement in turn is composed of quantification, taxonomy and valuation. The latter has received considerable attention in the last decade.

Three broad classifications in regard to valuation can be distinguished: (1) nominalism; (2) price level accounting; and (3) substantialism. The first applies to the measurement and reporting of data at its original (historic) cost. Price level accounting, a form of nominalism, either tries to correct original prices by a general price index or by more specific price indices. Substantialism tends to reflect the real economic value or current cost of transactions, income and wealth. All three forms of valuation are found in practice.

The historic cost model does not fully satisfy the socioeconomic requirements, and price-level accounting and/or current cost accounting also will have to be reflected in the internal and external measurement and reporting system. Current costs tend to portray more clearly and relevantly the economic activities carried out and the results of operations. Current cost (value) information is warranted for effective cost – benefit appraisals, cost calculations, resource allocations, performance assessments, and managerial planning and decision making. It can link the micro and macro accounting sphere, it serves the capital maintenance concept, and it spurs internal and external capital formation.

Various forms and methods of standardisation are feasible and it should, therefore, be made quite clear what it encompasses. Standardisation may involve:

   (i) more uniform application of accounting concepts, principles and rules, reporting procedures and legislation;

  (ii) adherence to more unified charts of accounts and statements, which specify the classification categories by economic units, industries and sectors, and which preferably are applicable on an international scale;

 (iii) greater systematisation of all accounting activities, particularly standardised plans of accounts. (This would not only include the classification charts but also the quantitative and qualitative aspects of data.)

Variations are feasible in each case. Basic procedures and forms of unification need not apply necessarily in the same way to all branches of accounting or to all countries, nor does standardisation need to be rigidly uniform. Some examples which have been met in earlier chapters are:

1. The French *Plan Comptable Général*

   This standardisation plan for enterprises is geared to the whole economic sphere and consists of the following fundamentals: a uniform terminology, a uniform classification of accounts, a standardised method for registration, and general rules of valuation on a historical cost basis. The objectives of the French system are: improvement of fiscal control, systematic information for social accounts and standardisation of presentation in company financial statements.

2. The German Framework of Accounts (*Kontenrahmen*)

   This system includes a standard chart of accounts and flowcharts for industries. The flowcharts present all transactions occurring in an enterprise and are integrated with the chart of accounts. The whole system is micro-oriented for the comparison of industrial data.

3. Standardisation in the USA

   The standardisation of accounting in the United States focuses largely on three aspects: generally accepted accounting principles, the presentation of the account layout, and the uniform pattern of reporting and costing for utilities and certain other industries, as required by federal agencies. The SEC provides a balance sheet model and a profit and loss statement for firms over which it has supervision, and requires strict adherence to this chart.

   The US Cost Accounting Standards Board, part of the US General Accounting Office, has outlined cost accounting standards to achieve comparability, reliability and consistency of cost data for contract purposes, while maintaining equity and adherence to sound accounting principles.

Standards (norms) of an international nature also need to be established. Efforts in this direction are being carried out by the United Nations and the International Accounting Standards Committee (see Chapter 14). The standards need to be linked with a conceptual framework, serving the various subsystems (or branches) of accounting, and must have true international validity. They require a stage, or phase, approach involving *primary* and *secondary* standards, perhaps as follows:

1. The development of certain *primary standards* for international operations, taking into account different economic objectives and circumstances.

2. The development of a set of *secondary standards* depending on regional or country circumstances. For example, standards pertaining to value-added measurement and reporting and the portrayal of indirect costs and benefits play a vital role in many economies. In essence, then, the secondary standards could be developed in

greater coordination with economic regions. Furthermore, different economic development objectives and requirements demand differently oriented standards.

As recently stated by Washington Sycip (Chairman of the International Federation of Accountants):

> Lately there has been considerable discussion on international accounting standards and laudable efforts have been made to harmonize such standards. The concept of harmonization should not mean having to apply a single principle or standard uniformly to all environments or circumstances no matter how different they are, but rather recognising that there could be alternative accounting principles or standards provided particular environments or circumstances present justify such alternative treatment. Areas of differences between developed and developing nations will continue to exist, particularly if the standards are always considered from the viewpoint of acceptability in the US and UK ... Since accounting deals with monetary, business and economic transactions, the stage of economic development of a country seems the more relevant when discussing accounting standards and practices. (Burton 1980)

Our concern should not only be with the development of a *financial accounting* theory and framework, but also with *management accounting* and *government accounting*. As discussed in the next section, there is a great need to set forth concepts, standards, and methods for these distinct branches of accounting, although it is hoped that they can be linked under a parent accounting framework and theory. However, certain concepts and standards may have to vary by economic environment, as the objectives of accounting may diverge (see Enthoven 1982).

9.4   Accounting Structures and Processes

Our review will cover accounting patterns and various factors that have influenced these, such as former colonial accounting practices and legal, professional and educational conditions. First of all, it is necessary to appraise accounting systems from an international comparative point of view.

Comparative Accounting Systems

Classification of systems was discussed in the previous chapter. One method of classification was suggested by the Committee on International Accounting of the AAA (1977). It identifies zones of 'accounting influence' and distinguished five of them:

1. British
2. Franco – Spanish – Portuguese
3. Dutch – German
4. US
5. Communist

Most developing countries, depending upon their historical background and state of economic development, feel one or more accounting zone influences. Knowing the origins of accounting in a country will facilitate a set of potential improvements and changes in its system. Current influences still have a very strong enterprise/financial accounting/stewardship basis, to the neglect of adequate training and practices in such areas as: managerial accounting, systems and procedures, controllership, government accounting and budgeting, national economic accounting and 'economic development accounting'.

Enterprise Accounting

Enterprise accounting lacks relevance in both its current practice and 'theory' in many developing countries (Briston 1978). Practice tends to be stewardship-oriented and geared towards tax, while the 'theory' is just a set of practical rules. Professional accountants may be hired to give tax and/or bookkeeping advice. The requirements of the commercial and tax code may cause accountants to be legal experts, and their expertise in 'real' accounting and control methods consequently may be limited. These requirements undoubtedly have hampered the enhancement of accounting. Assets and liabilities may be reflected inadequately, and the extent of foreign ownership concealed, for taxation, legislative or political purposes. Moreover, a clear segregation may not exist between current and capital items, or among capital items. Income statement details may not be broken down properly. Cash receipts are often confused with accrued sales. Accordingly, the amount of useful information generated by the enterprise accounting system for analysis and decision making is often scanty, unreliable and untimely. Financial statements are sometimes delayed as long as several years. Consequently, the system and its internal and external financial – and audit – reports are not relied upon by investors, bankers, national statistical institutes, government or even management.

In many countries the Companies Acts or other legislative requirements are so detailed that they force accountants to spend a large portion of their time keeping basic records. This limits the opportunity for relevant economic-accounting measurement and reporting tasks and services.

As an example of a structural socioeconomic problem, R. Dominguez, of the Inter-American Development Bank (SID 1976), mentions that accounting has played a rather insignificant role as a source of relevant, adequate and reliable information for analysing the financial condition and the results of enterprises, and as a useful instrument in decision making. He states (pp. 13–15):

> Many sectors of society do not properly recognize the part that accounting has to play in enterprise management, and they have not made appropriate use of it. Among entrepreneurs and managers, including those from the public sector, there is insufficient awareness of the value of accounting and of the information it may provide as an instrument of administrative and financial control. Business ownership, even of large-scale enterprises, is often concentrated among a few individuals. There may be no capital market; if there is one, its field of action is quite limited. This system of broadly based ownership faces a variety of difficulties, and the climate of trust and confidence needed to make it viable is, for several reasons, non-existent. Lacking broadly based investment by numerous minority share-holders, the need for the protection afforded by the regulation of enterprises of this kind has not been felt, and this extends even to the accounting aspects. Business affairs are frequently conducted in secrecy. Rather than relying on their clients' financial statements – in which they have little confidence – financial institutions emphasize other factors in their credit investigations, such as reputation and personal knowledge of the owners of the borrowing enterprises and substantial security pledged in the form of personal property.
>
> Financial accounting is often limited to the deficient recording of trans-actions; it is rudimentary and not kept up to date. It is maintained solely for the purpose of satisfying the formalities required by law and the tax authori-ties. The information provided by such records is consequently of little value in assessing the performance of an enterprise. Accounting methods and practices are usually outdated, even anachronistic, and there is no consistency in their application. In fact, accounting is not organized in such a way as to provide useful information. Most of the countries have not adopted – in some cases they have not even made efforts to adopt – a body of accounting standards to govern the recording of transactions and the presentation of financial statements. Accounting literature from the more developed coun-tries has had considerable influence, but this in itself is a problem because the developed countries have different practices for recording the same transactions. Add to this variances introduced locally, which quite often have not been based on sound technical grounds, and the problem of stan-dardization is compounded.

It is not surprising in a situation such as the one described above to find that financial statements (the vehicles for communicating accumu-lated and processed information) are excessively delayed, deficient and, consequently, of little use. Managers often lack the knowledge and training that would enable them to use accounting information or that would encourage them to try to introduce improved accounting systems. Also, there is a shortage of personnel having expertise in modern accounting techniques and modern management skills.

From a technical point of view, it often is not easy to determine the variety of accounting methods used for problems such as: fixed assets and inventory accounting and valuations; production costs determination; recording interest costs, deferred charges, prior year adjustments and investments in affiliates; converting financial statements from one currency to another; and recording revaluation, liabilities in foreign exchange, and exchange rate differences. The acute and continuing inflation in some countries has aggravated the situation, since financial statements based on historic costs are of little use in showing an enterprise's financial condition and results for evaluating its efficiency, or for preparing budgets and making financial plans. As an example of the difficulties faced, it was found in Nigeria (Enthoven 1975(a), p. 100) that:

> Accounting information is not effectively used by the enterpreneur. There are about 100 large companies, and these are mostly owned by or affiliated with, foreign firms. The small firms see no need for accounting services nor for managerial services. Generally the standard of financial management is deficient, and the lack of financial management and control has been largely responsible for the failure of many firms in Nigeria. Accounts are often kept carelessly. The inflation rate in Nigeria has been 10% or more per annum, and since the accounts are to be reflected at 'historical costs', it has been recognised that many of the items set forth in the balance sheet are quite unrealistic and misleading.

Auditing

Accounting data may be subjected to extensive and detailed checking, while insufficient care is taken to verify and review the control system. A proper accounting information system may be absent. However, in some countries obligatory audits of major firms to be filed with governments has not only improved accounting and spurred the profession, but has tended to influence positively capital formation and economic development.

As for internal auditing, little use is made of this in developing countries, even by enterprises which need it because of their complexity or volume of business. If an internal auditing system is set up, it often is not suitably structured and therefore its usefulness is considerably limited. The use of a corporate audit committee, as now required in the US, is seldom found in Third World enterprises. In general, external and internal auditing and a related auditing profession are not well developed in many Third World economies. Shortage of trained auditing staff is endemic.

Several countries have government Audit Corporations in addition to private auditing firms, e.g. Tanzania and India. These corporations audit government departments and public enterprises, although private firms also do audit some parastatals (government enterprises) due to a scarcity of qualified personnel. For example, at the large Tanzanian-owned public enterprise, the National Development Corporation, several private firms have been certifying the accounts of subsidiaries. Auditing standards, where these exist in developing countries, tend to be geared towards financial audits; very little is done about operational or economic audit norms and practices, although these countries have just as great a need for such appraisals. India, however, forms an exception in this regard.

A special feature of auditing in India is the 'Cost Audit', carried out for the government which is described (Enthoven 1977, p. 254) as:

> ... [the] verification of the correctness of cost accounts and adherence to the cost accounting plans and procedures. The financial auditor is not expected to make a detailed examination of cost records. Cost audit seeks to bring to light distortions and also the errors of omission and commission, if any, in the basic records, the bedrock of the balance sheet and profit and loss account. Thus cost audit is clearly different from financial audit.

Chartered accountants cannot perform 'Cost Audits' as the government specifically has assigned them to the Institute of Cost and Works Accountants. The reason apparently is that they should be independent from the certification of financial statements, and that they involve different skills.

In addition to a separate cost audit for certain industries, there exists the Bureau of Costs and Prices, a government agency. Its function is to establish acceptable norms for prices and costs. It is above all interested in the breakdown of cost, and makes comparative analyses. It furthermore determines whether industries are economically viable and how to direct them in the future. It feels that a better accountancy methodology is needed (Enthoven 1977, p. 262).

Management Accounting

Management accounting also tends to be highly underrated. The entrepreneurial and managerial classes frequently have an inadequate conception of the value of sound management accounting techniques for efficient planning, decision making and control. Cost records may be poorly maintained and void of realistic cost and allocation procedures. Firms often do not know the real cost of their products or whether departments are profitable; they may be reluctant to install and use effective cost accounting systems. The procedures used in determining costs may be deficient, and often the cost accounting system is not integrated with the financial accounting system. In general, the value of cost accounting as a tool for pricing policy, performance measurement, product and cost control and budgeting is still inadequately understood. Internal planning and control methods often are very weak, and accountants both in the private and public sector tend to spend a relatively small portion of their time on systems and procedures.

The deficiencies in this connection make accounting methods and the information derived from them largely unreliable, owing to the errors and omissions they contain and the opportunities for manipulations they offer. Furthermore, for taxation purposes, the entrepreneur may not want to keep accurate costs records. He may have to resort to other kinds of (confidential) records, which are generally incomplete, crude, and not integrated with his official accounting system, in order to determine – at least approximately and in an untechnical fashion – his actual costs and results of operations (Enthoven 1975(b), pp. 188 – 189). Indonesia is one of those many developing countries where management accounting, in particular, has been neglected due to a general historical occupation with financial accounting (Enthoven 1975(b), pp. 14 – 15). In contrast, however, well developed cost and management accounting professions and practices are found in India and Pakistan.

Management accounting has suffered the fate of not having a 'theory', notwithstanding that many techniques and methods have found universal acceptance. It is to be hoped that we have now entered the era of the scientific accounting base; the work of FASB in the United States (and its *Conceptual Framework*) is a good example. However, it has essentially been an *inductive* approach, and the *deductive* method has, to a large degree, been absent.

Management accounting, more so than financial accounting, faces the challenge of being economically relevant. The context in which management accounting must function tends to be broader: it deals with the effective and efficient allocation of financial, indirect, and human resources. Such allocations – based on sound and relevant measurements – require direct and indirect assessments as part of the objectives. Management accounting also uses non-accounting information to reach the objectives, which tend to be of an economic and social nature. Based on those elements, it sets forth normative models which serve this frame of reference.

The changing objectives to be encountered in the area of international management accounting show a close affinity to the international economic scene concerning the changing international economic and accounting focus. The principal changes in our opinion are the following:

1. Many governments, domestic and foreign, have taken a greater interest in what *enterprises contribute to the socioeconomic wellbeing* of the economy and its citizens. The contributory elements have become a major aspect in such assessments, and the social cost – benefit aspects have become a major underlying goal. The objective of

management also has changed from pure maximisation of income to growth and continuity. Therefore, its image elements, such as social goodwill and acceptance, have become important features. The role of the public sector in controlling – and even guiding – micro-operations has become a major feature. The foreseeable scarcity of many resources may well enhance such a trend.

2. The requirements of *social responsibility* are closely related to this. Alienation of the public by means of management practices is being prevented at all costs. The current era of social responsibility requires that the public should know 'what is going on'. Closely related to this is the reflection of social indicators and the need for corporate socioeconomic audits.

3 .The *growth of the large multinational enterprise* has forced changes in international accounting demands. Domestic and foreign parties (for example, governments) require a clear insight into the objectives of these entities and their contributions to the economy. This has forced upon us a whole series of different measurement demands: value added, transfer pricing, and employment and social welfare contributions, for example.

4. The *interdisciplinary involvement of management accounting* with behavioural science, organisation theory, economic science, sociology, quantitative methods and economic science must be reflected in our management accounting system. The interdisciplinary involvement may also be considered a resultant factor.

5. The concept of *what is meant by costs and benefits*, in contrast to expenditures and revenues, needs to be expanded to fit eco-accounting analysis, policy, and decision models. Cost – benefit notions cover a broad range of measurements, based on resources and activities, which tend to go beyond the direct aspects of an entity. Society now demands an insight into the application and benefit of resources used; this requires an enlargement of the accounting frame of reference. For example, the determination of profit or income in the micro sense may well cause capital consumption or depletion in a macro sense, as market forces are not a good basis for social cost – benefit analysis. All these criteria pertain to a rather broad underlying framework, the conceptual foundation and its quantitative characteristics, which set the bases for the development and use of techniques and norms (see Enthoven 1981).

Government Accounting

Government (parastatal) enterprises play a sizeable role in many developing countries. They can be found as public utilities or in transportation, industry, banking and mining. Accounting in these entities often has the same deficiencies as in private sector entities: for example, accounting procedures often reflect such a complicated system of checks and balances that efficacy and timeliness are hampered. Public sector accounting is still mainly seen as an accountability and control device for public receipts and expenditures.

In the government budgetary and planning field, inadequate attention generally is given to sound data estimation procedures, financial controls and supervision over execution. The accounting data on which budgets and plans have to be based are often deficient, while budget items are rarely assessed from a managerial (performance budget) point of view. A tremendous gap sometimes exists between budgetary estimates and actual receipts or expenditures, and the budgetary audit may be performed long after the end of the fiscal period, when it no longer serves its purpose. Productivity appraisals may not be made at all. Auditing in the government sector tends to be a highly neglected and outdated procedure. As for economic planning, limited use is made of accounting skills.

A. Premchand of the International Monetary Fund has outlined a number of shortcomings (SID 1976, pp. 34–35). First, accounting is too biased towards stewardship and thus the checking of the legality and propriety of transactions. However, even in this area, delays are so great that the usefulness of accounting is reduced. A related point is that systems are devoted to the recording of cash movements rather than cost measurements. Also, excessive rigidity and archaic procedures mean that public needs are not well served. Similar deficiencies are pointed out by the UN study *Government Accountancy in Economic Development Management* (UN 1977, pp. 13–14).

Just as in enterprise accounting, different types of government accounting (or funds) systems have evolved showing evidence of 'zones of influence'. This is referred to by Premchand (SID 1976, pp. 31–32):

In the British system, these funds usually are (1) a consolidated fund through which all transactions are carried out; (2) a contingency fund, which is more of an accounting entity than an operational fund, for meeting unforeseen expenditures pending legislative approval; and (3) a public account in which public monies are held in trust. In the American and other related practices, there is usually a general account forming the hard core of the accounting system, and a number of other special accounts set up for specific purposes. In the French system, the basic factor is the treasury itself, which maintains a sort of universal fund. The Latin American experience is somewhat more diversified, in that there are some countries that have only a single fund while some others have a large number of funds. A general feature of most of these systems, however, is that there is usually a single cash balance – no separate physical balances are maintained – although there are several exceptions to this in Latin American countries.

Funds budgeted for are made available to the spending agencies in several ways. In some of the countries that use the British system, there is usually a system of exchequer issues institutionalized in the office of the Paymaster General. In the French system, an annual decree indicates the amounts available for each agency. Funds are, however, retained by the treasury as payments are made for it. In the American and Latin American systems, a system of quarterly apportionments of funds to spending agencies is followed.

The expenditures incurred from these amounts and the revenues collected by the agencies are recorded in different ways in different systems. Revenues are generally recorded on a cash basis, although in a few Latin American countries they are recorded with reference to both the 'due' basis and the actual payments in the year. Expenditures are variously recorded. In the French system, expenditures are recorded by both the spending agency (on the basis of the delivery of goods and services) and the treasury (on the basis of the actual payments). In Latin American countries various procedures are in vogue, and expenditures may be recorded with reference to firm obligations, payment orders, transfer of funds to spending agencies, delivery of goods, or checks issued. In British and American systems expenditures are usually recorded on the basis of checks issued or paid, and actual cash disbursements.

The Government Accounting System in Zambia gives a fairly representative picture of the issues involved (Enthoven 1975(a), pp. 40–41):

> The Revenue and Expenditures of the Government, by calendar year, are based on the 'cash system'. A great amount of detail is presented in both the accounts and the budget, according to object classifications by ministries and departments. The broader accounts have been reflected according to functional classes; however, no proper system of performance and program budgeting exists as yet. No forward budget exists either.
>
> ... In regard to Government Auditing, the Auditor-General is hampered in his work by lack of a large number of qualified accountants. Consequently, the Auditor-General's report on the Accounts of the Republic have concerned themselves largely with unconstitutional and unauthorized expenditures of the various Ministries, while not having been able yet to focus on broader systems and policy aspects.

In Latin America, ILACIF (Latin American Institute of Auditing Sciences) is making extensive efforts to standardise public sector auditing. It is achieved through common operational rules based upon generally accepted professional standards. ILACIF is sponsored by the Latin American governments; it is associated with the International Organisation of Government Audit Institutions, and is one of the founding members of The International Consortium on Government Financial Management, a worldwide professional and technical group of government institutions.

The International Consortium on Government Financial Management, formed in 1978, still has to prove itself. However, its objectives – relating to the development of better government accounting and auditing – seem commendable. Specific areas of focus are: accounting, auditing, budgeting, data processing, debt administration and treasury management. An integral part will be the establishment of policies and standards for the use of automatic data processing. Another aspect is the harmonisation of policies, legislation and accounting systems applicable to multinational enterprises. In general, public sector accounting and auditing has not received the study and reform warranted, although some progress has been made in the mechanisation and processing of data and classification of transactions.

Macro Accounting

Most developing countries have national income and product accounts, while several have set forth input – output tables and flow of funds accounts, with various degrees of success. Although a fairly good frame of national accounts generally exists (usually based on the UN/OECD model), the basic data (e.g. accounting) are often incomplete or unreliable. Figures for the necessary inputs and outputs are often unsubstantiated. Statisticians and economists (at the statistical office, central bank, government agency, planning bureau) frequently compile and process accounting data without sufficient understanding of the accounting techniques involved, thus risking gross misinterpretations (Enthoven 1975(b), pp. 190 – 191).

The necessity to present 'value added' data with uniform classification and valuation criteria is generally not adequately grasped by accountants. The current data supplied may not be very meaningful for statistical and planning purposes. As stated before, audits of national accounts, and the underlying data accumulation and measurement procedures, are hardly done at all.

The current state of affairs of macro accounting in development is said to be that the system of classification (into sectors, accounts and transactions) is fairly well laid out in most countries, and harmonised to a certain degree internationally. However, the data base for all versions of macro accounting is highly deficient. Deficiencies in non-accounting data-collecting procedures also can be blamed for the lack of full and accurate data. For example: many transactions may not go through the market system, and incomes may be paid in commodities; and there is no adequate training in accounting concepts among those who collect data (SID 1976, pp. 58 – 61).

Legal and Statutory Aspects

In many countries accounting theory, methodology and practice are influenced strongly by requirements in companies acts, or in legal and tax decrees. The accounting statutes may set forth accounting standards (principles) and auditing standards to be applied, but such standards and rules are often based on foreign guidelines without domestic relevance. On the other hand, the absence of regulation in many countries does limit the comparability and usefulness of the information. The functions of capital markets and capital formation may be hampered and the users of financial statements may be deprived of adequate protection. Accounting practices accordingly may vary to serve those who prepare the statements.

As for some general observations on Africa, we find (Enthoven 1975(a), p. 112):

> Most countries have a Companies or Corporate Act, being essentially based on the 1947 – or earlier – UK Companies Act. In several instances it has been updated and has incorporated domestic requirements. Generally a need exists to bring it up to date, even revise the existing Act, and make it more applicable to the economic and financial requirements of the country/ region concerned. Instead of spelling out the accounting requirements in the Companies Act, it may be more desirable to set those forth in an Accountancy (Registration) Act, which may delineate, for example: the accounting concepts and rules; the auditing standards; a code of ethics; the accountancy qualifications and tests; registration requirements; and standardization criteria regarding measurements and reporting.

Professional and Institutional Aspects

Professional institutes in developing countries tend to be fairly weak. The existing institutional frameworks still tend to be somewhat outdated. Not enough attention is given to the *future* direction of accounting tasks and ways to introduce new approaches to the institutes' members. However, an increasing recognition exists of the need for accounting institutes which set standards in accounting and auditing, design codes of practice, run training and educational programmes, give qualification tests, do research, and exchange information with other accounting bodies.

Unfortunately, professional accounting has not been geared adequately to the economic development needs of countries; while professional training programmes and research are neither linked effectively to these needs, nor do they portray future requirements of accounting. Professional links between the various fields of accountancy are still inadequate, hampering their potential functions in the total economic framework. The institutional accounting format frequently suffers from insufficient professional interest, inadequate government encouragement and lack of support and compliance by private and public institutions.

On the other hand, a variety of professional accounting bodies have been organised without much substance and involvement.

In many countries, foreign accounting firms operate. They tend to follow foreign accounting/auditing pronouncements, which may not help develop useful local standards. In general, accounting firms are not involved adequately in social and economic programmes; nor do they assist sufficiently in fulfilling the accounting needs of smaller firms, either directly or through development institutions. Excellent exceptions have been found. Foreign firms, however, cater largely for the auditing of foreign entities, and for other services to be performed for these units.

According to Dominguez (SID 1976, p. 15), referring particularly to Latin America:

> Existing circumstances have caused accounting to be viewed as a second-rank profession in the developing countries. This attitude has created neither the resolve nor the enthusiasm needed to draw the most qualified candidates from the community into the study and practice of accounting (public and private). In short, circumstances have combined to work against the sound structuring of the accounting profession in the developing countries. For many years, accountants have attached more importance to merely recording transactions than to the coherent, relevant, and useful exposition of the mass of data contained in such records.

In English-speaking Africa and several parts of Asia, the existing professions have been following, to a large degree, the 'UK approach', reflecting a heavy accountability orientation. While this accountability approach has been very useful and will remain so, the needs of developing economies demand a somewhat different orientation. Sizeable efforts are now being made to localise the profession in many countries. To this extent domestic registration, regulations, laws and citizenship rules are being passed, and usually a national board of accountants, a registration board or similar body is being set up to localise the profession under the direct or indirect supervision of a government ministry. Regulations covering accounting measurement and reporting are frequently designed and enforced by a government agency.

Education and Training

Underlying the existing weaknesses and the scope for improvement in developing countries' accounting systems we find educational weaknesses. According to a worldwide survey by the 1978–79 Committee on International Accounting Operations and Education of the AAA, the principal shortcomings and requirements included the following (*Accounting Education and The Third World – Evaluation Report*, August 1979, pp. 7–9):

1. *Better upgrading of teachers*, development of adequate staff and better pay for teachers is needed.
2. *Teaching aids* (texts, cases, labs, projectors, etc.) tend to be deficient.
3. Training may be too much geared towards small practitioners' problems; the *more relevant economic analytical and decision making* aspects of accounting and auditing are not well covered.
4. Generally no *clearing house for information* and publications exists, and students have to feel their way around.
5. *Accounting as an intellectual discipline* is not well established; it is still too much taught as a technical skill only. Newer areas of accounting such as controllership, feasibility studies, operational auditing, management accounting, computer know-how, etc. are mostly poorly covered.
6. *Workshops and conferences* are needed for accounting educators, practitioners and students; they could bring together educators, practitioners and government officials to discuss issues and developmental requisites.

Accounting education structures and activities should take into account socioeconomic objectives. It is not very beneficial just to copy educational systems from abroad without assessing them in the light of a country's requirements. Accounting education and educators may have to answer such basic questions as: what are the country's accounting information needs? What is available *qua* skills and data? What sort of and how many accountants do we have to educate for the short, medium, and long term? Can they be trained partly in conjunction with other, related disciplines (economists, business administrators, lawyers, financial analysts, statisticians, government administrators, etc.)? Where and how shall we educate them? What should we teach and what materials should we use? How are we to produce the finances? Where do we get the staff etc.? And how should we go about all these things systematically? However, it is impossible and unnecessary to educate and train all accountants equally well in the various branches of accounting.

In order to address the educational issue, a certain restructuring of the branches of accounting (enterprise, government, and national) is needed in most developing economies. This is to be associated with a series of functional improvements of a professional, legal and statutory nature within a national, regional and international context.

A country's accounting education programmes may well have to focus more on: management accounting and decision-information systems; capital budgeting; cost – benefit analysis; project appraisals; internal auditing; national income accounting; government accounting and budgeting; and other planning and control aspects – in order to enable future accountants to be more useful in the micro- and macro-economic sectors.

Significant divergences in accounting training at academic, institutional, and other training centre levels exist in most developing countries. To train highly qualified accountants, a bachelor's degree programme is becoming desirable. After such a basic university or other academic degree, further academic training may be pursued leading either to a master's degree or to graduates participating in further training through an accounting institutional programme. However, the latter does not exist in all countries. It should be determined whether university training should become a requisite for the professional examinations, or whether professional and technical training institutes should grant their own certificates. The latter may well lead to an undesirable proliferation of technical and professional titles.

Many countries recognise only one type of 'official' accountant, i.e. the financial accounting oriented certified accountant/auditor, while other professionally trained accountants are not (yet) considered 'accountants'. This seems unrealistic for the present and future. Various official accounting designations should be given for various levels of skills according to the specialisation referred to and the level of sophistication. For example, at the upper level are the certified or registered (financial) accountants, certified management accountants, certified government accountants, and certified internal auditors; while at the middle (diploma) level are the licensed (diploma) or approved financial, cost, and public sector accountants. Lower levels (bookkeeping technicians) also should receive a diploma or certificate. Diploma-level training carried out at polytechnics or other institutions may have to be increased greatly, based upon an assessment of requirements.

Education therefore should not be solely concerned with high-level training at academic institutions; the middle and lower levels also need vast improvement. At the lower levels especially, correspondence courses and other types of institutional programmes (e.g. continuing education) may have to be reshaped or developed.

The accounting education modules for economic development activities may demand: (1) a conceptual socioeconomic foundation of accounting education and training; (2) a further specialisation in the various branches of accounting; (3) a closer link between the institutional, professional and educational programmes and continuous education; and (4) a greater focus on forecasting techniques, of both an internal and external nature. This also involves the ability to audit such areas effectively, including the measurement and verification of performance, social, and economic aspects, e.g. external effects (externalities).

Educational content requires both theoretical and practical emphasis. Research in the various fields of accounting also demands improvement; good teaching without accounting research of a basic and applied nature is rather hollow. It tends to be retrospective. Furthermore, training and research coordination between institutions of learning and professional institutes would well serve the whole future accounting framework. In many countries, a more effective accounting education *approach* is warranted, and attention should be given to reappraising the structure and content of accounting education. This may, for example, require a student to follow a degree programme with a broad base in economics, sociology and quantitative methods, with subsequent specialisation in major areas of accounting.

Future accounting programmes, in both developing and developed countries, may also have to undergo changes in curriculum and structure due to changing international developments and environments. More emphasis may have to be given to issue-oriented approaches, an interdisciplinary body of knowledge, and a strong pragmatic orientation. As accounting training will find itself increasingly part of the total socioeconomic scene, it will also need to respond to dynamic changes and to be future-oriented. Research of a basic and applied nature will have to be viewed as the key to future development and improvement. Continuing education also will become a major force in accounting education; consequently the institutions of learning will be supplying both a general and specific base. Continuing education programmes may be given in short-term specialised courses by professional institutions and other agencies. Cooperation between the institutions of learning, the profession, industry, and government also will have to become closer. There will be a trend to broaden and enhance the academic curriculum.

Although a clear understanding may exist regarding the impact and role of accounting to enhance economic activities, many countries have not, in our opinion, adequately appraised their accounting education directions and emphases. Common deficiencies are the concentration on stewardship accounting, while other areas are neglected, and lack of awareness at both governmental and private levels of the importance of good accounting and the corresponding requirements to improve accounting education levels.

The greater specialisation in accounting, by means of such specific areas as: financial (external) accounting and auditing; management (internal) accounting; systems and procedures; government and not-for-profit accounting; and accounting for economic analysis and policy – also demands better coverage from an educational, training, research, and other developmental point of view.

In order to achieve a better link between societal-practical demands and educational pursuits, the following steps are necessary:

1. An *accounting inventory and planning* framework should evaluate the types, levels and skills required for accountants. Such a layout is not only important for internal appraisals in both developing and

developed countries, but also for organisations supplying technical
accounting (educational) assistance.

2. *Better links* may have to be established between: governmental
   agencies, the accounting profession, industry, and educational
   institutions to enhance accounting training, research and developmental activities.

3. An *accounting education and development report* is needed, outlining a
   programme for international and regional development, to be submitted for implementation to countries and regional and international agencies. Such a report, with input from educators and
   practitioners around the world – possibly subdivided by region –
   might be along similar lines to the recently issued United Nations/
   World Bank Brandt Commission Report, dealing with international economic development. The report also should cover future
   accounting needs, the ways and means to satisfy them from a practical and educational point of view, and the scope for better
   theoretical norms. Such a comprehensive educational survey
   should be supported by the United Nations, the World Bank or
   other agency.

4. An *international association for accounting development* should be established, especially to cater for the requirements of Third World
   countries in the areas of accounting education, training, research
   and clearinghouse activities. International and regional certification and coordination of educational programmes would also have
   to be considered, broken down by levels and areas of competency.

5. *Accounting development centres* should be considered for countries and
   regions to upgrade accounting instructors and pursue research and
   writing in various fields of accounting. Internationally and
   regionally, a better *theoretical framework*, and related concepts, will
   have to be jointly explored and researched (see Enthoven 1982).

9.5   Summary

Accounting in developing countries is faced with a series of technical,
educational and operational problems, in addition to socioeconomic and
behavioural ones. The accounting weaknesses in these countries'
accountancy systems can be largely traced to historical, cultural and
educational factors.

The significance and function of accounting and auditing in all sectors
of the economy is not (yet) sufficiently recognised and in many countries
has a low status. Consequently, accounting does not have a great appeal
to students.

For a country's economic development, sound systems and methods
of accounting are required. Accounting is able not only to measure and

report economic events, but also to influence economic activities in the private and public sector. Much needs to be done yet to raise both the recognition and methodology of accounting in Third World economies.

References

Briston, R.J. (1978) 'The evolution of accounting in developing countries', *International Journal of Accounting*, Fall.

Burton, J.C. (ed.) (1980) *The International World of Accounting*, Arthur Young, Reston, Virginia, p. 86.

Enthoven, A.J.H. (1975a) Ford Foundation Study, *An Evaluation of Accountancy Systems, Developments, and Requirements in Africa*, University of North Carolina.

Enthoven, A.J.H. (1975b) Ford Foundation Study, *An Evaluation of Accountancy Systems, Developments, and Requirements in Asia*, University of North Carolina.

Enthoven, A.J.H. (1977) *Accountancy Systems in Third World Economies*, North-Holland.

Enthoven, A.J.H. (1980) 'International management accounting, its scope and standards', *International Journal of Accounting*, Spring.

Enthoven, A.J.H. (1981) *Accounting Education in Economic Development Management*, North-Holland.

Enthoven, A.J.H. (1982) *Accounting Education – Its Importance and Requirements*, Center for International Accounting Development, University of Texas at Dallas.

SID (1976) *The Role of Accountancy in Economic Development*, International Seminar, Society for International Development, Washington, DC, April.

United Nations (1977) *Government Accountancy in Economic Development Management*, ST/ESA/SER/E, 10, New York.

Part II

Problem Areas

10

Consolidation Accounting

R.H. PARKER

Both theory and practice in the field of consolidation accounting differ substantially from country to country. The differences are of four kinds:

- (a) differences in the rate of adoption of consolidated financial statements;
- (b) differences in the concept of a group for consolidation purposes;
- (c) differences in what is currently published by companies; and
- (d) differences in the techniques of consolidation.

The International Accounting Standards Committee and the EEC Commission are attempting to narrow these differences, but they are unlikely to be removed entirely. Awareness that there are important differences is itself relatively recent. The main aim of this chapter is to describe them and, so far as is possible, to explain them. The final section of the chapter looks at harmonisation.

Discussion in this chapter deals mainly with five countries: the USA, the UK, West Germany, France and the Netherlands. Consolidation practices in Japan are a recent development and are dealt with in Chapter 7. Those in countries such as Australia (see Ma and Parker 1983) and Canada are similar but not identical to those in the UK and USA. Australia, for example, has shown more reluctance than other countries to adopt equity accounting. In many countries, consolidation is still either non-existent or at a very primitive stage.

10.1   Rate of Adoption

Consolidated financial statements were first adopted in the USA. A number of American companies published such statements before the turn of the century (Bores 1934, Hein 1978, Mumford 1982) but it was the United States Steel Company, which was chartered in New Jersey in 1901 and published consolidated statements from its inception, that set a pattern.

The faster rate of adoption in the USA than elsewhere can be explained in part by the earlier development there of the *holding company*. One consequence of the wave of mergers in the United States at the turn of the twentieth century was the carrying on of commercial and industrial activities not by individual companies in isolation but by groups of companies. There were no legal or regulatory barriers to hold up new accounting techniques and a social climate existed in which innovation was highly regarded.

In Britain and Continental Europe, both holding companies and consolidated statements were a later development. In the UK it was not until the second wave of merger activity (1916 – 1922) that holding companies became an important form of business organisation. The earliest consolidated accounts appear to date from 1910 (Edwards and Webb 1984). The first British book on the subject, *Holding Companies and their Published Accounts* by Gilbert Garnsey, was published in 1923, by which time consolidation had, as Garnsey himself pointed out, become almost universal in the USA. When company law was extensively reformed in 1929, consolidated financial statements were not introduced as a legal requirement. Dunlop Ltd led the way during the 1930s, and by the end of the decade consolidation had become generally accepted. In 1939 the London Stock Exchange required consolidated statements as a condition of new issues. The Second World War then intervened and it was not until 1947 that group accounts (normally in the form of consolidated financial statements) were finally required by law.

Both the need for the new technique (the rise of the holding company) and its recognition came more slowly in the UK than in the USA. Garnsey stated that 'the natural reluctance of the people of this country to change is too well known to require any comment' and he placed the blame on the directors who were, under British law, responsible for published accounts. It is possible that the obligation (not present in the USA) to published the holding company's own balance sheet may have acted as a deterrent to the publication of a consolidated balance sheet.

Consolidated financial statements developed even later in Continental Europe. The earliest Dutch example, according to Bores (1934), was Wm. H. Müller & Co. of the Hague in 1926. German companies did not start consolidating until the 1930s and were not obliged by law to do so until 1965. French companies were even slower. In 1967 only 22 French companies published a consolidated balance sheet. Only from 1985 onwards are consolidated statements compulsory – and only for listed companies. Consolidated statements are still very rare in such countries as Italy, Greece and Luxembourg. This should, however, change in the 1990s as a result of the EEC seventh Directive (see section 10.5 below).

10.2 The Concept of a Group

The production of consolidated financial statements assumes that a group of enterprises can be regarded as an accounting entity. In defining the boundaries of such an entity, it is necessary to ask: (a) for whom is information about the entity intended? and (b) for what purpose is the information to be provided? (AAA Committee Report 1965) A British discussion paper, *The Corporate Report* (Accounting Standards Steering Committee 1975), distinguishes the following as legitimate users for whom information might be provided: (i) equity investors (ii) loan creditors (iii) employees (iv) managers (v) analyst-advisers (vi) business contacts (vii) government (viii) the public.

In the USA and the UK it has traditionally been assumed that it is for the first of these user groups, that is, existing and potential holders of ordinary shares (common stock) that group financial statements are to be prepared. Furthermore, the emphasis has been on the shareholders of the parent or holding company at the expense of minority shareholders in less than wholly owned subsidiaries. This is the 'parent company' concept of a group.

Such a concept has a number of weaknesses, apart from ignoring the interest of minority shareholders. For example:

(i) It assumes that a group consists of a parent company which dominates a number of dependent or subsidiary companies. It does not allow for the possibility that the group has been formed by the merger of two or more companies of approximately equal size. Nor does it allow for companies dominated by more than one company, or for companies over which another company exercises a significant influence but not control.

(ii) It ignores all interested parties other than equity shareholders.

The parent company concept is based on legal control. This is usually based on majority shareholdings and voting rights but can also be attained (where company legislation permits, as it does in West Germany) by the use of control contracts whereby one company places itself under the legal domination of another.

A possible alternative is the 'entity' concept of a group. This emphasises the economic unity of all enterprises in the group and gives equal importance to all shareholders, whether majority or minority. This way of looking at a group is also, it can be argued, more appropriate for such users as employees and managers. A group which consists of, say, two equally large companies can also be accommodated more easily under the entity concept.

Neither the parent company nor the entity concept, however, copes satisfactorily with enterprises which belong to more than one group or only partially to a group. In these cases there is neither a single parent company nor a minority interest. There is neither legal dominance nor an economic unit. These situations are, however, covered by the 'proprietary' concept which emphasises not legal control or economic unity, but ownership or proprietorship which gives the possibility of exercising 'significant influence' over commercial and financial policy decisions. Under this concept a proportionate share of the profit or loss for the year and a proportionate share of the assets and liabilities are brought into the consolidated statements, either item by item ('proportional consolidation') or on a 'one-line' basis (the 'equity method').

All three concepts need to be invoked to explain the law and practice in the five countries under consideration.

British law and practice are based mainly on the parent company concept. However, the equity method (based on the proprietary concept) is also standard practice, and elimination of 100% of intra-group profits (more appropriate to the entity concept) is generally accepted. The Companies Act makes no attempt to define a group, and indeed groups only exist for accounting purposes. SSAP 14 (1978), which deals with Group Accounts, defines a group as 'a holding company and its subsidiaries' (paragraph 8) and follows s.736 of the 1985 Companies Act (which repeats s.154 of the 1948 Companies Act) in defining a subsidiary and then deeming a company to be another holding company if, but only if, that other is its subsidiary. The criteria are (i) membership together with control of the board of directors *or* (ii) holding more than half in nominal value (not, be it noted, necessarily the same as voting power) of the equity share capital.

A 'related company' is a company (other than a subsidiary or holding company) in which an investing company holds, on a long-term basis, a qualifying capital interest (usually 20% or more of equity share capital carrying voting rights) for the purpose of securing a contribution to the investing company's own activities by the exercise of any control or influence arising from that interest (para. 92, Sch. 4, Companies Act 1985). A more usual term in British accounting practice has been 'associated company'. Related companies are usually also associated companies. An associated company is defined in SSAP 1 (as revised in 1982) as follows (italics added):

A company not being a subsidiary of the investing group or company in which.

(a) the interest of the investing group or company is effectively that of a partner in a joint venture or consortium and the investing group or company is in a position to exercise *significant influence*; or

(b) the interest of the investing group or company is for the *long term* and is *substantial* and, having regard to the disposition of the other shareholdings, the investing group or company is in a position to exercise a *significant influence* over the company in which the investment is made.

In the case of (b), where there is an interest of 20% or more of the equity voting rights, a significant influence is to be presumed unless it can be clearly demonstrated otherwise. Where there is an interest of less than 20% of the equity voting rights, it is to be presumed that significant influence is not exercised unless the investing group or company can clearly demonstrate otherwise (normally by a supporting statement from the investee concerned).

It will be noted that there are two types of associated company but, as we shall see later, the distinction is not of great importance in British practice.

American practice is in many ways the same as British in that it is based on the parent company concept plus the use of the equity method (but the term 'associated companies' is not commonly used). Extensive use is also made, however, of 'pooling of interests' ('merger accounting' in British terminology). Pooling of interests, which is discussed further in section 10.4, would seem to be based upon the entity concept and is difficult to reconcile with a parent company approach. Its use in the United States owes more to management's need to boost earnings per share than to theoretical considerations. Merger accounting has been less common in British practice (Lee 1974), partly because management's need for it has been less than in the USA (given the greater flexibility of accepted accounting procedures) and partly because of doubts about its legality. In 1980 it was held in *Shearer v. Bercain* that merger accounting was indeed illegal but the Companies Act 1981 legalised it retrospectively and also laid down rules for its application which have been supplemented in SSAP 23.

German law and practice are quite different from British and American and are based more on the entity concept. Unlike other countries, a group of enterprises exists as a legal entity, known as a *Konzern*. A *Konzern* is constituted if a dominant and one or more dependent enterprises are under unified management (*einheitliche Leitung*) (*Aktiengesetz*, s.18). The *Aktiengesetz* does not make a distinction between subsidiaries and associated companies and precludes the use of techniques such as the equity method and proportional consolidation consonant with the proprietary concept.

The entity (*Konzern*) envisaged by German law does not, however, include those parts of a group domiciled outside the Federal Republic. This is a significant weakness in the German application of the entity concept. It will be removed when the EEC seventh Directive is implemented.

French law and practice are based on the parent company and proprietary concepts. As already noted, consolidations are compulsory for *listed* companies from 1985 onwards. A distinction is made between *filiales* and *participations* (Law of 24 July 1966), terms which may be roughly translated as subsidiaries and associated companies. When a company owns more than half the capital of another company, the latter is considered to be the *filiale* of the former; and when a company owns between 10% and 50% of the capital of another company, the former is considered to have a *participation* in the latter.

In French practice a distinction is made between *sociétés multigroupes*, (joint ventures, the shares being held by a number of groups) and *sociétés associées au groupe* (companies over which a group exercises a significant influence). Although proportional consolidation is recommended for the former and the equity method for the latter, there are as yet no binding regulations in the matter and practice has varied considerably.

Dutch practice is fairly close to British. As in Britain, groups exist only for accounting purposes. Article 379(b) of the Civil Code requires that financial data concerning subsidiaries must, with or without data relating to the parent company and other group companies, be included in group annual accounts drawn up in accordance with the consolidation method. Subsidiaries, group companies and participating interests are defined in the Code.

Some Dutch companies use proportional consolidation for joint ventures. The equity method is widely used and, indeed, Dutch practice differs from that in other EEC countries in that the method is also used for both subsidiaries and associates in the holding company financial statements, so that the holding company's reported profit is the same as the consolidated profit. (There is further information on Dutch consolidation accounting in Chapter 6.3.)

10.3   Publication Requirements and Practices

The International Accounting Standards Committee recommends that a parent company which is not itself a wholly owned subsidiary should issue consolidated financial statements and that, with minor exceptions, it should consolidate all subsidiaries both domestic and foreign (IAS 3, *Consolidated Financial Statements*, 1976, paragraphs 34–7).

The practice of consolidation in the UK, West Germany, France, the Netherlands and the USA is by no means as simple as this, as Table 10.1

Table 10.1 Publication Practices of Some Major Companies

	Parent Company			Consolidated		
	Balance sheet	Income statement	Funds statement	Balance sheet	Income statement	Funds statement
UK						
British Petroleum	yes	no	no	yes	yes	yes
BAT Industries	yes	no	no	yes	yes	yes
Imperial Chemical Industries	yes	no	no	yes	yes	yes
USA						
Exxon Corporation	no	no	no	yes	yes	yes
General Motors	no	no	no	yes	yes	yes
American Telephone & Telegraph	no	no	no	yes	yes	yes
Germany						
Veba	yes	yes	no	yes	yes	yes*
Volkswagenwerk	yes	yes	no	yes	yes	yes*
Daimler – Benz	yes	yes	no	yes	yes	no
France						
Compagnie Française des Pétroles (CFP)	yes	yes	no	yes	yes	yes
Elf-Aquitaine	yes	yes	no	yes	yes	yes
Peugeot	yes	yes	yes	yes	yes	yes
Netherlands						
Philips	yes	yes	no	yes	yes	yes
AKZO	yes	yes	no	yes	yes	yes
Hoogovens	yes	yes	no	yes	yes	yes
International (Dutch/UK)						
Royal Dutch/Shell	yes	yes	yes	yes***	yes***	yes
Unilever	yes	yes/no**	no	yes	yes	yes

Notes: * as part of the Notes
** yes: Unilever NV; no: Unilever plc.
*** in accordance with Dutch legislation

demonstrates. Included in it are three large listed companies from each country, plus Royal Dutch/Shell and Unilever which are 'international' companies of joint British and Dutch nationality.

Several interesting conclusions can be drawn from the table:

(a) the US companies publish consolidated balance sheets, profit and loss accounts and funds statements, but do not publish any parent company statements (these are, however, filed with the SEC);

(b) the British companies publish the same as the American, plus the balance sheet, but not the profit and loss account (income statement) of the parent company;

(c) the Dutch companies publish the same as the British, plus the parent company's income statement (in practice often only the appropriation section is published).

(d) French and German companies are not uniform in their publication of funds statements. In Germany funds statements are usually published as part of the Notes;

(e) the 'international' companies have chosen slightly different ways of complying with the law and practice of their home countries.

Not apparent from the table is the German treatment of foreign subsidiaries. This is explained later in this section.

Practice is in part a reflection of the law. Both law and practice of publication in the five countries are summarised below. The differences in techniques are examined in section 10.4 and the likely effects of harmonisation in section 10.5.

Great Britain

'Group accounts', but not necessarily consolidated accounts, are required by s.229 of the Companies Act 1985 where a company has a subsidiary at the end of its financial year and is not itself a wholly owned subsidiary of another company incorporated in Great Britain. Group accounts are defined as accounts (financial statements) dealing with the state of affairs and profit or loss of the company and its subsidiaries. Group accounts must give a true and fair view of the state of affairs and profit or loss of the company and the subsidiaries dealt with thereby as a whole, so far as concerns members (i.e. shareholders) of the company (s.230). The parent company concept is thus quite explicitly supported by British legislation.

Group accounts will *usually* comprise a consolidated balance sheet and a consolidated profit and loss account (s.229; a consolidated funds statement is required by SSAP 10). Other forms are permissible if, in the opinion of the directors, a better presentation of the same or equivalent information can be achieved which can readily be appreciated by members. In particular, group accounts may take the form of:

(a) more than one set of consolidated accounts dealing respectively with the company and one group of subsidiaries and other groups of subsidiaries;

(b) separate accounts dealing with each of the subsidiaries;

(c) statements expanding the information about the subsidiaries in the company's own accounts; or

(d) any combination of the above (s.229).

Group accounts containing other than one set of consolidated accounts are very rare. SSAP 14 on Group Accounts comes out firmly in favour of a single set of consolidated financial statements except in exceptional circumstances.

United States

American consolidation practice is governed by the rules of the SEC and by relevant accounting standards. Consolidated financial statements must be filed each year by all companies subject to SEC jurisdiction (see Chapter 2), as must also the financial statements of the parent company (there are exceptions to this requirement and such statements are not usually published). Financial statements of unconsolidated subsidiaries and of companies accounted for by the equity method must also be filed (either or both may be omitted in certain circumstances).

Article 4 of Regulation S – X sets forth the SEC's requirements as to the form and contents of consolidated and combined financial statements. It requires *inter alia* that consolidated statements clearly exhibit the financial condition and results of operations of the registrant and its subsidiaries. It further requires the consolidation of majority-owned subsidiaries only; the reasons for inclusion and exclusion of subsidiaries; separate disclosure of minority interest in capital, in retained earnings and in consolidated income for the year; and elimination of inter-company transactions and items.

The accounting standards of most relevance are *Accounting Research Bulletin No. 51* and *Opinions Nos. 16 and 18* of the Accounting Principles Board.

ARB 51 (1959) states that the purpose of consolidated statements is to present, primarily for the benefit of the shareholders and creditors of the parent company, the results of operations and the financial position of a parent company and its subsidiaries essentially as if the group were a single company with one or more branches or divisions. A holding of more than 50% of the voting shares of another company is a condition pointing towards consolidation, but there may be exceptions, e.g. in the case of finance-related, real estate and foreign subsidiaries. Of the 600 companies' financial statements for 1983, analysed by AICPA in *Accounting Trends and Techniques 1984*, 419 consolidated all significant subsidiaries, 172 consolidated certain significant subsidiaries only and 9 did not present consolidated financial statements. 97 companies did not consolidate finance-related subsidiaries, 31 did not consolidate real estate subsidiaries and 17 did not consolidate foreign subsidiaries.

Opinion No. 16 (1970) specifies the elaborate criteria by which a purchase ('acquisition' in British terminology) is to be distinguished from a pooling of interests ('merger' in British terminology). The latter cannot apply where shares are acquired for cash; it *must* apply in certain specified circumstances where shares are acquired for a consideration other than cash. *Accounting Trends and Techniques 1984* reported 26 new business combinations accounted for as poolings of interests and 154 accounted for by the purchase method. Figures for the previous three years were similar.

Opinion No. 18 stipulates that the equity method should be used to account for investments in unconsolidated subsidiaries, for investments in corporate joint ventures, and for investments in companies in which at least 20% but not more than 50% of the voting stock is held and the investor has the ability to exercise significant influence over the operating and financial policies of the investee. The rules are very similar to those obtaining in the UK, although the useful British term 'associated company' is not commonly used.

West Germany

The provision of consolidated financial statements (*Konzernabschlüsse*) is required by s.329 of the German law relating to public companies (the *Aktiengesetz* of 1965). The dominant enterprise may be a public company (*Aktiengesellschaft* – AG), a limited partnership with shares (*Kommandit-gesellschaft auf Aktien* – KGaA) or one of the other forms of German business enterprises (see Chapter 5). Dominant AGs and KGaAs must prepare consolidated financial statements (balance sheets and income statements) and a group annual report including all *domestically* domiciled enterprises in the group. Where the dominant enterprise is not an AG or a KGaA (i.e. is another type of German enterprise or is an enterprise domiciled outside Germany), the board of management of the AG or KGaA which is closest to the dominant enterprise must prepare what are known as *partially* consolidated financial statements, but these may be dispensed with if the dominant enterprise itself publishes con-solidated financial statements (s.330).

The Publicity Law of 1969 extends certain provisions of the *Aktiengesetz*, including those relating to consolidation, to private com-panies (*Gesellschaften mit beschränkter Haftung* – GmbH), partnerships and sole traders above a certain size. Such enterprises are much more impor-tant in West Germany than in Britain and include such important enter-prises as Robert Bosch GmbH and the Flick Group which are in the top 20 German companies. Some German groups publish more than is required by law, especially those quoted on overseas stock exchanges.

The consolidation of foreign subsidiaries is an area where large Ger-man companies are increasingly going beyond their legal obligations.

Three patterns are found:

(a) The foreign subsidiaries are not consolidated, e.g. RWE.
(b) The foreign subsidiaries are included in the consolidated financial statements, e.g. Daimler – Benz and Volkswagenwerk.
(c) The foreign subsidiaries are included in a separate 'world' consolidation, published in addition to the 'domestic' consolidation, e.g. AEG – Telefunken, Thyssen and BASF.

France

Until very recently consolidated financial statements have not been a legal requirement in France. In practice, however, consolidated statements became increasingly common from the late 1960s and were greatly encouraged by the French equivalent of the SEC, the COB, which since 1 July 1971 has required companies making a public issue of shares to include consolidated financial statements in their prospectuses.

The implementation of the EEC seventh Directive will eventually lead to the widespread adoption in France of audited consolidated statements prepared in a uniform manner. In anticipation of full implementation, the law of 3 January 1985 requires *listed* companies to publish consolidated statements for financial years ending after 31 December 1984. Details are to be set out in a decree to be issued after consultation with the Conseil National de la Comptabilité (National Accounting Council).

The seventh Directive will also introduce into French law a number of Anglo-Saxon consolidation techniques. These have already been adopted by some companies (e.g. St. Gobain-Pont-à-Mousson) whose shares are quoted on UK or US stock exchanges.

The Netherlands

Consolidated financial statements have long been the norm in the Netherlands but it is only since the Act of 7 December 1983 (incorporated in the Civil Code) that they have been explicitly required by legislation, which defines subsidiaries, group companies and participating interests (see Chapter 6.4).

Details of practice are given in the periodic surveys of annual reports published by the Dutch Institute (e.g. NIVRA 1985). As discussed in section 10.4 below, the surveys show that, whilst equity accounting is more common, some Dutch companies use the proportional method of consolidation.

10.4   Techniques of Consolidation

There are considerable differences in the techniques of consolidation used in the five countries. In summary the most important points are as follows:

  (i) pooling of interests (merger accounting) is a recognised standard accounting practice only in the USA and the UK;
 (ii) the equity method is illegal in West Germany but is used in varying ways in the other four countries;
(iii) proportional consolidation is common in France and to a lesser extent in the Netherlands but is illegal in West Germany and very rarely found in practice in the UK and USA;
 (iv) the treatment of the 'consolidation difference' varies considerably from country to country.

Pooling of Interests

As explained in Chapter 2, a subsidiary acquired by a US company through an exchange of shares may, and in some cases must, be consolidated by a pooling of interests. In a pooling there is no revaluation of assets at the date of acquisition (as there normally would be in other methods) and no goodwill on consolidation emerges. The investment in the subsidiary in the acquiring company's books is valued at the book value of the equity interest acquired. The consolidated retained profits are simply the sum of the retained profits of the companies concerned. No distinction is drawn between pre- and post-acquisition profits. It is clear that a pooling of interests is likely to result in lower reported expenses (since depreciation is calculated on historical, not revalued, figures and there is no goodwill to be amortised) and thus higher reported annual earnings and earnings per share. Retained earnings will also be higher. A share premium will not be recorded by the parent company as a result of the merger.

The UK is the only country in the EEC where pooling of interests (merger accounting) is of any importance. As already noted in Section 10.2, it was retrospectively legalised in 1981 and was the subject of an accounting standard (SSAP 23) in 1985.

Equity Method

In Britain, use of the equity method is confined to consolidated financial statements. An 'associated company' is valued in the balance sheet at cost plus a proportionate share of the retained profits since the date of acquisition. The income statement does not include the detailed revenues and expenses (as would be the case for a subsidiary company). Instead, there is a figure for the proportionate share of the associate's profit before tax and extraordinary items, followed by separate figures for the share of tax and extraordinary gains/losses applicable to associated companies. The goodwill arising on acquisition is disclosed in the Notes but not, as it is in the USA, transferred out of the figure for investment to form part of amortisable goodwill. American practice also differs from British in that the equity method is used in the parent company financial statements as well as in the consolidated financial statements.

In Germany, as already noted, the equity method is effectively disallowed by statute. In France it is known as *mise en équivalence*. The value of a *participation mise en équivalence* (investment recorded by the equity method) is calculated by taking a proportionate share of the net assets of the investee. The effect of doing the calculation in this manner is, of course, to exclude any element of goodwill. There are few rules in practice about the use of *mise en équivalence*. Some French companies do not use it at all; some use it for all associated companies; some do not use it for joint ventures. A few large French companies follow American practice instead.

In the Netherlands, equity accounting is used in the financial statements of the parent company (for both subsidiaries and associated companies) as well as in the consolidated statements. The effect of this, of course, is to bring into the parent company statements the profits or losses of the group as a whole. Any goodwill arising is separately identified and either written off immediately to reserves or amortised through the profit and loss account. Negative goodwill is transferred to a revaluation reserve.

Proportional Consolidation

Proportional or pro rata consolidation is not allowed by law in Germany and is almost unknown in practice in the USA and the UK. It is, however, used by the British multinational Rio Tinto Zinc for joint ventures. It is quite common in France and the Netherlands.

As usual, French practice in this area is diverse. Some companies (e.g. Rhône-Poulenc) do not use the method at all; others (e.g. Compagnie Française des Pétroles) use it extensively. In the Netherlands it is used for joint ventures by companies such as Heineken. Philips, however, has abandoned this method of consolidation.

Consolidation Difference

'Consolidation difference' is a term which will be more easily recognised by Continental European than by Anglo-Saxon accountants. It refers to the difference which arises on consolidation because the amount paid by the investor company is greater or less than its proportionate share of the tangible and identifiable intangible net assets of the investee.

In the UK and the USA (except where pooling of interests is used), it is standard practice to make this calculation at the date of acquisition, to take the net assets at their current value at that date and to refer to the resulting balancing figure as 'goodwill on consolidation'. In the USA, goodwill on consolidation has to be amortised over a period of not more than 40 years (APB *Opinion No. 17*). In the UK, SSAP 22 requires that goodwill be either transferred immediately to reserves (i.e. not capitalised at all) or written off over a period not longer than its economic life. In practice, the former predominates. In the Netherlands goodwill on consolidation must be amortised over a period of not more than five years, although where it can reasonably be allocated to a substantially longer period, it may be written off over that period, provided that the latter does not exceed ten years. Most Dutch companies write it off immediately against reserves.

German practice has been quite different. A consolidation difference is calculated at the date of each balance sheet. The book value of the investee is defined to include share capital and reserves but not the *Bilanzgewinn* or *Bilanzverlust* (i.e. the profit or loss for the year before dividends but after transfers to or from reserves). This means that the size of the consolidation difference changes every year. Some companies split it into debit and credit portions. This method of treating consolidation differences is not, however, a statutory requirement and some German companies, e.g. Siemens, have adopted the Anglo-Saxon method.

Some French companies, for example, St. Gobain-Pont-à-Mousson, also use the Anglo-Saxon method, but most use a method akin to, but not the same as, the German method. The consolidation difference is calculated at the date of each balance sheet. The book value of the investee is defined to include the share capital, reserves and profit brought forward, but excludes the profit or loss for the year. In other words, the comparison is based on the investee's book value at the beginning of the year. Some companies separate out the goodwill element in the consolidation difference and disclose it separately.

As will be seen in the next section, one effect of the EEC seventh Directive will be the adoption by German and French companies of more Anglo-Saxon techniques of dealing with goodwill on consolidation.

10.5 Harmonisation

The previous sections of this chapter should have made abundantly clear both the scope for harmonisation and the considerable difficulties that are likely to be encountered.

The two attempts which have been made are very different in nature. The International Accounting Standards Committee, which has no direct means of enforcing its standards, has concentrated with some success on producing a standard which would encourage consolidation in countries where it is still underdeveloped, and on drawing up a list of practices acceptable to both American and British accountants. The Committee deliberately excluded from the standard (*Consolidated Financial Statements*, IAS 3 1976) two areas – pooling of interests (merger accounting) and the treatment of goodwill on consolidation – where practice is divergent. Merger accounting is now covered, however, in IAS 22 (of 1983) on business combinations.

The EEC has tackled the much more difficult task of producing a set of rules which will be enforceable by statute and which will be acceptable to countries of such diverse practices as the UK, West Germany, France, the Netherlands and Italy.

IAS 3 recommends that a parent company should issue consolidated statements unless it is itself a wholly-owned subsidiary. All subsidiaries should be consolidated, whether foreign or domestic, unless control is to be temporary or the subsidiary operates under conditions in which severe long-term restrictions on the transfer of funds impair control by the parent company over the subsidiary's assets and operations. Companies with dissimilar activities *may* be excluded from consolidation.

The standard recommends the use of the equity method for associated companies and for subsidiaries excluded from consolidation. Consonant with the parent company concept, it is expressly stated that the minority interest should be classified as a separate item and should not be shown as part of shareholders' funds. The standard also includes a number of disclosure provisions.

The requirements of IAS 3 are consistent with both British and American practice, but not with French or German. Proportional consolidation, for example, is ignored, as is the fact that German companies are precluded by statute from using the equity method.

Adoption of the EEC seventh Directive in 1983 was a notable event in the history of consolidation accounting. The Directive covers all the problem areas discussed in previous sections of this chapter (the concept of a group, publication requirements and techniques of consolidation) and it will have a major impact on consolidation law and practice in most of the member states.

Harmonisation will not, however, be complete since adoption was only made possible by allowing a number of options. These include the following (with the names in brackets of some member state(s) likely to take advantage of the options):

(1) Consolidation may be required where there is *de facto* control, even where there is no *de jure* control. (West Germany)
(2) Consolidation may be confined to those groups where the parent is a limited company. (UK, Ireland)
(3) Financial holding companies may be exempted if certain conditions are met. (Luxembourg)
(4) Small groups may be exempted, except where one of the companies in the group is listed on a stock exchange. (France)
(5) Merger accounting may be permitted under certain conditions. (UK, Ireland)
(6) Goodwill on consolidation may be deducted from reserves rather than written off over five years or its useful ecônomic life. (UK, Ireland)
(7) Tax-based valuations need not be eliminated if they are disclosed, along with the reasons for them. (All except UK, Ireland, Netherlands)
(8) The proportional method of consolidation may be required or permitted for joint ventures. (France, Netherlands)

The major conceptual problem faced by those who negotiated the Directive was the nature of a group and, in particular, the conflict between the parent company concept and the entity concept (see section 10.2 above). The first draft of the Directive (1976) leaned very strongly towards the latter concept. For example, *de facto* control rather than *de jure* control was the criterion of consolidation; consolidation was required even where the head of the group was not a company; and EEC-level consolidations were required when the head of the group was registered outside the EEC.

However, the Directive as finally adopted is based much more on the parent company concept, although it allows member states to bring in elements of the entity concept. One example of this is option (1) above. Options not mentioned above include the right of a member state not to insist on consolidation where one undertaking has the right to exercise a dominant influence over another undertaking pursuant to a 'control contract'. This option is for the benefit of member states other than West Germany, which is the only state where such contracts are common.

Another option gives the right to require a 'horizontal consolidation' of undertakings (such as Unilever) that are not linked vertically but are regarded as being managed on a unified basis. Also, there is an option that, so long as the parent's financial statements are attached, the parent's figures may be omitted from consolidation, where the parent does not carry on any industrial or commercial activity but holds shares in a subsidiary undertaking on the basis of a joint arrangement with one or more undertakings not included in the consolidation. An example of this last case is the parent company, Shell Transport and Trading plc, and its linked company, Royal Dutch Petroleum.

Also more in line with the entity concept than with the parent company concept is the provision of the Directive that consolidated financial statements are to be prepared where *either* the parent undertaking *or one or more* subsidiary undertakings is (using UK terminology) a public or a private company. This clearly allows undertakings other than companies to be included in consolidations. There is, however, as already noted, an option for parent companies to be exempted. It was observed that without the possibility of such an exemption the Directive would call for a consolidation of the economic interests of, for example, the Agnelli family in Italy or the Anglican Church in England (Ernst & Whinney 1980, p 18).

The publication requirements of the Directive are quite stringent and will lead to increased disclosure in most member states. In countries such as Italy, Greece, Spain and Portugal most companies will be publishing consolidated information for the first time.

So far as consolidation techniques are concerned, the Directive is based on acquisition (purchase) accounting but merger accounting (pooling of interests) is allowed as an option. This will be of most importance to the UK where interest in merger accounting appears to be increasing. The Directive prescribes equity accounting for associated companies but allows proportional consolidation as an option for joint ventures. In regard to the consolidation difference, goodwill is to be calculated as at the date of acquisition and based on a comparison of the fair values (rather than the historical costs) of the net tangible assets with the total purchase consideration. The Directive stresses the necessity for amortisation of goodwill over its economic life, but an immediate and clear deduction from reserves is allowed as an option.

Negative differences on consolidation are divided into two categories. Those that represent an expectation of future costs or unfavourable results can be credited to profit and loss account when those expectations are fulfilled. Those that arise for some other reason (e.g. a bargain purchase) can only be transferred to profit and loss account when they have been realised. A negative difference not so transferred is presumably treated as a reserve on consolidation, although it would also seem possible to follow the standard US practice (APB Opinion No. 16) of allocating it proportionately against the fair values of fixed assets other than investments.

10.6 Summary

Consolidated financial statements were adopted first in the USA, became general in the UK in the 1930s, but are a postwar innovation in much of Continental Europe. There is no worldwide agreement yet either on the relevant concepts or on the techniques of consolidation. There are still important differences in the laws and practices of the USA, the UK, the Netherlands, France and Germany but a considerable degree of harmonisation within the EEC will be brought about by the seventh Directive.

Three concepts can be distinguished: parent company, entity and proprietary. The most important technical differences relate to pooling of interests, the equity method, proportional consolidation and the 'consolidation difference' (of which goodwill is a part).

Harmonisation has been attempted by the International Accounting Standards Committee and the EEC Commission. International accounting standards have been published but are not being enforced in some countries. An EEC Directive has been adopted and will have a considerable impact in many countries when implemented.

References

AAA Committee Report (1965) 'The entity concept', *Accounting Review*, April, pp. 358–367.

Accounting Standards Steering Committee (1975) *The Corporate Report*, London.

American Institute of Certified Public Accountants (1984) *Accounting Trends and Techniques*, New York.

Bores, W. (1934) 'Geschichtliche Entwicklung der konsolidierten Bilanz (Konzernbilanz)', *Zeitschrift für handelswissenschaftliche Forschung*, vol 28.

Edwards, J.R. and Webb, K.M. (1984) 'The development of group accounting in the United Kingdom', *The Accounting Historians Journal*, Spring, pp. 31–61.

Ernst & Whinney (1980), *Consolidated Accounts in Europe*, Financial Times Business Information, London.

Garnsey, G. (1923) *Holding Companies and Their Published Accounts*, Gee.

Hein, L.W. (1978) *The British Companies Acts and the Practice of Accountancy 1844–1962*, Arno Press, New York.

Lee, T.A. (1974) 'Accounting for and disclosure of business combinations', *Journal of Business Finance and Accounting*, Spring, pp. 1–33.

Ma, R. and Parker, R.H. (1983) *Consolidation Accounting in Australia*, Longman Cheshire, Melbourne.

Mumford, M. (1982) 'The origins of consolidated accounts', University of Lancaster Accounting and Finance Working Party Series, No. 12, September.

Nederlands Instituut van Register accountants (NIVRA) (1985), *Onderzoek Jaarsverslagen 1983*, Amsterdam.

Further Reading

Busse von Colbe, W. and Ordelheide, D. (1984, 5th edn) *Konzernabschlüsse*, Galber, Wiesbaden.

Ernst & Whinney (1984), *The Impact of the Seventh Directive*, Financial Times Business Information, London.

McKinnon, J.L. (1984) 'Application of Anglo–American principles of consolidation to corporate financial disclosure in Japan', *Abacus*, June.

McKinnon, S.M. (1984) *The Seventh Directive, Consolidated Accounts in the EEC*, Kluwer Publishing and Arthur Young International.

Peat, Marwick, Mitchell & Co. (1984) *Consolidated Accounts, Seventh Directive.*

UEC Auditing Committee (1978) *The Preparation and Audit of Consolidated Financial Statements*, Gee & Co., London. (Originally published 1977 in German by IdW-Verlag, Düsseldorf.)

Walker, R.G. (1978) *Consolidated Statements*, Arno Press, New York.

11

Inflation Accounting

PATRICK KIRKMAN

Literature on inflation accounting has been readily available in the English-speaking world for fifty years (e.g. Sweeney 1936), although it was not until the 1970s that this subject became of widespread interest. In the 1950s and 1960s the average annual rate of inflation in most developed countries was below 4%, and accountants and businessmen were in most cases not seriously concerned about the effects of price changes on profit measurement. In the 1970s, there was a dramatic increase in the rate of price increases in most parts of the world, and many countries experienced 'double-digit' inflation which naturally produced more interest in inflation and its effects on accounting.

Largely as a result of these rates of inflation, several English-speaking countries began to experiment with inflation accounting systems in the late 1970s and early 1980s with information normally provided in supplementary form. During this period of experimentation, inflation rates began to fall – as can be seen from an examination of Table 11.1 – and the need for inflation accounting data began to be questioned as projected inflation rates went below the 5% per annum level. Published financial results showed that in these circumstances there could still be significant effects on profit measurement, although the impetus for adjustments naturally diminishes as inflation rates fall.

By the mid-1980s, therefore, the inflation accounting debate was not only about the type of system that should be used, but also about the real need for such a system. Users of financial statements had in most cases been unenthusiastic about the results of inflation accounting, and

Table 11.1 Annual Rates of Inflation — Selected Countries

	1971	1972	1973	1974	1975	1976	1977	1978	1979	1980	1981	1982	1983
United Kingdom	9.4	7.1	9.2	15.9	24.3	16.5	15.9	8.3	13.4	18.0	11.9	8.6	4.6
Ireland	8.9	8.7	11.3	17.0	20.9	18.0	13.7	7.6	13.2	18.2	20.4	17.1	10.5
France	5.5	6.2	7.3	13.7	11.8	9.2	9.8	9.1	10.5	13.6	13.4	11.8	9.6
West Germany	5.3	5.5	6.9	7.0	6.0	4.5	3.9	2.6	4.0	5.5	6.3	5.2	3.3
Belgium	4.3	5.5	7.0	12.7	12.7	9.2	7.1	4.5	4.6	6.7	7.6	8.7	7.7
Luxembourg	4.7	5.2	6.1	9.6	10.7	9.8	6.7	3.1	4.6	6.3	8.0	9.4	8.7
Netherlands	7.6	7.8	7.9	9.7	10.2	8.8	6.7	4.0	4.3	6.6	6.7	6.0	2.7
Italy	4.8	5.7	10.8	19.1	17.0	16.8	18.4	12.1	14.8	21.2	19.5	16.5	14.6
Denmark	5.8	6.6	9.3	15.2	9.6	9.0	11.1	10.0	9.6	12.3	NA	NA	6.9
Norway	6.2	7.2	7.5	9.4	11.6	9.2	9.1	8.1	4.8	10.9	13.6	11.4	8.4
Sweden	7.4	6.0	6.8	9.9	9.8	10.3	11.4	10.0	7.2	13.6	12.1	8.6	8.9
Spain	8.2	8.3	11.4	15.7	16.9	17.7	24.5	19.8	15.7	15.5	14.6	14.5	12.1
Switzerland	6.6	6.7	8.7	9.8	6.7	1.7	1.3	1.1	3.6	4.0	6.5	5.6	3.0
United States of America	4.3	3.3	6.2	11.0	9.1	5.8	6.5	7.6	11.5	13.5	10.2	6.0	3.2
Canada	2.9	4.8	7.6	10.9	10.8	7.5	8.0	8.9	9.2	10.2	12.4	10.8	5.8
Argentina	34.7	58.5	60.3	24.2	182.8	444.1	183.8	175.5	159.5	100.7	104.5	164.5	344.8
Brazil	NA	NA	15.5	24.9	30.2	35.3	40.5	38.3	50.2	77.9	95.7	89.3	135.8
Chile	20.0	77.5	354.0	504.5	374.7	211.9	92.0	40.1	33.4	35.1	19.7	9.9	27.3
Japan	6.1	4.5	11.7	24.5	11.8	9.3	8.1	3.8	3.6	8.0	4.9	2.7	1.8
India	3.3	6.3	16.8	28.8	5.6	(7.8)	8.5	2.5	6.4	11.5	13.1	7.7	12.0
Australia	6.1	5.8	9.4	15.1	15.1	13.6	12.3	7.9	10.9	10.2	9.7	11.1	10.1
New Zealand	10.4	6.9	8.2	11.1	14.7	17.0	14.3	11.9	13.7	17.2	15.4	16.1	7.4

Source: Derived from *United Nations Monthly Bulletin of Statistics, Consumer Price Index Information.*
Note: NA = not available.

many preparers questioned whether the benefits of disclosure were greater than the additional preparation and publication costs. In early 1985 it seemed likely, however, that the major English-speaking countries would continue to experiment with inflation accounting systems into the late 1980s, although the protest movement against the use of these systems was growing and there was certainly a possibility that inflation accounting recommendations might be partially or completely withdrawn.

The major objective of this chapter will be to provide information about recent international inflation accounting developments and to comment on possible future changes. It is not intended to examine all of these developments in detail, although references to more specialised material are provided, including articles which have studied the case for and against the various systems of inflation accounting and the effects and implications of the adoption of these systems. This aspect of the subject will be touched on only superficially in this chapter, although the author has examined these matters in more detail elsewhere (Kirkman 1978).

11.1 Terminology

There has been some controversy as to the subject matter that should be dealt with under the heading 'inflation accounting'. Some writers (e.g. AICPA 1963) have suggested that inflation accounting should only be concerned with accounting for changes in the general purchasing power of money. However, a complete study of accounting under inflationary conditions should be concerned with changes in both general and specific prices. In this chapter the term 'inflation accounting' will be used to cover all those methods of accounting which make some allowance for the effects of changing prices. This approach is now widely accepted in the academic world and the business sector.

There have also been differences of opinion concerning the best way to describe the major inflation accounting systems. The term 'general purchasing power accounting' will be used to describe all those accounting systems under which adjustments are made for general price changes. Other commonly used terms for this method are 'general price-level accounting' (frequently used in North America although there now appears to be an official preference for 'constant dollar accounting') and 'current purchasing power accounting' (the description adopted by the UK accountancy bodies).

The term 'current value accounting' is also widely used in inflation accounting literature. This term will be used to describe all those accounting systems which are concerned with the adjustment of historical costs to current values. The current value of an asset may be based on economic values, current replacement costs or net realisable values. In those countries which have experimented with current value accounting systems it has generally been decided that current values should be largely or completely based on current replacement costs. This system of accounting is now widely known as 'current cost accounting', although several European countries use the description 'replacement value accounting'.

11.2 United Kingdom

A small number of professional pronouncements on inflation accounting were issued in the UK in the seven years following the end of the Second World War (e.g., ACA, ICAEW and ICWA 1952). These documents had virtually no effect in the business sector, and the interest that had been aroused soon disappeared when inflation fell to a rate in the region of 4% per annum for most of the 1950s and 1960s. In the late 1960s, however, there was a significant change in the rate of price increases, and the Accounting Standards Committee (ASC) which was formed in 1969, decided that discussion material must be produced on this subject as quickly as possible.

Between 1971 and 1974 the ASC produced three documents on inflation accounting, all of which were concerned with changes in the general purchasing power of money:

(1) A discussion document and fact sheet, *Inflation and Accounts*, published in 1971 (12 pages).
(2) An exposure draft (ED8), *Accounting for Changes in the Purchasing Power of Money*, published in January 1973 (16 pages).
(3) A provisional statement of standard accounting practice (PSSAP7), *Accounting for Changes in the Purchasing Power of Money*, published in May 1974 (26 pages).

The latter document would probably have been a finalised statement of standard accounting practice if it had not been for the intervention of the UK Government in July 1973. At that time it was announced that a special committee of enquiry was to be set up 'to consider whether, and if so how, company accounts should allow for changes (including relative changes) in costs and prices'. The report of this committee, which eventually became known as the Sandilands Committee, will be considered later in this chapter.

The provisional standard published in May 1974 showed only a small number of changes from the 1971 and 1973 documents. The major recommendations contained in the 1974 statement were (paragraph 12):

  (a) Companies will continue to keep their records and present their basic annual accounts in historical pounds, i.e. in terms of the value of the pound at the time of each transaction or revaluation.
  (b) In addition, all listed companies should present to their shareholders a supplementary statement in terms of the value of the pound at the end of the period to which the accounts relate.
  (c) The conversion of the figures in the basic accounts into the figures in the supplementary statement should be by means of a general index of the purchasing power of the pound.
  (d) The standard requires the directors to provide in a note to the supplementary statement an explanation of the basis on which it has been prepared and it is desirable that directors should comment on the significance of the figures.

The provisional standard was issued at a time when the Sandilands Committee was considering what its recommendations should be on this subject, and it was not surprising that many companies decided to defer action until the official committee of enquiry produced its report. Nevertheless about 150 companies – about 6% of the total number of listed UK companies at that time – responded to the request of the accountancy bodies to publish the recommended information 'as soon as possible, and preferably not later than the first accounting period beginning after 30 June, 1974' (paragraph 44).

It is very difficult to assess what would have happened in the UK inflation accounting debate in the mid-1970s in the absence of government intervention. A finalised standard would probably have been issued, although there might have been protests from the business sector which had already been provided with much-needed taxation reliefs in the form of 100% capital allowances on plant and machinery and a generous stock relief system (these allowances were withdrawn in 1984). In the annual reports of those companies which produced supplementary general purchasing power (GPP) financial statements in 1974-5, there were numerous comments – mainly adverse – concerning the information value of the adjusted figures. Most of the protests were concerned with the unsatisfactory nature of the retail price index for adjustment purposes, and the inclusion in earnings of long-term purchasing power gains on monetary items. The treatment of these gains has been a major problem area in most inflation accounting proposals.

On the other hand, the advocates of GPP accounting stressed the simplicity of the system – adjustments need only be calculated once a year at the end of the financial year – and the probability that the costs incurred would be comparatively small once the age analysis of fixed assets had been prepared. There were serious doubts, however, amongst the users of financial statements as to whether any significant benefits were likely to accrue from the publication of GPP financial statements, especially when specific prices were moving at a very different rate from prices generally. There was, therefore, a significant amount of support for the view expressed in the Sandilands Committee Report that 'if UK company accounts are to show more adequately than at present the effect of changes in prices, it is accounting that must be changed, not the unit of measurement in which accounts are expressed' (paragraph 415).

The 364-page report on *Inflation Accounting* (the Sandilands Report) was completed in July 1975, although it was not published until September 1975. The committee recommended that all companies should as soon as practicable adopt an accounting system to be known as current cost accounting, the main features of which were (paragraph 519):

(a) Money is the unit of measurement.
(b) Assets and liabilities are shown in the balance sheet at a valuation.
(c) Operating profit is struck after charging the value to the business of assets consumed during the period, thus excluding holding gains from profit and showing them separately.

These recommendations were accepted with some reservations by the UK accountancy bodies, and a 94-page exposure draft, *Current Cost Accounting (ED18)*, was eventually published by the ASC in November 1976. This document did not, however, prove to be acceptable to members of the major accountancy bodies. In particular, the members of the largest professional body – the Institute of Chartered Accountants in England and Wales – were not satisfied with the recommendation that current cost accounting (CCA) statements should be made compulsory, and a resolution to this effect was passed at a special meeting in July 1977.

If the replacement of historical cost accounts by CCA statements had been the only objection to the proposals contained in ED 18, a compromise could probably have been arranged; for example, it could have been decided that CCA statements should be published in supplementary form. There were, however, several other objections. To many accountants the proposals appeared to be extremely complicated and subjective, especially for companies which were not listed on the Stock Exchange, and there also appeared to be numerous auditing problems. The omission of purchasing power losses and gains on monetary items was also heavily criticised, especially by the banks and other financial institutions.

The result of the objections to ED 18 was a new set of proposals issued by the ASC in November 1977 under the title *Inflation Accounting*

– *an Interim Recommendation*. These proposals, which became known as 'the Hyde Committee Guidelines', were extremely brief (only 12 pages), and were concerned only with the provision of supplementary profit statements for companies listed on the Stock Exchange. Three adjustments were suggested. The cost of sales and depreciation adjustments were (as in ED 18) based on the difference between historical and current cost accounting figures. In many companies these two adjustments had already been shown to reduce profits by a substantial amount. The third adjustment – the gearing adjustment – was based on the proposition that the effect of inflation accounting on profits will vary according to the capital gearing structure (usually described as leverage in North America) of the organisation.

The introduction of a gearing adjustment – which had not been included in the profit statement under the Sandilands Report and the ED 18 recommendations – was an acceptance by the ASC that monetary adjustments could not be completely ignored in an inflation accounting system. The suggested calculation in the case of an industrial company produced an 'add-back' to profit based on the following formula:

$$\frac{\text{Net monetary liabilities}}{\text{Total capital employed}} \times \begin{array}{l}\text{Total of depreciation and}\\\text{cost of sales adjustments}\end{array}$$

If, therefore, a large part of capital was made up of monetary liabilities – loan stock, bank finance etc. – the addition to profit would be relatively large because a substantial part of the inflationary 'loss' on depreciation and inventories would be borne by the providers of debt finance. If, on the other hand, virtually all the finance of the company were provided by equity shareholders, the addition to profit would be relatively small. In 1978 over 300 companies published supplementary CCA statements based on the Hyde Committee Guidelines. There was, therefore, some support for these proposals, despite argument concerning the theoretical correctness of the gearing adjustment (Fielding 1979).

The next development was the issue of an exposure draft (ED 24) – *Current Cost Accounting* – in April 1979. The recommendations contained in ED 24 were similar to those contained in the Hyde Committee Guidelines. There were, however, some important changes. For example, it was suggested that the supplementary CCA statement should be published by companies with a turnover in excess of £5m (subject to a small number of exceptions). It was also recommended that there should be a published CCA balance sheet, and that the gearing adjustment should be split into two parts – a monetary working capital adjustment (MWCA) and a revised gearing adjustment figure. The MWCA was primarily introduced in order to allow for the fact that cash retailers and other similar organisations are able to finance inventory increases by taking extra credit from suppliers. In these circumstances a large cost of sales adjustment is probably inappropriate, as inflationary losses are in effect partly or wholly borne by creditors. The overall effect of the MWCA in the manufacturing sector was small, although there were some companies which showed sizeable losses or gains.

By the beginning of 1980 the number of companies publishing CCA statements had increased to about 500. The accountancy bodies therefore decided that a standard (SSAP 16) should be issued in March 1980 to apply to accounting periods starting on or after 1 January 1980. As in ED 24 the major recommendation was for the publication of a CCA profit statement and balance sheet. There was, however, a significant change in the scope of the standard: the companies covered were those listed on the stock exchange (about 2,200 companies) plus all unlisted companies which satisfied at least two of the following three criteria (based on the UK proposals for implementing the EEC's fourth Directive) – (1) turnover of £5 million or more; (2) total assets of £2.5 million or more; and (3) employees numbering 250 or more (probably about 3,000 companies). There were a small number of exceptions; for example, insurance companies, investment trusts and unit trusts. The CCA data could be published as the main or supplementary accounts, although historical cost data had to be provided. The vast majority of companies publishing this information have shown CCA data in supplementary form.

The form of disclosure suggested in the standard is shown in Table 11.2. This format was not compulsory – experimentation was encouraged – although most major UK companies adopted a similar method of presentation. The major adjustments that were necessary in order to arrive at the CCA operating profit were those in respect of depreciation, cost of sales and monetary working capital. At a later stage in the profit and loss account the gearing adjustment was calculated as part of a revised retained profit figure. All these adjustments had to be disclosed, either in the CCA statement or in note form.

The adjusted balance sheet had to show CCA figures in respect of fixed assets and stocks. These assets had to be shown at their value to the business which was in most cases the current replacement cost of identical or similar assets of the same age and condition. The double entry for these adjustments was shown in the current cost reserve. Other balance sheet items were not normally adjusted.

The most controversial aspect of these recommendations was the gearing adjustment which was heavily attacked from both theoretical and practical viewpoints. In addition, there were major international

Table 11.2 Example of Presentation of Current Cost Accounts

Y Limited and Subsidiaries
Group Current Cost Profit and Loss Account for the year ended
31 December, 1980

1979 £'000		1980 £'000
18,000	Turnover	20,000
2,420	Profit before interest and taxation on the historical cost basis	2,900
1,320	Less: Current cost operating adjustments*	1,510
1,100	*Current Cost Operating Profit*	1,390
170	Gearing adjustment	166
180	Interest payable less receivable	200
10		34
1,090	Current cost profit before taxation	1,356
610	Taxation	730
480	*Current Cost Profit Attributable to Shareholders*	626
400	Dividends	430
80	Retained current cost profit of the year	196
16.0p	Current cost earnings per share	20.9p
5.2%	Operating profit return on net operating assets	6.0%

Statement of Retained Profits/Reserves

1979		1980
80	Retained current cost profit of the year	196
1,850	Movements on current cost reserve	2,054
Nil	Movements on other reserves	Nil
1,930		2,250
14,150	Retained profits/reserves at the beginning of the year	16,080
16,080	Retained profits/reserves at the end of the year	18,330

Summarised Group Current Cost Balance Sheet as at 31 December, 1980

1979 £'000	£'000		£'000	1980 £'000
		Assets Employed:		
	18,130	Fixed Assets		19,530
		Net Current Assets:		
3,200		Stock	4,000	
700		Monetary Working Capital	800	
3,900		Total Working Capital	4,800	
(400)		Proposed Dividends	(430)	
(600)		Other Current Liabilities (net)	(570)	
	2,900			3,800
	21,030			23,330
		Financed by:		
		Share Capital and Reserves:		
3,000		Share Capital	3,000	
12,350		Current Cost Reserve	14,404	
3,730		Other reserves and retained profit	3,926	
	19,080			21,330
	1,950	Loan Capital		2,000
	21,030			23,330

Source: Statement of Standard Accounting Practice 16, UK Accountancy Bodies 1980.
Note: *These adjustments would comprise items relating to depreciation, cost of sales and monetary working capital.

comparability problems as this adjustment frequently produces very different results from the purchasing power adjustment recommended in the US standard. This was a very important difference in the case of multinational companies with strong UK and US interests.

The initial response by major companies to SSAP 16 was reasonably satisfactory, with over 90% of the companies listed on the stock exchange providing CCA data. There was a much less satisfactory response, however, from those private companies which came within the stipulated size criteria. No official figures have been provided concerning the companies in this category, although unofficial estimates suggest that well under 25% of these companies published CCA statements.

With the fall in the rate of inflation in the early and mid-1980s, the enthusiasm for SSAP 16 began to wane and an increasing number of listed companies decided to stop publishing CCA data. The stock exchange recommendation that listed companies should follow the standard appeared to have little effect, as no action was generally taken in the case of non-disclosure. The auditor's brief comment about the omission of these data also appeared rather ineffective, and by the end of 1984 the percentage of listed companies publishing the recommended data was probably in the region of 50%.

The reaction of the UK accountancy bodies to these criticisms was to issue a new exposure draft (ED 35) *Accounting for the Effects of Changing Prices* in July 1984. Its recommendations were similar to those of SSAP 16, although there were some changes of emphasis. For example, it was suggested that:

(1) All public limited companies should be subject to the new standard, except for wholly owned subsidiaries and financial companies. There would be no size test as in SSAP 16, and private companies would not be affected by the standard.
(2) Where current cost accounts are *not* shown as the main accounts, the information disclosed should be given in a note to the main accounts and not in supplementary current cost statements (as in SSAP 16).
(3) Adjustment calculations should be very similar to those required in SSAP 16, although it is suggested that two additional methods of calculating the gearing adjustment should be accepted.
(4) A balance sheet should not be regarded as essential, although information should be provided regarding CCA figures for fixed assets and inventories.

These recommendations were attacked from many quarters in the latter part of 1984, and there were expected to be some significant changes before a new standard proved to be acceptable. At the end of 1984 the target date for the new standard was the second quarter of 1985, in order to replace SSAP 16 before its expiry. However, because of the opposition which the new exposure draft produced, ED was abandoned.

SSAP 16 was withdrawn in 1985 without immediate replacement, although eventually there will probably be a new standard which may in some respects be very similar. It seems probable, however, that there will be some changes concerning the gearing adjustment, and the required information may be shown in simplified form as a note to the main financial statements. The latter requirement will almost certainly have legal implications, especially as far as the auditor's report is concerned.

By the end of 1987 we may therefore have a revitalised inflation accounting standard in operation in the UK. It is possible, however, that the protest movement against the publication of inflation accounting data could grow to such an extent that the recommendations could be completely withdrawn and no new standard issued. Much will depend on the rate of inflation. A rate of below 5% per annum could sound the death knell for inflation accounting, although this will in effect be an admission that the UK accountancy profession has failed in its attempts to find a satisfactory method of measuring the effects of price changes in financial statements.

11.3 Europe (excluding the UK)

There have been very few important inflation accounting developments in Europe (excluding the UK) in the last decade. Rates of inflation have varied very significantly. In a small number of countries, for example Germany and Switzerland, price increases were kept down to an average rate of about 5% per annum in the latter part of the 1970s and the early 1980s and current rates are in the region of 3%. As a result of this, and memories of hyper-inflation in Germany in the 1920s and 1940s, there has been very little enthusiasm for inflation accounting, and the West German government was reluctant to allow any provision in EEC Directives for member states to use inflation accounting systems.

In several other countries annual rates of inflation reached double-digit levels in the late 1970s. France, Ireland, Italy and Spain had the highest average levels of inflation in that period (see Table 11.1) although these rates have dropped very significantly in recent years. It was therefore surprising that inflation accounting systems were not more seriously considered in the late 1970s.

The EEC fourth Directive – published in July 1978 – did after a lot of argument contain provisions which allowed member states to introduce inflation accounting systems. The valuation rules contained in the Directive were based on historical cost principles, although Article 33 did allow member states to permit or require companies to value tangible fixed assets and inventories on a replacement or other appropriate inflation accounting basis.

The main pressure for the replacement value clause in the fourth Directive came initially from the Netherlands, where replacement value systems have been used by a small but significant number of companies for many years (see Chapter 6 for more information on this subject). In more recent years support has come from other countries, including the UK and Ireland. There has, however, been little experimentation with inflation accounting in company financial statements outside the UK although this subject has been examined in some detail in several countries.

In France, a government-sponsored committee recommended in November 1976 that companies listed on the stock exchange should produce supplementary financial statements based on GPP principles. These recommendations were not accepted by the French government, although legislation concerning the revaluation of assets was introduced in the Finance Acts of 1977 and 1978. This legislation, which was mandatory for listed companies but optional for most other companies, laid down that all long-term assets should be revalued at their value to the enterprise at 31 December 1976. Initial regulations were concerned with non-depreciable assets, although it was eventually decided that all long-term assets should be revalued. Earnings figures were little changed, however, as any additional depreciation was cancelled out by an equivalent revaluation surplus in the latter part of the profit statement. (See Chapter 4.)

In the 1980s very little progress was made in France on this subject, although documents were issued by the professional accountancy body (Ordre des Experts Comptables et des Comptables Agréés) in 1981 and 1984 (see Chapter 4). These documents suggested that adjustments could be made in supplementary form for the effect of prices changes on depreciation, cost of sales and monetary items. The permissive nature of these recommendations and the lack of tax incentives suggest that there will be little response by the business sector, especially now that inflation rates appear to be falling.

In West Germany, a statement on inflation accounting was issued in October 1975 by a committee of the German Institute of Accountants (Institut der Wirtschaftsprüfer). This document recommended that the effect of changing prices on profit should be shown in supplementary notes included in the annual reports and accounts. The supplementary information was expected to be audited. The suggested form of the supplementary material was as follows:

Additional depreciation based on the replacement cost of   ....
   fixed assets

Amount necessary to maintain the real value of inventories   ....

                                                                        ——

Total of necessary adjustments (inflationary profits)   ....

                                                                        ——

The official statement recommended that only equity-financed assets should be brought into account in the calculation of the relevant amounts. To help in this calculation, the statement suggested that it should be assumed that equity funds provided finance for fixed assets before the purchase of inventories. The adjustments for depreciation and inventories were therefore reduced in a similar way to the gearing adjustment recommendation in the UK. No adjustments were required in the main financial statements, although comments have occasionally been provided in accompanying notes; for example, Siemens has commented on the effect of price changes on profits on several occasions.

However, this type of adjustment has not been very much used in Germany because of low rates of inflation and the lack of taxation incentives. There was also a feeling in government circles that countries should attack inflation rather than introduce inflation accounting; but academics have carried out a considerable amount of research on this subject, largely because of the very high rates of inflation that were experienced in the 1920s and 1940s (e.g. Sweeney 1927; Schmidt 1930).

In the Netherlands, replacement value accounting systems have been used since the 1920s, largely as a result of the teaching of Prof. Th. Limperg Jr. of the Municipal University of Amsterdam. Full usage in published financial statements has, however, been restricted to a small number of influential companies – for example Philips Gloeilampenfabrieken – although a significant number of companies make partial adjustments, especially for fixed assets and depreciation.

There is no legislation in the Netherlands requiring the adoption of inflation accounting systems, although occasional statements on this subject have been issued by the major accountancy body (Nederlands Instituut van Register Accountants) and by a tripartite committee representing employers, trade unions and accountants (The Council for Annual Reporting). New company legislation, based on the EEC fourth Directive, was enacted in December 1983. This laid down that corporate bodies could value tangible fixed assets and inventories on a current cost basis, although there is no compulsion to use this method of accounting, and taxation is still largely based on historical costs. It seems probable, therefore, that the Act will not produce any significant changes in company attitudes towards inflation accounting systems (see Chapter 6).

In the remaining EEC countries there have been no important inflation accounting developments, although in countries such as Italy there have occasionally been taxation concessions based on current value depreciation or the LIFO (last in, first out) system of inventory valuation. Outside the EEC, however, a few large companies have decided to use partial inflation accounting systems. For example, in Sweden, Alfa Laval provides an inflation-adjusted profit statement and Volvo publishes a considerable amount of replacement cost data in note form. In Switzerland, several large companies use inflation accounting systems; for example, Ciba-Geigy and Sulzer are heavily committed to current cost accounting and use this system extensively in their main accounts.

It is difficult, therefore, to generalise about inflation accounting in a European context. There does, however, appear to be a great reluctance to depart from historical cost accounting principles, due in some countries to the close links between taxation computations and financial reporting. In countries where there has been a considerable degree of flexibility concerning the content and presentation of financial statements, as in the Netherlands, a few leading companies do provide some inflation accounting data, usually based on current replacement costs. The number of companies publishing full current cost data, in the Netherlands and elsewhere in Europe, is however very small.

11.4 North America

The great volume of writing on inflation accounting in North America has had surprisingly little effect on the annual reports of major US companies although supplementary data have been published in the 1980s. In the 1960s and 1970s a few firms published supplementary GPP financial statements. Probably the best known of these was the Indiana Telephone Corporation which published GPP statements for many years before it was taken over in the late 1970s. In addition, there has been widespread use of the LIFO method of inventory valuation which does make some allowance for the effects of changing prices on profits. The LIFO method is accepted in the US for taxation purposes, unlike the UK, Canada and many other countries. Accelerated methods of depreciation accounting are also accepted for taxation purposes, and they have been used fairly extensively.

Most of the inflation accounting publications of the AICPA have been concerned with GPP accounting. For example, in 1963 a detailed research study was produced on *Reporting the Financial Effects of Price-Level Changes*. This created very little interest amongst business organisations and in 1969 the AICPA accepted in another document, *Financial Statements Restated for General Price-Level Changes*, that this type of financial information was 'not required at this time for fair presentation of financial position and results of operations in conformity with generally accepted accounting principles in the United States'. These comments were made at a time when the rate of inflation in the USA was very low – below 3% per annum – and the subject was not considered again until rates of inflation began to rise at a fairly rapid rate in the mid-1970s.

The Financial Accounting Standards Board, which was set up in 1973, reopened discussions on this subject, and an exposure draft on *Financial Reporting in Units of General Purchasing Power* was issued in 1974. This document suggested that supplementary GPP financial statements should be provided in financial years commencing on or after 1 January 1976. There was in this case an adverse reaction from businessmen and accountants, many of whom suggested that GPP financial statements would not provide sufficient benefits to compensate for the extra costs involved. In addition, the SEC made it clear that it would prefer a reporting system based on replacement costs.

In June 1976, the FASB announced that it was deferring further consideration of the 1974 exposure draft, as GPP financial information 'is not now sufficiently well understood by preparers and users, and the need for it is not now sufficiently well demonstrated, to justify imposing the cost of implementation upon all preparers of financial statements at this time'. Probably no more than ten American companies published GPP financial statements, although one large corporation – the Shell Oil Company – has provided this type of information in its annual report for several years.

The inflation accounting debate in the USA entered a new stage in 1976 when the SEC published *Accounting Series Release No. 190* which required the disclosure of replacement cost information by major listed companies in the return submitted to the SEC at the end of each financial year. There was *no* requirement that this information should be published in the annual report for shareholders. The corporations affected by these regulations were those listed on recognised Stock Exchanges which had total inventories, gross property, plant and equipment (before deducting accumulated depreciation) in excess of $100 million, and which comprised more than 10% of total assets at the beginning of the most recent financial year. The commencement date of these provisions was the first financial year ending on or after 25 December 1976. The stipulated replacement cost data were as follows:

(1) The current cost (both gross and net of accumulated depreciation) of newly replacing the productive capacity of property, plant and

equipment at the end of each year for which a balance sheet was required.

(2) The current replacement cost of inventories at the end of each year for which a balance sheet was required. If the net realisable value of inventories was less than the replacement cost, this fact was to be stated and the excess disclosed.

(3) Depreciation (using the straight line method) for the two most recent financial years based on the average current cost of productive capacity.

(4) The approximate amount which the cost of sales would have been for the two most recent financial years if it had been calculated by estimating the replacement cost of goods and services at the time sales took place.

The main objective of these regulations was to provide information for investors to assist them in obtaining an understanding of the current costs of the business. An adjusted profit figure did *not* have to be provided, although many analysts used the replacement cost figuies as an aid in the production of revised profit figures. There was no requirement that purchasing power losses and gains on monetary items should be disclosed, a serious deficiency as far as many inflation accounting advocates were concerned. Nevertheless, the users of financial statements were able for the first time to obtain replacement cost information, though it is by no means clear what use was made of these data.

The reaction of the business sector toward the SEC regulations was rather hostile, mainly because of the amount of time involved in preparing the replacement cost data and the supposed lack of value in such figures. One of the most detailed studies of this subject (O'Connor and Chandra 1978) suggested that the compliance costs in the first year of implementation ranged from $15,000 to $360,000, with a typical estimate of about $100,000. Most of the internal staff interviewed during this survey doubted whether the replacement cost data would be useful either internally or externally. In addition, it was considered that the data were 'too subjective, too piecemeal, and had little to do with the actual economics of the reporting entity' (p.3). Also, external analysts were sceptical about the value of the additional information; for example, 70% of the analysts questioned in the survey stated that in their opinion the SEC requirements were not the best solution to the problem of reporting the effects of changing prices.

After the issue of the SEC's replacement cost regulations, the FASB decided to concentrate on the objectives of financial statements in the hope that this would help in the search for a more satisfactory method of income measurement. Their interim conclusions were published in December 1977 in the form of an exposure draft, *Objectives of Financial Reporting and Elements of Financial Statements of Business Enterprises*. This exposure draft was followed in November 1978 by Statement of Financial Accounting Concepts No. 1 — *Objectives of Financial Reporting by Business Enterprises*. This document recommended that 'financial reporting should provide information that is useful to present and potential investors and creditors and other users in making rational investment, credit and similar decisions'. It was also suggested that the information provided should 'help investors, creditors and others assess the amounts, timing, and uncertainty of prospective net cash inflows to the related enterprise' (p.viii). These pronouncements certainly seem to have had a significant influence on recent FASB publications.

Following the publication of the 'objectives' statement, the FASB returned to the subject of inflation accounting, and in December 1978 a new exposure draft appeared on *Financial Reporting and Changing Prices*. This document recommended that major US corporations should publish supplementary financial statements based on either general purchasing power or current cost principles. Corporations that presented current cost data were also asked to provide information on holding gains or losses, net of inflation, and a statement of the current cost of inventory and property, plant, and equipment at the end of the fiscal year. The current cost method appeared to be the preferred basis of adjustment unless depreciation charges and the cost of goods sold were relatively small, or price changes affecting assets were approximately the same as the change in the general price level.

In October 1979, Statement of Financial Accounting Standards No. 33, *Financial Reporting and Changing Prices*, was issued by the FASB. This applied to public enterprises with either (1) inventories and property, plant and equipment (before deducting accumulated depreciation) amounting to more than $125 million or (2) total assets amounting to more than $1 billion (this latter clause was primarily intended to cover banks and other financial institutions).

The major change from the 1978 exposure draft was that *both* general purchasing power and current cost statements had to be published. The required GPP information was:

(a) income from continuing operations adjusted for the effects of general information;
(b) the purchasing power gain or loss on net monetary items.

In addition, the following current cost information had to be disclosed:

(a) income from continuing operations on a current cost basis;
(b) the current cost amounts of inventory and property, plant and equipment at the end of the fiscal year;
(c) increases or decreases in current cost amounts of inventory and property, plant and equipment net of inflation.

It was stressed that it had been decided 'to allow flexibility in the choice of format so that enterprises may experiment to find methods of presentation which they believe to be most effective in their present circumstances' (paragraph 203). Financial data adjusted for changing prices were also required.

The number of corporations affected by the standard in 1984 was in the region of 1,300, all of which appeared to comply with the standard, as non-compliance accompanied by an audit qualification almost inevitably causes the SEC to reject the financial statements. For a corporation listed on one of the stock exchanges, this could lead to withdrawal of a stock exchange listing.

Major American corporations have had over four years of experience in the production of supplementary inflation accounting statements. In most cases the method of presentation has been very similar to that suggested in the standard. An example can be seen in the published data of Eastman Kodak shown in Table 11.3. It should be noted that an adjusted balance sheet is not provided. There was no recommendation regarding this matter in the standard.

The requirements contained in FAS 33 were accompanied by a statement that the standard would 'be reviewed comprehensively after a period of not more than five years' (paragraph 5). A new exposure draft was issued early in December 1984. This was similar to FAS 33, although the requirement for the publication of GPP data within the income statement was withdrawn. The new accounting standard (FAS 82) was issued in 1985, although a rate of inflation below 3% in 1984/5 had led some accountants to call for the complete withdrawal of pronouncements on inflation accounting. The USA has therefore fallen in line with other English-speaking countries in restricting supplementary income statement disclosures to CCA data.

In Canada, the production of financial statements has been influenced by both American and British ideas. As in the UK and the USA, initial inflation accounting proposals were based on supplementary GPP financial statements (CICA 1975), but there was not enough support for these proposals to be implemented. In the following year a discussion paper was produced on current value accounting (CICA 1976), but this was not followed by an exposure draft, although further discussion documents were produced at provincial level, for example in Ontario.

In December 1979 an exposure draft, *Current Cost Accounting* was issued and this was eventually followed by an accounting standard, *Reporting the Effects of Changing Prices* in October 1982. The standard requires companies to publish supplementary inflation accounting data and is operative for financial years commencing on or after 1 January 1983. The companies affected by this standard are those having equity or debt traded in a public market and having either inventories and

Table 11.3 Eastman Kodak — Extract from Annual Report for 1983

Notes to Financial Statements

Statement of Earnings Adjusted for Changing Prices

(in millions) For the Year ended December 25, 1983	Per financial statements (Historical cost)	Adjusted for general inflation (Constant dollar)	Adjusted for changes in specific prices (Current cost)
Sales	$10,170	$10,170	$10,170
Cost of goods sold (excluding depreciation)	6,467	6,467	6,467
Sales, advertising, distribution, and administrative expenses (excluding depreciation)	2,024	2,024	2,024
Depreciation expenses	652	814	805
Investment income	122	122	122
Interest expense	117	117	117
Other income and (charges)	(12)	(12)	(12)
Provision for income taxes	455	455	455
Net earnings	$ 565	$ 403	$ 412
Loss from decline in purchasing power of net monetary assets		$ 8	$ 8
Increase in values of inventories and property, plant and equipment held during the year:			
Measured in constant dollars			$ 422
Measured in current cost*			90
Difference between the increase in the general price level and the increase in specific prices			$ 332

Note: *At December 25, 1983, the current cost of property, plant and equipment, net of accumulated depreciation, was $8,475 million and the current cost of inventory was $2,710 million.

5-Year Comparison of Selected Supplemental Financial Data Adjusted for the Effects of Changing Prices*

	1983	1982	1981	1980	1979
	(in millions, except per share)				
SALES					
Per financial statements	$10,170	$10,815	$10,337	$9,734	$8,028
Constant dollar	10,170	11,161	11,319	11,768	11,022
NET EARNINGS					
Per financial statements	565	1,162	1,239	1,154	1,001
Constant dollar	403	1,055	1,187	1,236	1,157
Current cost	412	1,014	1,165	1,164	1,070
NET EARNINGS PER COMMON SHARE					
Per financial statements	3.41	7.12	7.66	7.15	6.20
Constant dollar	2.43	6.46	7.34	7.65	7.17
Current cost	2.49	6.21	7.21	7.22	6.60
NET ASSETS					
Per financial statements	7,520	7,541	6,770	6,028	5,391
Constant dollar	11,666	11,990	11,443	11,014	10,692
Current cost	11,691	12,225	11,975	12,322	12,927
LOSS FROM DECLINE IN PURCHASING POWER OF NET MONETARY ASSETS	8	17	76	144	168
DIFFERENCE BETWEEN INCREASE IN THE GENERAL PRICE LEVEL AND INCREASE IN SPECIFIC PRICES	332	124	572	(312)	
CASH DIVIDENDS DECLARED PER COMMON SHARE					
Per financial statements	3.55	3.55	3.50	3.20	2.90
Constant dollar	3.55	3.66	3.83	3.87	3.98
MARKET PRICE PER COMMON SHARE AT YEAR-END					
Actual	75½	85⅜	71⅛	69½	48¼
Constant dollar	74¼	88⅜	78	84	66¼
AVERAGE CONSUMER PRICE INDEX (1967 = 100)	298.4	289.1	272.4	246.8	217.4

Notes: (a) * Constant dollar and current cost data in average 1983 dollars.
(b) There is no cost of sales adjustment in the earnings statement because of the extensive use of the LIFO (last-in first-out) method of inventory valuation.

property, plant and equipment (before depreciation) totalling $50 million or more, or total assets (after depreciation) of $350 million or more.

Most of the required data are of a CCA nature and should include figures in respect of the cost of goods sold and depreciation, current and deferred taxation, and the income before extraordinary items. Figures in respect of the financing (or gearing) adjustment and the purchasing power loss or gain on monetary items are also required. A CCA balance sheet is *not* required, although the current cost of inventories and property, plant and equipment should be disclosed. Changes during the latest reporting period in CCA terms should also be provided, together with comparative information concerning the change in general price terms.

The response to the Canadian standard has been disappointing. About 300 companies are covered by the standard, but less than 25% have published data in accordance with it. This figure might have been much smaller if the American SEC had not required Canadian companies quoted on US stock exchanges to file data in accordance with the standard.

The Canadian standard is therefore a strange mixture of American and British influences. The adopted model is primarily of CCA origin and therefore nearer to the UK standard, although a small amount of GPP data does have to be disclosed. The standard does in some ways, however, follow the American approach in that no balance sheet is required and that the information published has to be in supplementary form. Future developments are likely to be more influenced by US practices, as most leading Canadian companies are now quoted on US stock exchanges.

11.5 South America

Most countries in South America have experienced extremely high rates of inflation in recent years, and consequently there have been more experiments with inflation accounting systems than in any other continent. In most cases, adjustments have been initiated by governments, mainly for taxation purposes, although the accountancy profession in some of these countries has made determined efforts to change historical cost accounting systems.

In Brazil, inflation accounting adjustments have been used since the 1950s. A comprehensive system of inflation accounting was set up in 1964 as part of a national strategy for reducing the harmful effects of inflation. Under this system, fixed assets and investments (not inventories) were compulsorily adjusted at the end of each financial year, based on changes in an official government index. Depreciation was based on the restated asset figures. There was also an adjustment for working capital items which was intended to provide an allowance for the maintenance of the purchasing power of inventories and net monetary items. The stipulated adjustments were made in the main financial statements – both the profit statement and balance sheet – and the revised profit figure was accepted for taxation purposes. The controversial subject of purchasing power gains on long-term monetary liabilities was not considered as part of these regulations, probably because the vast majority of long-term loan agreements are now linked to a price index.

A few changes have been made to the Brazilian inflation accounting procedures in the last ten years. For example, a new Corporation Law was passed in 1976 requiring all companies to prepare their primary financial statements in a recommended inflation accounting form for fiscal years commencing after 1 January 1978. The basic principles behind the system have not changed very significantly since 1964, except that the mechanics of the system are now laid down in more detail. The working capital adjustment has, however, been replaced by an 'inflationary loss' calculation which is largely made up of exchange and monetary losses, although the gross loss has to be reduced by any gains on correction of the balance sheet (Fleming 1979).

In Argentina, the accountancy profession has been heavily involved in the development of inflation accounting proposals, and a statement was issued in 1972 recommending the publication of supplementary GPP financial statements from 1973 onwards. It was envisaged that eventually these statements would replace historical cost information (Argentina Technical Institute of Public Accountants 1972). Compliance was poor initially, as was shown by a study of companies listed on the Buenos Aires Stock Exchange which showed that only 11% provided inflation-adjusted financial information and only 4% disclosed an adjusted profit figure (Zeff 1980). There has, however, been some improvement in recent years because of a pronouncement by the organisation which regulates the accounting profession in Buenos Aires. This body recommended that GPP data should be provided for financial years ending 1 October 1979 or later. Inflation-adjusted financial statements have also been accepted for tax purposes.

In Chile, rates of inflation over the last decade have been high, and the accountancy profession has made efforts to introduce GPP accounting. There was initially little government support for these proposals, although in 1975 it was reported that Chile had become the first country to accept a comprehensive GPP accounting system for both financial reporting and taxation purposes (Zeff and Ovando 1975).

In several other countries in South and Central America, discussion documents have been produced on inflation accounting although very little effective action has been taken. In Mexico several documents have been produced by the Mexican Institute of Accountants and, in 1983, it was recommended that supplementary statements showing the effects of inflation should be published by all companies. In other countries, for example Peru and Uruguay, the restatement of fixed asset figures for depreciation purposes has been accepted for many years, although the major objective behind these changes has been a reduction in taxation commitments rather than a revised system of accounting.

In 1985, therefore, inflation accounting information was being produced in several South American countries. In most cases a general price index is used for adjustment purposes, partly because of the absence of satisfactory specific asset indices. As a result, it seems unlikely that current value accounting systems will become extensively used in South America, although this part of the world will probably continue to be fertile ground for inflation accounting experiments.

11.6 Australasia

In Australia a substantial amount of literature has been produced on inflation accounting. Particularly important contributions have come from R.J. Chambers, one of the best known advocates of a system based on net realisable values, and R.S. Gynther, a strong supporter of current cost accounting. (Some of the contributions of these writers are mentioned in the further reading section at the end of this chapter.) Another notable contributor on this subject has been R.L. Mathews, who was the chairman of the government-sponsored committee which examined the Australian taxation system (*Report of the Committee of Inquiry into Inflation and Taxation 1975*). This committee recommended, among other things, that the business taxation system should be adjusted for specific price changes. The government reaction to these recommendations has been disappointing; a limited inventory relief system (the trading stock valuation adjustment) was introduced in 1976 but this was soon withdrawn.

There has been little disclosure of CCA information in financial reports. A small number of companies have, however, been prepared to experiment with partial CCA systems. In particular, the Broken Hill Proprietary Company based depreciation on current costs for many years. In addition, a few listed companies, e.g. British Petroleum, John Fairfax and the Direct Acceptance Corporation, have published supplementary CCA information.

The Australian Accounting Standards Committee (AASC), which used to prepare discussion documents and exposure drafts for the two professional accountancy bodies, the Institute of Chartered Accountants in Australia and the Australian Society of Accountants, produced several documents on inflation accounting. In December 1974 the AASC issued a preliminary exposure draft *A Method of Accounting for Changes in the Purchasing Power of Money.* A further preliminary exposure draft *A Method of Current Value Accounting* was issued in June 1975. The Australians were, therefore, able to debate the comparative merits of GPP accounting and current value systems at approximately the same time, as comments on both exposure drafts were required by 31 December 1975.

The majority of Australian accountants appeared to prefer the current value accounting proposals, and it was decided to issue a provisional statement on *Current Cost Accounting* (DPS 1.1) in October 1976. The original intention was that a standard should be issued requiring companies to publish supplementary CCA statements for accounting periods commencing on or after 1 July 1977. The suggested speed of implementation was, however, strongly criticised by many Australian accountants and businessmen, as was the recommendation that CCA statements should eventually become the principal basis for published financial statements.

As a result of these criticisms an amended provisional statement was issued in August 1978. This was only concerned with the disclosure in supplementary form of CCA information about fixed assets, depreciation, inventories and the cost of goods sold. Recommendations concerning monetary items were contained in a separate exposure draft, *The Recognition of Gains and Losses on Holding Monetary Resources in the Context of Current Cost Accounting,* issued in July 1978. The latter document produced a very adverse response and a revised exposure draft was issued in August 1979.

A detailed consideration of the responses took place in 1980 and a draft standard was prepared in April 1981. This was circulated to interested parties, and a small number of minor amendments were incorporated into another published draft which was circulated to all members of the professional accountancy bodies in August 1982. However, at the end of 1983 it was decided that an accounting standard would *not* be issued, primarily because of strong opposition in the business sector. However, the draft standard was converted into a statement of accounting practice (SAP 1 – *Current Cost Accounting*) to provide guidance for those companies producing CCA statements.

At the end of a protracted discussion process the Australian accountancy bodies have therefore decided that there was insufficient public support for a standard. In its place a 'statement of accounting practice' has been issued which does not have the same power. As a result, only about ten companies published full CCA data in 1983/4 out of a total of nearly 1,000 companies listed on the stock exchanges.

This is a very sad result for those accountants who have spent years seeking to set up a comprehensive CCA system in Australia.

Similar problems have been experienced in New Zealand. Initially, an exposure draft, *Accounting for Changes in the Purchasing Power of Money*, was issued by the New Zealand Society of Accountants in December 1974. The suggested GPP approach did not produce much support, and in August 1976 a new exposure draft (ED 14) was issued on *Accounting in Terms of Current Costs and Values*. Meanwhile, the government set up a special committee (the Richardson Committee) to look at all aspects of inflation accounting. The report of this committee was published in December 1976 (*Report of the Committee of Inquiry into Inflation Accounting*). The members of the Committee had the great advantage that two major government-sponsored reports were available to them – the Sandilands Report in the UK and the Mathews Report in Australia. The result of their efforts was a very comprehensive report of 268 pages.

The recommendations of the Richardson Committee were in many respects similar to those contained in the Sandilands and Mathews Reports. For example, it was recommended that revised cost of sales and depreciation figures should normally be based on current replacement costs. The approach on monetary items was, however, very different as it was suggested that an additional charge should be made against profits for the maintenance of the purchasing power of circulating monetary assets. Monetary liabilities were not to be taken into account in this calculation. The revised profit figure after these adjustments was to be described as CCA operating profit. Further adjustments were then to be made to arrive at 'the profit attributable to the owners'.

There was little response by government to these recommendations, and as a result the New Zealand Society of Accountants issued a guideline document (GU -1) in 1978 and an exposure draft (ED25 – *Current Cost Accounting*) in 1981. These documents were followed by an accounting standard (CCA 1 – *Information Reflecting the Effect of Changing Prices*) in April 1982. The standard requires all companies which have securities listed on the New Zealand stock exchange to publish supplementary CCA statements for financial periods commencing on or after 1 April 1982.

The recommendations contained in the New Zealand standard are similar to those contained in the UK standard (SSAP 16), although there are slight differences in the calculation of the monetary working capital and gearing adjustments. The CCA profit statement and balance sheet are, however, expected to be in supplementary form, and there is no provision for CCA data to be shown in place of the historical cost accounts.

The response by New Zealand companies to this standard has been very disappointing, with less than 10% of the 200 companies listed on the stock exchange publishing full CCA data. The stock exchange has recommended that listed companies should comply with statements of standard accounting practice but there has been no effective action in the case of non-compliance.

A great amount of work has therefore been carried out on inflation accounting proposals in Australia and New Zealand. The response of the business sector has, however, been unenthusiastic, and with inflation rates dropping it now looks as if the overall effects of the many pronouncements issued will be extremely small.

11.7 Other Countries

There have been very few inflation accounting developments in Africa and Asia despite high rates of inflation. In the vast majority of cases, however, the accountancy profession is at an early stage of development and most accountants prefer to await developments in Europe, North America and Australasia.

On the African continent the only country that has produced a detailed statement is South Africa, where a *Guideline on Disclosure of Effects of Changing Prices on Financial Results* was issued by the National Council of Chartered Accountants in August 1978. This document was only concerned with the profit statement and was similar to the UK's Hyde Committee Guidelines. A few South African companies published inflation-adjusted data in response to this statement, but the overall level of response was poor and it was decided that an accounting standard would not be issued.

In Asia several countries, such as Indonesia, Japan and Korea, have over the past thirty years introduced temporary legislation permitting the use of inflation-adjusted fixed asset and depreciation figures. In most cases the recommended adjustments were concerned with taxation computations rather than financial reporting. In Japan the Ministry of Finance appointed a study group in 1978 to monitor inflation accounting developments in the UK and North America, but this did not lead to any positive action.

One country that has experienced very high rates of inflation in recent years has been Israel. The Institute of Certified Public Accountants in Israel has produced an inflation accounting 'opinion' as a result of which several major companies have produced GPP statements, e.g. Dubek.

Developments in Africa, Asia and many other parts of the world may be influenced by the pronouncements of the International Accounting Standards Committee which has produced several documents on this subject. An accounting standard (IAS 6 – *Accounting Responses to Changing Prices*) was published in June 1977. This stated that 'enterprises should present in their financial statements information that describes the procedures adopted to reflect the impact on financial statements of specific price changes, changes in general level of prices, or of both. If no such procedures have been adopted that fact should be disclosed'. A further standard (IAS 15 – *Information Reflecting the Effects of Changing Prices)* was issued in June 1981; this applies to financial statements for periods beginning on or after 1 January 1983. The required information, which covers depreciation, cost of sales and monetary items, should show the effects of changing prices and may be in either a general purchasing power or current cost form. These data should be provided on a supplementary basis unless information is presented in the primary financial statements. There was no detailed evidence available regarding the effect, if any, of this standard in early 1985.

11.8 Summary

Over the last two decades there has been extensive international experimentation with inflation accounting systems, largely as a result of the high levels of inflation during the 1970s and early 1980s. Before this there had been some academic writings, although these had produced little response in the business sector, apart from areas such as South America where inflation had been rampant for many years.

In the 1970s there were several discernible trends in the search for more satisfactory systems of accounting measurement under inflationary conditions. In the early part of the decade, several English-speaking countries experimented with, or at least considered the adoption of, supplementary GPP financial statements. By the end of the decade, however, there was a significant measure of agreement that GPP statements without current value information did not provide any great improvement in published financial information, although in South America there were few alternatives available in the absence of national price data relating to specific assets. The US standard, published in 1979, was in some respects rather different from documents published in other English-speaking countries, in that GPP figures were required as well as current cost information, although GPP data is not required in the USA from 1985 onwards.

In the late 1970s and early 1980s there was a strong movement in favour of CCA systems largely based on the Sandilands Committee recommendations in the UK that asset values and the associated profit figures should be based on current values rather than historical costs.

Initially it was suggested that the CCA data should take the place of the historical cost figures, but this approach was soon abandoned and most companies provided these data in supplementary form.

Initially, the major problem in reaching agreement on CCA systems centred around the very controversial matter of monetary losses and gains, on which subject different recommendations were produced in all five of the major English-speaking countries – UK, USA, Canada, Australia and New Zealand. When systems were put into operation other problems emerged, especially the calculation of current replacement values when technological change had produced very significant changes in asset efficiency and construction.

In the mid-1980s the character of the debate changed as projected inflation rates fell below 5% per annum and an increasing number of accountants began to doubt the value of inflation accounting. In 1985/6 important decisions will have to be made in the UK and USA regarding the issue or abandonment of accounting standards. These decisions will undoubtedly have a great effect on the continued use of inflation accounting data, although the work of the 1970s and early 1980s should be of value in those countries that continue to experience high rates of inflation.

It seems extremely likely therefore that by the end of the 1980s the historical cost accounting system will still be in extensive use internationally, despite the many assaults that have been launched against it in the last decade. There will probably continue to be experimentation with inflation accounting systems in primary statements in a few countries (mainly in South America) but these will most likely be very limited. The disclosure of supplementary inflation accounting data may continue on a limited scale, although continued inflation below 5% per annum will probably lead to the eventual demise of these systems. Accountants will therefore have to hope that high rates of inflation do not re-emerge in the 1990s, as we do not seem to have learned from the experiences of the last decade how profit should be measured under inflationary conditions (Mumford 1979).

References

Fielding, J. (1979) 'The gearing adjustment – what is the best method?', *Accountancy*, May pp. 73-74.

Fleming, R. (1979) 'New concepts in Brazilian accounting for inflation', *The Accountant's Magazine*, April, pp. 162-165.

Kirkman, P. R. A. (1978, 2nd edn) *Accounting under Inflationary Conditions*, Allen & Unwin.

Mumford, M. (1979) 'The end of a familiar inflation accounting cycle', *Accounting and Business Research*, Spring.

O'Connor, M. C. and Chandra, G. A. (1978) *Replacement Cost Disclosures: A Study of Compliance with the SEC Requirement,* National Association of Accountants.

Schmidt, F. (1930) 'The impact of replacement value', *Accounting Review,* September, pp. 235-242.

Sweeney, H. W. (1927) 'Effect of inflation on German accounting', *Journal of Accountancy,* March, pp. 180-191.

Sweeney, H. W. (1936) *Stabilized Accounting,* Holt, Rhinehart and Winston.

Zeff, S. A. and Ovando, H. Z. (1975) 'Inflation accounting and the development of accounting principles in Chile', *The Accountant's Magazine,* June, pp. 212-214.

Zeff, S. A. (1980) 'New inflation accounting rule', *World Accounting Report,* February, p. 8.

American Institute of Certified Public Accountants (1963) *Reporting the Financial Effects of Price-Level Changes,* and (1969) *Financial Statements Restated for General Price-Level Changes.*

Argentine Technical Institute of Public Accountants (1972) *Dictamen Number 2.*

Association of Certified Accountants (1952) *Accounting for Inflation.*

Australian Accounting Research Foundation (1978, revised in 1979) *Exposure Draft – The Recognition of Gains and Losses on holding Monetary Items in the Context of Current Cost Accounting.*

Canadian Institute of Chartered Accountants, Accounting Research Committee (1975) *Exposure Draft – Accounting for Changes in the General Purchasing Power of Money.*

Canadian Institute of Chartered Accountants, Accounting Research Committee (1976) *Discussion Paper – Current Value Accounting.*

Inflation Accounting – the Sandilands Report (1975) HMSO.

Institute of Chartered Accountants in England and Wales (1952) Recommendation N15, *Accounting in Relation to Changes in the Purchasing Power of Money.*

Institute of Chartered Accountants in Australia and Australian Society of Accountants (1976, amended 1978) *Current Cost Accounting* (DPS 1.1).

Institute of Cost and Works Accountants (1952) *The Accountancy of Changing Price Levels.*

Report of the Committee of Inquiry into Inflation and Taxation – The Mathews Report (1975) Australian Government Publishing Service.

Report of the Committee of Inquiry into Inflation Accounting – The Richardson Report (1976) New Zealand Government Printer.

Further Reading

Backer, M. (1973) *Current Value Accounting,* Financial Executives Research Foundation.

Barton, A. D. (1977) 'The macro-economic effects of current cost accounting', *Australian Accountant,* March, pp. 83-88.

Baxter, W. T. (1975) *Accounting Values and Inflation,* McGraw-Hill.

Carsberg, B. & Page, M. (1984) *Current Cost Accounting,* Institute of Chartered Accountants in England and Wales.

Chambers, R. J. (1966) *Accounting, Evaluation and Economic Behavior,* Prentice-Hall.

Chambers, R. J. (1975) *Accounting for Inflation – Exposure Draft,* University of Sydney.

Coenenberg, A. G. and Macharzina, K. (1976) 'Accounting for price changes', *Journal of Business Finance and Accounting,* July, pp. 53-68.

Davidson, S., Stickney, C. P. and Weil, R. L. (1976) *Inflation Accounting,* McGraw-Hill.

Drummond, C. S. R. & Stickler, A. D. (1983) *Current Cost Accounting,* Methuen.

Edwards, E.O. (1975) 'The state of current value accounting', *Accounting Review,* April,   pp. 235-245.

Edwards, E. O. and Bell, P. W. (1961) *The Theory and Measurement of Business Income,* University of California Press.

Gee, K. P. and Peasnell, K. V. (1976) 'A pragmatic defence of replacement cost', *Accounting and Business Research,* Autumn, pp. 242-249.

Goudeket, A. (1960) 'An application of replacement value theory', *Journal of Accountancy,* July, pp. 37-47.

Gynther, R. S. (1966) *Accounting for Price-Level Changes: Theory and Procedures,* Pergamon Press.

Gynther, R. S. (1974) 'Why use general purchasing power?', *Accounting and Business Research,* Spring, pp. 141-156.

Kennedy, C. (1978) 'Inflation accounting: retrospect and prospect', *Economic Policy Review,* March, pp. 58-64.

Kirkman, P.R.A. (1985) *Inflation Accounting in Major English-Speaking Countries,* Institute of Chartered Accountants in England and Wales.

Largay, J. A. and Livingstone, J. L. (1976) *Accounting for Changing Prices,* John Wiley.

Mallinson, D. (1980) *Understanding Current Cost Accounting,* Butterworths.

Muis, J. S. (1975) 'Current value accounting in the Netherlands: fact or fiction?', *The Accountant's Magazine,* November, pp. 377-379.

Parker, R. H., Harcourt, G. C. and Whittington, G. (eds) (1985) *Readings in the Concept and Measurement of Income,* Philip Allan.

Revsine, L. (1973) *Replacement Cost Accounting,* Prentice-Hall.

Rosenfield, P. (1972) 'The confusion between general price-level restatement and current value accounting', *Journal of Accountancy,* October, pp. 63-68.

Stamp, E. (1977) 'ED18 and current cost accounting', *Accounting and Business Research,* Spring, pp.83-94.

Sterling, R. R. (1970) *Theory of the Measurement of Enterprise Income,* University Press of Kansas.

Stickler, A. D. and Hutchins, C. S. R. (1975) *General Price Level Accounting: Described and Illustrated,* CICA, Toronto.

Tweedie, D. P. and Whittington, G. (1984) *The Debate on Inflation Accounting,* Cambridge University Press.

Westwick, C.A. (1980) 'The lessons to be learned from the development of inflation accounting in the UK', *Accounting and Business Research,* Autumn, pp. 357-373.

Whittington, G. (1983) *Inflation Accounting – An Introduction to the Debate,* Cambridge University Press.

12

Foreign Currency Translation

JOHN FLOWER

12.1 Introduction

The Translation Problem

The special problem of consolidation to be faced by multinational groups is that the component financial statements are denominated in different currencies. To prepare the consolidated balance sheet of a group consisting of a British holding company and its American subsidiary, the two balance sheets must be denominated in the same currency. One cannot add together the holding company's assets valued in terms of pounds and the subsidiary company's assets valued in terms of dollars – one of the currencies must be changed. It is normal to denominate consolidated financial statements in the currency of the holding company, since the main users of the consolidated statements are the shareholders and creditors of the holding company. Therefore it is the financial statements of the subsidiary that are changed from being denominated in terms of dollars to being denominated in terms of pounds. This process of transformation is *not* termed 'conversion', this term being reserved for the situation where a sum of money in one currency is exchanged for an equivalent sum in another currency. The assets of the subsidiary are not touched, they remain abroad. All that happens is that their value is reexpressed in terms of another currency. The term used for this process is 'translation'. In accounting terminology, the subsidiary's financial statements are translated from dollars to pounds.

The fact that there are several fundamentally different ways of doing this gives rise to a fascinating area of empirical and theoretical study, which is rapidly changing. It is of very considerable practical importance because the balance sheets, and particularly the profit figures, of multinationals are greatly affected by the method chosen.

The Source of the Problem

Translation presents problems because exchange rates are not fixed. If, for example, the exchange rate between the pound and the dollar were always that £1 was equal to $2, there would be no grounds for differences of opinion as to the translated pound value of an American asset with a book value of $200 – it is of course £100. However, exchange rates are not fixed. Table 12.1 shows the exchange rate of the pound against the dollar, the mark and the cruzeiro over the last 22 years. It can be seen that there have been very substantial fluctuations, which have increased in intensity in recent years.

Table 12.1   The Rate of Exchange of £1 to Three Major Currencies

Date	USA Dollar	West Germany Mark	Brazil Cruzeiro
31.12.63	2.80	11.09	1.75
31.12.64	2.79	11.21	5.16
31.12.65	2.80	11.14	6.19
31.12.66	2.79	11.18	6.19
31.10.67	2.78	11.12	7.55
31.12.67	2.41	9.62	6.53
31.12.68	2.38	9.55	9.13
31.12.69	2.40	8.84	10.44
31.12.70	2.39	8.73	11.85
31.12.71	2.55	8.33	14.38
31.12.72	2.35	7.50	14.59
31.12.73	2.32	6.27	14.20
31.12.74	2.35	5.66	16.95
31.12.75	2.02	5.29	18.34
31.12.76	1.70	4.02	21.01
31.12.77	1.91	4.01	30.59
31.12.78	2.03	3.72	42.56
31.12.79	2.22	3.85	94.59
31.12.80	2.38	4.67	156.22
31.12.81	1.91	4.30	243.84
31.12.82	1.61	3.84	407.94
31.12.83	1.45	3.95	1,427.39
31.12.84	1.15	3.66	3,622.00

Source: UN Monthly Bulletin of Statistics.

The fact that exchange rates are not fixed creates two problems for the accountant:

(a) what is the appropriate rate to use in translating an asset/liability that was acquired at a time when the rate was not the same as the present rate?

(b) how should one account for the gain or loss that arises from the change in rates?

For example, suppose that the American subsidiary of a British company acquired an asset, say inventory, costing $1,000 on 31 December 1983, when the exchange rate was $1.45 to £1. A year later, on 31 December 1984, the subsidiary still holds the asset, which is included in its balance sheet at its historical cost of $1,000. In preparing the consolidated balance sheet at 31 December 1984 two problems arise. First, what value should be placed on the asset, inventory, in the balance sheet? Two possible values suggest themselves under historical cost accounting:

(i) The cost, in terms of sterling, at the date of acquisition. This is achieved by translating the dollar cost using the exchange rate at the date of acquisition, that is $1,000 × £1/$1.45 = £690. The exchange rate at the date of acquisition of an asset is known as the 'historic rate'.

(ii) The pound equivalent at the balance sheet date, 31 December 1984, of the dollar cost (that is the dollar cost translated at the 1984 rate) $1,000 × £1/$1.15 = £870. The rate of exchange at the current balance sheet date is known as the 'closing rate'.

Secondly, if the latter figure (£870) is used in the 1984 balance sheet, how is the difference between this figure and the asset's value as presented in the 1983 balance sheet (£690) to be dealt with? A rise in value of an asset of £180 will have to be accounted for.

The first problem is the more significant, since it concerns the value to be placed on the assets and liabilities of the company. This affects not only the balance sheet but also, ultimately, the calculation of profit, since, by definition, the company's profit is the increase in its net worth over a period. For this reason more attention is given to this problem in this chapter, the following six sections being devoted exclusively to the translation of assets and liabilities. The second problem is largely concerned with presentation – how should the gain or loss be described, and where should it be placed in the financial statements? This problem is considered in section 12.9, where it will be found that it is quite significant. The treatment to be accorded to the loss or gain in the financial statements will affect many important accounting variables such as net profit and earnings per share.

12.2   The Diversity of Translation Practice

The Three Traditional Translation Methods

In practice, assets and liabilities are translated using either the historic rate or the closing rate. However there is no basic agreement throughout the world as to which rate should be used to translate which type of asset. Three different translation methods have been in widespread use:

(i)   The closing rate method, which uses the closing rate for all assets and liabilities.

(ii) The current/non-current method, which uses the closing rate for current assets and current liabilities, and the historic rate for all other assets and liabilities.

(iii) The monetary/non-monetary method, which uses the closing rate for monetary items (i.e. money and amounts to be received or paid in money, e.g. debtors, creditors, loans, debentures etc.) and the historic rate for non-monetary items (i.e. most fixed assets and inventory).

An Example

The application of these three methods is illustrated using a simple example. On 31 December 1983, the American subsidiary of a British company acquired the assets and liabilities listed in the first column of Table 12.2. To ease the exposition, it is assumed that no transactions took place in 1984, so that the subsidiary's balance sheet in terms of local currency (dollars) at 31 December 1984 (drawn up in accordance with the historical cost convention) is identical to that of a year earlier. Table 12.2 shows how the subsidiary's balance sheet is translated into pounds using each of the three methods described above.

The net worth of the subsidiary in terms of pounds is found by deducting the translated value of the liabilities from that of the assets. It can be seen that the three methods give widely differing figures for the subsidiary's net worth: closing rate method, £870; current/non-current method, £1230; monetary/non-monetary method, £330. The net worth of the subsidiary at 31 December 1983 was £690. There is no dispute over this figure since all the assets and liabilties were acquired on that day, so in the 1983 balance sheet the closing rate and the historic rate are the same. The change in the subsidiary's net worth since 1983 represents a gain (closing rate method and current/non-current method) or a loss (monetary/non-monetary method). This gain (loss) clearly arises from the translation process, since no gain or loss is shown in the

Table 12.2

Foreign subsidiary translated balance sheet at 31.12.84

	Foreign subsidiary balance sheet at 31.12.83 and 31.12.84 (Note: no transactions in 1984) Local currency	Closing rate method		Current/Non-current method		Monetary/Non-monetary method	
		Exchange rate	Translated value	Exchange rate	Translated value	Exchange rate	Translated value
Fixed assets (Plant)	$1,000	CR 0.87	£ 870	HR 0.69	£ 690	HR 0.69	£ 690
Current assets							
Inventory	$2,000	CR 0.87	£1,740	CR 0.87	£1,740	HR 0.69	£1,380
Debtors	$2,000	CR 0.87	£1,740	CR 0.87	£1,740	CR 0.87	£1,740
Total assets	$5,000		£4,350		£4,170		£3,810
Long-term liabilities	$3,000	CR 0.87	£2,610	HR 0.69	£2,070	CR 0.87	£2,610
Current liabilities	$1,000	CR 0.87	£ 870	CR 0.87	£ 870	CR 0.87	£ 870
Total liabilities	$4,000		£3,480		£2,940		£3,480
Net worth at 31.12.84 (Total assets less total liabilities)	$1,000		£ 870		£1,230		£ 330
Note:							
Net worth at 31.12.83	$1,000	0.69	£ 690	0.69	£ 690	0.69	£ 690
Gain (Loss) on translation	Nil		£ 180		£ 540		(£ 360)

Note: Exchange Rate at 31.12.83 HR (Historic Rate) $1 = £0.69; at 31.12.84 CR (Closing Rate) $1 = £0.87

subsidiary's dollar financial statements. Therefore it is described in Table 12.2 as gain (loss) on translation. In practice it is often described as gain (loss) on exchange. This is rather confusing since no exchange of assets has in fact taken place.

The Translation Gain Examined

It is startling to note the wide variations in the gain or loss on translation: a loss of £360 under the monetary/non-monetary method, compared with a gain of £180 under the closing rate method and an even bigger gain of £540 under the current/non-current method. It is instructive to examine these gains and losses a little more closely. At the start of 1984, one dollar was worth £0.69, and at the end of the year £0.87. Hence the holding company records a gain of £0.18 for every dollar-denominated asset that it held during 1984. This is clearly the case where the asset involved is cash (e.g. a dollar bill). However, where the book value in terms of dollars of an asset, such as plant or inventory, remains constant over the year in accordance with accounting convention, then the exchange rate fall will lead to the recording of a sterling gain in respect of these assets. In the same way a loss of £0.18 will be recorded for each dollar owed.

Table 12.3 explains how this gain or loss is recorded under each of the three translation methods:

(i)   Under the closing rate method, all the assets and liabilities are revalued at 31 December 1984 using the new closing rate. Hence the gain is calculated on the whole of the holding company's net investment in the subsidiary.

(ii) Under the current/non-current method, the non-current assets and liabilities, being translated at historic rates, retain their original value in terms of pounds. Hence no translation gain is recorded in respect of these assets and liabilities. The gain is recognised only in respect of current assets and liabilities.

(iii) In the case of the monetary/non-monetary method, a similar principle is followed: the gain is calculated only on the monetary items. Since, in this example, the net monetary assets are negative (the liabilities exceed the monetary assets), a loss is registered.

The three methods produce widely differing figures for the translation loss because of different assumptions as to which classes of assets and liabilities are affected by changes in exchange rates.

Table 12.3 Net Gains and Losses on Translation

Method of translation	Assets/liabilities subject to translation gain (loss)	Net amount of relevant assets less liabilities	Gain (loss) per $ of net assets	Net gain (loss)
Closing rate	All assets/liabilities	+ $1,000	£0.18	£180
Current/non-current	Current assets/liabilities	+ $3,000	£0.18	£540
Monetary/non-monetary	Monetary assets/liabilities	− $2,000	£0.18	(£360)

12.3   The American Initiative

The existence of these three methods of translation, which produce such fundamentally different valuations of overseas assets and losses or gains on translation, represents a disturbing state of affairs. Clearly not all three methods can be correct for the same purpose.

The Americans were the first to do something concrete about the problem. The American Institute of Certified Public Accountants set about tackling it in a systematic way. First it commissioned a member of its research staff, Leonard Lorensen, to undertake a thorough research study (Lorensen 1972). It is probably no exaggeration to describe the report as one of the best pieces of academic research applied to a major practical problem in accounting; certainly it is one of the most influential. The report established and clearly set out a universally applicable 'temporal principle'. Under historical cost accounting this turns out to mean something broadly similar to the monetary/non-monetary method.

The Temporal Principle

The essence of the temporal principle is that the valuation method used for the subsidiary's assets and liabilities in its own balance sheet should be retained in the translated accounts. There are several different methods used in valuing assets in the balance sheet. They may be classified as follows:

(i) *Historical cost*: the amount of cash (or resources of equivalent value) actually paid out in the past in order to acquire the asset.

(ii) *Current replacement cost (CRC)*: the amount of cash that would have to be expended by the company at the balance sheet date to acquire a similar asset.

(iii) *Net realisable value (NRV)*: the amount of cash that the company would receive (net of expenses) if it were to sell the asset at the balance sheet date.

(iv) *Value of future receipts*: debtors and amounts receivable are stated at the amount of cash that the company expects to receive in the future. Similarly, creditors and other liabilities are stated at the amount of cash that the company expects to be obliged to pay out in the future in order to redeem the liability.

For each of these four methods of valuation one can state a date which pertains to the money amount at which a subsidiary's asset is valued and hence the date of the exchange rate to be used in its translation.

   (i) *Historical cost* – the date of the acquisition of the asset, hence the
       appropriate historic rate.
  (ii) and (iii) *CRC* and *NRV* – the balance sheet date, hence the
       closing rate.
  (iv) *Value of future receipts* – the future date on which the asset or
       liability will be converted into cash, hence the appropriate
       future rate.

Future or Closing Rate for Debtors and Creditors?

However, Lorensen came to the conclusion that the closing rate, and
not the future rate, should be used for the translation of assets
(liabilities) valued at the amount of future receipts (payments). There
are a number of reasons for this decision – some pragmatic, some more
theoretical. Thus the appropriate future rate is often not known when
the balance sheet is being prepared, and the best (or at least the most
objective) estimate of it is the closing rate.

   Furthermore, if a future (or forward) rate is quoted on the foreign
exchange market, which is different from the current (or spot) rate, the
difference between the two rates will normally be offset by differences in
interest rates; that is, interest rates will be higher in a country where the
forward rate is lower than the spot rate (see the discussion on the 'Fisher
effect' in Section 12.9). In order for interest charges to be allocated to
the right period, the closing rate should be used to translate loans. If the
future rate were used, interest would be anticipated. For example, a
company could record instant profits simply by investing in bonds
denominated in a currency whose forward rate stood at a premium in
relation to its spot rate.

   Finally, if there were a change in exchange rates between the balance
sheet date and the date when the debt or liability were liquidated, it can
be argued that the gain (or loss) would be caused by an event of the later
period (i.e. when the rate changes) and should be recorded in that
period. For all these reasons, the closing rate and not the future rate is
used in the application of the temporal principle.

The Generality of the Temporal Principle

The temporal principle is generally consistent with the monetary/non-
monetary method under historical cost accounting. Using this temporal
principle, assets measured on a current or future basis (including
monetary assets) are translated at closing rate, and assets which are
stated at historical cost (as is generally the case with non-monetary
assets) are translated at historic rates. The main difference for a pure

version of the monetary/non-monetary method is that inventories measured at net realisable value would be translated at a historic rate. However, the beauty of the temporal principle is that it is not tied to the historical cost convention. It provides the rules for the translation of financial statements prepared in accordance with other valuation conventions. Thus, if certain of the subsidiary's assets are valued at current replacement cost as at the balance sheet date, then clearly the closing rate should be used. The same principle applies when assets are stated in terms of net realisable value as at the balance sheet date. A rather more complicated situation arises when the subsidiary's fixed assets are revalued as at a date that is not the same as that of the closing balance sheet. However, clearly the historic rate at the date of revaluation should be used.

It is the general applicability of the temporal principle which makes it so attractive to many accounting theorists and which has convinced them, on essentially *a priori* grounds, that it provides the correct solution to the translation problem.

FAS 8

The Financial Accounting Standards Board (FASB) accepted the recommendations of the Lorensen Study with few reservations. In October 1975 it issued 'Statement of Financial Accounting Standards No. 8' (FASB 1975), which made the use of the temporal method (i.e. the application of the temporal principle) obligatory for financial statements relating to accounting years beginning on or after 1 January 1976. No alternative methods were permitted.

FAS 8 caused a furore, particularly from companies that found themselves obliged to report substantial losses on translation in their consolidated accounts. During the 1970s the dollar weakened against many major currencies, such as the yen, the mark, and even the pound. With the application of the temporal method, American multinationals were obliged to report translation losses on foreign currency borrowings (even long-term borrowings), whilst no translation gain could be reported in respect of the foreign fixed assets that had been acquired with the proceeds of these borrowings. Under other translation methods no such loss is reported. Under the current/non-current method, no gain or loss is reported on either the fixed assets or the long-term liabilities. Under the closing rate method, the gain on the assets offsets the loss on the liabilities. Many American companies did not like the enforced change. Thus, after 1975, there began a spirited public debate over the temporal method, that started in America and spread to the rest of the world. This is the subject of an excellent article by Nobes (1980). In this debate it was soon agreed by most parties that the current/non-current method should be rejected, and thus the issue was reduced to a straight fight between the temporal method and the closing rate method.

12.4   The Temporal Method vs. the Closing Rate Method

The opposition between the temporal method and the closing rate method throughout the accountancy world is probably the most important aspect of the translation problem. Note, however, that this opposition would not arise under current value accounting, when the two methods would give the same results. It is the author's opinion that, for the reasons set out in section 12.3, only the temporal method can be justified for use with historical cost accounting. The fundamental objection of the accounting theorist to the closing rate method under historical cost accounting can be stated very simply as follows. The closing rate method when applied to an asset stated in the foreign subsidiary's balance sheet at historical cost, produces a translated figure which has no meaning: it is not the historical cost in terms of the home currency, nor in terms of the foreign currency; neither is it the current replacement cost nor the net realisable value. 'The number is in fact nothing except the product of multiplying two unrelated numbers' (Lorensen 1972, p. 107). This fault of the closing rate method is so fundamental that, in the opinion of most serious accounting theorists, it makes the use of the method quite unacceptable.

The case for the closing rate method was set out by the British Accounting Standards Committee in ED21 (issued in September 1977), notably paragraphs 9 and 10:

9.   The closing rate method is based on the concept that a reporting company has a net investment in a foreign operation and what is at risk from currency fluctuations is the net investment . . .

10. The closing rate method possesses the following advantages:
(a) It deals effectively with the situation where fixed assets located overseas have been financed by foreign currency borrowings and a change in the exchange rate results in offsetting gains and losses.
(b) The relationship existing between balances in accounts as originally prepared in a foreign currency is preserved in the translated accounts whereas this is not the case where historical rates are used for translating certain assets.
(c) It is not necessary to maintain sterling records of fixed assets and

inventories located overseas which would be required if historical
rates were to be used.

(d) It is simple to operate and the results are easily understood by
users of accounts.

Ease of Operation

The advantages listed in paragraph 10(c) and (d) are the more
straightforward and can be easily disposed of. It is certainly true that the
closing rate method is easier to operate. However, the practical difficulties of applying the temporal method should not be exaggerated.
Once the historical cost of fixed assets, in terms of the home currency,
has been established, it is valid for all future balance sheets. It is the closing rate method that demands annual modifications to the value of
assets. Thus advantage (c) is really very trivial. Moreover, ease of
operation is not a very respectable reason for choosing an accounting
method, particularly when the differences in asset values involved may
be very substantial. Finally, it is wrong to state that the results of the
application of the closing rate method are easily understood by users of
accounts, except in the facile sense of being the output of a simple
arithmetic operation. As stated earlier, the exact significance of the
translated value (at the closing rate) of the historical cost of an asset is so
complex as to defy understanding.

Preservation of Relationships in the Subsidiary's Financial Statements

Paragraph 10(b) refers to an interesting and somewhat disturbing aspect
of the temporal method (i.e. the temporal principle as used with
historical cost accounting): that the process of translation can change the
relationship between individual items in the financial statements. This
arises because different exchange rates are used to translate different
items: the historic rate is used for fixed assets and the closing rate for
most other items. Thus the relative weight of fixed assets in the
translated balance sheet will be different from that shown in the subsidiary's foreign currency balance sheet. This will affect, among other
matters, the debt/equity ratio. More significantly, in the translated
profit and loss account, the weight given to depreciation (derived from
fixed assets translated at a historic rate) will be different from that shown
in the foreign currency accounts. If the foreign currency has fallen in
value (relative to the home currency) since the fixed assets were
acquired, this will have the effect of increasing the relative importance of
the depreciation expense in the translated profit and loss account. This
could well turn a profit reported in the subsidiary's foreign currency

Table 12.4   Example of How the Temporal Method Translates a Loss as a Profit

	Foreign currency accounts ($)	Translation factor	Translated accounts (£)
Profit and Loss Account for 1984			
Trading profit	90,000	£1/$1.15	78,261
Less depreciation	100,000	£1/$1.61	62,112
Net profit/(loss)	(10,000)		16,149
Balance sheet at 31/12/84			
Fixed assets: cost	1,000,000	£1/$1.61	621,118
less depreciation	200,000	£1/$1.61	124,224
	800,000		496,894
Current assets (cash)	200,000	£1/$1.15	173,913
Total assets	1,000,000		670,807
Less long-term liabilities	500,000	£1/$1.15	434,783
Net worth (equity)	500,000		236,024

Data: Foreign Ltd bought all its fixed assets in 1982.
　　　　All transactions assumed to take place at year end.
　　　　Exchange rates: 31/12/82 £1 = $1.61
　　　　　　　　　　　31/12/84 £1 = $1.15
Note: Debt/equity ratio　　　　　1:1　　　　　　　　1:0.54

accounts into a loss in the translated accounts. This point is demonstrated in a detailed example presented in Table 12.4. The closing rate method does not suffer from this disadvantage. As the same exchange rate is used for all items, the translated accounts are always an exact model of the original foreign currency accounts.

To proponents of the temporal method this is a highly awkward result and they need all their ingenuity to explain how it is right for a profit in one currency to be turned into a loss when translated into another currency. However, there are good arguments to be made. First, it should be stressed that the purpose of translation is to permit the preparation of consolidated accounts. As a general rule, the translated figures of the subsidiary's assets, liabilities, revenues and expenses are aggregated with those of the holding company in the consolidated financial statements. The foreign subsidiary's separate entity is lost in the consolidated accounts. Hence, the fact that it has a certain debt/equity ratio as an individual company is irrelevant from the viewpoint of the consolidated financial statement. Conversely, if a person wishes to examine the financial position of the foreign subsidiary as a separate entity (e.g. a minority shareholder or a creditor of the subsidiary), then he should look to its separate foreign currency accounts. The group accounts are irrelevant for this purpose. The creditor of a subsidiary company cannot normally demand repayment of his debt from the holding company, nor can a minority shareholder expect dividends to be paid out of group profits. In order to obtain a proper picture of the *subsidiary's* financial position, its financial statements should not be translated. It may be that the financial statements are confusing because they are denominated in an unfamiliar currency (e.g. the British creditor of an Italian company may be bemused by the item: *Rimaneze: materie prime: L29,256,673,696*). In this event it may be helpful to translate the entire financial statement into a more understandable currency. There is general agreement that for this operation the appropriate exchange rate to use is the closing rate, since the operation is quite different from the translation process analysed in this chapter, which is to facilitate the preparation of consolidated financial statements.

However, while the above argument goes part of the way towards explaining why the relationships in the subsidiary's financial statements are irrelevant for the consolidated statements, it is still uncomfortable that a profit in the subsidiary's own (foreign currency) profit and loss account can be translated into a loss in the consolidated profit and loss account. One may legitimately ask the question: which financial statement is presenting the true and fair view – the subsidiary's foreign currency accounts or the translated version incorporated into the consolidated account? If the temporal method is correct, then the answer to this question must be that both financial statements are correct. The subsidiary's own financial statements present a true and fair view in relation to its creditors and shareholders; the consolidated financial statements (incorporating the subsidiary's translated accounts) present a true and fair view in relation to the shareholders of the holding company. How is this possible?

It will be recalled that a profit can be translated into a loss only when certain assets (i.e. fixed assets and inventory) are valued in the accounts at historical cost. When this convention is followed the persons for whom the accounts are prepared (i.e. the shareholders) interpret the book value of the assets as being the amount of finance that is tied up in these assets. The amount tied up in the fixed assets is expressed in terms of the currency in which the finance was provided. In the case of a holding company owning assets abroad via a subsidiary, the position is that ultimately these assets have been financed by the holding company's shareholders. When the assets were acquired they made a financial sacrifice. It is of no consequence for the argument whether this sacrifice was voluntary or involuntary, or whether the acquisition of the assets was facilitated by a remittance of cash from the holding company or by a reduction in the dividend from the subsidiary. The essential point is that in a past year the holding company's shareholders made a financial sacrifice and that this sacrifice is measured in terms of the amount of home currency foregone in that year. Hence the requirement to state the subsidiary's assets in the consolidated financial statements at their historical cost in terms of the home currency. The position of minority shareholders of the foreign subsidiary is rather different. Their sacrifice was in terms of their own currency. When subsequently the foreign currency falls in value relative to the home currency, the sacrifice made by the holding company's shareholders will become valued rather more highly than that made by the subsidiary's minority shareholders; hence the paradox of a profit being translated into a loss.

To summarise, the answer to paragraph 10(b) is, firstly, that the relationships in the foreign subsidiary's financial statements are largely irrelevant for the consolidated financial statements. Secondly, where they are relevant, the relationship produced by the application of the temporal method is the correct one from the viewpoint of the shareholders of the holding company. Naturally, these problems are due to the use of historical cost accounting and would not arise under a current value system.

The 'Net Investment' Concept

Finally, paragraph 10(a) has to be considered. This is closely tied up with the statement in paragraph 9 that the closing rate method is based on the concept that a reporting company has a net investment in a foreign operation and what is at risk from currency fluctuations is that net investment. This statement is rather brief. The full line of reasoning can be presented as follows:

(a) In many cases, in practice, foreign subsidiaries are largely autonomous; decisions as to which assets to acquire or hold, and on trading operations, are taken by the local board of directors.

(b) Additionally, these foreign subsidiaries are often largely self-financing, using local loans and retained profits.

(c) In these circumstances, the holding company's main interest in the subsidiary is the annual dividend. If this is satisfactory, the holding company will not concern itself in detail with the subsidiary's financial position or operations.

(d) Hence the holding company is not interested in the detailed assets, liabilities, revenues and expenses of the subsidiary; its interest is in the net investment in the subsidiary which is the source of the only tangible benefit, the annual dividends.

(e) The value of this net investment is best reflected in translating the net worth at the closing rate. If only one rate is to be used it has to be the closing rate.

(f) Since the net worth is to be translated at the closing rate, all the other items in the balance sheet must be translated at the same rate, if the balance sheet is to balance.

This line of reasoning appears very strong when one considers the case of a devaluation of the home currency. In the normal situation of a foreign subsidiary with net monetary liabilities (i.e. total liabilities exceeding monetary assets), the application of the temporal method will lead to a fall in the value of the subsidiary's translated net worth; the translated value of the fixed assets will remain unchanged but the translated value of net liabilities will increase. This hardly seems logical. After the devaluation, the foreign currency is worth more in terms of the home currency than before: the net investment which is expressed in terms of the foreign currency should also be worth more. An alternative argument is that, following the devaluation, the annual dividend from the subsidiary will probably be worth more in terms of the home currency. This will certainly be the case if one makes the reasonably conservative assumption of no change in the annual dividend in terms of the foreign currency. The net investment in the foreign subsidiary, the source of these dividends, should therefore be worth more on the principle of an investment being valued as the net present value of future receipts. This is essentially the case set out in paragraph 10(a).

The paradox created by the application of the temporal method is most obvious when the net worth of the foreign subsidiary can be established without difficulty. For example, the holding company may own only 51% of the foreign subsidiary's shares, the remaining 49% being quoted on the local stock exchange. The market price of these shares gives an arguably accurate and objective assessment of the value of the holding company's net investment. On this basis of valuation, it will generally be found that the value of the net investment in terms of the holding company's currency will have increased. In these circumstances, it is particularly galling for the holding company to have to report a loss on translation.

This argument appears both logical and coherent. The answer of the proponents of the temporal method is simple. The above procedure may be appropriate where the holding company's investment in the foreign subsidiary is presented in the holding company's balance sheet as a single item, that is, in the same way that the interest in an associated company is commonly presented. However, it is not appropriate where the assets, liabilities, revenues and expenses of the subsidiary are incorporated as such in the group's consolidated financial statements. Essentially the above line of argument falls down in two places. First, the method of valuation that is appropriate for the net worth is not necessarily appropriate for each of the individual assets and liabilities: this line of reasoning leads directly to the nonsense of the historical cost of an asset being translated at the closing rate. Secondly, if a subsidiary is, in fact, a largely independent entity then it is not appropriate to consolidate fully this subsidiary in the group's consolidated financial statements.

Consolidated financial statements are defined in SSAP14 (ASC 1978) as 'one form of group accounts which present the information contained in the separate financial statements of a holding company and its subsidiaries as if they were the financial statements of a single entity'. In addition, section 229(3)(d) of the Companies Act 1948 states that a subsidiary need not be incorporated into the group accounts if 'the business of the holding company and of the subsidiary are so different that they cannot reasonably be treated as a single undertaking'. The use of the terms 'single entity' and 'single undertaking' in these quotations is very significant. It is clear that the existence of a single entity is a precondition for the preparation of consolidated financial statements. Thus the closing rate method which is consistent with the concept of the holding company having a net investment in a semi-autonomous foreign subsidiary should not be used in the preparation of consolidated financial statements. The conclusion is inescapable:

either the foreign subsidiary is largely autonomous, in which case fully consolidated accounts should not be prepared. In this case the holding company's investment in the subsidiary would normally be presented in its balance sheet as a single item (perhaps using the equity method) with the subsidiary's full financial statements joined to the holding company's financial statements as an annex. Whether the closing rate method should be used in this procedure is not considered further in this chapter;

or the holding company and the foreign subsidiary may be considered a single entity in which case the appropriate translation method to use is the temporal method which, in the words of paragraph 11 of ED 21, 'is based on the concept that a single enterprise is reporting and foreign operations are an extension of the activities of the parent body', which is precisely the concept on which all consolidated financial statements are based.

However, although the author is personally convinced on this matter, the argument has been settled (at least temporarily) in favour of the closing rate method. In December 1981 the FASB finally gave way to the considerable pressure to which it had been subjected and issued a new standard, FAS 52 (FASB 1981), which effectively reversed FAS 8 and prescribed the use of the closing rate method under most circumstances.

12.5 FAS 52

Even the most convinced opponents of FAS 8 admit that FAS 52 is not a very impressive document. It is badly written and the intellectual basis for most of its provisions is unclear: this reflects the fact that the statement is based not so much on research and reasoning, as on the opinions of the preparers and users of accounts. FAS 52 was adopted by the FASB by the smallest possible majority: by four votes to three, the minority including the Chairman of the Board, Donald Kirk. In fact the most stimulating part of the statement is the note of dissent written by the dissenting members. However, for good or ill, FAS 52 is now the effective standard in the United States, and American accountants are obliged to apply it – at least until the next change.

In the introduction to FAS 52, the FASB states that the objectives of translation are to:

(a) provide information that is generally compatible with the expected economic effects of a rate change on an enterprise's cash flows and equity;
(b) reflect in consolidated statements the financial results and relationships of the individual consolidated entities as measured in their functional currencies in conformity with US generally accepted accounting principles. (FASB 1981, p. 3.)

In setting these objectives the FASB clearly had in mind the two major criticisms of the temporal method that are discussed in section 12.4: objective (a) refers to the paradox that an upward revaluation of the local currency leads to a loss on translation, and objective (b) refers to the paradox of a profit being translated as a loss. Therefore, even at the stage of setting the objectives, the FASB appears to have made up its mind against the temporal method. Objective (a) is remarkable for the proposition that accounts should reflect *expected* economic effects. In the author's opinion, this is a revolutionary departure from generally accepted accounting principles, which are based on the principle of measuring reality as evidenced by the past (in the case of historical cost) or by the present (in the case of replacement cost or realisable value). When objective (b) is analysed more closely, it becomes clear that it is virtually identical with the imposition of the closing rate method. For in order to preserve in the consolidated financial statements the results and relationships of the subsidiary's own statements, it is necessary that every item should be multiplied by the same factor (i.e. the translated statements must be a linear transformation of the local currency statements). If the same factor has to be used for all items, then clearly it has to be the closing rate.

Given these objectives, it was inevitable that FAS 52 should come to the conclusion that the financial statements of foreign entities, as expressed in their functional currencies, must be translated at the closing rate. The only interest in the statement is to find out what is meant by the term 'functional currency'. This is a new concept introduced for the first time in FAS 52, which gives the following definition: 'an entity's functional currency is the currency of the primary economic environment in which the entity operates' (FASB 1981, p.3). It seems clear that for the great majority of foreign entities the functional currency will be the local currency; for these cases, FAS 52 provides for the straightforward application of the closing rate method. There are two main exceptions to this general rule:

(a) where the foreign operations are a direct and integral component or extension of the parent company's operations (in this case it is felt that the primary economic environment is that of the parent company);
(b) where the foreign entity operates in a highly inflationary economy (defined as one where prices double in three years) – in this case, FAS 52 prescribes the completely arbitrary rule that the functional currency is to be that of the parent company.

In the exceptional cases where the financial statements of the foreign entity are not expressed in its functional currency, they must be translated into the functional currency using the temporal method. FAS 52 uses the term 'remeasurement' for this process, which is very confusing as it differs in no way from other forms of translation.

In effect, FAS 52 is based on the principle that in general the parent company and its foreign subsidiaries should be considered as distinct and separate entities. The consolidated balance sheet is nothing more than the arithmetic sum of the balance sheets of these distinct entities, adjusted for intra-group items. Although, in order to perform the arithmetic, the balance sheets of the foreign subsidiaries must first be translated at the closing rate, in no sense does the currency of the parent company predominate over those of its subsidiaries. Essentially, all the currencies are treated as equal. The valuation of the assets of the foreign subsidiaries remains based in their foreign currencies. The consolidated balance sheet is based on multiple functional currencies. FAS 52 rejects the concepts used by the author in section 12.4 to justify the temporal method: that the consolidated accounts are prepared for the benefit of the shareholders of the parent company and should present the returns on investments in terms of the currency provided by these shareholders. The main reason for the dissent of three members of the FASB was that they could not accept this rejection: they believed that more meaningful consolidated results were attained by measuring costs, cost recovery, and exchange risk from a dollar perspective rather than from multiple functional currency perspectives.

The FASB resolved the closing rate versus temporal method argument by changing the nature of the consolidated accounts of multinational companies. It took this step to resolve the problem facing American companies in the quite exceptional foreign exchange conditions of the late 1970s. It remains to be seen whether it proves to be a lasting solution.

12.6   The British Approach

In the search for a solution to the translation problem, the British have tended to play second fiddle to the Americans. In fact the Accounting Standards Committee issued no standard on the subject until after FAS 52 had shown the way. Before the Second World War, most British companies used the current/non-current method. This is referred to as the accepted method in one of the most interesting early articles on translation in which Professors Baxter and Yamey of the London School of Economics criticised its shortcomings and pointed out that the significant line of demarcation in the balance sheet lay between money and non-money items (Baxter and Yamey 1951). However, British accountants did not follow this lead. The monetary/non-monetary method never became widely used in Britain. Instead, there was a marked swing towards the closing rate method. The 1978 Survey of Published Accounts (ICAEW 1979) reported that 251 out of 267 companies that gave information on the matter used the closing rate method.

In the period when FAS 8 was the effective standard in the United States (1975 – 1981), the ASC found itself in a very difficult position. It could not come out against the closing rate method which was so firmly entrenched in British accounting practice. On the other hand it was reluctant to ban the temporal method, which would have created difficulties for British companies that were quoted on the New York Stock Exchange and which were obliged to comply with FAS 8. Hence the ASC made no decision until after the issue of FAS 52. Then, in May 1983, the ASC issued SSAP 20 (ASC 1983) which, in relation to the translation of assets and liabilities, is virtually identical to FAS 52. It specifies the closing rate for most situations and the temporal method 'where the trade of the foreign enterprise is more dependent on the economic environment of the investing company's currency than that of its own reporting currency' (words very similar to those used in FAS 52). The main difference is that SSAP 20 specifies that, where a foreign enterprise operates in a country with a very high rate of inflation (not defined), its local financial statements should be adjusted to reflect current price levels before translation.

For most thoughtful British accountants the position is rather humiliating. Britain has played a very minor role in the great debate on translation. And when finally the ASC dared to issue a standard, it was virtually a copy of the American standard. It would seem that, in this field at least, the centre of accounting thought is situated on the western side of the Atlantic.

12.7   Other Countries and the IASC

In the rest of the European Community the situation is even less satisfactory than in Britain. In many countries it has been quite common and perfectly legal for groups not to publish consolidated accounts; in 1985 this is still the case in Italy. Where there *is* an obligation to publish group accounts, it does not always extend to the consolidation of foreign subsidiaries, as in Germany. This was discussed in Chapter 10.

The European Community has not yet succeeded in harmonising methods of translation. The seventh Directive on consolidated accounts (passed on 13 June 1983) makes no reference to translation methods except in the requirement that the bases of foreign currency translation be disclosed in the notes to the accounts. Thus, in most of Europe, the choice of method is left to the company. Graham (1982) reports the results of a survey of 199 European multinational companies. This reveals a wide diversity of practice with a certain preference for the closing rate method. Only a minority of companies uses a historic rate method, generally for fixed assets; these are often companies with investments in countries whose currencies have suffered substantial devaluation. However, often it is difficult to discover the precise method used, since many companies do not provide this information.

International Accounting Standard 21

Given the diversity of accounting practice around the world, it is not surprising that the International Accounting Standards Committee had difficulties in preparing a standard on the subject of translation. It was not until July 1983 that it published International Accounting Standard 21, *Accounting for the effects of changes in foreign exchange rates* (IASC 1983). It is no accident that this appeared after FAS 52, for clearly the IASC had first to wait for the FASB to make up its mind. IASC 21 follows closely the line taken in FAS 52. The accounts of a foreign subsidiary should be translated at the closing rate, except when it is integral to the operations of the parent. For foreign subsidiaries affected by high rates of inflation a choice of method is permitted – either translation using the temporal method (as required in FAS 52) or translation at the closing rate after the foreign currency accounts have been adjusted for the change in prices (as required in SSAP 20). In fact, nowhere does IASC 21 make any provision that is in conflict with FAS 52 or SSAP 20.

Since IASC 21 is essentially a passive document that meekly follows the line established by FAS 52, its interest to the student of accounting theory is limited. However, it is well written and gives a relatively clear explanation of the issues involved and of the reasons for the choices made. Since it is also quite short (about 2,000 words), it can be recommended as worthwhile reading.

12.8 Translation of the Profit and Loss Account

In order to present a complete set of consolidated accounts it is necessary to translate the foreign subsidiary's profit and loss account. The procedure to be followed differs according to the method used to translate the balance sheet.

The Temporal Method

With the temporal method it is easy to discover the principle to be followed: for each item of revenue and expense, the rate of exchange to be applied is that ruling at the date when the underlying transaction is recognised in the books of account. For sales, this will normally be the date of delivery; for goods and services paid for in cash, this will be the date of payment; for goods and services obtained on credit, it will be the date when the goods or services were received since, if a balance sheet were drawn up at this date, the amount owing would be translated at the rate on that date. In theory, every transaction should be translated at its appropriate rate; in practice, a reasonably close approximation will often be obtained by using the average rate for the period, or a weighted average where there are marked seasonal fluctuations. Two elements of expense require special attention.

(a) *Depreciation*: the rate of exchange to be used for the translation of depreciation expense is clearly the same as that used for the translation of the underlying asset, that is, the historic rate for assets valued at historical cost, and the closing rate for assets valued at current value. This procedure is one of the main causes of the 'profit translated as a loss' paradox that was referred to in section 12.4.

(b) *Cost of goods sold*: the cost of goods sold will normally include an element of stock, which should be translated at the rate of exchange appropriate for this asset.

The Closing Rate Method

There is no general agreement on how to translate the profit and loss account when the closing rate method is used to translate the balance sheet. FAS 52 specifies the use of the exchange rate at the date when the revenues and expenses are recognised but, since this is generally impractical, it permits the use of an appropriate weighted average. SSAP 20 permits the use of either the average rate or the closing rate, explaining that commentators on the exposure draft were evenly divided between the average rate and the closing rate. This is one of the main points of difference between SSAP 20 and FAS 52. The advantage of the closing rate is that it preserves the relationships in the foreign currency accounts. The advantage of the average rate is that interim accounts do not have to be restated (i.e. the annual profit will be equal to the total of the profits reported in the interim accounts). Most UK companies use the closing rate.

In the author's opinion the lack of agreement over the rate to be used for the profit and loss account is a clear indictment of the lack of theoretical basis for the closing rate method. The proponents of the method have no basic principles to which they may turn for a solution to this problem.

12.9   Accounting for Translation Gains and Losses

This section considers the problem of how translation gains and losses are to be presented in the consolidated financial statements. It might be felt that there is no problem: since profit may be defined as the increase in value of net assets, it follows that, if the translated value of an asset or liability is different from its previous translated value, a gain (or loss) is automatically created which must be shown in the income statement as an element of the profit for the year. The temporal method follows this reasoning and requires that all translation gains and losses be included in the income statement. This simple rule has not found favour with accountants either in the United States or in Britain. It was the aspect of FAS 8 which was criticised more than any other.

When there have been wide fluctuations in exchange rates, as has been the general experience over the past decade, translation gains and losses can be very substantial for a group with significant foreign interests. They may well be the largest single item in the income statement, turning a loss into a profit or vice versa. Therefore attention is given as to how the effects of translation gains and losses may be tempered. There are two classical ways of reducing the impact of an item on the year's profit:

(a) in the income statement, by placing it 'below the line';
(b) in the balance sheet, by including it with the reserves.

'Below the Line' Treatment

Some accountants claim that translation gains and losses should not form part of the profit of the year, but should be shown 'below the line' in the income statement, as extraordinary or unusual items. Accounting for unusual items is dealt with in International Accounting Standard No. 8 (1978), which gives the following definition: 'unusual items are gains or losses that derive from events or transactions that are distinct from the ordinary activities of the enterprise and therefore are not expected to recur frequently or regularly'. If this definition is accepted, translation gains and losses cannot be treated as unusual items. Clearly the foreign operations of most multinationals are part of their ordinary activities; furthermore, as shown by the data in Table 12.1, significant changes in exchange rates have occurred frequently in the past and can be expected to recur. For these reasons there has been little support for the proposition that translation gains and losses should be shown 'below the line'. It is, however, of interest that the FASB considered this approach as a comparatively innocuous way of modifying FAS 8.

Reserves in the Balance Sheet

Both FAS 52 and SSAP 20 specify that the gain or loss arising on translation under the closing rate method should be transferred directly to the reserves in the balance sheet and not pass through the profit and loss account. FAS 52 uses the term 'separate component of equity' rather than 'reserve', but the difference from SSAP 20, which states that the gain or loss 'should be recorded as a movement on reserves', is only one of terminology. However, there is a more substantial difference between FAS 52 and SSAP 20 over the subsequent treatment of this item. FAS 52 states that the amount of the gain or loss should be transferred out of the 'separate component of equity' into the income statement upon the complete or substantially complete liquidation of the investment in the foreign entity, being reported as part of the gain or loss on liquidation. SSAP 20 is silent on this matter, but the ASC intends to deal with it when it reviews its standard on depreciation. It should be stressed that both gains and losses are treated in exactly the same way. Hence the 'separate component of equity' and the reserve could well have debit balances.

One of the main reasons why both FAS 52 and SSAP 20 exclude translation gains and losses from the income statement is the belief of those who drew up these statements that these amounts are not real gains and losses but rather a difference thrown out by the translation process. Hence FAS 52 refers to them as 'translation adjustments' and SSAP 20 as 'exchange differences'.

SSAP 20 gives the following explanation for its treatment of exchange differences:

> The results of an operation of a foreign enterprise are best reflected in the group profit and loss account by consolidating the net profit or loss shown in its local currency financial statements without adjustment. If exchange differences . . . were introduced, the results from trading operations, as shown in the local currency financial statements, would be distorted. Such differences may result from many factors unrelated to the trading performance or financial operations of the foreign enterprise; in particular, they do not represent or measure changes in actual or prospective cash flows. It is therefore inappropriate to regard them as profits or losses and they should be dealt with as adjustments to reserves.

The author accepts the point that it may well be appropriate to exclude the 'exchange difference' when assessing the performance of foreign subsidiaries, but he rejects entirely the notion that this 'exchange difference' does not represent a genuine gain or loss to the holding company. Once the holding company has decided to place certain values on its foreign-based assets and liabilities (which it has no hesitation in including in its consolidated balance as the correct values), it cannot deny that the gain or loss which stems automatically from this decision is also genuine.

The reasoning in FAS 52 is much more difficult to understand because the four assenting members of the FASB could not agree on the nature of translation adjustments. The disagreement is set out in paragraphs 112 – 115 or FAS 52, where it is stated that there are two views. The first view is that 'the translation adjustment reflects an economic effect of exchange rate changes . . . an unrealised component of comprehensive income . . . that should be reported separately from net income'. The second view is that the translation adjustment is 'merely a mechanical byproduct of the translation process'. The author has some sympathy with the first view; he disagrees on how the 'component of income' should be reported. He has no sympathy with the second view which seems to imply that items may be included in the balance sheet that have no real meaning.

One of the main criticisms of the treatment of translation losses set out in SSAP 20 and FAS 52 is that they run counter to the principle of prudence, which is one of the most fundamental of the generally accepted accounting principles. Thus consolidated income can be overstated by the building up of debit balances in the balance sheet which do not represent genuine assets. One way in which this can be done involves foreign currency *transaction* (not translation) gains. So far, this chapter has considered only the translation of the foreign currency accounts of subsidiaries. However, the holding company itself may hold assets or owe liabilities that are denominated in foreign currency, or receive income or incur expenses in foreign currency. There is general agreement that the temporal method of translation should be used for the determination of the amount at which they should be stated in the accounts of the holding company. Any difference between the translated value in the balance sheet and the value previously stated is considered to be a *transaction* gain or loss and is included in the profit and loss account. Normally, following a change in exchange rates, the holding company will report foreign exchange transaction gains and losses on its liabilities and monetary assets that are denominated in foreign currency. There is no dispute over the correctness of this procedure.

The foreign subsidiary in its own (foreign currency) accounts will also, quite correctly, report transaction gains and losses on its own monetary assets and liabilities that are denominated in foreign currency (i.e. currency other than the subsidiary's own currency). Thus, when the holding company has made a loan to its subsidiary, denominated in the holding company's currency, the subsidiary will report a transaction gain or loss on this loan following a change in exchange rates. This is a genuine gain or loss from the point of view of the subsidiary as a separate entity (e.g. from the viewpoint of its minority shareholders).

Problems may arise when the subsidiary's accounts are incorporated in the consolidated accounts. No problem arises when the temporal method is used: the subsidiary's profit or loss is calculated in terms of the holding company's currency and no gain or loss arises on the loan denominated in the holding company's currency. A problem does arise when the closing rate method is used. Under both FAS 52 and SSAP 20, the subsidiary's entire profit and loss account is translated at the closing (or average) rate – including the transaction gain on the loan from the holding company. It is clearly quite wrong to include such a gain in consolidated profit for it relates to an intra-group transaction. Furthermore, it seems bizarre to report to the holding company's shareholders an exchange gain on an item that is denominated in their own currency.

To deal with this problem, FAS 52 provides that exchange gains and losses on inter-company loans of a long-term-investment nature should be excluded from consolidation; but gains and losses on other intercompany loans are to be consolidated. Thus it is still possible under FAS 52 to report a profit on an inter-company loan.

In the author's opinion, the fact that FAS 52 had to resort to *ad hoc* rules to deal with particular situations is a clear indication of the conceptual weakness of the closing rate method. It is not possible to deal with all problems by inventing *ad hoc* rules. For example, FAS 52 does not deal with a rather similar problem: the overstatement of the exchange gain in the consolidated accounts when the subsidiary reports an exchange gain on an asset denominated in a foreign currency that strengthens against the subsidiary's functional currency but weakens against the holding company's currency.

12.10   Inflation in the Foreign Country

Translation is no Substitute for Inflation Accounting

High rates of inflation in foreign countries often present problems for accountants. For example, as shown in Table 12.5, in the period 1970–1984 prices in Brazil increased very rapidly, at greatly more than the rate experienced in Britain. There was a corresponding fall in the exchange value of the cruzeiro. In such a situation the closing rate method produces unsatisfactory results, as can be demonstrated by a simple example. Assume that in 1970 the Brazilian subsidiary of a UK company bought a plot of land for 10,000,000 cruzeiros (or £843,882 at the 1970 exchange rate). In the absence of any adjustment for inflation in the Brazilian accounts, this asset will be shown in the subsidiary's 1984 balance sheet at its historical cost, i.e. 10,000,000 cruzeiros. Translated at the closing rate, the value of the land in the 1984 consolidated accounts is £2,761 (10,000,000 cr. × £1/3,622 cr.). This hardly seems a 'true and fair' value to place on this asset. This is an example of the 'disappearing plant' phenomenon: that, over time, plant located in highly inflationary economies tends to disappear from the consolidated balance sheet. To counter this, it is often suggested that, in these circumstances, historical rates should be used to translate fixed assets. This is the approach of FAS 52, which prescribes the use of the temporal method for the translation of the financial statements of subsidiaries that are located in highly inflationary economies. In the present example, if the temporal method were used, the land would be stated in the consolidated balance sheet at £843,882 – its cost in terms of pounds. Although the temporal method gives a more satisfactory result, it must

Table 12.5   Brazil and Britain: Exchange Rates and Prices

Year	Exchange rate Cruzeiros to £1	Retail Price Index Brazil	Britain
1970	11.85	100	100
1984	3,622.00	30,000	500

be made quite clear that its use is in no way a means of adjusting for inflation. The figure of £843,882 represents neither the shareholders' original investment adjusted for inflation in Britain (this is given by the original cost in pounds multiplied by the change in the British price index, i.e. £4,219,410 being £843,882 × 500/100) nor the current value of the land in Brazil (which may be approximately the original cost in cruzeiros multiplied by the increase in the Brazilian price index i.e. 3,000,000,000 cruzeiros, being 10,000,000 cr. × 30,000/100). The position is quite clear. Translation can never be a substitute for the adjustment for inflation of the subsidiary's financial statements.

Methods of Inflation Accounting

However, there is, at present, no general agreement on how this adjustment should be made. There are two widely accepted methods of preparing inflation-adjusted financial statements: current cost accounting (CCA) and general purchasing power accounting (GPP) (see Chapter 11). It is highly desirable that the same method be used in preparing the financial statements of both the holding company and its subsidiary. It is natural that the subsidiary should follow the holding company in this matter, since the consolidated financial statements are prepared for the benefit of the holding company's shareholders and creditors. Thus, if the holding company's inflation-adjusted accounts are based on CCA, the subsidiary's accounts will have to be adjusted using CCA before being incorporated into the consolidated financial statements. In this way consistency is assured. This adjustment process does, however, present rather different problems dependent on whether CCA or GPP is used.

Current Cost Accounting

CCA is based on the concept of replacement cost. In the case of a foreign subsidiary, the question arises as to whether this means replacement cost in the foreign market or in the home market. It would seem clear that the appropriate market to use is that of the country where the assets are located. The implicit assumption behind replacement cost accounting is that the asset will be replaced by one of equivalent productivity in its present location. A plot of land in the Brazilian jungle is quite a different asset from a plot of land in Central London. This is even more obvious when one considers the market value of inventory: a pound of coffee in Brazil is far less valuable than a pound of coffee in London. In both cases the local market should be used as the reference point. Where there are difficulties in observing replacement costs directly, an approximation can be made by using a local specific price index. Applying this technique to the example of the Brazilian subsidiary for the 1984 balance sheet, the historical cost of the land should be multiplied by the increase between 1970 and 1984 in the index that measures the cost of land in Brazil. The result will be the current cost in 1984 of the land in terms of cruzeiros which should then be translated into pounds using the closing (1984) rate.

To summarise, the basic procedure with CCA is first to adjust the historical cost of the assets using a local specific price index, then to translate using the closing rate (as suggested by the temporal principle).

General Purchasing Power Accounting

The basic principle underlying GPP is that the cost of assets is restated in terms of purchasing power. The concept of purchasing power has meaning only in relation to 'purchasers'. In this case the purchasers concerned are the shareholders. In the past, they (or rather the directors on their behalf) invested a certain amount of their wealth in certain assets. The current balance sheet indicates how much of this initial investment remains tied up in the assets. In order for this to be shown in terms of purchasing power, the original cost of the assets has to be multiplied by the increase in the general price index. A general price index is used as the best available measure of the purchasing power of shareholders' money.

However, should the index used be the foreign price index or the parent country price index? The authoritative analysis of this most interesting problem is given by Rosenfield (1971). He shows that there are two possible procedures:

  (i) 'First translate, then restate': the foreign currency cost of the asset is translated into the parent currency using the historic rate. This gives the parent currency cost at the date of acquisition, which is then adjusted by the subsequent increase in the parent general price index. Applying this procedure to the example of the Brazilian asset gives a figure of £4,219,410 (10,000,000 cr × (£1 ÷ 11.85 cr) × 5). The figures are taken from Table 12.5.
 (ii) 'First restate, then translate': the foreign currency cost of the asset is adjusted by the increase in the foreign general price index. This gives the updated foreign currency cost, which is then translated at the current exchange rate. Applying this procedure to the Brazilian example gives a figure of £828,272 (10,000,000 cr × 300 × (£1 ÷ 3,622 cr)).

The two methods produce different results for the reason that changes in the exchange rate between two currencies do not reflect exactly the difference in the rate of inflation in the two countries.

The 'first translate, then restate' method is the only one that results in consistent consolidated financial statements. The holding company's assets are stated in terms of the shareholders' purchasing power invested in them; therefore the subsidiary's assets should be stated in similar terms. The shareholders are, normally, located in the parent country and receive accounts expressed in the currency of the parent country. Their initial investment was in terms of the parent currency. This raises a strong presumption that the purchasing power that is being measured is that of the parent currency. The holding company shareholders have invested a certain amount of their wealth in the assets of the foreign subsidiary; the sacrifice that they made, in terms of purchasing power, is measured by the original investment in the parent currency (the currency in which the sacrifice was made) multiplied by the subsequent increase in the general price level in the parent country.

The 'first restate, then translate' method should not be used because it would result in the holding company's assets, which have been adjusted for the increase in the price level in the parent country, being added to assets (i.e. those of the subsidiary) which have been adjusted for the increase in the price level of the foreign country. As Rosenfield points out, this implies the use of 'more than one standard for the unit of measure in terms of general purchasing power and may lead to undesirable results such as ambiguity, unintelligibility and noncomparability'.

To summarise, the correct procedure with GPP is first to translate using the temporal method (the historical cost of assets being translated at historic exchange rates) and then to adjust the translated amounts using the general price index of the home country.

This result is remarkably inconvenient! If the converse were the case (i.e. if 'first restate, then translate' were correct), life would be much simpler for three reasons:

1. The same rule would apply to both CCA and GPP.

2. One could make the generalisation that for inflation-adjusted accounts the current rate of exchange should be used for translation. The application of the temporal method to accounts that have already been adjusted for inflation (i.e. expressed in terms of values at the balance sheet date) requires the use of the current rate for all items. In this case the temporal method and the closing rate method produce identical results. It is interesting to speculate that the controversy between proponents of these two methods may one day be rendered obsolete by the universal adoption of current cost accounting.

3. If the subsidiary's foreign currency financial statements have already been stated in terms of GPP (perhaps to fulfil a local legal requirement), strict adherence to the correct procedure would imply that this process be reversed to produce historical cost accounts that would serve as input to the 'first translate, then restate' procedure. This is not only extra work but also strikes one as a rather strange thing to do.

The advantages of choosing the 'first restate, then translate' rule for GPP are obvious, and many accountants would be tempted to use it. In principle they would be wrong.

12.11   The Economist vs. The Accountant

Economists and some accountants criticise the translation methods described in the previous sections as leading to the calculation of asset values and exchange gains and losses that are not in accordance with economic reality. Dufey (1972) gives an amusing example of the French subsidiary of a US-based car manufacturer whose main activity was the manufacture of engines which it exported to assembly plants in Germany. In 1969 a devaluation of the French franc of between 10 and 20% seemed imminent. This would have produced translation losses of several million dollars in the consolidated financial statements. Accordingly, the American head office ordered the French subsidiary to keep its working capital to an absolute minimum, which implied reducing the level of its operations. However, the manager of the French subsidiary was in favour of expanding operations. The expected devaluation of the French franc would result in an automatic increase in his selling price, which would lead to a substantial increase in profits, since the other costs would not increase in the same proportion. The devaluation would lead to an increase in the subsidiary company's value, at least when valued in terms of French francs.

Walker (1978) argues that the foreign subsidiary's value should be taken as the net present value of future cash flows. He states that 'economic analysis recognises that a devaluation of the foreign subsidiary's local currency will not automatically reduce the parent currency value of the foreign subsidiary's net assets as is suggested by the accounting approach'. But although he analyses in detail the effect of a devaluation on a foreign subsidiary's cash flow, he is unable to arrive at any general rule. There are practical difficulties of estimation, but 'despite these difficulties, the economic analysis of exchange risk is clearly the right approach'.

In fact one suspects that most accountants would not take exception to Walker's two main conclusions: that balance sheet values of assets determined in accordance with generally accepted accounting principles are poor indicators of economic values; and that it is very difficult to estimate future cash flows. Most accountants would probably add that it is not intended that the balance sheet should reflect economic values.

A number of influential voices have recently warned against the adjustment of accounting principles (especially those on translation) away from what is theoretically sound merely in order to affect the behaviour of businessmen (Zeff 1978, Solomons 1978). It is hoped and intended that businessmen will react to economic reality, which does not alter with, for example, a different accounting presentation of translation gains or losses.

Aliber and Stickney's Research

A startling alternative view has been proposed by Aliber and Stickney (1975). By the use of two economic theories they prove that changes in exchange rates have no effect on the values of foreign subsidiaries. The theories are:

(i) The purchasing power parity theorem which states that, between two countries, changes in the exchange rate are proportional to changes in the relative price levels.

(ii) The 'Fisher effect' which states that, between two countries, the differential in the interest rates earned on similar financial assets is equal to the expected change in the exchange rate.

The Purchasing Power Parity (PPP) Theorem

The implications of the PPP theorem can be examined using a simple example. At the start of a year, a British company constructs two identical factories: one in Britain that costs £100,000 and one in Ruritania costing $100,000, the exchange rate at that time being £1 = $1. It undertook the investment in the expectation of a 20% annual return, anticipating an annual cash flow in perpetuity of £20,000 in Britain and $20,000 in Ruritania, after charging the annual cost of replacing worn-out plant. During the next twelve months, prices in Ruritania rise by 50%. The anticipated annual cash flow from the Ruritanian factory is now $30,000. Prices in Britain rise by 10%; the anticipated annual cash flow there is now £22,000. The new exchange rate, as predicted by the PPP theorem, is £1.10 = $1.50. The future cash flows of the two factories at this new exchange rate are identical; hence the factories' values are identical. The change in the exchange rate has not affected the value of the Ruritanian factory.

The implications for translation are most interesting. If historical cost is used as the basis of valuation of assets, the British factory will be shown in the balance sheet at £100,000. For the Ruritanian factory to be shown in the consolidated balance sheet at the same value, the historical cost in terms of local currency ($100,000) must be translated at the historic exchange rate. If assets are stated at the net present value of future cash flows, the situation is a little more complex: the British factory has a value of £110,000 (i.e. £22,000 × 100 ÷ 20) and the Ruritanian factory a value of $150,000 (i.e. $30,000 × 100 ÷ 20). To achieve identical values, the Ruritanian factory's present value must be translated at the current exchange rate. If the PPP theorem is correct, this analysis proves to be a convincing justification of the temporal method (historical cost translated at historic rates; present values translated at current rates).

The 'Fisher Effect'

The 'Fisher effect' will be illustrated using the same example. The two factories, one in Britain and the other in Ruritania, are each financed by a local loan. Lenders demand a 5% real return after taking into account the expected rates of inflation as before. Hence the nominal rate of interest will be 15.5% in Britain and 57.5% in Ruritania. After twelve months, the exchange rate will have moved from £1 = $1 to £1.10 = $1.50. This is all as predicted by the 'Fisher effect': the interest rate differential (1.575 ÷ 1.155 = 1.36) is identical to the change in the exchange rate (1.50 ÷ 1.10 = 1.36). In other words, a person with £100,000 who invested it in Britain at the start of the year would be exactly as well off as if he had invested it in Ruritania. In the first case he would have £115,500 at the end of the year; in the second case he would have $157,500 which, at the current exchange rate of £1 = $1.36, is worth £115,500. If this were not the case, if for example the return in Britain were higher, arbitrage between the two markets should cause the gap to close; investors would invest less in Ruritania, lend more in Britain, bringing about lower interest rates in Britain and higher interest rates in Ruritania as the markets adjusted to the relative shortage and glut of funds.

The implications for accounting are interesting. Since the real rate of interest is the same for both loans, one would expect their financing cost, as reported in the consolidated profit and loss account, also to be the same. Since the interest costs of the Ruritanian loan are so much higher than those of the British loan, this can only be achieved by deducting, from the interest cost of the Ruritanian loan, the fall in its sterling value, i.e. by translating the loan at the closing rate. If this is done, the financing cost of the Ruritanian loan, in terms of sterling, becomes:

Interest:
  57.5% of $100,000 = $57,500 × £1 ÷ $1.36 =   £42,167
Less fall in value of loan:
  Start of year:
    $100,000 × £1 ÷ $1   = £100,000
  End of year:
    $100,000 × £1 ÷ $1.36 = £ 73,333   £26,667

                                                     £15,500

The net cost of the Ruritanian loan (£15,500) is, of course, equal to the interest cost of the British loan.

The temporal principle is again vindicated. In this case it is the rather old-fashioned current/non-current method that is shown to be incorrect. Also the example shows that the practice of excluding translation gains and losses from income is of doubtful validity, since the true cost of financing a foreign loan can be established only after taking into account both the interest payments and the exchange loss or gain relating to the capital value of the loan.

It should be noted that Aliber and Stickney (1975) were in error in stating that their analysis of the 'Fisher effect' showed the temporal principle of translation to be wrong. They were correct in stating that it showed that financial liabilities were not subject to exchange risk since the total financing cost will be the same no matter where the liability is located. However, they inferred from this that the capital value of a foreign loan should not be adjusted for changes in the exchange rate. This is incorrect. Only by taking into account the loss (or gain) on the loan can the true cost of financing be shown.

There is one slight snag in this almost idyllic partnership of economic theory and accounting practice. Are the two economic theories (the PPP theorem and the 'Fisher effect') in fact correct? This was investigated by Aliber and Stickney. For the PPP theorem they analysed data for 48 countries over the period 1961 to 1971 and compared the change in the exchange rate predicted by the theorem with the observed change. Figures for the average annual deviation are given in Table 12.6. It is noticeable that there is a clear central tendency and that for a majority of countries (29 out of 48) the average deviation was less than 2%. Thus, over the longer period (11 years in this case), the data support the theorem. However, in the shorter run, the theorem is far less successful. Since the 11-year average is calculated from a number of positive and negative deviations that to a large extent offset each other, the deviation in any given year is generally higher than the 11-year average. Aliber and Stickney found that this was the case with 68% of the countries; in fact 42% of the year-to-year deviations were greater than ± 3%.

Table 12.6   A Test of the PPP Theorem

Average deviation from expected exchange rate	Number of countries
more than 3%	3
2% to 3%	8
1% to 2%	9
0% to 1%	6
0% to − 1%	9
− 1% to − 2%	5
− 2% to − 3%	3
more than − 3%	5
Total	48

Source: Aliber and Stickney, 1975

Aliber and Stickney performed a similar analysis to test the 'Fisher effect' using data for seven developed countries for the same period. The average annual deviation for the 11-year period was only 0.8% with no country worse than 2%. However, the deviations in any given year were higher: 28% were over ±2%. The conclusion that might be drawn from this empirical investigation is that both the PPP theorem and the 'Fisher effect' are reasonably good representations of the real world in the long run: say over 10 years. It is therefore reasonable to use these theories as a basis for the development of accounting practice. They are a poor representation of the world in the short run, which means that economic theorists have not yet eliminated exchange risk; but neither have they yet invented a better theory on which to base accounting practice.

12.12   Summary

Translation is the necessary re-expression of the foreign currency financial statements of a foreign subsidiary into the parent's currency for consolidation. Since exchange rates alter, there are decisions to be made about the exchange rates to be used for the translation of the various items in the subsidiary's financial statements. The most obvious choice is between the historic rate ruling at the time of the transaction and the current rate at the time of the balance sheet.

Traditional methods of translation are: (i) the closing rate method which uses only current rates; (ii) the current/non-current method (CNC) which uses historic rates for non-current balances; and (iii) the monetary/non-monetary method which uses historic rates for non-momentary balances. Naturally, as exchange rates change, different methods lead to different results, including the size of gains and losses on translation.

A new approach was made in the early 1970s by the AICPA who commissioned a research project, leading to ARS 12 and FAS 8, which introduced the temporal principle of translation. The temporal principle translates a balance at the exchange rate ruling at the date that the valuation basis was established. Under historical cost accounting, this leads to results similar to the MNM method. However, the temporal principle applies equally well for current value or any other system of accounting.

There was considerable opposition to the enforced application of the temporal method in the USA, particularly from companies that preferred to use the closing rate method. The relative merits of the temporal method and of the closing rate method were discussed in a lengthy debate which was ultimately resolved in favour of the closing rate method. In 1981 the FASB issued FAS 52, which made the closing rate method the normal standard; the temporal method was only to be applied in certain well-defined, exceptional circumstances. The same line was followed by the ASC (in SSAP 20) and the IASC (in IAS 21).

There has been much controversy over how the translation gain or loss should be treated in the accounts. FAS 8 provided that the gain or loss should be included in income, but this was reversed by FAS 52, which states that it must be reported as an element of equity. The situation is complicated by the problem of how to treat gains and losses on foreign exchange transactions.

Further complications arise when the foreign subsidiary is located in a highly inflationary economy. The subsidiary's accounts must be adjusted for inflation. The method to be used to adjust for inflation is closely connected with the choice of translation method.

Finally, two important economic theorems in the field of foreign exchange have been considered: the Purchasing Power Parity (PPP) theorem and the Fisher Effect. The surprising conclusion was reached that these two theorems provide considerable support for the temporal principle.

References

Aliber, R.Z. and Stickney, C.P. (1975) 'Measures of foreign exchange exposure', *The Accounting Review*, January.

Baxter, W.T. and Yamey, B.S. (1951) 'Theory of foreign branch accounts', reprinted in W.T. Baxter (1978) *Collected Papers in Accounting*, Arno Press.

Dufey, G. (1972) 'Corporate finance and exchange rate variations', *Financial Management*, Summer.

Graham, N. (1982) 'Europe's divers routes to exchange rates problems', *Accountancy*, December.

Lorensen, L. (1972) *Accounting Research Study No. 12: Reporting Foreign Operations of US Companies in US Dollars*, AICPA, New York.

Nobes, C.W. (1980) 'A review of the translation debate', *Accounting and Business Research*, Autumn.

Parkinson, R.M. (1972) *Translation of Foreign Currencies – a Research Study*, CICA, Toronto.

Patz, D. (1977) 'A price parity theory of translation', *Accounting and Business Research*, Winter.

Price Waterhouse (1980) *International Survey of Accounting Principles and Reporting Practices*, Butterworth.

Rosenfield, P. (1971) 'General price-level accounting and foreign operations', *Journal of Accountancy*, February.

Smith, A.F. (1978) 'Temporal method: temporary mode', *Management Accounting (US)*, February.

Solomons, D. (1978) 'The politicization of accounting', *Journal of Accountancy*, November.

Walker, D.P. (1978) *An Economic Analysis of Foreign Exchange Risk, Research Committee Occasional Paper No. 14*, ICAEW, London.

Zeff, S.A. (1978) 'The rise of economic consequences', *Journal of Accountancy*, December.

ASC (1977) *Exposure Draft 21, Accounting for Foreign Currency Transactions*, Accounting Standards Committee, *Accountancy*, October.

ASC (1978) *SSAP 14, Consolidation Accounting*, CCAB Accountancy Bodies, London.

ASC (1983) *SSAP 20, Foreign Currency Translation*, CCAB Accountancy Bodies, London. (Printed in *Accountancy*, May 1983).

FASB (1975) *Statement of Financial Accounting Standards No. 8: Accounting for the Translation of Foreign Currency Transactions and Foreign Currency Financial Statements*, Financial Accounting Standards Board.

FASB (1981) *Statement of Financial Accounting Standards No. 52: Foreign Currency Translation*, Financial Accounting Standards Board.

IASC (1978) *IAS 8, Unusual and Prior Period Items* ..., International Accounting Standards Committee.

IASC (1983) *IAS 21 Accounting for the Effects of Changes in Foreign Exchange Rates*, International Accounting Standards Committee.

Further Reading

For an introduction to translation, see IAS 21.

For an analysis of the temporal and other methods, see Lorensen (1972).

For a defence of the closing rate method, see Parkinson (1972).

For the economic aspects of translation, see Walker (1978) and Aliber and Stickney (1975).

For a review of the translation debate, see Nobes (1980).

For the case in favour of purchasing power parity, see Patz (1977).

13

Foreign Exchange Risk Management

DAVID P. WALKER

13.1 Introduction

A discussion of the management of foreign exchange risk may seem a little out of place in a text on comparative international accounting, but it is certainly true that the different accounting rules prevailing throughout the world have a major impact on how multinational corporations define and hence manage their currency exposures. The purpose of this chapter is to discuss the strategic choices facing today's multinational company in the management of foreign exchange risk and, indirectly, to show how these choices can be affected by accounting practices.

All corporate exposure management strategies must address two fundamental issues. First, since there is no single definition of exposure to foreign exchange risk, which definition or definitions of exposure should a company be concerned with? If the answer embodies more than one definition, priorities and the trade-off between the alternatives should be clearly understood and defined. Secondly, given a company's definition(s) of exposure, what is the corporate attitude towards risk? Is the company seeking to maximise foreign exchange gains, or minimise exchange losses? Also, what time frame is being considered – is the intention to smooth short-term results at the expense of longer-term trends, or vice versa?

13.2 Alternative Definitions of Foreign Exchange Risk

The starting point for the formulation of a company's foreign exchange risk management programme must be to decide exactly what the company has at risk. Quite simply, an asset, liability or income stream is said to be 'exposed' to exchange risk when a currency movement will change, for better or for worse, its parent or home currency value. Exposure is therefore a neutral concept. It merely signifies that a company has assets, liabilities or income streams denominated in currencies other than its own. The 'risk' element is that the currency movement may produce adverse results.

All foreign currency denominated assets, liabilities and income streams are therefore exposed to exchange risk. Basically, this exposure is of two types. First, there is the exposure inherent in a foreign currency transaction, known as 'transactional exposure'. This consists of both trading items (foreign currency invoiced trade receivables and payables) and capital items (foreign currency dividend and loan payments). Second, there is the exposure associated with the ownership of foreign currency denominated assets and liabilities.

Transactional exposure is usually clear and well-defined. If a US company invoices an export customer for, say, 10 million French francs ('FF'), then for the period between the contract date and the date the receivable is settled the exporter has an exposure of FF 10 million. If the franc were to depreciate by 5 per cent against the US dollar during this period, a realised loss of 5 per cent of the exposure would have been incurred. This kind of foreign exchange exposure is now fully recognised by almost all participants in international business. Hence there is no need here to discuss it further.

The exposure inherent in ongoing foreign operations is, however, much more problematical. Confusion has arisen from the fact that accounting practice and economic logic give two very different pictures of the way in which currency fluctuations affect the value of foreign operations. Briefly, the accounting approach is concerned essentially with translation adjustments in a company's consolidated accounts, whereas economic or cash flow exposure is concerned with the effect of currency movements on the future cash flows produced by foreign operations. The first type of effect gives rise to unrealised adjustments, whilst the latter leads to gains and losses which will actually be realised. Let us now analyse these two interpretations of exposure.

13.3 Accounting Exposure

Accounting ('translation') exposure arises on the consolidation of foreign subsidiaries' accounts into the parent currency denominated group financial statements. This process requires the application of a rate or rates of exchange to foreign subsidiaries' accounts so that they can be translated into the parent currency. Since both balance sheets and income statements must be consolidated, they both generate translation exposures.

Balance Sheet Exposure

As explained in Chapter 12, certain items in a foreign subsidiary's balance sheet may be translated at their historical exchange rates (the rate prevailing at the date of acquisition or at the date of any subsequent revaluation). Hence their parent currency translated values cannot be altered by currency movements – such assets and liabilities cannot be exposed in the accounting sense. Other items, however, are translated at current or 'closing' exchange rates (the rate prevailing at the balance sheet date). Even when the value of such items is fixed in terms of the foreign subsidiary's currency, the parent currency translated value will alter from year to year if the exchange rate of the foreign subsidiary's host country changes vis-à-vis the parent currency. Therefore all foreign currency items which are consolidated at current rates are exposed in the accounting sense.

To illustrate how balance sheet exposure can be measured, let us take the case of a US company which has a UK subsidiary. The US parent's balance sheet exposure in UK pounds (UKP) consists of three elements:

1. All balance sheet accounts of the foreign (UK) subsidiary which are denominated in the subsidiary's local currency (UKP) and which are to be translated into the parent currency at the closing exchange rate.
2. The foreign (UK) subsidiary's UKP tax-related exposures arising from the foreign (non-UKP) currency debtors/creditors – third party and intercompany – on the UK subsidiary's balance sheet. For example, if the UK subsidiary has a Deutsche mark (DM) 100 debtor outstanding at balance sheet reporting date, then this represents a sterling asset exposure equivalent to (DM 100 × $t_{UK}/100$), where t is the percentage tax rate. This arises because an appreciation of the UKP against the DM means that the DM debtor is worth less in UKP terms. Since the resulting foreign exchange loss in the UK is tax deductible, the appreciation of the UKP has generated a UKP cash inflow (local tax credit). The corollary of this is that the UK subsidiary has an after-tax asset exposure of [DM 100 $(100 - t_{UK})/100$].

3. The after-tax UKP exposures arising from the UKP debtors/ creditors – third party and intercompany – on other (non-UK) subsidiaries' balance sheets. For example, if a French subsidiary has a UKP 100 creditor then this represents a UKP liability exposure equivalent to $[UKP\ 100(100 - t_F)/100]$. An appreciation of UKP against the FF means that the UKP creditor increases in value in FF terms. Part of this exposure (i.e. $UKP100 \times t_F/100$) is absorbed by the French tax authorities. The balance represents a UKP liability exposure to the French company.

The measurement of balance sheet exposure is a relatively straight-forward process. To calculate the three elements, the subsidiaries' projected balance sheets must be disaggregated by currency and the effective marginal tax rates must be ascertained and applied. The sum of these three parts gives the balance sheet exposure which will generate the foreign exchange gain/loss at the next reporting date.

Income Statement Exposure

Foreign exchange gains/losses here derive from the process of translating each unit's income statement into the parent currency consolidated statement. As with balance sheet translation, this is a two-step process. The foreign currency items on each unit's income statement must first be translated into its local currency and then (for foreign units) this local currency income statement must be translated into the parent currency.

To illustrate the kind of effects which income statement exposure generates, consider the case of a UK subsidiary (US parent) whose expenses are entirely denominated in pesetas and which sells entirely in the local UK market. How would the consolidated income statement be exposed to currency movements?

Projected cost of goods sold (less inventory on hand assuming FIFO inventory accounting) represents a short peseta exposure – if the peseta depreciates against the US dollar, group consolidated expenses are reduced. Just as with balance sheet exposure, however, this short position must be tax-effected. Hence the projected exposure consists of both a peseta exposure (projected peseta expense multiplied by a factor of $(100 - t_{UK})$) and a UKP exposure (projected expense multiplied by (t_{UK}), where t_{UK} is the percentage effective tax rate). On the reverse side, projected UKP sales represent a long UKP exposure to the US parent. There are no tax effects here since there can be no realised foreign exchange gains/losses.

The measurement of income statement exposure requires the application of this kind of analysis to each unit's projected income statement, categorised by currency. Quantification is achieved by applying alternative exchange rate assumptions to the basic formula:

$$\text{Exposure} \quad \times \quad \frac{\text{Percentage exchange}}{\text{rate change}} \quad = \quad \frac{\text{Foreign exchange}}{\text{gain/loss}}$$

One of the key variables of the income statement measurement process is the exposure period. This will reflect the company's operating characteristics and, specifically, should incorporate the concept of a price adjustment lag. This lag is defined as the length of time it will take to raise selling prices in order to offset the adverse impact of a currency movement on operations as measured in parent currency terms. The assumption here is that prices can be increased so that projected net income measured in parent currency terms can be protected. If this is not possible, the loss becomes a permanent one – hence the price adjustment lag is a key determinant of the exposure period.

13.4 Economic or Cash Flow Exposure

The theoretical value of an asset is represented by the net present value (NPV) of the future net cash flows (after-tax) which the asset is expected to produce. In the valuation of foreign assets the only additional step required is that the NPV of cash flows (including indirect cash flows generated by the subsidiary but arising elsewhere in the corporate group, such as trading profits, management fees, and royalties) must then be translated into the parent currency at some rate of exchange. The NPV of a foreign subsidiary should therefore be defined as follows:

$$NPV_o = \sum_{t=0}^{n} \frac{(CIF_t - COF_t)ER_t}{(1 + d)^t}$$

where

NPV = net present value (parent currency equivalent)

CIF = cash inflows (denominated in foreign subsidiary's local currency)

COF = cash outflows (denominated in foreign subsidiary's local currency), including tax payments

ER = exchange rate (parent currency value of one unit of foreign currency)

d = discount rate (the rate of return required by the parent company for its investment in the foreign subsidiary)

t = period t

n = the last period in which cash flows are expected

The economic evaluation of exchange risk should therefore be defined as the possibility that the parent company denominated NPV of the foreign subsidiary's future cash flows will be adversely affected by exchange rate movements. In other words, exposure is that component of a firm's value (future cash flows) which is related to the future exchange rate scenario.

This exchange rate impact will comprise two different kinds of effects, analogous to the price and quantity effects of basic economic theory. A change in the foreign subsidiary's exchange rate will not only have the automatic effect of altering the 'price' at which future local currency (LC) cash flows are transformed into the parent currency (ER in the above equation), but it may also change the quantity (CIF – COF) and timing (t) of these cash flows. Hence the economic analysis of exchange risk is concerned with estimating the effects of currency movements on foreign operations' future LC cash inflows (sales revenues) and cash outflows ('physical' input and financing costs). A conceptual framework expressed diagrammatically in Figure 13.1 will now be outlined for

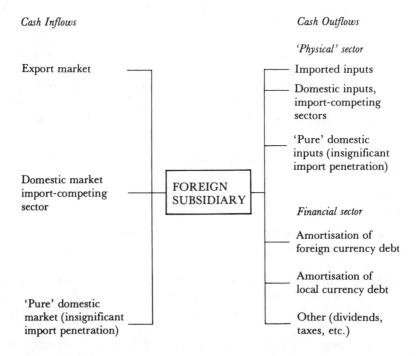

Figure 13.1   A Framework for the Analysis of Cash Flow Exposure

economic exposure analysis, using the simple case of a devaluation of a foreign subsidiary's host currency (hereafter referred to as 'the devaluation').

Cash Inflows: Sales Revenues

A change in the subsidiary's host country exchange rate (irrespective of whether it moves in relation to the parent currency) can have two types of effect on the subsidiary's sales revenues. It can alter the size of the market in which the subsidiary sells its output ('market size' effect) and/or it may alter the share of this market which the subsidiary holds ('market share' effect). The direction and incidence of these effects will vary according to the market characteristics of the subsidiary. These market characteristics can be categorised into three market types: the export sector; the import-competing sector of the domestic market; and the 'pure' domestic market (i.e. zero or insignificant import penetration). The devaluation (market size and share) effects for each of these three market categories are as follows:

(i) Export sector

Whilst a devaluation will have little or no effect on the total size of the export market, it will have a favourable market share effect. Hence the LC revenues produced by the foreign subsidiary's exports should be increased. The export-oriented subsidiary may reduce its foreign (that is, 'foreign' to the host) currency selling price by the devaluation percentage (maintaining the LC equivalent), which will presumably lead to a higher sales volume. Alternatively, it can maintain its foreign currency prices (raising the LC equivalent), thereby increasing by the devaluation percentage the LC revenue per unit of an unchanged sales volume. In other words, devaluation should produce increased sales and/or higher profit margins – either way, LC export revenues should benefit from the devaluation. They may not benefit by the full devaluation percentage, however, since foreign markets may be the subject of increased competition from other exporters.

(ii) Domestic market, import-competing sector

As in the export sector, the market share effect will be favourable because it will increase the competitiveness of local vis-à-vis foreign goods. Hence subsidiaries selling goods which compete with imports in the domestic market should also produce increased revenues, unless overseas exporters are willing and able to suffer a fall in revenue denominated in their own currencies. Typically, then, a devaluation will lead to an increase in the LC price of imported goods, in the short term at least. The long-run outcome may be that foreign suppliers move their production facilities to devaluation-prone markets. Foreign subsidiaries located in the devaluing country and operating in the import-competing sector of the domestic market will therefore benefit, again in the form of increased sales volume and/or higher profit margins.

Devaluation will also have a positive effect on nominal domestic income because of the foreign trade multiplier. However, the rising price of imports and import-competing goods in the devaluing country may reduce real income. More importantly, domestic demand is likely to be dampened by the government deflationary measures which usually accompany devaluations. The favourable market-share effects of a devaluation may therefore be partly offset by adverse effects on the total size of the domestic market.

(iii)   Pure domestic market

Foreign subsidiaries operating in this market category are most likely to lose from a devaluation, since there will be no favourable market-share effects to offset the probable adverse domestic income effect.

Cash Outflows

For analytical purposes it is useful to make the distinction between 'physical' input (labour, raw material, and plant) costs and 'financing' (working capital and borrowing) costs:

(i)   Physical sector

Devaluation will increase the LC cost of physical inputs for most firms operating in the devaluing country. The extent of input price increases will depend on such macroeconomic factors as the pre-devaluation employment situation, the effectiveness of the government deflationary programme and the speed with which inputs can be shifted between different sectors of the economy. Within this general pattern, Shapiro (1975) has proposed a three-fold classification of the production function into imported, traded domestic, and non-traded domestic inputs. Clearly, those companies which import a large proportion of their inputs will be hardest hit by a devaluation. Their costs may not rise by the full devaluation percentage, however, if competition from domestic producers forces overseas suppliers to absorb part of the cost increase. Even firms using mainly domestic inputs will be subject to rising costs, since expansion in the export- and import-competing sectors will force up factor prices. This will, of course, affect traded rather than non-traded input costs, which will be least affected by the devaluation.

(ii)   Financial sector

Devaluation will have a twofold impact on financing costs, since it will alter companies' working capital requirements as well as the cost of borrowing. In terms of working capital requirements, it has been argued above that a devaluation may lead to increased sales revenues and rising input costs. If this is the case, larger cash and inventory balances will be required and customers' credit needs will be larger, resulting in additional working capital requirements.

The effect on borrowing costs will depend on the currency denomination of the company's liability structure. The obvious impact on the cost of foreign (that is, 'foreign' to the host) currency-denominated loans is that the effective interest rate will be increased. Not so obvious, however, is the effect on domestic interest rates. These usually rise when a currency comes under pressure and devaluation is expected. Also, interest rates will remain high after a devaluation if continuing inflationary pressures are expected. Hence, the interest cost of almost all loans is likely to rise as a result of devaluation – the only exception is the company's existing fixed-rate domestic debt.

After adjusting expected future LC cash inflows and outflows for the 'quantity' effect of a devaluation, the cash flow analysis must finally take account of the 'price' effect. The adjusted net LC cash flow which the subsidiary is now expected to produce is therefore translated into the parent currency at the new rate of exchange, giving the parent-currency-denominated net cash flow. If the loss on translation at the new rate (the 'price' effect) is more than offset by an improvement in LC cash flows (the 'quantity' effect), the parent company will benefit from the devaluation since the value of its foreign subsidiary is increased. If the reverse is true, the parent company should consider neutralising the exposure by, for instance, changing the financing, sourcing and marketing structure of its subsidiary.

Clearly, however, such an analysis of future cash flows is a very difficult and complex task. It requires the estimation of such variables as the devaluation reactions of competitors (price elasticity of supply), consumers (price elasticity of demand) and the local government (will price controls be introduced?). Nevertheless, it is essential that each firm try to measure its currency exposures. How can this be done in practice?

Measurement of Cash Flow Exposure

This exposure concept is very difficult to translate into a quantifiable form; there seem to be three approaches. The narrow approach is the most common. This considers solely the actual cash flows which are to be transferred between the foreign subsidiary and the parent company over the exposure period. These consist of intercompany trade payments, dividends, and quasi-dividend flows (e.g. management fees, royalties) and intercompany debt servicing. The main strength of this approach is that it is easy to calculate. It is very limited, however, since it excludes foreign subsidiary cash flows which are generated but not repatriated during the exposure period.

The second approach focuses on the parent currency value of the available net cash flow (surplus or deficit) produced by each unit. 'Availability' here refers to the extent to which the local net cash flow can be used or funded by the parent. Utilisation takes such forms as dividend and quasi-dividend remittances (management fees, royalties), intercompany debt servicing and intercompany trade flows. Parent company funding of deficit units normally takes the form of a loan or equity injection. Local exchange controls and local borrowing capacity are key determinants of availability.

The third and broadest approach includes the total net cash flow produced by the foreign subsidiary over the exposure period, regardless of whether this is planned to be remitted or is 'available' for remittance. It should be added, of course, that once funds are repatriated they are no longer exposed.

Whatever the focus, the measurement of cash flow exposure requires an evaluation of how the parent currency value of each unit's projected cash flows (broken down by currency) will be affected by currency movements. To illustrate, consider the case of a subsidiary currency (UKP) appreciation. The following sterling cash flows will increase in parent currency (US dollar) terms:

— local (UK) sales receipts and UKP-invoiced export receipts;
— local payments for inventory and UKP-invoiced import payments;
— local payments for selling, general, administrative, and financial costs;
— local tax payments, adjusted for the foreign exchange loss on foreign currency (non-UKP) cash inflows and the foreign exchange gain on foreign currency cash outflows.

Once these projected flows have been isolated and quantified for the exposure (price adjustment plus receivables collection/payables turnover) period, cash flow exposure can be calculated by again applying alternative exchange rate scenarios to the basic formula.

Does Foreign Exchange Risk Matter?

Currency depreciation is almost always associated with a relatively high rate of inflation, especially in a floating rate system. In our earlier conceptual analysis of the devaluation case, the effects of inflation were ignored. Yet inflation will have an important influence on a subsidiary's

LC cash flows and, as Shapiro (1975) has shown, its effects will generally be the opposite to those of devaluation.

For example, inflation will have an adverse market-share effect on sales revenues in the export- and import-competing sectors, whilst it will have a favourable (nominal) income effect on domestic demand. It will drive up the cost of physical inputs in domestically sourced production functions, whilst not affecting imported inputs. Indeed, it is only in the financial sector that the impact of devaluation and inflation will be similar: both can be expected to increase working capital and borrowing costs.

In sum, then, devaluation will tend to favour companies in the export- and import-competing sectors and those which are domestically sourced and financed. Inflation will tend to have the opposite effects. It should also be added, of course, that inflation and currency depreciation are experienced simultaneously. Indeed, this interaction between the opposing processes of inflation and currency depreciation poses the question of whether exchange risk really exists at all. If the adverse (beneficial) effects of LC depreciation are simultaneously and exactly offset by the beneficial (adverse) effects of LC inflation, then does exchange risk exist? This is the essence of a view which has gained much influence in the academic world (Aliber and Stickney 1975, and Aliber 1974).

The rationale of this view is based on two economic theorems: the purchasing power parity (PPP) theory and the interest rate theory of exchange rate expectations (the Fisher effect). These are discussed in Chapter 12; their specific relevance to exchange risk is examined here. The rationale of both theorems is based on arbitrage: commodity arbitrage in the first case, and covered interest arbitrage in the second.

The PPP theory states that the difference between the inflation rates of two countries tends over time to equal the rate of change of the exchange rate between their two currencies. The implication is that:

> . . . if gains and losses from exchange rate changes tend over time to be offset by differences in relative inflation rates, it matters little in which currency the firm buys its inputs or sells its products, since any devaluation (revaluation) of a foreign currency will sooner or later be offset by a correspondingly higher (lower) rate of inflation in that currency. (Giddy 1977)

According to the Fisher effect, the difference between the interest rates of two currencies should equal the expected rate of change of the exchange rate during the appropriate maturity period. Hence:

> . . . it would not matter in which currency the firm borrowed or loaned funds, given a sufficiently long time horizon, since any exchange loss (gain) would eventually be offset by an interest rate advantage (disadvantage). (Giddy 1977)

The question 'does exchange risk matter?' now becomes an empirical one. If these two theories hold (see Chapter 12) then it does not matter in which currencies a firm buys/sells or borrows/lends since the effects of currency movements will be offset by countervailing changes in inflation and interest rates. In the long run, the rate of return on the asset side and the cost of capital on the liability side both adjust to offset the effects of currency movements. In the long run, exchange risk does not exist.

Unfortunately, however, both the PPP theorem and the Fisher effect fail a crucial real-life test – they do not hold in the short run. When the theorems are tested on an annual basis there are significant deviations from the projected exchange rate path, and the correlations are much worse for quarterly tests. In other words, whilst the long-term trend is accurately reflected in the PPP and Fisher paths, in the short run actual exchange rates will deviate around these paths. Hence, exchange risk stems from deviations from the expected rate (indicated by the forward rate or interest rate differential). These unexpected exchange rate changes cause a variability in cash flow, and it is this which constitutes the firm's exchange risk.

13.5 Alternative Strategies for Managing Foreign Exchange Risk

Two fundamental exchange risk management strategies can be distinguished, which we will call 'aggressive' and 'defensive'. (In practice, of course, these fundamental strategies rarely exist – rather, companies will tend to lie somewhere on a spectrum of risk/return trade-offs between the two polar types.) The difference between these two approaches can be most easily demonstrated by reference to the case of a single and one-off export sale. The aggressive exporter would try to invoice the sale in what he expected to be a hard currency (relative to his own currency), and he would only cover the currency receivable when the forward rate of exchange was more favourable than the spot rate which he expected would prevail at the settlement date. Exchange forecasts therefore play a key role in the invoicing and forward-cover decisions. In contrast, the defensive firm would try to invoice the export sale in its home currency. Where this is not possible the exposed receivable would be automatically covered, irrespective of the view of future currency movements. Indeed, such firms would not be concerned with exchange rate forecasts since their cover policy is automatic.

These two strategies can also be applied to decisions of a more fundamental and long-term nature. As regards currency of financing, for instance, the aggressive firm would choose that currency-denomination of debt which would minimise expected effective interest costs (i.e. interest cost plus expected exchange gain/loss). In contrast, the defensive firm would match either the currency-denomination of assets with liabilities (minimising translation exposure) or the currency-denomination of cash inflows with outflows (minimising cash flow exposure), depending on how the firm defined exchange risk. Either way, a lower level of 'risk' is traded off against higher expected effective interest costs.

Which of these two ideal types should international companies lean towards as the basis for their exposure management strategies? A key factor here will clearly be the company's ability to forecast exchange rates and, in particular, its ability to 'beat' the forward rate.

The Forecasting Debate

Dufey and Giddy (1978) have distinguished three situations, within the present flexible exchange rate system, which have an important bearing:

(i) *Foreign Exchange Market Biases.* These occur because market imperfections, such as government controls and intervention, cause the forward rate to deviate in a systematic way from the market's actual expectation of future spot rates. This is the kind of bias which is illustrated, *ex post*, by the finding (Kettell, 1978) that the forward buying rate of US dollars and Deutsche marks consistently underestimated actual future dollar/sterling and Deutsche mark/sterling rates in 1975 and 1976. When treasury management is aware of this, a selective forward-cover policy, for example, is worthwhile. Hence, in 1975–76, a company selling dollars or Deutsche marks for sterling would have done consistently better by taking the spot rate at settlement date rather than the forward rate; conversely, the buyer of dollars or Deutsche marks for sterling should have taken the forward rate.

(ii) *Special Forecasting Abilities.* This is similar to (i), in that once again there are profitable opportunities to be gained from aggressive currency management, but this time the opportunities arise because the firm has an unusual forecasting ability. The firm must have access to information not available to most other market participants, or access to some special expertise in interpreting generally available information, if it is consistently to 'beat' the forward rate.

Apart from the fact that both give rise to profit opportunities, the above two cases have one other thing in common – they are much less likely to prevail in our present flexible rate system than in the Bretton Woods era. Under the Bretton Woods system, even in its deteriorating stages in the late sixties, the forecasting game consisted of the following three-step procedure:

1. balance of payments trends showed the pressures on a currency;

2. the level of central bank foreign exchange reserves (including borrowing facilities) gave an indication of when the situation became critical;

3. then came the crucial step of predicting which one of the rather limited policy options the nation's economic decision makers would resort to in a crisis: internal deflation, interventionism and exchange controls, or devaluation.

Clearly, the success or failure of forecasting depended largely on step (3) and there was no doubt that some participants did very well. Some US corporations, for example, spent considerable resources on analysing both the power structure and the economic ideology of key decision makers in various countries (see, for example, Shulman, 1970). Moreover, since the downside risks of actions taken on the basis of these forecasts were quite limited, and also as more people caught on to this game, forecasting became more and more self-fulfilling.

This has changed considerably. The actions of monetary authorities have become much less predictable, even under 'dirty' or managed floating. Short-term pressures on currencies have both increased and are no longer in one direction only. These developments mean that currency forecasting has become much more difficult, in terms of both the likelihood of making the right decision and the costs associated with getting the forecast wrong. This brings us to the third and most likely situation which may now prevail:

(iii) *Efficient Foreign Exchange Markets*. Here, the foreign exchange markets are reasonably efficient, and financial management normally knows of no systematic biases or constraints on market rates. Management's currency expectations are synonymous with those of the market, as generally embodied in forward rates. Unlike (i) and (ii) above, profit opportunities are rare, occurring only when there is discernible bias in the forward rate because of government intervention and exchange controls. In this situation the aim of international financial management should be to arrange the affairs of a company so that, whatever the exchange rate change may be, its detrimental effects on expected returns are minimised.

13.6   Defensive Strategies for Three Prototype Firms

Rather than use an abstract microeconomic model of the firm, we will introduce three prototypes, each of which exemplifies a particular kind of international operation. The aim here is to develop the sort of financial policies, appropriate for each of these three types, which will minimise the effects of a given exchange rate change. The three prototypes are: the capital equipment producer who occasionally exports one of his products; the producer of consumer goods who has developed a significant export market; and the multinational company with interrelated operations in many countries.

The Occasional Exporter

The occasional exporter is a paradoxical animal. This type of company hardly exists in reality, yet it seems that conventional exchange risk analysis is concerned exclusively with the problems faced by such a firm. The company usually produces for the domestic market but occasionally it obtains an order from abroad, and here it runs into a problem. If the export sale is invoiced in foreign currency, its debtors are subject to exchange risk. (The exporter could denominate the contract in his own currency, of course, but this simply throws the risk on to the overseas company, which may be unwilling to accept it.)

Conventional wisdom suggests that the solution to this kind of exchange risk problem lies in using the forward exchange markets. During the negotiations our exporter checks the forward rates quoted for the time the payment is to be received. This exchange rate is then used to decide whether or not the receipt in terms of the exporter's home currency is attractive enough to go through with the export sale.

Simultaneously with the agreement of an export sale, the exporter enters into an offsetting forward exchange transaction. This takes the form of a promise by the export company to deliver at some date in the future a certain amount of foreign currency (the export debtor amount). In return its contracting party, usually a bank, would promise to pay the exporter at the time a fixed amount of domestic currency. This amount is, of course, determined by the forward exchange rate prevailing at the time when all commitments are made.

Should the spot rate at settlement date – or, indeed, any appropriate forward rate available during the credit period – be more favourable than the contracted (forward) rate, our exporter will have incurred an opportunity loss. However, this is not really relevant. The firm has made the decision to sell on the basis of a certain receipt (abstracting from the credit risk) at which the export transaction was deemed to be profitable and worthwhile. Of course, with the covering transaction he has avoided the loss resulting from a possible depreciation of the foreign currency over the credit period; in doing so he has also foregone the possibility of a gain if the foreign currency appreciates. The rationalisation for this is that the exporter is in the business of making and selling a product, and not in the foreign exchange business.

The important point to emphasise, however, is that this 'classical' covering operation will only work for a particular type of business. Should the amount that our exporter receives through the forward market be below his minimum selling price, he will simply sell his equipment in the domestic market – and this is precisely the problem. How many firms really do have this ready alternative? A far more frequent situation is the one represented by our second prototype.

The Significant Exporter

The distinguishing feature of the significant exporter is that he has permanently committed substantial resources to servicing the foreign market(s). A depreciation of the foreign currency will shrink not only the value of foreign receivables already booked, a one-time loss, but it may also affect future cash flows. The real problem, then, is the effect on the future stream of home currency revenues. What action can management take to alleviate this problem? One obvious option is for our exporter to raise foreign currency prices. The long-run validity of the purchasing power parity theorem suggests that the cash flow effects of a currency movement will be offset by countervailing inflation rate changes. In the long run, then, foreign currency selling prices can be increased sufficiently to re-establish the home currency value of the export revenues to their former level. This assumes that the exporter can adjust his selling prices quickly in response to the relatively high inflation/currency depreciation rate in his export markets. However, lengthy price adjustment lags are often an important source of exchange risk to the individual firm. (Hence a company may take forward cover against the foreign currency receipts which it expects to collect during the price adjustment period.)

This 'long run' argument also assumes that the exchange rate is located on its long-run equilibrium path. In the short run, however, exchange rates deviate significantly from their expected long-run paths – hence the definition of foreign exchange risk in terms of unexpected exchange rate movements. Moreover, these deviations are sufficiently large to concern management: a 'temporary' adverse deviation of an exchange rate from its expected path for a few months could have a drastic effect on our exporter's cash position, rate of return on assets, and management performance reviews. If the currency depreciation in the export market exceeds the compensating foreign currency price increases, the rate of return on export operations will obviously fall. It will be little comfort to the outgoing management that the exchange-rate/inflation-rate relationship will correct itself in the long run – management may not be able to afford to wait that long.

How could the classical hedging policy outlined above for the 'occasional exporter' help in such a situation? Let us assume our significant exporter makes regular (monthly) shipments, and bills accordingly on 90-day terms. How would it look if he sold his expected foreign currency receipts forward at each shipment date, instead of waiting for the currency to be remitted and then exchanging these funds through the spot market? There are two possible conditions which might have a bearing on such action: the relative transaction costs and the relative stability of the spot and forward markets.

Foreign exchange transaction costs consist of two elements: foreign exchange commissions and the spread between buying and selling rates. If transaction costs are higher in one market than the other, this might influence the choice between spot and forward markets. This issue can be settled quickly: foreign exchange commissions on forward contracts are either the same or higher than those on spot deals, and spreads tend to be larger in the forward market. Hence transaction costs in the spot market tend to be smaller. More important for our analysis is the stability of spot versus forward rates, which can be measured by the expected deviation from the current rate (spot or forward) for a given future time period. If this deviation should be less in the forward market than in the spot market it can be argued that exchange risk will be reduced by taking the forward rate.

To illustrate: assume that our exporter receives a regular (monthly) amount of foreign currency. This he must convert into his own currency, either through the spot market as he receives the foreign exchange or by selling the expected amount receivable on a 90-day forward basis (or whatever period is appropriate to his billing procedures). Assuming forecasting environment (iii) above, where the firm is unable consistently to predict forward rates, his exchange rate expectations will not influence the 'spot versus forward' choice. Yet if he were to expect greater variability from one period (month) to the next in one market versus the other, he would prefer to go through the market which has less variability since he would expect its scope for unpleasant surprises to be smaller.

During the Bretton Woods era, the spot rate was expected to fluctuate less than the forward rate because central banks (with a very few, albeit notable, exceptions) concentrated their stabilising interventions in the spot market. This left forward rates free to fluctuate around the spot rates, as interest rate differentials and expectations about the future spot rates fluctuated. In the post-Bretton Woods era, however, the volume of official intervention in spot markets seems to have been considerably reduced for most currencies. (The major exceptions are the European Monetary System currencies.) A corollary of this is that the volatility of spot rates relative to forward rates of major currencies has increased. In testing three pairs of currencies (dollar/lira, dollar/sterling and dollar/Deutsche mark) for the floating years 1972 – 74, Dufey and Min (1975) found that the percentage deviations from one period to the next were virtually the same for the spot and forward rates for all three pairs.

Can our second type of exporter now use the forward market to protect profits from his export sales? We have seen that the major advantage of going through the forward market for our occasional exporter was that he was able to avoid an unprofitable transaction by taking account of the forward rates. Yet what about the exporter who has developed a significant export market and whose very existence depends on this market? If he does not like the promised rate received through the forward market he has very little choice, besides shutting down his operation. He must continue to sell in the export market, his only hope being that either the 'temporary' exchange rate/inflation rate imbalance will reverse itself in the not too distant future or that he may be able to take some policy action.

Only prayer might help our firm as regards the first possibility. The second option is of more interest. Our exporter can, of course, seek out opportunities for further raising his selling prices and lowering his costs. Yet we are assuming here that our exporter is already selling at the maximum price which his markets will bear. Similarly, the question must be asked whether the firm really needs a depreciation of the currency in its export market in order to look for opportunities for cost reduction. The only type of cost reduction we are concerned with here is one caused directly by the currency movement. Clearly, in so far as inputs denominated in the depreciating currency are being used or can be used in the production process, some relief will be obtained. Whether this is possible or not is largely a matter of the specific production process. Treasury and operating management must routinely explore this opportunity after a change in the exchange rate/inflation rate relationship. The result of this exploration is a significant determinant of a firm's exchange risk.

The focus of attention here, however, is on the scope for financial management action, and specifically on the exposure implications of the currency-of-financing decision. Currency-of-financing policy is potentially a very powerful exposure management tool. If a company's operations generate exposed assets or cash inflows, these exposures can be neutralised by creating financial liabilities or cash outflows in the same currencies. The net asset or cash flow variability resulting from the deviations of an exchange rate from its expected path can thus be neutralised. In concrete terms this principle suggests that a company which has built a significant export market in foreign currencies should hold a portion of its liabilities in the currency(ies) of its export markets, so that it gets relief from the very event that degenerates its operating margins.

The Multinational Company

The term 'multinational company' is used here to refer to companies which have interrelated operations in many countries. Since the shift from a discussion of the case of the exporter to that of the multinational enterprise appears to be a giant step we will deal here with the simplest case possible: a company with one foreign manufacturing subsidiary.

Again, the important question is how the currency movement will affect the benefits (future cash flows) derived by the parent from its foreign venture. Remember that the long-run validity of the PPP and Fisher theorems means that the cash flow effects of currency movements are offset, in the long run, by countervailing changes in relative inflation and interest rates. So what we are concerned with here is the impact of unexpected deviations of an exchange rate (either short-term oscillations or structural changes) from its long-run path. This impact will consist of the price and quantity effects.

The first and obvious result is that foreign currency revenues will be repatriated to the parent company at a different rate of exchange. What ultimately counts, of course, is the effect on profits in terms of the currency which the parent company uses as a base currency and, more importantly, in which the company's shareholders hold their wealth. The second type of impact is that an exchange rate change will affect the quantity of future local currency (LC) cash flows generated by foreign operations. This is the focus of financial analysis: how will the LC cash flows produced by the subsidiary be affected by, say, a depreciation of the LC? The macroeconomic adjustment process provides us with the relevant variables for such an analysis, as explained in section 13.4. As far as operating profit is concerned, three relevant market sectors can be distinguished in which the subsidiary buys its inputs and sells its output: the export market, the import-competing sector of the domestic market, and the 'pure' domestic market (zero or negligible import penetration).

The analysis of the 'extreme case' is relatively simple. For instance, a subsidiary that sells its output in the export market and buys its inports in the 'pure' domestic sector will undoubtedly experience a rise in LC operating profits, if the LC devaluation is greater than the compensating price-level change. This should be sufficient to convert into an increased flow of home currency (HC) units for the parent – the beneficial 'quantity' effect more than outweighs the adverse 'price' effect.

At the other extreme is the case of a subsidiary which sells its output in the 'pure' domestic market (where it faces strong competition from other local producers) while it obtains the bulk of its inputs from, say, its foreign parent. If the devaluation again overcompensates for higher LC inflation, then in this case LC profitability will suffer, and the situation will look worse in terms of the HC (i.e. 'quantity' as well as 'price' effects are adverse).

Many permutations lying between these two extremes are possible, yet the essential point has been made: the effect of an unexpected exchange rate change on the profitability of foreign operations for the parent company depends entirely on the specific operating pattern of that subsidiary. Any management policy that does not take account of such differences is suboptimal. More particularly, the effects of a currency movement are determined by four factors: the origin of the subsidiary's inputs, the destination of its output, the degree of competition in input and output markets, and the degree of flexibility of the operation. Given the unpredictability of currency markets, the last factor is a key determinant of the susceptibility of a subsidiary to changes in exchange rates. To the extent that it can or cannot switch its sourcing and selling patterns between foreign and domestic markets and/or raise its prices, the exchange risk situation will be more or less serious.

This cash flow analysis now leads us to the question of changes in stock values. The starting point here is that the economic values of assets are determined by future cash flows: as expectations about such future flows change, so do asset values. For example, the plant and equipment of the subsidiary whose export revenues are favourably affected by a currency depreciation in relation to its cost stream will be worth more, regardless of whether or not this increased value is reported by our accounting methods. Yet what about current assets and liabilities?

Inventories are relatively easy to evaluate. If the currency movement has caused the unit LC price of our final product to increase, the LC value of inventories should rise proportionately. The resulting economic value for the parent should be computed by translating the increased LC value at the new exchange rate into home currency units.

The analysis becomes more controversial as we proceed to LC-denominated monetary items, especially cash, debtors and creditors. Let us again consider the exporting subsidiary whose profits increased because of the depreciation. A certain level of LC cash is required to conduct operations. What will happen to the value of this LC cash as the LC depreciates vis-à-vis the HC? As regards its economic value the answer will depend on the function that this monetary asset performs for the subsidiary and, most importantly, whether this function changes because of the exchange rate change.

In the case where the subsidiary's export sales volume is unchanged but where it is able to raise its LC selling price by the depreciation percentage (thus leaving the foreign currency price of its output unchanged), the normal level of LC cash balance required to continue operations will very probably stay unchanged. Since it still performs the same service for the subsidiary, it would seem that its economic value to both subsidiary and parent company is unchanged. In other words, its HC value is unchanged. Alternatively, if the subsidiary increases its volume of operations because of the currency movement and therefore increases the necessary level of liquid funds, a loss would be incurred. The difference between the old and the new (higher) cash balance must come from funds that otherwise would have been transferred to the parent as profit. Instead, these funds are now tied up 'forever' and become part of the investment base – in an ongoing firm they are committed forever. This change in the required cash balance should be included with the change in operating cash flows for that period in order to calculate the overall impact of a currency movement on the firm.

The same kind of analysis also holds for the subsidiary's debtors and creditors. For example, an increase in LC creditors would free LC funds and provide the parent company with additional HC cash. The analysis of creditors is important, for all borrowings can be viewed as such after allowances are made for maturity.

All this will be anathema to those who think about these matters in accounting terms. Just the thought of LC cash not decreasing in value in terms of the home currency by the same percentage as the LC depreciation will cause considerable consternation. It may help to emphasise that the cash balance that concerns us here must be regarded as an integrated element of that bundle of assets and liabilities that make up an ongoing foreign subsidiary. It cannot be compared with a discretionary cash balance left in another country, which is obviously subject to exchange risk.

To sum up, then, the general rule governing economic loss or gain on current assets and liabilities is as follows: to the extent that the exchange rate causes additional (or fewer) net current assets to be required, a one-time loss (or gain) is incurred. This loss (or gain) for the parent is equal to the additional HC funds forgone.

The Multinational's Risk-Minimising Financing Policy

Now that we have analysed the economic effects of currency movements on a firm's profitability, we can turn to the problem of an appropriate currency-of-financing pattern. The rules we developed earlier for the 'significant exporter' can again be applied. If exposure neutralisation is the company's objective, its liability portfolio should be structured in such a way that the outflow on liabilities (effective interest costs) offsets as much as possible the change in the inflow on assets (operating profits).

The rationale of this approach is clear. Manufacturing companies expect to make a profit because of their ability to exploit certain specialised market opportunities – to make cars, chemicals or computers. The role of financial management is to protect this expected profit from unexpected changes in financial market (interest and exchange rate) conditions. Protection can be achieved by manipulating operating and/or financial variables. The operating response consists of structural or business opportunities to create matched currency cash flow patterns – altering sourcing, product, plant location, market selection, credit, pricing and currency-of-invoicing policies. However, the currency-denomination of operating variables is determined largely by intrinsic business conditions (production and marketing factors). Such constraints are far less important as regards financial variables, although even here credit availability is a problem in certain environments. Generally, then, adjustments to offset exchange risk will occur on the liability rather than the asset side.

How can this general principle be implemented? The basic step is to estimate how deviations around the expected exchange rate will affect the operating cash flows of the firm as a whole. This may not be an easy task. As indicated above, operating cash flows can be affected positively, negatively or not at all by a currency movement, depending on where the firm buys its inputs and sells its output, and on the pricing and locational flexibility of these markets. Having established how net operating cash flows will be affected, it is then a straightforward task to choose the risk-minimising liability structure. A unit should be financed in the currency(ies) against whose value its operating cash flows are positively correlated. Take the case of a French subsidiary exporting to Germany. Here the operating returns of the subsidiary are positively correlated with movements in the Deutsche mark and so the subsidiary should be financed in Deutsche marks. A depreciation of the Deutsche mark would then reduce not only cash inflows (operating returns) but also cash outflows (effective interest costs). In this way the change in the net cash flow on the asset side can, to some extent at least, be offset by a change on the liability side. The firm's cash flow (economic) exposure to exchange risk is thereby reduced.

13.7   Summary

Two kinds of exposure to exchange risk are distinguished: the exposure inherent in foreign-currency-denominated transactions and the exposure associated with the ownership of ongoing foreign-currency-denominated assets and liabilities. It is the second kind of exposure which is the problematical area. There are two opposing viewpoints here: the 'accounting' (translation) approach and the 'cash flow' (economic) approach.

Accounting exposure indicates the possibility that those foreign currency denominated items (balance sheet and income statement) which are consolidated into a company's published financial statements at current exchange rates will show a translation loss (or gain) as a result of currency movements since the previous reporting date. This is an arbitrary indication of the real effect of an exchange rate change on the value of a company's foreign operations, for two reasons. First, as indicated in Chapter 12, different countries, and different firms within individual countries, use a variety of methods to value their foreign assets and liabilities and hence to calculate translation gains and losses. Thus two otherwise identical firms could show different levels of exposure and different translation gains and/or losses merely because of differences in their foreign currency translation procedures. The second and fundamental weakness of accounting exposure is that it ignores the future effects of currency movements on cash flows.

In contrast, cash flow exposure is concerned with the effects of an exchange rate change on the parent currency value of the future cash flows generated by a company's foreign operations. The cash flow impact consists of both 'price' effects (the effect on the price at which future local currency cash flows are transformed into the parent currency) and 'quantity' effects (the effect on the quantity and timing of these local currency cash flows). The cash flow analysis therefore recognises that a devaluation of a foreign subsidiary's host currency vis-à-vis the parent currency will not automatically reduce the parent currency value of the foreign subsidiary's 'exposed' net assets or liabilities, as suggested by the accounting approach.

The choice of exposure definition (accounting, cash flow or both) can only be made by each company's policymakers. This choice becomes crucial when the accounting and cash flow approaches give very different pictures of a company's exposure – indeed, a company can be 'long' according to one definition and 'short' according to another. In this situation senior management must decide where its priorities lie. Irrespective of this choice, however, both exposure types should be monitored. Many companies place primary emphasis on cash flow exposure, for example, but also monitor accounting exposure so that management action can be taken if the expected impact on financial reports reaches an unacceptable level. The starting point for exposure management, then, is exposure measurement. Whilst both accounting (balance sheet and income statement) exposure and cash flow exposure are difficult to measure, reasonably firm quantification is possible. This requires a sophisticated firm-specific analysis of financing, sourcing and selling patterns, tax effects, and price adjustment lags.

The effects of inflation on a foreign subsidiary's local currency cash flows are generally opposite to those of devaluation. The interaction of these two opposing processes has led to the view that, in the long run,

exchange risk does not exist. This view is based on the long-run acceptance of the PPP theorem (relative inflation rates equal the rate of
change of the exchange rate) and the Fisher effect (interest rate differentials equal the expected rate of change of the exchange rate). In the short
run, however, these two theorems do not hold. Hence we are left with
the view that exchange risk stems from the short-run deviations of an
exchange rate from its expected long-run path.

Once a company has defined its exposure to foreign exchange risk, it
must decide how this exposure should be managed. Two fundamental
attitudes towards foreign exchange risk have been identified, which we
have called 'aggressive' and 'defensive'. A key factor in a company's
choice between these two strategies will be its ability accurately to
forecast exchange rates – specifically its ability to predict the forward
rate. In contrast to the Bretton Woods era, in today's flexible exchange
rate environment such forecasting is very difficult. Hence a generally
defensive exposure management strategy is recommended: the aim
should be to arrange the affairs of a company so that, whatever the
exchange rate change may be, its detrimental impact is minimised. This
general principle is then applied to three prototype international firms:
the occasional exporter, the significant exporter, and the multinational
company.

For the occasional exporter the classical exposure management
operation – cover all exposed transactions on the forward currency
markets – is the obvious defensive approach. For the other two prototypes, however, this strategy is much less appropriate. For the significant exporter and the multinational company, economic exposure to
exchange risk can only be minimised by structuring the group's
liabilities in such a way that the change in cash inflows (operating
revenues) induced by a currency movement is offset as much as possible
by a countervailing change in cash outflows (effective interest costs).

References

Aliber, R.Z. (1974) 'The short guide to corporate international finance', University of
    Chicago, unpublished paper.
Aliber, R.Z. and Stickney, C.P. (1975) 'Accounting measures of foreign exchange
    exposure: the long and short of it', *Accounting Review*, January.
Dufey, G. and Giddy, I.H. (1978) 'International financial planning: the use of market
    based forecasts', *California Management Review*, Fall.
Dufey, G. and Min, S. (1975) 'A comparison of the variability of spot and forward
    rates', unpublished working paper, Graduate School of Business Administration,
    University of Michigan.
Giddy, I.H. (1977) 'Exchange risk: whose view?' *Financial Management*, Summer.
Kettell, B. (1978) 'The forward rate as an accurate predictor of future spot rates', in
    T.W. McRae and D.P. Walker (1978) *Readings in Foreign Exchange Risk Management*,
    MCB Publications.

McRae, T.W. and Walker, D.P. (1978) *Readings in Foreign Exchange Risk Management*, MCB Publications.

Shapiro, A.C. (1975) 'Exchange rate changes, inflation and the value of the multinational corporation', *Journal of Finance*, May.

Shulman, R.B. (1970) 'Are foreign exchange risks measurable?', *Columbia Journal of World Business*, June.

Part III

Harmonisation

14

Harmonisation of Financial Reporting

CHRISTOPHER NOBES

The preceding chapters make it clear that there are major differences in the financial reporting practices of companies in different countries. This leads to great complications for those preparing, consolidating, auditing and interpreting published financial statements. Since the preparation of *internal* financial information often overlaps with the preparation of published information, the complications spread further. To combat this, several organisations thoughout the world are involved in attempts to harmonise or standardise accounting.

'Harmonisation' is a process of increasing the compatibility of accounting practices by setting bounds to their degree of variation. 'Standardisation' appears to imply the imposition of a more rigid and narrow set of rules. However, within accounting, these two words have almost become technical terms, and one cannot rely upon the normal difference in their meanings. Harmonisation is a word which tends to be associated with the transnational legislation being promulgated by the Commission of the European Economic Community;[1] standardisation is a word especially associated with the International Accounting Standards Committee. In practical effect, the 'harmonisation' of the EEC

---

1. This ten-country organisation is also known as the Common Market. Its members in 1985 were Belgium, Denmark, France, Greece, Ireland, Italy, Luxembourg, the Netherlands, the United Kingdom and West Germany. Spain and Portugal have negotiated for entry in 1986.

has been more powerful and detailed than the 'standardisation' of the IASC.

This chapter starts by looking at the purposes of and obstacles to standardisation. There follow sections on the work of the IASC and other international bodies. Finally, there is a section on the nature and progress of harmonisation in the EEC.

14.1   Reasons for and Obstacles to Standardisation

Reasons for Standardisation

It is increasingly the case that the products of accounting in one country are used in various other countries. Consequently, the reasons that make national accounting standards desirable also apply internationally. The pressure for international standardisation comes from those who prepare and use financial statements. We will now look at their interests more closely.

Investors and financial analysts need to be able to understand the financial statements of foreign companies whose shares they might wish to buy. They would like to be sure that statements from different countries are reliable and comparable, or at least to be clear about the nature and magnitude of the differences. They also need confidence in the soundness of the auditing.

For this reason, various intergovernmental transnational bodies from the EEC Commission to the United Nations are interested, among other things, in protecting investors within their spheres of influence. Also, in cases where foreign shares are quoted on the domestic stock exchange of an investor, that stock exchange will often demand financial statements which are consistent with domestic practices. In addition, those companies which wish to issue new shares more widely than on their domestic markets will see the advantages of standardised practices in the promotion of their issues.

These pressures will also be felt by companies which do not operate multinationally. However, for multinationals, the advantages of standardisation are much more important. The great effort of financial accountants to prepare and consolidate financial statements would be much simplified if statements from all round the world were prepared on the same basis. Similarly, the task of preparing comparable internal information for the appraisal of the performance of subsidiaries in different countries would be made much easier. Many aspects of investment appraisal, performance evaluation and other decision-making uses of management accounting information would benefit from standardisation. The appraisal of foreign companies for potential takeovers would also be greatly facilitated. Multinational companies would also find it easier to transfer accounting staff from one country to another.

A third group which would benefit from standardisation are the international accountancy firms. Many of the clients of the large Anglo-American accountancy firms have at least one foreign subsidiary or branch. The preparation, consolidation and auditing of these companies' financial statements would become less onerous if accounting practices were standardised. Also, the accountancy firms would benefit from the added mobility of staff.

The revenue authorities throughout the world have their work greatly complicated when dealing with foreign incomes by differences in the measurement of profit in different countries. It should be admitted, however, that revenue authorities have *caused* many of the differences, for example the influence of tax on continental accounting (see Chapters 4 and 5) and the use of LIFO in the United States (see Chapter 2). Governments in developing countries might find it easier to understand and control the operations of multinationals if financial reporting were standardised, particularly as this would imply greater disclosure in some cases. International credit grantors like the World Bank must also face the difficulties of comparison. Other organisations that would benefit from greater international comparability of company information are labour unions who face multinational employers. All these groups might benefit from standardisation.

Examples of the Need for Standardisation

Much of this book has been devoted to the analysis of international differences in accounting. The number and magnitude of the differences make clear the scope for standardisation. Let us take one basic accounting problem: the valuation of inventories. An indication of the importance of standardisation can be obtained by noting the differences in practice. An estimate was made of the potential impact of the IASC's standard on inventory valuation (IAS 2). This involved a study of the differences in practice in the member countries of the IASC before the standard's introduction (Mason 1976). Examples of the differences from IAS 2 were that, in 13 of the 23 countries, a minority of companies did not follow the 'lower of historic cost and net realisable value' basis; in 17 countries some companies used 'prime cost' as the measure of cost; and in eight countries the basis of valuation was not disclosed.

On more controversial issues, like deferred tax and accounting for changing prices, the variations in practice may be much wider. As will be shown, even compliance with the present standards of the IASC would leave much of this diversity intact.

Obstacles to Standardisation

The most fundamental of obstacles to standardisation is the size of the present differences between the accounting practices of different countries. Using the type of classifications of accounting systems discussed in Chapter 8, there are several significant differences even within the Anglo-Saxon class, let alone between that class and the Franco-German. These latter differences go to the root of the reasons for the preparation of accounting information. The general dichotomy between shareholder/fair-view presentation and creditor/tax/conservative presentation is an obstacle sufficiently difficult not to be overcome without major changes in attitudes and law.

Indeed, it is not clear that it *should be* overcome. If the predominant purposes of financial reporting vary by country, it seems reasonable that the reporting should vary. However, standardisation is concerned with similar users who receive information from companies in different countries. It may be that the relevant companies should be required to produce two sets of financial statements: one for domestic and another for international consumption. This is discussed further at the end of section 14.2.

Another obstacle is the lack of strong professional accountancy bodies in some countries. This means that any body such as the IASC, which seeks to operate through national accountancy bodies, will not be effective in all countries. The alternative to this, a world-wide enforcement agency, is also lacking. The EEC Commission may prove to be such an agency for one part of the world, as is discussed in section 14.4.

A further problem is nationalism. This may show itself in an unwillingness to accept compromises which involve changing accounting practices towards those of other countries. This unwillingness may exist on the part of accountants and companies or on the part of states who may not wish to lose their sovereignty (Fantl 1971). Another manifestation of nationalism may be the lack of knowledge or interest in accounting elsewhere. A rather more subtle and acceptable variety of this is the concern that it would be difficult to alter internationally-set standards in response to a change of mind or a change of circumstances.

Table 14.1   Board Members of IASC until 1987

Australia	The Netherlands
Canada	Nigeria
France	South Africa
Germany (Federal Republic)	Taiwan
Italy	United Kingdom and Ireland
Japan	United States
Mexico	

Another difficulty which has recently been highlighted is the effect of 'economic consequences' on accounting standards (see Chapter 12). To the extent that economic consequences of standards vary by country and to the extent that they are taken into account by those who set standards, this could be a force for disharmonisation.

These are the major general obstacles to international standardisation. The following sections look at the progress of several organisations in overcoming them.

14.2   The International Accounting Standards Committee

History and Purpose of the IASC

Of the many bodies working for international standardisation to be looked at in this chapter, the IASC is perhaps the most important and the most successful (apart from the EEC Commission which operates in a more restricted area). The IASC was founded in 1973 and has a small secretariat based in London. The original board members were the accountancy bodies of nine countries: Australia, Canada, France, Japan, Mexico, the Netherlands, the United Kingdom and Ireland, the United States and West Germany (Benson 1976). These nine, plus four other countries (see Table 14.1) make up the main board of IASC until 1987, when the influence of the founder members will be reduced, as explained below. In 1985, there are about 90 member accountancy bodies from about 70 countries.

Initially the IASC was independent from all other bodies, but from 1983 onwards a close connection was established with the body which replaced ICCAP in 1977: the International Federation of Accountants (IFAC), which will be discussed later (Hepworth 1979). The membership of IFAC and the IASC is now identical (Burggraaff 1982). The former concentrates on such matters as auditing, management accounting, and the International Congresses of Accountants (see Chapter 1). The latter is only concerned with international accounting standards. Members of IFAC/IASC pay their subscriptions to IFAC, which then funds 10% of the IASC budget, the remaining 90% being provided by the board members.

Since 1983, the board has consisted of up to 17 members: nine or ten developed countries, three or four developing countries and up to four other organisations, perhaps drawn from the IASC's consultative group (which includes such bodies as the World Bank, the International Confederation of Trades Unions and the International Federation of Stock Exchanges).

The aim of the IASC is 'to formulate and publish in the public interest accounting standards to be observed in the presentation of financial statements and to promote their worldwide acceptance and observance.' (IASC 1982; the word 'basic' preceded the words 'accounting standards' in the original 1973 version.) The member bodies of IASC agree to support the standards and to use 'their best endeavours' to ensure that published financial statements comply with the standards; to ensure that auditors enforce this; and to persuade governments, stock exchanges and other bodies to back the standards (IASC 1983).

The Standards

A list of IASC standards is shown as Table 14.2. These are preceded by exposure drafts prepared by sub-committees of the board. In order to be published, an exposure draft must be approved by a two-thirds majority

Table 14.2   IASC Statements (early 1985)

Preface (revised October 1982).
Objectives and Procedures (including the Constitution; revised October 1982).

IAS 1 — Disclosure of accounting policies.
IAS 2 — Valuation and presentation of inventories in the context of the historical cost system.
IAS 3 — Consolidated financial statements.
IAS 4 — Depreciation accounting.
IAS 5 — Information to be disclosed in financial statements.
IAS 6 — Accounting responses to changing prices (superseded by IAS 15).
IAS 7 — Statement of changes in financial position.
IAS 8 — Unusual and prior period items and changes in accounting policies.
IAS 9 — Accounting for research and development activities.
IAS 10 — Contingencies and events occurring after the balance sheet date.
IAS 11 — Accounting for construction contracts.
IAS 12 — Accounting for taxes on income.
IAS 13 — Presentation of current assets and current liabilities.
IAS 14 — Reporting financial information by segment.
IAS 15 — Information reflecting the effects of changing prices.
IAS 16 — Accounting for property, plant and equipment.
IAS 17 — Accounting for leases.
IAS 18 — Revenue recognition.
IAS 19 — Accounting for retirement benefits in the financial statements of employers.
IAS 20 — Accounting for government grants and disclosure of government assistance.
IAS 21 — Accounting for the effects of changes in foreign exchange rates.
IAS 22 — Accounting for business combinations.
IAS 23 — Capitalisation of borrowing costs.
IAS 24 — Related party disclosures.

---

of the board. A subsequent standard must be approved by a three-quarters majority.

It is the countries influenced by the Anglo-American tradition which are most familiar with setting accounting standards and are most likely to be able to adopt them professionally. It is not surprising, then, that the working language of the IASC is English, that its secretariat is in London, that all the Chairmen and Secretaries have been from countries using Anglo-Saxon or Dutch accounting, and that most standards closely follow or compromise between US and UK standards.

Consequently, the IASC's standards generally allow a range of practices. For example, research and development expenditure may be carried forward according to IAS 9 under similar conditions to those in SSAP 13, whereas such expenditure cannot be carried forward under FAS 2. Similarly, IAS 12 allows partial accounting for deferred tax, like SSAP 15, whereas APB 11 requires full accounting.

However, there are some cases where international standards are more demanding with regard to disclosure. For example, IAS 9 calls for disclosure of the year's R and D expense (paragraph 23), whereas SSAP 13 does not. However, the US standard calls for greater disclosure than the UK standard, which helps to explain why the international standard also does. To a large extent, any extra demands of international standards are at present ignored in the US and the UK (e.g. ICAEW 1983). The original intention of the IASC was to avoid complex detail and to concentrate on basic standards. However, the list of standards shown in Table 14.2 includes some, like *Accounting for Construction Contracts*, which might not be thought to be 'basic'. Further, the contents of some standards could be criticised as being unnecessarily detailed. For example, the details for the ascertainment of net realisable value (paragraphs 28–31 of IAS 2) could be thought excessive in the context of the great diversity of practice on much more fundamental matters within inventory valuation. However, in the author's opinion, these are exceptions, and the standards are generally commendably clearly presented.

Enforcement

The success of member accountancy bodies' 'best endeavours' to promote the work of the IASC varies to some degree. The problem is one of enforcement. The IASC has no authority of its own and therefore must rely on that of its members. It has been seen in earlier chapters that the influence of professional accountancy bodies in the formulation of accounting rules also varies widely between countries. In France and Germany, for example, the *Ordre* and the *Institut* have little room (and inadequate authority) to influence accounting practice because of the strength and detail of company law and the *plan comptable*. The more powerful bodies like the *Conseil National de la Comptabilité* or the *Commission des Opérations de Bourse* are not members of the IASC (see Chapter 4).

At the other extreme, in the UK, Ireland, New Zealand and Canada, accounting standards are set by the professional bodies which belong to the IASC. Consequently it has been possible for the IASC's standards to be introduced. Taking the UK and Ireland as an example, standards are brought into line with IASC standards wherever possible. They either state that compliance automatically ensures compliance with the IASC standard, or the differences are stated.

In between these two extremes is the United States. The two bodies most directly concerned with the setting and enforcement of domestic standards, the FASB and the SEC, are not members of the IASC. However, the AICPA which is the US representative on the IASC is influential. Also, the FASB is sympathetic to the work of the IASC, though it does not directly take the IASC's views into account.

One tell-tale sign of the problems of enforcement is the gradual weakening of the commitments required from member bodies. At one stage, members were required to use their best endeavours to ensure that companies who broke international standards would disclose this fact. Now the IASC Preface calls for companies that *observe* the standards to disclose this fact. In the case of the UK and Ireland, the professional bodies have moved away from the idea of audit qualifications for breaches of IASC standards or even for lack of disclosure of breaches. It is probably the case that most UK accountants are not very conversant with the content or status of IASC standards.

Is the IASC Successful?

In order to answer this question it is necessary to establish the criteria by which success should be measured. We might start by looking at the stated objectives of the IASC, though we need to confirm that these are reasonable and useful objectives before adopting them as the measure for the IASC's success. The IASC's objectives are to publish and promote the acceptance of standards on a worldwide basis. These objectives might be thought to be too ambitious in one respect and not ambitious enough in another.

To attempt worldwide standardisation seems a hopeless and unnecessary target. The greatest benefits will come from standardisation among countries where there are companies which publish financial statements and which have foreign investors, auditors, parents or subsidiaries. This means that the context of success might more sensibly be seen as the developed western world and those developing countries with which it has significant economic links. To try to bring the accounting of the Soviet Union into line, for example, would not only have very few benefits but would also be impossible at present.

Secondly, to *publish and promote* standards is not a sufficient aim. Fortunately, in the IASC's 1982 Preface and Constitution, the more fundamental aim of harmonising accounting practices is recognised. What is needed is progress towards an easier and surer comparability of published financial statements from different countries, or at least disclosure of the nature and significance of the differences.

Let us take these revised objectives as a measure of the IASC's success. It is clear that substantial progress has been made since 1973 in the issue of standards and in the adaptation of the national standards of some member countries of the IASC. This is a mark of success, although it relates to those Anglo-Saxon countries on which the IASC's standards are based. Nevertheless, a fully standardised system of financial reporting, for listed companies in English-speaking countries for example, would be a major achievement. To this end, many of the companies listed on the Toronto Stock Exchange in Canada have been persuaded to state that they comply with IASC standards. It is also the case that the differences between the UK and the USA have declined since 1973. However, to infer that the IASC has caused this would probably be mistaken. For example, the US adoption of the current rate method of currency translation (FAS 52, 1981; see Chapter 12), and the UK move to capitalisation of leases (SSAP 21, 1984) were not mainly caused by a desire for transatlantic harmonisation.

Such international progress as there is does not extend throughout the developed western world, let alone 'worldwide'. Advances towards standardisation in such countries as France and West Germany have been or will be brought about by governments or government-backed bodies like the COB or the EEC Commission. Certainly, direct influence by the IASC on the practice of financial reporting in France or West Germany is very slight. For example, the handbook of the *Institut der Wirtschaftsprüfer* contains no mention of IASC standards (and obviously the all-important German company laws contain no reference to them, not least because at present (1985) the laws pre-date the IASC).

One researcher has proposed that standardisation will only move ahead effectively if each of six 'vital countries' supports it (Mason 1978; and see Chapter 1). These countries are France, Japan, the Netherlands, the UK, the US and West Germany. At present, the IASC is not a body with sufficient power to be effective in all these countries directly. We must look to the EEC Commission for harmonisation covering four of the six.

Nevertheless, there is probably some IASC influence in continental European countries. The most obvious example is in Italy, where listed companies (a small but important group) are required to follow IASC standards. This is part of a major change towards Anglo-Saxon types of financial reporting and auditing for listed and state companies in Italy. There has also been IASC influence in the move towards consolidated accounting in continental Europe (see Chapter 10). Anglo-Dutch consolidation practices are clearly predominant in the EEC's seventh Directive on Company Law, which requires consolidation. However, it is useful to be able to point to the internationally agreed IAS 3 on the subject; and countries such as France have enthusiastically moved towards adoption of consolidation on that basis, whereas they might have found it more difficult if this were seen as 'following the UK'. More generally, there may be great long-run benefit from bringing together senior accountants from major countries to discuss technical and theoretical problems. The enhanced level of understanding of each other's practices should assist harmonisation eventually, perhaps via a different agency such as the EEC.

There is a second major area where we may look for IASC achievements towards the underlying aim of harmonisation. For those developing countries that did not have accounting standards, a ready-made IASC set has proved attractive. Kenya, Malaysia, Nigeria, Pakistan, Singapore and Zimbabwe fit into this category. It is obviously preferable for them to adopt an internationally recognised set of standards, from a body to which they belong, than to follow the standards of any one country. However, the six countries above have a feature in common: they have inherited a British legal and commercial structure. This makes it less surprising that IASC standards seem suitable to them; perhaps they would have followed similar UK standards anyway, though that path might have been slower and less comfortable for them. An important point in this context is whether IASC standards are suitable for such countries. This is examined in the next section.

There has been some empirical analysis of the effects of the IASC. Evans and Taylor (1982) examined compliance with IAS standards in five of the six 'vital' countries. They suggest that the IASC has had little influence. Nair and Frank (1981) look more widely at the degree of harmonisation over the period 1973 to 1979. They arrive at no stronger a conclusion than that 'the period of the IASC's existence has coincided with a growing harmonisation of accounting standards'.

Appropriate Standards and Dual Standards

Before leaving the discussion of international standardisation, two connected points raised earlier should be considered. They are both contained in the suggestion (AISG 1975) that companies should prepare a set of primary financial statements which obey the accounting standards most suitable for the majority of users in their own country. A secondary set should be prepared using other accounting standards which would be more appropriate for particular intended users in other countries. Alternatively, there could be an internationally agreed set of standards (perhaps the IASC's) which would be used in all countries when preparing secondary accounts for foreign users.

Thus, the first point is whether Anglo-Saxon standards are suitable for the majority of businesses in continental Europe or in developing countries. These standards have developed in the context of loose company law, large stock exchanges, widely held ownership, and large, well-trained bodies of auditors. It is not at all obvious that British accounting would be more suitable for the bulk of German companies than German accounting is! It is quite possible that a standardised system like the French *plan comptable* might be more suitable than Anglo-Saxon accounting for developing countries with few listed companies,

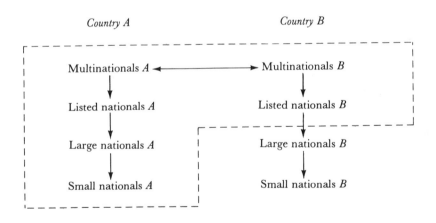

Notes: 1. See text for an explanation of this figure.
2. I am grateful to Geoff Mitchell, formerly of the IASC, for the idea behind this figure.

Figure 14.1 Dual Standards

sophisticated shareholders or highly qualified accountants (Briston 1978).

For the above reason, it may be sensible (as well as easier) to direct harmonisation attempts at listed companies. These are an easily defined set that has many shareholders and is most involved in international trade and capital raising. For this set, Anglo-Saxon accounting does seem the appropriate system upon which to harmonise, because it stresses the true and fair view, substance over form, independent audit, consolidation, shareholder orientation, and so on.

In practice, dual standards already exist to some extent. This is formally the case in Italy, as has been mentioned; but it is also the practice in Scandinavia for large companies to volunteer to prepare Anglo-Saxon-style financial reports. Similarly, many large French and German companies that wish to raise money in London or New York volunteer to have Anglo-Saxon audits and to prepare worldwide consolidations. IASC standards would be a very suitable, neutral basis for any formal adoption of this idea. Such harmonisation would be easier to implement than the standardisation discussed in the earlier parts of this chapter. Many of the obstacles to standardisation on a single set of rules would become irrelevant, and clear advantages would flow from having the most suitable financial statements for domestic and, separately, for international comparative purposes.

The above arguments may be illustrated with the aid of Figure 14.1. Country A is an Anglo-Saxon country, country B is not. The two-headed arrow at the top of the figure represents the main object of harmonisation. However, it is difficult to see how Multinational B could adopt international standards unless *either* other listed companies in Country B did so as well, *or* dual standards were implemented. Otherwise, various listed companies in the same country would be obeying different rules. Furthermore, precisely what constitutes a 'multinational' is hard to define. By an extension of this argument, it appears to be the IASC view that *all* companies in countries A and B should be targets for harmonisation. However the arguments in the above paragraph might lead to the alternative conclusion that the companies within the dotted line should harmonise on IASC standards, leaving the bulk of the companies in country B unaffected, at least initially (Gray 1981).

Whether the listed companies in country B should also prepare financial statements using domestic rules would be a matter for country B. The Italian answer seems to be negative, and to some extent this could be the case in other continental countries where large, public or listed companies have special financial reporting rules. Perhaps surprisingly, this also approximately describes the case of the USA, where the minority of companies that are SEC-registered have greatly increased reporting and audit requirements compared to the majority of companies.

14.3   Other International Bodies

This section looks at the nature and importance of some other bodies concerned with international aspects of accounting. The *Groupe d'Etudes* is left until discussion of EEC harmonisation later in this chapter.

International Federation of Accountants

This body came into being in 1977 after the Eleventh International Congress of Accountants. It aims to develop a coordinated international accountancy profession. A predecessor body, called the International Coordination Committee for the Accountancy Profession, which had been formed in 1972 after the Tenth Congress, was wound up in favour of the IFAC.

The IFAC has a full-time secretariat in New York and comprises an assembly of about 90 accountancy bodies from about 70 countries.

The work of the IFAC includes the setting of international guidelines for auditing, ethics, education and management accounting; involvement in education and technical research; and organising the international congress about every five years (Cummings and Chetkovich 1978).

As well as the ICCAP, another body was wound up in 1977 when the IFAC was formed – the Accountants' International Study Group. This group was formed in 1966 and comprised members from professional bodies in Canada, the UK and the US. Its purpose was to study and report on accounting practices in the three countries. Twenty studies were issued, mainly on financial reporting matters (Choi and Mueller 1984).

Union Européenne des Experts Comptables, Economiques et Financiers

The UEC is a regional accountancy group, founded in 1951, with a membership of professional bodies from most European countries. There is a permanent secretariat in Munich and a number of sub-committees covering a wide range of subjects, including auditing and accounting practices, professional regulations and tax systems. The sub-committees plan to promote research and publication of studies and recommendations, and to influence professional bodies and governments in the above areas. There have also been a *Journal UEC* (until 1980), a multilingual *Lexicon UEC*, and other publications. Statements include those on Disclosure of Accounting Policies (1974), the Audit Report (1975), Professional Ethics (1975) and Auditor Independence (1977) (see McDougall 1979).

There are other regional groups which are less well developed than the UEC. The two most important are the Inter-American Accounting Association (IAAA), which covers the two American continents, and the Confederation of Asian and Pacific Accountants (CAPA) (Choi and Mueller 1984). CAPA can be traced back to 1957, though it was not formally organised until 1976. It includes very many countries, and it may be that its members are too heterogeneous in their environmental make-up to constitute a 'viable accounting cluster' (Choi 1981, p.31). So there may be problems in defining a region for the purpose of accounting harmonisation (Parker 1982).

In the case of CAPA countries, perhaps a more successful regional grouping involves a sub-set of them: the ASEAN Federation of Accountants (AFA) formed in Bangkok in 1977 (Choi 1979). Choi (1981) suggests that one function of the AFA is 'to buffer individual ASEAN countries against the wholesale adoption of international accounting pronouncements that may not be suitable to local circumstances'.

Non-Accounting Bodies

One of the factors that drives accountants and their professional bodies towards better national and international standards is the possibility that other bodies will intervene or gain the initiative. At present, with the regional exception of the EEC Commission, such international bodies have influence rather than power. The Organisation for Economic Co-operation and Development (OECD) researched and published recommendations for accounting practice in 1976: the *Code of Conduct for Multinational Enterprises* (Enthoven 1976). This mainly concerns disclosure requirements. It is voluntary, but it may influence the behaviour of large and politically sensitive corporations. Since 1976, there has been a survey of accounting practices (OECD 1980), but no agreement as to how to achieve harmonisation (Denman 1980). It seems clear that part of the OECD's aim in this area is to protect developed countries from any extreme proposals that might have come from the United Nations, which is interested in the regulation of multinational businesses.

In 1977, the UN published a report (Benson 1978, Sahlgren 1979) in this area which proposed very substantial increases in disclosure of financial and non-financial items by transnational corporations. The UN went further and set up an 'Intergovernmental Group on International Accounting Standards and Reporting' which intended to publish standards for multinational companies (Wong 1980). However, progress has been slow, perhaps partly because of differences of stance towards multinationals between host and parent countries.

14.4   EEC Harmonisation

Reasons for and Obstacles to EEC Harmonisation

The objects of the Treaty of Rome (of 1957) include the establishment of the free movement of persons, goods and services, and capital. This involves the elimination of customs duties, the imposition of common tariffs to third countries and the establishment of procedures to permit the coordination of economic policies. More specifically, the EEC's Common Industrial Policy (of 1970) calls for the creation of a unified business environment, including the harmonisation of company law and taxation, and the creation of a common capital market.

The reasoning behind these objectives includes the fact that the activities of companies extend beyond national frontiers, and that shareholders and others need protection throughout the EEC. In order to achieve this and to encourage the movement of capital, it is necessary to create a flow of reliable homogeneous financial information about companies from all parts of the EEC. Further, since companies in different EEC countries exist in the same form and are in competition with each other, it is argued that they should be subject to the same laws and taxation.

The obstacles to harmonisation of financial reporting and company law have been discussed in section 14.2. Of particular importance here are the fundamental differences between the various national accounting systems in the EEC. They include the differences between creditor/secrecy in the Franco-German systems and investor/disclosure in the Anglo-Dutch systems; between law/tax-based rules and professionally set standards. These large differences have contributed towards the great variations in the size and strength of the profession. The smaller and weaker professional bodies in Franco-German countries are an obstacle to movements towards accounting and auditing of an Anglo-Dutch type (see Chapter 1).

The Groupe d'Etudes

Before discussing the moves of the EEC Commission towards harmonisation, it will be useful to describe the body which represents the opinion of professional accountancy bodies to the various institutions of the EEC. The *Groupe d'Etudes* (or the EEC Accountants' Study Group) is an informal committee of accountants from each EEC member country which was formed at the request of the Commission. It was formed in 1966 and is based in Brussels. The UK and Ireland joined as observers in 1971, just over a year before entering the EEC. The UK representative is appointed by the Consultative Committee of Accountancy

Bodies, and the Irish representative by the Insitute of Chartered Accountants in Ireland. The *Groupe d'Etudes* is not an official organ of the EEC, and its budget is met by contributions from the participating professional bodies.

The main work of the *Groupe d'Etudes* concerns liaison with the EEC Commission and Parliament. It is to the advantage of these two bodies (and to the combined profession) that accountants should speak with one voice (and, incidentally, with one tongue: French) on such matters as draft Directives on company law.

The basic differences in accounting and accountants between different EEC countries have caused difficulties for the *Groupe d'Etudes*. The Anglo-Dutch representatives have found it difficult to persuade their Franco-German colleagues that the *Groupe* should express opinions on corporation tax harmonisation, insolvency or the format of the proposed European company, because these matters fall outside the direct sphere of influence of the professional bodies in France and Germany. However, major changes have occurred since 1971. The *Groupe* has been largely won round to many Anglo-Saxon concepts like the predominance of the 'true and fair view' and all that that entails for secret reserves, tax-based depreciation, inflation adjustments, and so on. This has probably had an impact on the EEC Commission's Directives on the harmonisation of accounting which are now to be discussed.

Directives and Regulations

The EEC Commission achieves its harmonising objectives through two main instruments: Directives, which must be incorporated into the laws of member states; and Regulations, which become law throughout the EEC without the need to pass through national legislatures. The concern of this section will be with the Directives on company law and with two Regulations. These are listed in Table 14.3, which also gives a brief description of their scope. The company law Directives of most relevance to accounting are the fourth and seventh (see Chapter 10 for the latter). The fourth will be discussed in more detail below, after an outline of the procedure for setting Directives.

First, the Commission, which is the EEC's permanent civil service, decides on a project and asks an expert to prepare a report. In the case of the fourth Directive, this was the Elmendorff Report of 1967. Then an *avant projet* or discussion document is prepared. This is studied by a Commission working party and commented on by the *Groupe d'Etudes*. This may lead to the issue of a draft Directive which is commented on by the European Parliament (a directly elected assembly with limited powers) and the Economic and Social Committee (a consultative body of employers, employees and others). A revised proposal is then submitted to a Working Party of the Council of Ministers. The Council, consisting of the relevant ministers from each EEC country, must vote unanimously if a Directive or Regulation is to be adopted. In the case of a Directive, member states are required to introduce a national law within a specified period, though they often exceed it, as discussed below in the case of the fourth Directive. Table 14.3 includes UK implementation dates, as an example.

Table 14.3 Company Law Directives and Regulations Relevant to Corporate Accounting (mid-1985)

Directives	Draft dates		Date approved	UK law	Purpose
First		1964	1968	1972	Ultra vires rules etc.
Second	1970,	1972	1976	1980	Separation of private from public companies, minimum capital, distributable income
Third	1970, 1975	1973,	1978		Mergers
Fourth	1971,	1974	1978	1981	Formats and rules of accounting
Fifth	1972,	1983			Structure, management and audit of public companies
Sixth	1975,	1978	1982		De-mergers
Seventh	1976,	1978	1983		Group accounting
Eighth	1978,	1979	1984		Qualifications and work of auditors
Ninth	—				Links between public company groups
Tenth	1985				International mergers of public companies
Vredeling	1980	1983			Employee information and consultation
Regulations					
Societas Europea	1970,	1975			A European company subject to EEC laws
European Economic Interest Grouping	1973,	1978	1985		A legal form for multinational joint ventures

The Fourth Directive

The exact effects of any Directive on a particular country will depend upon the laws passed by national legislatures. For example, there are dozens of articles in the fourth Directive which begin with such expressions as 'member states may require or permit companies to . . .'. Given this flexibility, the effects on the accounting of different countries have been included in the relevant chapters. However, it seems appropriate to consider here the general outline of the Directive and the process whereby it took its ultimate form.

The Directive (EEC Commission 1978) covers public and private companies in all EEC countries. Its articles include those referring to valuation rules, formats of published financial statements and disclosure requirements. It does not cover consolidation, which is left for the seventh Directive. The fourth Directive's first draft was published in 1971, before the UK, Ireland and Denmark had entered the EEC or had representatives on the *Groupe d'Etudes*. This initial draft was heavily influenced by German company law, particularly the *Aktiengesetz* of 1965. Consequently, valuation rules were to be conservative, formats were to be prescribed in rigid detail, and disclosure by notes was to be very limited. Financial statements were to obey strictly the provisions of the Directive.

The influence of the UK and Ireland on the EEC Commission, Parliament and *Groupe d'Etudes* was such that a much amended draft was issued in 1974. This introduced the concept of the 'true and fair view'. Another change by 1974 was that some flexibility of presentation had been introduced. This process continued and, by the promulgation of the finalised Directive, the 'true and fair view' was established as a predominant principle in the preparation of financial statements (Article 2, paragraphs 2 – 5). In addition, the four principles of the UK's SSAP 2 (accruals, prudence, consistency and going concern) were made clearer than they had been in the 1974 draft (Article 31).

More rearrangement and summarisation of items in the financial statements were made possible (Article 4). There were also calls for more notes in the 1974 draft than the 1971 draft, and more in the final Directive than in the 1974 draft (Articles 43 – 46). Another concern of Anglo-Dutch accountants has been with the effect of taxation on Franco-German accounts. The extra disclosures called for by the 1974 draft about the effect of taxation are included in the final Directive (Articles 30 and 35).

The fact that member states may permit or require a type of inflation accounting is treated in more detail than in the 1974 draft (Article 33). As a further accommodation of Anglo-Dutch opinion, a 'Contact Committee' of EEC and national civil servants is provided for. This was intended to answer the criticism that the Directive will give rise to laws which are not flexible to changing circumstances and attitudes. The Committee looks at practical problems arising from the implementation of the Directive, and makes suggestions for amendments (Article 52).

The fourth Directive was supposed to be enacted in members states by July 1980 and to be in force by January 1982. In fact it was enacted in Denmark and the UK in 1981, and in France and the Netherlands in 1983. By mid-1985, Belgium and Luxembourg had also implemented the Directive, leaving the other four countries in the bad books of the Commission.

The implementation in the UK was brought about by the 1981 Companies Act. The changes included compulsory formats and detailed valuation requirements (Nobes 1983), which also affect the Netherlands and Ireland in a similar way. In other countries the introduction of the 'true and fair view' as an over-riding requirement, the requirements for extra disclosures, and the extension of publication and audit to many more companies are significant (see Chapters 4 and 5).

It is clear that neither asset valuation, nor formats, nor disclosure will be completely standardised as a result of the laws consequent upon the fourth Directive. However, *harmonisation* will be considerable and inevitable, although UK financial statements, for example, have been much less affected than was feared by some UK accountants. The present degree of harmonisation might reasonably be welcomed by shareholders and accountants throughout the EEC, once the initial inertia against change is overcome.

Nevertheless, there is a very loose compromise between the opinions of those countries which are in favour of adjustments for price changes (the Netherlands, at one extreme) and those which are against them (West Germany, at the other extreme). There is a requirement that the difference between the adjusted figures and historic cost must be shown. However, there is no requirement that all member states must demand at least some adjustments; there will be no standardisation on current cost or current purchasing power adjustments; and there is no direction about whether adjusted statements should be the main or supplementary ones, or whether merely adjusting notes should be provided.

Other Directives

The second Directive concerns a number of matters connected with share capital and the differences between public and private companies (see Nobes 1983). The draft fifth Directive and the draft Vredeling Directive concern attempts by the Commission to improve the involvement of employees in companies. There are proposals for informing employees and consulting them on important matters, and for employee involvement in the management of public companies (Lyall 1984,

Nobes 1984). The seventh Directive concerns consolidated accounting, and is considered in Chapter 10. The eighth Directive was watered down from its original draft which might have greatly affected the training patterns and scope of work of accountants, particularly in the UK. However, its main effect now will be to decide on who is allowed to audit accounts in certain countries with small numbers of accountants, such as Denmark and West Germany.

European Company

One of the draft Regulations in Table 14.3 concerns a totally new type of company which will be registered as an EEC company and will be subject to EEC laws. It will be called the *Societas Europea* (SE). However, progress is very slow, partly because member states may not wish to lose sovereignty over companies operating in their countries, and partly because member states have so far found it impossible to agree upon a company structure with respect to supervisory boards.

It has been easier to agree upon proposals for a form of joint venture organisation for EEC companies. The Regulation on the 'European Economic Interest Grouping' is based on the successful French business form, the *groupement d'intérêt économique* – as used, for example, by the aviation business, Airbus Industrie. It provides a corporate organisation which can be smaller and of shorter duration than the SE. The members of the Grouping will be autonomous profit-making entities, whereas the Grouping itself will provide joint facilities or enable a combination for a specific purpose (Drury 1976).

14.5   Summary

There are many interested parties who would benefit from international standardisation. These include shareholders, stock exchanges, multinational companies, accounting firms, trade unions and revenue authorities. The scope for standardisation is great because the international variations in practice are very large. However, the obstacles are important, too. The fundamental causes of differences remain and these are backed up by nationalistic inertia. At present, the lack of an international enforcement agency is crucial.

However, a number of bodies *are* working for standardisation of accounting rules and disclosure, notably the IASC which has rapidly published a substantial list of international standards. These are heavily influenced by practices in the UK and the US, and have the most effect in English-speaking countries. Enforcement in other areas of the world is difficult because of underdeveloped accountancy professions or because the rules for financial reporting are made by governments. It may be that the development of dual standards for domestic and foreign reporting would be an easier solution, which would preserve differences in accounting that result from national differences of an economic, social and legal nature.

There are other bodies concerned with standardisation on a worldwide or regional basis. However, the most powerful source of change towards harmonisation among leading countries in world accounting is the EEC Commission. Harmonisation of accounting is one of the many aims of the Commission as part of its overall objective to remove economic barriers within the EEC.

Harmonisation will come about through EEC Directives and Regulations. It is particularly the fourth and the seventh Directives on company law which are affecting accounting in Europe. The fourth Directive is causing important changes in most EEC countries in formats of accounts or disclosure or valuation procedures. The seventh Directive will harmonise consolidation practices. However, because of differing opinions among the member states, there are no requirements concerning inflation accounting. This will restrict the degree of harmonisation.

References

Benson, H. (1976) 'The story of international accounting standards', *Accountancy*, July.

Benson, H. (1978) 'A corporate report from the UN', *Accountancy*, May.

Briston, R. (1978) 'The evolution of accounting in developing countries', *International Journal of Accounting*, Fall.

Burggraaff, J.A. (1982) 'IASC developments: an update', *Journal of Accountancy*, September.

Choi, F.D.S. (1979) 'ASEAN Federation of Accountants: A new international accounting force', *International Journal of Accounting*, Fall.

Choi, F.D.S. (1981) 'A cluster approach to accounting harmonisation', *Management Accounting* (USA), August.

Choi, F.D.S. and Mueller, G.G. (1984) *International Accounting*, Prentice-Hall, Chapter 12.

Cummings, J.P. and Chetkovich, M.N. (1978) 'World accounting enters a new era', *Journal of Accountancy*, April.

Denman, J.H. (1980) 'The OECD and international accounting standards', *CA Magazine*, February.

Drury, R.R. (1976) 'The European cooperation grouping', *Common Market Law Review*, pp. 7 – 35.

Enthoven, A.J.H. (1976) *Social and Political Impact of Multinationals on Third World Countries*, AAA 60th Annual Meeting.

Ernst & Whinney (1979) *The Fourth Directive – Its Effect on the Annual Accounts of Companies*, Kluwer.

Evans, T.G. and Taylor, M.E. (1982) '"Bottom line compliance" with the IASC: A comparative analysis', *International Journal of Accounting*, Fall.

Fantl, I. (1971) 'The case against international uniformity', *Management Accounting*, May.

Gray, S.J. (1981) 'Multinational enterprises and the development of international accounting standards', *Chartered Accountant in Australia*, August.

Hepworth, J.A. (1979) 'IASC – the future', in W.J. Brennan (ed.) *The Internationalization of the Accountancy Profession*, CICA, Toronto.

Lyall, D. (1984) 'Compulsory disclosure to employees – the Vredeling Directive', *Accountant's Magazine*, February.

Mason, A.K. (1976) 'International reporting of inventories', *The Accountant*, 7 October.

Mason, A.K. (1978) *The Development of International Financial Reporting Standards*, International Centre for Research in Accounting, Lancaster University, Chapter 6.

McDougall, E.H.V. (1979) 'Regional accountancy bodies', in W.J. Brennan (ed.) *The Internationalization of the Accountancy Profession*, CICA, Toronto.

Nair, R.D. and Frank, W.G. (1981) 'The harmonization of international accouting standards, 1973–1979', *International Journal of Accounting*, Fall.

Nobes, C.W. (1980) 'Harmonization of accounting within the European Communities', *International Journal of Accounting*, Spring.

Nobes, C.W. (1983) 'The origins of the harmonising provisions of the 1980 and 1981 Companies Acts', *Accounting and Business Research*, Winter.

Nobes, C.W. (1984) 'Another look at the draft Fifth', *Accountancy*, August.

Parker, R.H. (1982) 'Why are Australian accounting standards different?', *Australian Accountant*, August.

Reece, N.J. (1978) 'A guide to EEC proposed legislation', *Accountants Digest* No. 64, ICAEW, London (updated version No. 91, Summer 1980).

Sahlgren, K.A. (1979) 'The work of non-accountant international bodies', in W.J. Brennan (ed.) *The Internationalization of the Accountancy Profession*, CICA, Toronto.

Watts, T.R. (1979) *Handbook on the EEC Fourth Directive*, ICAEW, London.

Wong, E.H. (1980) 'International standards of accounting and reporting', *Australian Accountant*, August.

Accountants International Study Group (1975) *International Financial Reporting*.

EEC Commission (1978) *Fourth Directive on Company Law*, reprinted in *Trade and Industry*, 11 August 1978.

IASC (1973) *Agreement*.

IASC (1977) *Preface to International Accounting Standards*.

IASC (1982) *Constitution of the International Accounting Standards Committee*.

IASC (1983) *Preface to International Accounting Standards*.

ICAEW (1983) *Financial Reporting, 1983–84*, London, p.134.

OECD (1980) *International Investment and Multinational Enterprises*.

For a useful summary of international bodies, see Cummings and Chetkovich (1978).

For reasons for and obstacles to harmonisation, see Mason (1978).

For an analysis of the fourth Directive, see Ernst & Whinney (1979), Watts (1979) and Nobes (1980) and (1983).

For a guide to the machinery and Directives of the EEC, see Reece (1978).

15

Classification and Harmonisation of Corporate Income Taxes

CHRISTOPHER NOBES

15.1 Introduction

The Relevance of this Chapter

This book has been concerned mainly with international aspects of published financial reporting. Therefore, although it may be clear that this chapter's subject matter is of considerable interest and importance, it may not be immediately clear how it fits in here. However, there are several good reasons for its inclusion. First, even in Anglo-Saxon countries, corporate taxation obviously has some significant effects on net profit figures and other financial reporting matters. More importantly, it has been shown that, in some Continental countries, the rules relating to corporate income taxation have a dominant effect on financial accounting measurement and valuation rules.

Secondly, an understanding of the differences between corporate taxation in different countries is a necessary introduction to a study of international business finance and management accounting. However, it is often poorly covered or omitted from books on these subjects. Hence it was decided to provide a fairly detailed introduction here. Thirdly, the classification and harmonisation aspects of taxation are useful further illustrations of the processes described in Chapters 8 and 14.

Differences in Taxes

The two fundamental types of difference between corporate income taxes might be called tax bases and tax systems. The international differences in corporate income tax bases (or definitions of taxable income) are very great. Although in all countries there is *some* relationship between accounting income and taxable income, in France and Germany the relationship is much closer than it is in the UK and the US. Further, it has been pointed out throughout this book that the underlying measurement of accounting income itself varies substantially by country. These two points, which are of course linked, mean that similar companies in different countries may have vastly different taxable incomes.

The second basic type of difference lies in tax systems. Once taxable income has been determined, its interaction with a tax system can vary, in particular with respect to the treatment of dividends. Corporations, unlike partnerships whose business income in most countries is taxed as though it were all distributed at the end of each tax year, may have both retained and distributed income for tax purposes. If business income is taxed only at the corporate level and only when it is earned, then different shareholders will not pay different rates of personal income tax. If income is taxed only on distribution, taxation may be postponed indefinitely. On the other hand, if income is taxed both when it is earned and when it is distributed, this creates 'economic double taxation' which could be said to be inequitable and inefficient (see section 15.3).

These differences in tax bases and tax systems could lead to several important economic effects: for example, on dividend policies, investment plans and capital raising methods. Such matters are not dealt with extensively here. Neither are the important issues of transfer pricing and double taxation which in practice help to determine taxable profits and tax liabilities (see, for example, Benke and Edwards 1980; Chown 1977).

15.2   Tax Bases

The obvious way to classify corporate income taxation bases is by degrees of difference between accounting income and taxable income. As should be clear from Chapters 2 to 7, the influence of taxation on accounting varies from the negligible in the UK to the dominant in France. Such is the importance of this difference for accounting that a simple classification of tax bases would look much like a simple classification of accounting systems. For example, a two-group classification in either case might put the UK, the US and the

Netherlands in one group, and France, Germany and Japan in the other.

In the former group the requirement for financial accounting to present a 'fair' view to shareholders pre-dates and overrides any taxation rules. Consequently many adjustments to accounting profit are necessary in order to arrive at the tax base: taxable income. In the other group, the needs of taxation have been dominant in the evolution of accounting and auditing. Consequently, the tax base corresponds closely with accounting profit. It is a complaint of Anglo-Saxon accountants that the importance of this taxation effect is not even disclosed. However, as has been discussed, the EEC's fourth Directive should remedy this for Continental countries.

Tax bases have been discussed elsewhere, country by country (James and Nobes 1983, Chapter 13; Chown 1977; Saunders 1977; Commerce Clearing House 1984). Here it is intended to discuss some of the differences between countries by topic. In general, the details relate to 1984.

Depreciation

Naturally, in all the countries studied in detail in this book, the Revenue Authorities take an interest in the amount of depreciation charged in the calculation of taxable income. This concern varies from fairly precise specification of rates and methods to be used (as in most countries), to an interference only where charges are unreasonable (as in the Netherlands). As has been pointed out in earlier chapters, the vital difference for *financial reporting* is that accounting depreciation must usually be kept the same as tax depreciation in Franco-German countries but not under Anglo-Saxon-Dutch accounting. An interesting effect of this difference is that there is little need for the concept of deferred taxation in Franco-German countries.

Examples of the specification of rates and methods for depreciation of fixed assets for tax purposes are shown below:

(i) In the UK for 1986–87, machinery is depreciated at 25% on a reducing balance basis. There is a complete separation of this scheme of 'capital allowances' from the depreciation charged by companies against accounting profit. Unlike other countries, the UK does not give any depreciation tax allowance for most commercial buildings.

(ii) In the US, there are depreciation ranges for different assets. Normally, fixed assets are written off for tax purposes using the 'accelerated cost recovery system'. The most common form of this involves a five-year write-off period, with 15%, 22% and three sets of 21% in the successive years. Buildings normally have a 15-year write-off period. In addition, there is a tax credit of 10% of investment. There are other accelerated allowances from time to time.

(iii) In the Netherlands, depreciation is determined by individual companies. Straight-line depreciation may be used for any asset, and reducing balance for all assets except buildings. Companies may change from one method to another if there are good business reasons. Since 1978, there has been a system of investment incentives (WIR). Typical levels are: new non-residential buildings 14%, plant 12%.

(iv) In France, depreciation is allowed by tax law on a straight-line basis for nearly all assets at the following rates: industrial and commercial buildings 5%, office or residential buildings 4%, plant and fixtures 10–20%, vehicles 15–25%. It is possible to use a reducing balance basis for plant. The rates to be used are expressed as multiples of the straight-line rates depending on the asset's life. It is possible to change the basis. Accelerated depreciation is allowed for R&D, certain regions, anti-pollution and energy-saving assets.

(v) In Germany and Japan, depreciation rates are specified by tax law. Straight-line and reducing balance are available, except that straight-line is mandatory for buildings in Germany. The following rates apply in Germany: buildings 2.5%, plant 10%, office equipment 20%, office furniture 10%, vehicles 20–25%. It is possible to change methods only from reducing balance to straight-line. Accelerated allowances are available for assets in Berlin and Eastern border areas, and for anti-pollution.

Allowances for Inflationary Gains on Inventories

The second largest adjustment made during the calculation of corporation tax liabilities in the UK between 1978 and 1984 was 'stock relief' (James and Nobes 1983, Chapter 13). This partially allowed for the fact that, during periods of inflation, an important element of accounting and taxable profits is an unrealised gain due to holding trading stocks. This is not part of operating profit and there may be liquidity problems if it bears corporation tax.

In the US and Japan, the last in, first out (LIFO) system of inventory costing is allowed as long as it is used for both financial and tax accounting. During inflation this reduces stock valuation and increases the cost of sales expense, thus reducing accounting and taxable profits. In the other countries mentioned above, there is neither stock relief nor a deliberate use of LIFO to correct for holding gains. LIFO is allowed in Germany in those unusual cases where it corresponds with physical reality; in the Netherlands, where it is commercially sensible; and in France, never.

Capital Gains

The taxation of corporate capital gains varies substantially by country. In the UK a proportion of capital gains is added to taxable income. In 1986, with corporation tax at 35%, the proportion is 1/7; this means that the capital gain bears 30% taxation, which is the same rate as the original individual capital gains tax.

In the Netherlands, Germany and Japan, capital gains are added to taxable income in full. In the US and France, short-term capital gains are fully taxed (US, under one year; France, under two years), but long-term capital gains are taxed at a reduced rate. Roll-over relief provisions also vary internationally.

Losses

Different treatment of losses can have important effects on taxable profits. These are illustrated in Table 15.1.

Dividends Received

The degree to which the dividends received by a company must be included has an important effect on its taxable income. In the UK and Japan, domestic dividends are not taxed in the hands of a recipient company. In the US, dividends from companies in which there is an 80% or higher holding are not taxed. However, 15% of dividends from other companies are taxed. In France, dividend income is fully taxed unless

Table 15.1 Operating Loss Reliefs (Years)

	Carry back	Carry forward
UK	1	No limit
US	3	15
France	3	5
W. Germany	2	5
Netherlands	3	8
Japan	1	5

there is a holding of at least 10% or FF 10m, in which case only 5% of
dividend income is taxed. In Germany, dividends are fully taxable. In
the Netherlands, a minimum 5% holding relieves dividends from tax.

Expenses

In the UK, the US and the Netherlands, a number of expenses deducted
in the calculation of profit may not be allowed in the calculation of taxable income. In France and Germany, what is deducted for financial
accounting generally depends on what is allowed for tax purposes. Most
countries are more generous than the UK in allowing expenses for taxation. For example, most of them allow entertainment expenses to be
deducted. In the three other European countries there are also greater
allowances for bad debts and various other provisions.

Other Taxes

A very important complicating factor in determining overall tax
burdens is the existence and degree of deductibility for national corporate income tax purposes, of other types of taxes on companies. In
most countries there is some form of payroll tax or social security tax. In
the UK there are local property 'rates'. In West Germany there are
regional income taxes, capital taxes and payroll taxes. In France there is
a business licence tax. In Italy there is a regional corporation tax. In
general, these taxes are deductible in the calculation of national corporation tax. However, because of these taxes, the total tax burden is
much higher than might be thought at first sight in countries like Germany, where regional taxes are important.

15.3   Tax Systems

The preceding section has shown that the definition of taxable income
varies greatly by country. The way in which taxable income is taxed
depends upon the tax *system*. This also varies by country. Systems which
have been used in the recent past in the countries studied in this book
can be classified into three types.

Classical Systems

'Classical' systems are perhaps the easiest to explain. It is their alleged defects which other systems are designed to correct. Under a classical system, like most others, dividends paid are not deductible in the calculation of taxable income. Moreover, these dividends are fully taxable in the hands of the recipients. Interest payments, as in most systems, are usually tax deductible, though this is not an essential feature of classical systems. By 1985, the US, the Netherlands and Luxembourg had been using classical systems for many years, as had Australia. The UK used such a system from 1965 to 1973.

There are two main criticisms of classical systems; both rest upon what has been called the 'economic double taxation' of dividends whereby distributed income is taxed both to corporation tax and then to personal income tax. First, this double taxation is said to be inequitable when compared to the treatment of the distributed income of unincorporated businesses. Income of such businesses, whether physically distributed or not, bears no corporation tax but bears current income tax in the hands of the owners of the businesses. Such single taxation would not be so easy to arrange for corporations. This is because retained profit *does* exist, both in reality and for tax purposes, and so, if there were no separate corporation tax, taxation could be indefinitely postponed if companies delayed distribution. The alternative of taxing income only at the corporate level would mean that all individual recipients would have borne the same rate of tax. This would be unacceptable as part of an otherwise progressive income tax system. Thus, double taxation of the *distributed* income of corporations results from a desire by governments to ensure proper taxation of *retained* income.

The second case against economic double taxation is that it introduces a bias against the distribution of dividends. Since both total income and then distributed income are fully taxed, the larger the distribution, the larger is the total tax borne by a company and its shareholders. It might be thought that such an encouragement to retain profits would promote investment. However, more subtle economic thinking might suggest that profitable and efficient investment would be more likely to follow if companies distributed their profits and then shareholders allocated these funds through the new issue market to the most profitable companies. Unfortunately it is not proven that companies with a good earnings record will remain the most profitable (Whittington 1971).

It should also be noted about this second argument that, even if there were no effective corporation tax on distributed income (i.e. no double taxation), there would still be a bias against distribution if there were an income tax which had to be paid only when dividends were distributed.

The two cases against the economic double taxation of dividends have given rise to other systems of taxation which are designed to mitigate these effects of classical systems.

Imputation Systems

A frequently used way of mitigating the effects of economic double taxation is to impute to the recipients of dividends some of the tax paid by a corporation on the income out of which the dividends are paid. Imputation systems are used in EEC countries, apart from the Netherlands, Greece and Luxembourg, and also in Canada. Tables 15.2 and 15.3 illustrate the contrast between the UK's pre-1973 classical system and its imputation system in 1982–83. (The 1984 Finance Act in the UK has provided for the tax rate to fall gradually from 1983 onwards, to 35% in 1986.) In the UK there is a 'basic rate' of income tax, which is the marginal rate for a majority of taxpayers; it has been assumed that this is 30%, that the classical corporate tax rate is 40%, and that the imputation rate is 52% as it was in the UK between 1973 and 1983. Also, for simplicity, accounting and taxable income are assumed to be equal. The tax credit in the UK is linked to the basic rate of income tax for administrative simplicity. In 1982–83, when the basic rate was 30%, the tax credit was 30/70 or 3/7. Under the pre-1973 system there was a withholding of standard rate income tax at source.

A comparison of Tables 15.2 and 15.3 shows that, for shareholders who pay only basic rate tax, the UK imputation system fully removes the double taxation of dividends. The total tax (£5,200 in the tables) under the imputation system does not alter as the level of dividends rises. However, the case is different when there are shareholders who pay a higher rate of personal income tax. Then there is still a double taxation and the bias against distibution remains. Table 15.4 illustrates this by showing that total taxation is higher when there is a larger payout, not only under the classical system but also under the imputation system.

The present UK system, like most existing imputation systems, involves *partial* imputation. That is, only part of the corporation tax paid by companies is imputed to shareholders. In 1983–84, the part imputed was 39.56% but in 1985–86 it was 64.29% as Table 15.5 shows.

The partial imputation systems of France, Belgium, Denmark and Ireland are broadly similar to that in the UK. However, only the UK and Irish systems base the size of the tax credit on an income tax rate. A summary of rates is shown as Table 15.6. It can be seen, for example, that France has a corporation tax rate of 50% and a (partial) imputation of 50% of the amount of corporation tax underlying any dividend. Apart from the size of the tax credit, French imputation works in the same way as that in Table 15.2.

Unlike these systems, Table 15.6 shows that the West German and Italian systems involve *full* imputation. This removes the economic double taxation of dividends. It means that the eventual effect of the whole federal taxation system for distributed income is as though there were no

Table 15.2 Classical and Imputation Systems (low payout)

		Classical £	Imputation £
Company			
income (say)		10,000	10,000
corporation tax (40%)		4,000	(52%) 5,200
distibutable income		6,000	4,800
distibution (say) gross		2,000	
less income tax deducted at source (30%)	600		
net	1,400		cash 1,400
retained income		4,000	3,400
Shareholders (basic rate)			
dividend: cash received		1,400	1,400
income tax deducted at source		600	0
tax credit received (3/7)		0	600
gross dividend		2,000	'grossed up' dividend 2,000
income tax liability (30%)		600	600
less tax already deducted		600	0
less tax credit		0	600
tax due		0	0
Total tax		(4,000 + 600) 4,600	5,200

Table 15.3   Classical and Imputation Systems (high payout)

		Classical £		Imputation £
Company				
income (say)		10,000		10,000
corporation tax (40%)		4,000	(52%)	5,200
distributable income		6,000		4,800
distribution (say) gross		5,000		3,500
less income tax deduction (30%)	1,500			
net	3,500		cash	
retained income		1,000		1,300
Shareholders (basic rate)				
dividend: cash received		3,500		3,500
income tax deducted at source		1,500		0
tax credit received ($\frac{3}{7}$)		0		1,500
gross dividend		5,000	'grossed up' dividend	5,000
income tax liability (30%)		1,500		1,500
less tax already deducted		1,500		0
less tax credit		0		1,500
tax due		0		0
Total tax	(4,000 + 1,500)	5,500		5,200

Table 15.4   Classical and Imputation Systems (higher rate taxpayers)

	Classical £		Imputation £
Low payout			
Company (as Table 15.2)			
Shareholders (50% marginal rate)			
dividend: cash received	1,400		1,400
income tax deducted at source	600		0
tax credit received ($\tfrac{3}{7}$)	0		600
gross dividend	2,000	'grossed up' dividend	2,000
income tax liability (50%)	1,000		1,000
less tax already deducted	600		0
less tax credit	0		600
tax due	400		400
Total tax	$(4,000 + 600 + 400)$ 5,000		$(5,200 + 400)$ 5,600
High payout			
Company (as Table 15.3)			
Shareholders (50% marginal rate)			
dividend: cash received	3,500		3,500
income tax deducted at source	1,500		0
tax credit received ($\tfrac{3}{7}$)	0		1,500
gross dividend	5,000	'grossed up' dividend	5,000
income tax liability (50%)	2,500		2,500
less tax already deducted	1,500		0
less tax credit	0		1,500
tax due	1,000		1,000
Total tax	$(4,000 + 1,500 + 1,000)$ 6,500		$(5,200 + 1,000)$ 6,200

Table 15.5   UK Partial Imputation, 1985–86

	£
Company	
income	1,000
corporation tax (40%)	400
	600
dividend	600
	0
Shareholders	
cash receipt	600
tax credit ($\frac{3}{7}$)	257.14
'grossed up' dividend	857.14

$$\text{partial imputation} = \frac{257.14}{400} = 64.29\%$$

Note: if the tax credit remains the same for 1986–87, the proportion will become 79.59%

separate corporation tax. However, as was mentioned in the last section, this is much too simple a picture to give an accurate impression of overall taxation, which needs to include other federal and local taxes. Note also in Table 15.6 that the German system has a higher rate for retained than for distributed profits.

Most continental European systems of taxation also contain 'withholding taxes' whereby some proportion of dividends is deducted at source. The presence of such a tax is not a differentiating feature for the classification of tax systems. Eventual tax burdens are not affected, since the withholding tax can be set against tax liabilities or reclaimed by most recipients of dividends. The main purpose of withholding taxes is to reduce evasion, particularly by holders of bearer shares and by foreign shareholders.

One rather more interesting feature of imputation systems is the way in which they ensure that tax credits are not granted to shareholders whose companies have not paid adequate corporation tax to cover the credits. In the UK an Advance Corporation Tax (ACT) equal to the size of tax credits is charged on all distributions. It is not an extra tax but merely an advance payment of the corporation tax bill. This helps the government's cash flow and also ensures that there is always revenue to cover the tax credits. This would otherwise have been a problem in the UK because of the possibility of large accounting profits, dividends and tax credits existing simultaneously with small *taxable* profits and cor-

Table 15.6   EEC Corporation Tax Systems in 1984

Country	Imputation introduced	National corporation tax rate %[2]	Tax credit as proportion of dividend	Tax credit as % of underlying CT
Belgium	1963	45	54.5	66.6
France	1965	50	50	50
UK	1973	45	42.9 (i.e. 30/70)	52.41
Ireland	1976	50	53.8 (i.e. 35/65)	53.8
W. Germany	1977	56 & 36	56.25	100
Denmark	1977	40	15	22.5
Italy	1977	36[3]	56.25	100
Netherlands	(Classical)	43	—	—
Luxembourg	(Classical)	40	—	—
Greece	(Classical)	48.48[4]	—	—

Source for columns 3 and 4: Sections A and B of *European Taxation* Supplementary Service, International Bureau of Fiscal Documentation.

Notes: 1. Withholding taxes have been ignored throughout.
2. In many cases (e.g. UK, Luxembourg and Greece) there are lower rates for smaller profits or companies.
3. There is also a deductible local income tax of 15% making a total of 46.37%.
4. i.e. 45% plus a surcharge.

poration tax payments, due to heavy capital allowances and stock reliefs.

There is also an ACT system in Ireland. In France, an extra tax called the *précompte* operates in those unusual cases where taxable income is too low to cover tax credits. A similar 'compensatory' tax exists in Germany.

Split-Rate Systems

A second way to reduce the effects of double taxation is to charge a lower rate of tax on distributed income than on retained income. The West German system up until the end of 1976 was a split-rate system with a 51% rate for retained income and a 15% rate for distributed income. The Austrian split-rate system continues.

It is possible to reorganise a partial imputation system into a split-rate system with identical tax liabilities and therefore, presumably, identical economic effects (Nobes 1980). Therefore it could be said that, for the purposes of classification, split-rate systems and partial imputation systems are in the same category.

Other Ways to Mitigate Double Taxation of Dividends

There are many other ways to reduce double taxation. In the US and Greece, for example, the classical system is modified in that there are allowances of a certain amount of investment income received by an individual each year which is exempted from personal income tax. Alternatively, the 'primary dividend' system allows companies to deduct some proportion of dividends in the calculation of their taxable incomes. Such a system has operated in Sweden and Iceland.

15.4 Harmonisation

The existing differences between effective taxation burdens in different countries give rise to great difficulties for the Revenue Authorities who tax multinational companies. These companies themselves put considerable effort into reducing overall taxation by moving capital and profits around the world. However, these are matters of international business finance and management accounting rather than the province of this chapter. The existence of these differences has not yet given rise to the same plethora of proposals and committees for international harmonisation as have the differences between accounting systems. However, within the EEC, harmonisation of taxation is in progress. Many Directives on the harmonisation of VAT and other forms of indirect taxation have been passed. Direct corporate taxation, which we are concerned with here, has also been the subject of proposals for harmonisation. Progress in this area has been even slower than in company law and accounting because of the reluctance of governments to lose any control over direct taxation, which is such an important source of revenue and a regulator of the economy.

The Treaty of Rome calls for the elimination of customs duties between member states, the introduction of common tariffs with third countries, and the removal of barriers to the free movement of persons, capital, goods and services. The interest in taxation shown by the EEC Commission, which is the guardian of the Treaty of Rome, stems from this desire to promote free movement. The free movement of goods and services implies particularly the harmonisation of indirect taxes. Similarly the free movement of people and capital implies the harmonisation of direct taxes. If there were no harmonisation of taxes and if barriers to movement were eliminated, there might then be encouragement or obstruction of flows of people, capital and so on to particular countries within the EEC for purely fiscal reasons.

It is the aim of harmonisation (Dosser 1973, Burke 1979) that the conditions of competition and the returns to capital and effort should not be significantly affected by differences in effective tax burdens. Just by having looked briefly at the corporate taxation systems in some EEC countries, it should be clear that the scope for harmonisation is considerable. So far, the EEC Commission's proposals have only covered tax systems rather than tax bases. The Commission's activity in this area will now be outlined.

In 1962, the Neumark Committee (1963) recommended to the Commission that a split-rate system should be adopted. Later the van den Tempel Report (1970) described the three types of corporation tax systems, and recommended the classical system. However, the Commission's draft Directive (EEC Commission 1975, Nobes 1979) on the harmonisation of corporate taxation proposed the imputation system. This must be partly due to the fact that a majority of EEC countries were already using such a system or had plans to introduce one. In 1975, Belgium, France and the UK were using an imputation system. Since then, Germany, Denmark, Ireland and Italy have introduced one. (See Table 15.6, column 2.)

Some of the reasons for choosing an imputation system have been mentioned. They include the fact that the tax credit reduces the bias against distribution and favours small investors (lower rate taxpayers). Also, the system should reduce the incentive for evasion by lowering the effective marginal rate of tax on dividends. In addition, since the corporation tax rate tends to be higher under an imputation system, there is a fairer comparison between the rates of tax borne on company retained profits and partnership profits (European Taxation 1976, OECD 1974).

Article 3 of the draft Directive proposes that there shall be imputation systems in operation with a single rate of tax between 45 and 55%. Also, Article 8 proposes that imputation credits shall be between 45 and 55% of the corporation tax that would have to be paid on a sum equal to the taxable income out of which the dividend could be paid (i.e. on the dividend increased by the corporation tax; see Table 15.6). The rates in force in the EEC in 1984 are shown in Table 15.6, which reveals that little notice has been taken of these proposals even in recently introduced imputation systems. Other proposals are that there should be a compensatory tax like an ACT or a *précompte* (Article 9); that there should be a withholding tax of 25% unless shares are registered, as in the UK (Articles 14–17); and that tax credits should be available to shareholders irrespective of their member state (Article 4). This last requirement is clearly designed to promote the free movement of investors' capital. These various requirements would necessitate important adjustments in some EEC countries, as Table 15.6 suggests.

The draft Directive has been criticised on many grounds. The omission of a proposed treatment for capital gains is important. Unless their taxation is also harmonised, there will be much wasteful manoeuvring in order to create capital gains in favourable member states rather than *income* in any state or capital gains in unfavourable states. Another criticism is that other corporate taxes, like net worth, turnover and local taxes, must be included in the harmonisation. More generally, the different rules relating to the calculation of taxable income need attention if total effective tax burdens are to be harmonised. A further criticism is that some countries in the EEC are intrinsically less attractive to companies for economic, geographical and political reasons; and that these countries need advantageous corporate tax regimes if they are to encourage investment and employment. Therefore, to harmonise taxation without altering these other factors might give rise to undesirable regional side-effects.

The 'opinion' of the European Parliament (Official Journal 1979) on the draft Directive has stressed the need to include the problem of different tax bases as well as tax systems. Partly as a result of this and partly because member states are not enthusiastic about changing their tax systems or losing flexibility, the 1975 draft Directive – and that concerning the taxation of financial institutions (EEC Commission 1978) – have been delayed and may need considerable amendment. However, the proposals may give an indication of the direction of future changes in corporation tax in the EEC. In 1985 various draft directives are in preparation on loss carry forwards, capital gains, depreciation rules, and so on.

Summary

Corporate taxation plays an important role in some countries' financial accounting practices. Also, a knowledge of corporate taxation is important for international business finance. A comparative international analysis of corporate taxation is not easily found elsewhere; hence this present chapter. There is discussion here on differences in tax bases and in tax systems.

Tax *bases* differ in their treatment of depreciation, stock holding gains, capital gains, losses, dividends received, certain expenses and many other matters. The importance of taxes other than national corporate income taxation also varies.

Tax *systems* differ mainly in respect of their treatment of dividends. Classical systems treat corporations and their owners quite separately, giving rise to 'double taxation of dividends'. Other systems try to mitigate this for equity and efficiency reasons. For example, imputation systems give shareholders credit for some or all of the corporation tax underlying their dividends. Such systems are now predominant in the EEC and favoured by the Commission. Split-rate systems achieve a similar effect by taxing distributed income at a lower rate than retained income.

Harmonisation of *systems* is proposed by the Commission in a draft Directive, on which progress is slow. So far, there are no official proposals for the harmonisation of tax bases, without which the harmonisation of systems would make little sense.

References

Benke, R.L. and Edwards, J.D. (1980) *Transfer Pricing: Techniques and Uses*, National Association of Accountants, New York.

Burke, R. (1979) 'Harmonisation of corporation tax', *Intertax*, June–July.

CCH (1984 and later editions) *United States Master Tax Guide*, Commerce Clearing House, Chicago.

Chown, J.F. (1977) *Taxation and the Multinational*, Longman.

Dosser, D. (1973) *British Taxation and the Common Market*, Charles Knight, Chapters 1, 4 and 6.

European Taxation (1976) International Bureau of Fiscal Documentation, Amsterdam, vol. 16, nos. 2, 3, 4, pp. 41–51.

James, S.R. and Nobes, C.W. (1983), *The Economics of Taxation*, Philip Allan.

Nobes, C.W. (1979) 'Fiscal harmonisation and European integration: comments', *European Law Review*, August.

Nobes, C.W. (1980) 'Imputation systems of corporation tax in the EEC', *Accounting and Business Research*, Spring.

Pennington, R.R. (ed.) (1974 etc.) *Business Taxation* series, Oyez Publishing.

Saunders, M.R. (1977) *Tax Planning for Business in Europe*, Butterworth.

van den Tempel, A.J. (1970) *Corporation Tax and Individual Income Tax in the EEC*, Brussels.

Whittington, G. (1971) *The Prediction of Profitability*, Cambridge University Press, Chapters 4 and 5.

EEC Commission (1975) *Proposal for a Directive concerning the Harmonization of Systems of Company Taxation and of Withholding Taxes on Dividends*, COM(75) 392 final, Brussels.

EEC Commission (1978) *Proposal for a Directive on the Application to Collective Investment Institutions* (of the 1975 draft Directive), COM(78) 340 final, Brussels.

Neumark Committee (1963) *EEC Reports on Tax Harmonization*, International Bureau of Fiscal Documentation, Amsterdam.

OECD (1974) *Theoretical and Empirical Aspects of Corporate Taxation*, Paris.

Official Journal of the EEC (1979), C140; see also report in *Intertax*, October 1979.

Further Reading

For a more detailed account of tax systems, see Saunders (1977), Pennington (1974 etc.) and James and Nobes (1983).

For discussions on the effects of different tax systems see *European Taxation* (1976 and 1978) and OECD (1974).

Glossary

Australia

AARF	Australian Accounting Research Foundation
AASC	Australian Accounting Standards Committee
ASA	Australian Society of Accountants
ASRB	Accounting Standards Review Board
ICAA	Institute of Chartered Accountants in Australia
NCSC	National Companies and Securities Commission

Canada

CICA	Canadian Institute of Chartered Accountants

France

CNC	Conseil national de la comptabilité
CNCC	Compagnie nationale des commissaires aux comptes (body of state-registered auditors)
COB	Commission des opérations de bourse (French equivalent of US Securities and Exchange Commission)
OECCA	Ordre des experts comptables et des comptables agréés (French professional accountancy body)
SA	Société anonyme (public company)
Sàrl	Société à responsabilité limitée (private company)

Germany

AG   Aktiengesellschaft (public company)
AktG   Aktiengesetz (law on public companies and public companies with personally liable shareholders)
AO   Abgabenordnung (regulations on tax administration and procedure)
BFH   Bundesfinanzhof (Supreme Tax Court)
BGH   Bundesgerichtshof (Federal Supreme Court)
BGHZ   Entscheidungen des Bundesgerichtshofes in Zivilsachen (Decisions of the Federal Supreme Court in Civil Cases)
BStBl   Bundessteuerblatt (Federal Tax Bulletin)
EG   Europäische Gemeinschaften (European Communities)
EStG   Einkommensteuergesetz (income tax law)
EStR   Einkommensteuerrichtlinien (income tax regulations)
GenG   Genossenschaftsgesetz (law on cooperative societies)
GmbH   Gesellschaft mit beschränkter Haftung (private company)
GmbHG   Gesetz über Gesellschaften mit beschränkter Haftung (private company law)
GoB   Grundsätze ordnungsmässiger Buchführung (orderly bookkeeping principles)
HFA   Hauptfachausschuss (Research Committee of the German Institute)
HGB   Handelsgesetzbuch (Commercial Code)
IdW   Institut der Wirtschaftsprüfer (German Institute of Accountants)
KG   Kommanditgesellschaft (limited partnership)
KGaA   Kommanditgesellschaft auf Aktien (public company with personally liable shareholders)
OHG   Offene Handelsgesellschaft (general partnership)
PublG   Publizitätsgesetz (publicity law)
RGZ   Entscheidungen des Reichsgerichtshofes in Zivilsachen (Decisions of the Imperial Supreme Court in Civil Cases)
WP   Wirtschaftsprüfer

Japan

BADC   Business Accounting Deliberation Council
JICPA   Japanese Institute of Certified Public Accountants

Netherlands

BV   Besloten Vennootschap met Beperkte Aansprakelijheid (private company)

Fl	Florins/guilders
NIvRA	Nederlands Instituut van Registeraccountants (Dutch Institute of Accountants)
NV	Naamloze Vennootschap (public company)

UK and Ireland

APC	Auditing Practices Committee
ASC	Accounting Standards Committee
CACA	Chartered Association of Certified Accountants
CCAB	Consultative Committee of Accountancy Bodies
CIPFA	Chartered Institute of Public Finance and Accountancy
ICAEW	Institute of Chartered Accountants in England and Wales
ICAI	Institute of Chartered Accountants in Ireland
ICAS	Institute of Chartered Accountants of Scotland
ICMA	Institute of Cost and Management Accountants
PLC	Public limited company
SORP	Statement of Recommended Practice
SSAP	Statement of Standard Accounting Practice

USA

AAA	American Accounting Association
AICPA	American Institute of Certified Public Accountants
APB	Accounting Principles Board
ARB	Accounting Research Bulletin
ASR	Accounting Series Release (of SEC)
CCH	Commerce Clearing House, Chicago
FAF	Financial Accounting Foundation
FASB	Financial Accounting Standards Board
GAAP	Generally accepted accounting principles
GAAS	Generally accepted auditing standards
GASB	Government Accounting Standards Board
IRS	Internal Revenue Service
NAA	National Accounting Association
SEC	Securities and Exchange Commission

International

AAC	African Accounting Council
AFA	ASEAN Federation of Accountants
AISG	Accountants International Study Group

CAPA   Confederation of Asian and Pacific Accountants
EEC   European Economic Community
IAPC   International Auditing Practices Committee
IASC   International Accounting Standards Committee
ICCAP   International Co-ordination Committee for the Accountancy
            Profession
IFAC   International Federation of Accountants
OECD   Organisation for Economic Cooperation and Development
SID   Society for International Development
UEC   Union Européenne des Experts Comptables, Economiques
            et Financiers (European Union of Accounting, Economic
            and Financial Experts)
UNO   United Nations Organisation

Principles and methods

CCA   Current cost accounting
CNC   Current/non-current
CPP   Current purchasing power
FIFO   First in, first out system of inventory valuation
GPP   General purchasing power
HCA   Historical cost accounting
LC   Local currency
LIFO   Last in, first out system of inventory valuation
MNM   Monetary/non-monetary

Further Reading

More definitions and abbreviations may be found in:

Nobes, C.W. (1984) *The Pocket Accountant*, Basil Blackwell and *The Economist*.
Parker, R.H. (1984) *Macmillan Dictionary of Accounting*, Macmillan.

Index